Also by Mark Bittman

The Food Matters Cookbook

Food Matters: A Guide to Conscious Eating with More Than 75 Recipes

How to Cook Everything

How to Cook Everything Vegetarian

The Best Recipes in the World

Fish: The Complete Guide to Buying and Cooking

How to Cook Everything: The Basics

How to Cook Everything: Bittman Takes On America's Chefs

Mark Bittman's Quick and Easy Recipes from The New York Times

With Jean-Georges Vongerichten

Simple to Spectacular

Jean-Georges: Cooking at Home with a Four-Star Chef

Mark Bittman's
Kitchen Express

404 Inspired Seasonal Dishes You Can Make

in 20 Minutes or Less

Mark Bittman

Simon & Schuster Paperbacks

New York   London   Toronto   Sydney

Simon & Schuster Paperbacks
A Division of Simon & Schuster, Inc.
1230 Avenue of the Americas
New York, NY 10020

First Simon & Schuster trade paperback edition June 2011

SIMON & SCHUSTER PAPERBACKS and colophon are registered trademarks
of Simon & Schuster, Inc.

For information about special discounts for bulk purchases,
please contact Simon & Schuster Special Sales at
1-866-506-1949 or business@simonandschuster.com.

The Simon & Schuster Speakers Bureau can bring authors to your live event. For more
information or to book an event, contact the Simon & Schuster Speakers Bureau at
1-866-248-3049 or visit our website at www.simonspeakers.com.

Designed by Linda Dingler

Manufactured in the United States of America

4   6   8   10   9   7   5

The Library of Congress has cataloged the hardcover edition as follows:

Bittman, Mark.
Mark Bittman's Kitchen Express : 404 inspired seasonal dishes you can make in 20 minutes or less / Mark Bittman.
p. cm
1. Quick and easy cookery. 2. Cookery, International. I. Title.
TX833.5.B548   2009
641.5'55—dc22   2008054823

ISBN 978-1-4165-7567-2
ISBN 978-1-4165-7898-7 (ebook)

CONTENTS

INTRODUCTION

The simple format of *Kitchen Express* belies all that it has to offer. Here are 101 incredibly fast and easy recipes for each season—404 in all. The experienced home cook can play with each to great advantage, yet at their core, they're recipes presented in the simplest form possible, understandable and readily executed by anyone who's done some cooking.

As a group, they are precisely imprecise. This is unusual for recipes, but it's long been my belief that the most specific recipes are the most limiting. Specificity is fine for baking, where the chemistry among the ingredients often determines success or failure. But in savory cooking, where amounts can vary wildly—there's almost never a critical difference between one onion and two: A "head" of broccoli might weigh one or one-and-a-half pounds; a steak may be three-quarters to an inch and a half thick—to try to force cooks to follow recipes demanding precision robs them of the ability to improvise, to relax, to substitute, to use their own judgment.

Jacques Pepin once remarked to me that the old adage about never stepping foot in the same river twice holds true for recipes also: You don't start with the same amount of ingredients, they're not at the same temperature, they're not the same age or from the same place, the ambient temperature and humidity are probably different, as are your equipment and mood. Everything is different, and the results will be too.

These little recipes acknowledge that up front. I don't really care how much garlic you use in most recipes, so "some" is as good as "a teaspoon." Similarly, garnishes are garnishes: You use more, you use less, you leave them out—it shouldn't matter. "A carrot" in a soup could certainly be a big one or a small one, and so on. So I rarely give *exact* measurements, unless proportions are critical.

This style of cooking is about three things: speed, flexibility, and relaxation. If you read one of these recipes, if it inspires you, and if you have the ingredients (or something approximating them) to throw it together—then go into the kitchen, assemble what you need, and have at it. Twenty minutes later, max, you'll be eating something delicious. What's wrong with that?

HOW TO USE THIS BOOK

There are some givens here, and it's worth taking a moment to understand them. I've organized *Kitchen Express* by seasons, not because I think grilling in winter or braising in summer is "inappropriate," but because I wanted to feature the right ingredients at the right time. To me, the organization is not dogmatic, but it is realistic, and it jibes with the current trend among savvy eaters to avoid, for example, Southern Hemisphere fruit in winter. As it happens, asparagus is best in spring, broccoli in fall and spring, corn in summer, and so on. You can cook what you want when you want it, of course, but I think that as you're browsing in *Kitchen Express,* you're best off starting with the season in which you find yourself; chances are you'll find something appealing right there, one that not only uses the best ingredients available but suits your mood. (When all is said and done, grilling in winter works only occasionally for those of us who have real winters, and braising in summer usually requires a pretty hefty dose of air-conditioning.)

How fast are the recipes? In general the speed with which you execute them depends not on how fast you chop (almost everyone chops better and faster than I do, and I can do any of these in 20 minutes or so) but on how well you're organized, and how well you multitask.

If you're the kind of person who organizes everything ahead of time, then spends a while chopping and assembling the ingredients, then hovers over the stove and watches everything develop, stirring and turning carefully and lovingly, that's great, but you should figure that these dishes will take you a little longer. These recipes were developed for the type of cook who gets the oil hot while chopping an onion, cooks the onion while peeling and chopping the carrot, adds the carrot and goes on to dice the meat, and so on—a kind of fast, steady, sequential cooking that is more grandmotherly and short-order than it is haute cuisine.

In fact, this is definitely *not* haute cuisine. It's very good food, done quickly. The idea here is to provide quick, satisfying dishes—delicious dishes. Many are complete meals, but I've often suggested appropriate accompaniments and serving suggestions to fill them out when necessary. These, of course, are optional. Most often they feature quick-cooked or pre-bought ingredients: bread, steamed broccoli, couscous. This doesn't mean that if you have time you can't make brown rice, or your own bread, or a more complicated vegetable dish.

And if you have even less time, open a jar of high-quality pickles; steam a plate of vegetables in the microwave; broil some eggplant slices; shred some cabbage or lettuce and serve the meat or seafood on that (it will wilt and collect the flavorful juices); quickly stir-fry a single vegetable in the same pan you used to cook the main course; have sliced fruit on the side; use a fast-frozen vegetable like peas, rutabaga, or corn; make a quick raw-vegetable salad by grating or chopping whatever you'd like and dressing it in a little oil and vinegar. You get the idea.

By the same token, cooking methods are flexible, especially when it comes to grilling, broiling, or using a grill pan. Do what your equipment and the weather allow. In terms of equipment, I only assume that your kitchen is stocked with a food processor and *probably* a blender.

Generally, the quantities in the recipes here are designed for three or four people. But again, the specifications are loose enough so that it won't take much to tweak them for fewer or more servings to make a meal more substantial, or plan ahead for leftovers. You can also combine the dishes in this book to make a larger dinner or pull together a buffet; check out some suggestions on page 203.

How and when you use the dishes in *Kitchen Express* is equally flexible. Some foods become trans-seasonal simply by swapping out a key ingredient (see "Some Simple Substitutions" on page 15). Others transcend the seasons or may have multiple—or more specific—uses worth highlighting. For help finding recipes using a tool besides the seasonal chapters or the index, see "More Ways to Navigate *Kitchen Express*," beginning on page 17.

A WORD ABOUT INGREDIENTS

The simpler the cooking, the more important the ingredients. The dishes in *Kitchen Express* sometimes feature sophisticated combinations, and the occasional odd ingredient, but at their core they are extremely simple, and they rely on good ingredients (which you're more likely to find in season).

Even when, for the sake of speed, I call for convenience foods like canned beans, stock, or tomatoes, if you can use homemade or fresher versions, the dishes will be all the better. In any case, all your ingredients should be as high quality as you can find. If fresh tomatoes are real and tasty, use 'em, but whenever they're not, canned tomatoes are a better option. And whenever you have time to make stock or beans, for example, from scratch, you should—refrigerate or freeze them for future use and your *Kitchen Express*–style dishes will shine more brightly.

Like many modern cooks, I use extra-virgin olive oil for my cooking fat all the time, unless I want a more neutral flavor (in which case I use grapeseed or another oil), or a different flavor (like peanut), or a higher smoke point (in which case most oils are better than olive). In theory at least, all extra-virgin olive oil is high quality; for other oils, look for those that are cold-pressed or minimally processed.

I use a lot of really fast-cooking ingredients here: boneless meats, plenty of seafood, quick-cooking vegetables, grains like couscous (which is actually not a grain but a pasta) and bulgur (which steeps faster than rice cooks). As a result, as often as not, your rinsing, trimming, peeling, and chopping will take as long as your cooking. (As most veteran cooks know, shopping is the most time-consuming aspect of cooking, so if you keep a well-stocked pantry, you're miles ahead of the game.)

I'm assuming everything you start with is thawed, your shrimp is peeled, your mussels are scrubbed, your poultry is boned, and so on. The cooking methods I use are the quickest: sautéing (which I often call simply "cooking"), boiling, steaming, and grilling (or broiling; anything that can be grilled can be broiled, and vice versa). And I rely heavily on those convenience foods we don't think of as such: prosciutto and bacon, Parmesan and soy—these are ingredients that are front-loaded with time and labor so that we can use them to flavor dishes quickly.

Finally, I have tried my best to make these recipes as uncomplicated as possible, and—counter to my inclinations, and to most of the work I've done in other books—have avoided spelling out as many variations and substitutions as possible. Every cook with even a minimum of experience will quickly realize that string beans can be swapped for asparagus when the latter is unavailable, or that ground turkey (or even ground salmon, or shrimp) can almost always be substituted for ground beef. (See the table on page 15 for some more examples of easy substitutions.) You can't make a roast chicken without a chicken, it's true, but very few of the ingredients in these (or other) recipes are sacred. The goals are these: Get good food onto the table, fast, and have fun doing so.

THE *KITCHEN EXPRESS* PANTRY

Over the years, I've cooked substantial meals in the tiniest, most poorly equipped kitchens—even non-kitchens—that you can imagine. So I can say with the utmost confidence that the size of your larder is less important than how you stock it. It's equally true that the more you cook—and the more varied your recipe repertoire— the deeper your pantry will be, as you collect a range of global ingredients that reflect the way you like to eat.

Since this book assumes you're an enthusiastic cook, it also assumes you already have a well-stocked pantry. What follows, then, are specific lists of the foods you should keep handy if you want to cook in the style I'm outlining here.

Must your pantry contain these exact staples? Of course not. You will naturally gravitate toward the flavors and ingredients you prefer, and I've noted the cases that reflect some of these potential preferences. But cooking at home becomes exponentially easier, faster, and more spontaneous when you have basic foods at arm's reach.

In the Cupboard

These are all shelf-stable products that should be stored at room temperature (cool room temperature is best, though obviously not always possible), preferably in the dark (or at least out of direct sunlight). This list starts with the ones you're likely to use most, and I've noted the semi-perishable foods to consider freezing or refrigerating if you don't go through them fast. In general, replace anything else on this list every year or so.

Oils: Extra-virgin olive oil, and at least one vegetable oil (I like grapeseed or peanut oil) for when you want something neutral for Asian cooking or at other times when olive oil is too strong. Sesame oil is nice for drizzling, and a little goes a long way. Choose high-quality, minimally processed oils for the purest flavors; and if you don't go through them very fast, store the bottles in the fridge.

Vinegars: Sherry vinegar (which is higher in acidity than other types) is my favorite, though a good white wine vinegar is also useful. Balsamic and rice vinegars have no replacements, and with their relatively low acidity they work more like condiments than stronger vinegars.

Sauces: Soy, hot pepper, nam pla (Thai fish sauce), hoisin sauce, and maybe Worcestershire sauce are the only ones you need. If you don't make your own salsa or barbecue sauce, then maybe you want good-quality store-bought bottles of these on hand, too.

Condiments: Mustard (maybe more than one kind), ketchup, and mayonnaise (again, if you don't make your own). Though I'm not a fan of vinegary pickles and relishes, a lot of people are. And capers are endlessly useful. Once all these condiments are open, store them in the fridge if you're worried about leaving them at room temperature for long.

Canned Tomatoes and Paste: Whole plum tomatoes are better than diced. Just break them up with your hands right in the can and pull out the tough core; or take them out and roughly chop as you would a fresh tomato. If you don't need the juice, refrigerate it to drink or use later. The handiest way to buy tomato paste is in tubes, but if you can't find it that way, small cans or jars are fine. When I say "a can of tomatoes" I mean the standard-size can (which runs about 15 ounces), unless a large (28-ounce) can or other quantity is specified.

Stock: This is a tough one because premade stock is not a tenth as good as even the fastest batch you can whip up yourself; but it's undeniably convenient. So if you find a brand you can tolerate, keep it on hand. Water is a good substitute in most cases, and I rely on it more and more.

Rice: White long-grain rice can be ready in 20 minutes; short-grain is a little faster. Brown rice takes about twice as long. But the good news about all of these (as well as the grains that follow) is that once cooked, they keep in the fridge for several days and reheat well in the microwave. So cooking in bulk ahead of time is an option, too.

Quick-Cooking Grains: White or whole wheat couscous (which is actually a pasta) and bulgur require only steeping. If you're willing to wait 20 to 30 minutes for grains to get tender, you might want to try steel-cut oats, cracked wheat, kasha, or quinoa.

Pasta: Like rice, pasta can be ready by the time the main recipe is. Include enough time to bring a pot of water to a boil (putting a lid on it really helps speed things up). Keep long strands or cut noodles handy—whatever you like. The thinner the pasta, though, the quicker the cooking time, so if you're really pressed, think angel hair.

Asian Noodles: Rice sticks, rice vermicelli, and bean threads (sometimes called glass noodles) all get tender after 10 minutes or so of soaking in hot water. Soba, somen, udon, and dried Chinese egg noodles require cooking but generally take less time than Italian pasta; the fresh kinds take only a minute or two.

Beans: Chickpeas, cannellini, pinto, and black beans. Canned beans are one solution, since you obviously can't cook dried beans in less than 20 minutes (though lentils and split peas almost make the cut). But if you cook a pot of lightly seasoned dried beans, then freeze them in small portions along with some of the cooking liquid, you can essentially stock your own "canned" beans. Only these will be infinitely better. (When I say "a can of beans" I mean the standard can, about 15 ounces, which equals about two cups.)

Crackers, Croutons, and Breadcrumbs: Preferably homemade. Tightly sealed, they'll keep longer than you think. Panko breadcrumbs are my favorite store-bought variety because they're big and crunchy.

Flours: For the cooking in this book, you generally won't need more than small quantities of white flour—usually for dredging—or sometimes cornmeal. If you don't bake regularly, refrigerate or freeze flours in tightly sealed containers or bags.

Dried Fruit, Including Dried Tomatoes: They keep so well, don't take up much room, and quickly add heft, flavor, and nutrition to many pasta, meat, and poultry dishes.

Chocolate, Nuts, and Seeds: Not just for snacking, but for cooking too. Almonds, hazelnuts, and peanuts are basic, as are sesame, pumpkin, or sunflower seeds; shredded unsweetened coconut is also useful. Keep them in the freezer if you don't use them within a month. For chocolate I generally stick to bittersweet with a high percentage of cacao. Unsweetened cocoa powder is nice to have around, and it keeps forever, too.

Onions, Shallots, Garlic, and Ginger: The so-called aromatic vegetables. Keep them at room temperature as long as possible, then move them to the fridge if they start to shrivel. If you want to keep a knob of ginger for a long time, wrap it well and freeze it, or trim off any rough spots and drop it into a small jar of vodka, close the lid, and store it in the fridge.

Potatoes and Sweet Potatoes: You won't have time to bake or roast them with the recipes here, but they cook fast if you cut them small or grate them.

Canned Fish: Oil-packed chunk light tuna is what I recommend for the dishes in this book. It also wouldn't hurt to keep a can each of whole sardines and anchovies and good-quality Alaskan salmon on hand.

Canned Vegetables: None—with the sole exceptions of chiles, like chipotle in adobo sauce, roasted green chiles, or roasted red peppers.

Salt and Pepper: Kosher salt rather than iodized table salt. (Good sea salt, like fleur de sel, is also handy; use it as a condiment.) Whole peppercorns to grind as you use them are a must. If you haven't done so already, invest in a good grinder; you'll notice the difference immediately.

Spices: You can't have too many, but start with cumin, mustard, saffron, cinnamon, coriander, dried chiles, and blends like curry and chili powders. I try to toast and grind my own, but it's not always practical; buy ground when necessary.

Herbs: Few dried herbs are worth the price, but oregano, thyme, rosemary, dill, and tarragon can be useful. I shop at Penzey's (www.penzeys.com) for dried herbs and spices.

On the Counter

A Big Bowl of Fresh Stuff: Seasonal fruit, including tomatoes. Vegetables that don't require refrigeration, like chiles, avocados, and squashes.

Bread: A crusty loaf, a package of pita, or whole wheat or rye sandwich bread.

In the Fridge

Bacon and/or Pancetta: Buy the good stuff in small quantities, either thick-cut or in chunks or slabs. These cured meats keep for a couple of weeks in the fridge; months if you wrap them well and freeze them.

Smoked Ham and/or Prosciutto: Ditto here; when you want thin slices (which you will), just slice your own from larger pieces.

Fresh Meat, Fish, or Poultry: If you shop every few days (or more often) chances are you have something in the fridge for dinner tonight. See the section on substitutions (page 15) for ideas about how to work what you've got into the dishes described in the book.

These days, cooking with seafood warrants a special mention. If you want to choose species that are fished or farmed sustainably—and you should—or if you're worried about mercury or other contaminants, then you have to do a little research, and not just once but on an ongoing basis. I suggest using the Monterey Bay Aquarium's "Seafood Watch" (www.montereybayaquarium.org). The list and its rankings change frequently, and though I don't consider it perfect, this organization provides the most reliable and accessible tool for helping you make informed decisions.

The recipes here are designed to be flexible, so I usually call simply for "fish" and provide some guidance if necessary in the headnote. The exceptions are when I call for salmon (use wild if at all possible), scallops, tuna (not bluefin), sardines and anchovies, clams or mussels, crab, squid, lobster, and shrimp (again, wild), for which tasty, safe, and sustainable options are readily available, and substitutions are a little trickier.

Leftover Cooked Meat, Fish, or Poultry: These increase your options, as do cooked deli meats like roast beef, corned beef, rotisserie chicken, and turkey. All of these have a life beyond sandwiches, as some of these recipes suggest.

Eggs: Essential.

Cheese and Dairy: Parmesan—the real stuff, from Italy—is a must, and keeps for months as long as you buy it in chunks, not pre-grated. Other cheeses: sharp cheddar, Gruyère or another nutty melting cheese, and something fresh like mozzarella, feta, goat cheese, or queso fresco. For cooking, half-and-half or heavy cream is more useful than milk, but if you drink milk you already have it around, so that's fine. Butter: unsalted, please. And sour cream and/or yogurt: At least occasionally, I prefer the full-fat kinds.

Long-Keeping Vegetables: Carrots, celery, broccoli, cauliflower, cabbage, Brussels sprouts, eggplant, string beans, and summer squashes all keep for at least a week and are available virtually all year long. I also try to keep some fresh greens in the house for salads or stir-fries.

Long-Keeping Fruit: Lemons, always. Limes are nice for a change and virtually interchangeable with lemons. Oranges and grapefruit in the winter; apples and pineapples when they're good.

Olives: Pick your favorite kinds; they're virtually interchangeable.

Miso: Keeps forever and can produce a complex-tasting stock, sauce, dressing, or marinade in minutes. White is the mildest, red is the strongest, and brown (made with rice or barley) falls somewhere in between.

Fresh Herbs: Tricky. They can be expensive, and they have a short shelf life, but they're invaluable in quick-cooking dishes. So I suggest you always have a bunch of parsley in the fridge. Beyond that, pick, say, one or two fresh herbs—oregano, sage, basil, chives, rosemary, cilantro, whatever—to buy each week. All fresh herbs store best like flowers in a little jar of water. Cover the tops loosely with a plastic bag and pluck leaves or stems as you need them.

In the Freezer

Meat and Poultry: Ground meat, chops, steaks, cutlets, and chicken parts all do well in the freezer provided they're well wrapped to prevent freezer burn. (The only problem is that you've got to plan in advance before using them.) It's safest to thaw animal foods in the refrigerator, but this process can take a couple of days. Your second choice is to soak the food in cold water. (The microwave does not thaw properly.) Fish doesn't keep well in most home freezers.

Frozen Vegetables: No apologies. I'm a fan of frozen peas, edamame, and other fresh beans (like lima, fava, or black-eyed peas). Frozen corn kernels, spinach, and hearty greens like mustard or collards, rutabagas, and bell peppers are good, too. I don't bother with carrots or string beans, or anything sauced or seasoned.

Frozen Fruits: These are fine for cooking and smoothies. Frozen raspberries, blackberries, and blueberries are better than frozen strawberries.

A Loaf of Really Good Bread: I keep a couple of baguettes in the freezer all the time. It's not always possible to monitor the progress of the bread on the counter, and you don't want to be stuck without any.

Anything You Make Yourself: Tomato sauce, beans, and stock especially. I can't stress this enough.

Some Simple Substitutions

You can change virtually any recipe in the book according to season and work around whatever ingredients you have on hand (and remember that you can read this list back and forth from left to right or right to left).

FOODS	EASY SUBSTITUTIONS
Lettuce and salad greens like arugula, mesclun, iceberg, romaine, spinach, and so on	Raw, they're all virtually interchangeable.
Tender greens for cooking, like spinach or arugula	Watercress, thinly sliced napa cabbage
Heartier greens for cooking, like kale, chard, mustard, or bok choy	All interchangeable; cooking time will vary depending on thickness.
Shallots	Any onion, especially red
Parsnips	Carrots
Fennel	Celery
Cauliflower	Broccoli
Asparagus	String beans
Brussels sprouts	Cabbage
Fava beans	Lima beans or edamame (frozen are fine)
Jicama	Radishes, especially daikon
Eggplant	Zucchini
Apples	Pears
Mango	Papaya
Strawberries	Pineapple
Basil	Cilantro, mint, chives, or even parsley
Shrimp	Scallops, squid, or crawfish; or cut-up chicken or pork
Lump crabmeat	Cooked lobster or shrimp
Boneless chicken breasts	Boneless chicken thighs (they generally take a little longer to cook); pork, turkey, or veal cutlets
Chicken (cutlets, boneless parts, or cut up for stir-fry)	Pork (chops, tenderloin medallions, or cut-up shoulder), or turkey
Ground beef	Ground pork, turkey, chicken, or lamb
Beef steaks	Pork or lamb chops
Nam pla (Thai fish sauce)	Soy sauce
Sour cream	Yogurt

MORE WAYS TO NAVIGATE
KITCHEN EXPRESS

Dishes That Double as Appetizers

These make fabulous first courses in a more formal meal (you can also start with salad or soup, of course; see pages 227 and 230 of the Index). For finger food, see the list on page 20.

Wild Mushroom Crostini (page 128)
Snap Peas with Walnuts and Roquefort (page 175)
Seared Fish with Lettuce Leaves (page 176)
Garlic-Ginger Shrimp (page 180)
Mark's Famous Spicy Shrimp (page 180)
Carne Cruda (page 190)
Herbed Fresh Cheese Patties (page 198)
Sausage and Grape Bruschetta (page 40)
Black and Blue Tuna (page 47)
Grilled Watermelon and Shrimp Skewers (page 50)
Crab Cake Burger (page 51)
Egg and Carrot Cake with Soy (page 70)
White Bean Toasts (page 79)
Figs in a Blanket (page 80)
West Indian Pork Kebabs (page 99)

Brown-Bag Lunches

Leftover pasta, soup, and main courses; salads and cold sandwiches—these are all no-brainers for workplace lunches. So here are some of the less obvious one-dish meals that travel well from fridge to desk or corporate kitchen; some of them benefit from reheating. Some can be eaten as is, at work or (if you're lucky) on a bench, or at a park or beach.

Breakfasts and Brunches You Can Eat Any Time of the Year

Change the fruit, vegetables, or seasonings and these eye-openers are fine in any season.

Hangtown Fry (page 160)

Blueberry Pancakes (page 29)

Muesli with Raspberries (page 29)

Matzo Brei with Cherries (page 30)

Tomato, Goat Cheese, and Basil Strata (page 30)

Mediterranean Poached Eggs (page 69)

Spicy Escarole with Croutons and Eggs (page 69)

Huevos Rancheros (page 70)

Breakfast Burritos (page 70)

Brunch Baked Eggs (page 71)

Migas (page 33)

Desserts You Can Eat Any Time of the Year

Some desserts are bound to their season, but you can enjoy many others year-round. Then there are those that change character, and season, when you change the fruit.

Lemon Mascarpone Mousse (page 153)

Grapefruit 'n' Cream Shake (page 153)

Orange Fool (page 154)

Almond Tart (page 155)

Nutella Fondue (page 155)

Deconstructed Raspberry Soufflés (page 198)

Rose Water Whipped Cream with Honeydew (page 198)

Grilled Angel Food Cake with Fruit Salsa (page 199)

Ginger-Lemon "Ice Cream" (page 64)

Peach Lemon "Cheesecake" (page 65)

Fresh Fruit Gratin (page 65)

Blueberry Ricotta Cheesecakes (page 63)

Apricot Cream Upside-Down Pie (page 64)

Ice Cream Sandwich (page 66)

Caramelized Pears with Mascarpone (page 109)

Finger Food for All Occasions

Perfect for cocktail parties or picnics. Serve these with toothpicks alongside, or cut them into bite-size triangles, squares, or chunks, before or after preparing. For a list of more substantial knife-and-fork appetizers, see page 17.

Recipes That Barely Disturb the Kitchen

No recipe in this book leaves you with a sink full of dirty dishes, but here are those which really can be made in one pan or pot, with a minimum of mess.

Udon Noodles with Green Tea Broth (page 161)

Tuna and Bean Salad (page 170)

Fast Fish Soup (page 164)

Classic Caesar Salad (page 165)

Tuna with Pineapple, Cucumber, and Avocado (page 48)

Ice Cream Sandwich (page 66)

Pound Cake with Mascarpone and Marmalade (page 110)

Brown Sugar Apple in the Microwave (page 111)

The Easiest of the Easiest

Of all the recipes in *Kitchen Express*, these are the ones that give the biggest rewards for the smallest amount of work.

Zuppa di Pane (page 119)

Avocado, Citrus, and Radicchio Salad (page 125)

Mussels in White Wine and Garlic (page 133)

Citrus-Braised Fish Fillets or Steaks (page 135)

Chicken Piccata (page 141)

Sausage and Potatoes (page 142)

Linguine with Butter, Parmesan, and Sage (page 149)

Warm Milk Toast (page 152)

Chive Salad (page 167)

Lemon Parmesan Chicken (page 186)

Avocado Soup with Crab (page 32)

Sesame Shrimp Toasts (page 92)

Mussels in Tomato–White Bean Sauce (page 92)

Nutella Fondue (page 155)

The Best Recipes for Picnics

Any sandwich—and there are dozens of them here—is fine for a picnic. But here are some additional, perhaps unexpected, ideas.

The Best Recipes for Reheating

Any soup can be reheated; here are some other dishes that you can warm on the stove, in the oven, or in the microwave.

The Best Do-Ahead Recipes for Potlucks

Need to carry a dish to someone else's house? Try one of these.

Recipes for Hot Sandwiches

Terrific dishes for serving between two pieces of bread, stuffed into a split roll or pocket pita, wrapped up in a large warm tortilla, or open-face on thick slices of toast.

Sweet Sauerkraut with Kielbasa (page 142)

Hangtown Fry (page 160)

Eggs Bhona (page 160)

Jerk Chicken (page 54)

Spiced Chicken with Mango Salsa (page 55)

Spicy Grilled Pork with Peach Marmalade (page 56)

Korean Barbecued Beef (page 58)

Grilled Skirt Steak with Tomatillo Salsa (page 58)

Northern Beans with Spanish Chorizo (page 87)

Ham Steak with Redeye Gravy (page 100)

Recipes to Toss with Pasta

All of these are moist enough to serve as a sauce when mixed with a pound or more of cooked pasta.

Fish Braised in Lemon with Tomatoes and Red Peppers (page 177)

Chicken with Bacon, Shallots, and Brandy (page 140)

Mark's Famous Spicy Shrimp (page 180)

Mediterranean Chicken (page 183)

Chicken with Green Olives (page 185)

Zucchini with Tomatoes and Chorizo (page 46)

Garlicky Rabe with Pancetta and Pine Nuts (page 85)

Fried Endive with Butter and Lemon Sauce (page 86)

Seared Tuna with Capers and Tomatoes (page 90)

Braised Fish with Zucchini (page 88)

Chicken Puttanesca (page 96)

Recipes to Serve over Asian Noodles or Rice

Not every stir-fry dish mandates rice or noodles, but on the other hand, why not? The meal expands almost instantly.

Crisp Tofu and Asian Greens with Peanut Sauce (page 131)

Shrimp with Black Bean Sauce (page 133)

Chicken in Spicy Basil-Coconut Sauce (page 136)

Ketchup-Braised Tofu with Veggies (page 174)

Garlic-Ginger Shrimp (page 180)

Spicy Chicken with Lemongrass and Lime (page 184)

Broiled Eggplant with Miso-Walnut Vinaigrette (page 39)

Stir-Fried Corn and Clams (page 52)

Chicken with Chinese Long Beans and Lemongrass (page 54)

Hot-and-Sour Beef and Okra Stir-fry (page 59)

Stir-fried Mixed Vegetables with Ginger (page 85)

Eggplant Stir-fry (page 86)

Crisp Tofu 'n' Bok Choy (page 87)

Stir-fried Shrimp with Chestnuts and Napa Cabbage (page 90)

Stir-fried Chicken with Nuts (page 93)

Chicken Teriyaki Skewers (page 96)

Soups You Can Chill

Perfect hot-weather soups.

Peanut Soup (page 117)

Cauliflower Soup (page 117)

Asparagus Leek Soup (page 163)

Zucchini and Dill Soup (page 31)

Curried Coconut–Butternut Squash Soup (page 73)

Summer

The explosion of universally

available fruits and vegetables makes cooking
naturally quicker and more varied in summer than
it is in other seasons, with the possible exception of
fall. And the fact that this produce includes items
almost everyone loves—tomatoes, corn, stone fruit,
and much more—makes pleasing people easy. Almost
as interesting to the cook is the abundance of herbs:
These allow you to vary your favorite dishes by doing
little more than switching a tablespoon of this for a
tablespoon of that.

1.

Blueberry Pancakes

Substitute cornmeal for up to half of the flour, for crunch.

Combine two cups flour, two teaspoons baking powder, one-quarter teaspoon salt, and one tablespoon of sugar. Whisk two eggs with one and one-half cups milk and two tablespoons melted butter. Add wet ingredients to dry; stir to combine (it's OK if there are some lumps). Cook with butter—make them big or small, your call—scattering blueberries on top of each cake; flip after the batter begins to bubble. Serve however you like.

2.

Muesli with Raspberries

In the winter, try this with dried cherries.

In a large bowl combine rolled oats (*not* the quick-cooking kind) with a mixture of chopped nuts and seeds; the usual ratio is three parts oats to two parts extras, but do whatever you like. Toss in some shredded coconut, a little brown sugar and cinnamon, and a pinch of salt. Serve with yogurt and fresh raspberries, drizzled with honey. Store the leftovers as you would granola.

3.

Matzo Brei with Cherries

To go savory, skip the maple syrup and add some fresh chopped sage or rosemary and lots of black pepper.

Pit a couple of cups of tart cherries (or use frozen; don't bother to thaw them). For every egg (or two if you want more egg than cracker), run a sheet of matzo under cold water until it's barely soft. Fry the damp crackers in lots of butter over medium-high heat, tossing and breaking them up a bit. When they start to crisp up, add the cherries and cook until dry. Then stir in the scrambled eggs with a pinch of salt and cook them until just set. Serve drizzled with maple syrup.

4.

Deviled Eggs with Crab

Buy fresh crabmeat if you can or use chopped cooked shrimp.

Make hard-cooked eggs; meanwhile, combine crabmeat with a spoonful each of Dijon mustard and mayonnaise or yogurt, lemon juice, diced red bell pepper, paprika, and cumin; sprinkle with salt and pepper. Run eggs under cold water, shell and halve them, and mash the yolks into the crab mixture; stuff the whites. Sprinkle the top with chopped parsley (or caviar for that matter).

5.

Tomato, Goat Cheese, and Basil Strata

You can assemble this the night before and refrigerate until you're ready to bake.

Heat the oven to 400°F. Soften a chopped onion in butter; off heat, stir in chopped fresh tomato, six beaten eggs, a cup fresh shredded basil, a splash of milk or cream, and a sprinkle of salt and pepper. Top with bread cubes and dollops of goat cheese. Bake until just set, about 20 minutes; put under broiler quickly to brown top if necessary.

6.

Gazpacho

Try peaches or melons instead of tomatoes, or add anchovies for more flavor.

Core and seed ripe, juicy tomatoes and cut into chunks. Peel and seed a cucumber and roughly chop. Peel a clove or two of garlic. Cut the crusts from a couple of thick slices of good white bread and tear them up. Puree everything in a blender with salt, pepper, lots of olive oil, and a splash of sherry vinegar, adding just enough water (or ice) to thin the mixture. Serve garnished with a drizzle of olive oil and chopped basil or mint leaves.

7.

Zucchini and Dill Soup

Add fresh ricotta, sour cream, or yogurt while pureeing, for richness.

Grate a couple of zucchini. Cook a chopped onion in butter until softened, then add the zucchini and stir until softened, five minutes or so. Add vegetable or chicken stock and bring to a boil; simmer for about five minutes, then puree until smooth. Season with salt and pepper and lots of fresh chopped dill.

8.

Shrimp and Tomato Soup

Amazing with good tomatoes.

Boil one pound of shell-on shrimp in six cups of water until just pink; drain, reserving the liquid. Cook a chopped shallot in some olive oil (you can use the same pot), sprinkle with salt and pepper, and deglaze with a splash of white wine or dry vermouth. Add the reserved liquid and let bubble a bit; peel and chop the shrimp. Cut two or three ripe tomatoes into wedges and add them to the pot, along with the shrimp and chopped fresh tarragon. When just warmed through, serve in shallow bowls.

9.

Melon Soup with Pancetta

Sweet and salty.

Puree the flesh from a cantaloupe or honeydew with lemon juice and a little white wine or water until smooth. Put the soup in the freezer to chill (along with some serving bowls if you like) while you frizzle some thin ribbons of pancetta or prosciutto in a little olive oil. When crisp, add several grinds of black pepper and remove from heat. To serve, put the soup in bowls, and top with ham, chives, salt, and pan drippings.

10.

Avocado Soup with Crab

Lightning-fast luxury; instead of the crab, try cooked shrimp or lobster.
Or use tortilla chips, ripe tomato chunks, or crumbled queso fresco.

Puree a couple of ripe avocados with two cups of whole milk and a pinch of salt. Season a mound of fresh lump crabmeat with minced fresh red chiles, chopped cilantro, and a squeeze of lime or orange juice. Serve the soup with a scoop of the crab.

11.

Smoke 'n' Spice Fish Soup

Almost any seafood works here, as do bits of cooked chicken.

Chop an onion, a carrot, and a couple of celery stalks and cook in olive oil with minced garlic and salt and pepper until soft. Chop as much canned chipotle as you like (for less heat, remove the seeds) and add it to the soup along with some of its sauce (adobo) and six cups of chicken or fish stock (or water). Boil, then lower the heat a bit and add two or three chopped ripe tomatoes. When the mixture boils again, lay a couple white fish fillets in the soup, turn the heat to low, cover, and cook for about five more minutes. Break the fish into large chunks and serve with a dollop of sour cream, chopped cilantro, and warm tortillas.

12.

Charred Tomato Bisque

Good hot or cold.

Heat the broiler. Cut four or six large ripe tomatoes into thin slices and spread them out on a rimmed baking sheet, along with three smashed garlic cloves, olive oil, salt, and pepper. Broil until the tomatoes are beginning to blacken, turning as necessary, about eight minutes total; remove the garlic as soon as it turns golden. Puree everything with a cup of cream and a half-cup of basil leaves. Warm gently in a saucepan or chill for a few minutes in the freezer. Serve with grilled cheese sandwiches or breadsticks.

13.

Migas

Crouton hash, really; in place of the beans, any kind of protein works, from eggs (raw or hard-boiled) to nuts to sliced chorizo.

Cut several slices of old bread into cubes. Heat a film of olive oil in a large skillet and fry the bread, seasoning with salt, pepper, pimentón, and cumin as it cooks. Remove to a large bowl, add a little more oil to the pan if necessary, and cook precooked or canned chickpeas until they're golden and beginning to crisp. Cut a bunch of Swiss chard into ribbons and add that to the pan. Stir-fry until the greens wilt, then toss the mixture with the bread cubes. Serve with lemon wedges.

14.

Goat Cheese Salad

Serve on a bed of greens, on slices of toasted bread, or on a baked potato.

Mash soft goat cheese with a tiny bit of minced garlic, salt and pepper, chopped fresh mint, thinly sliced red onion, chopped ripe tomato, and olive oil. Add a handful of pine nuts or pistachios if you like.

15.

Panzanella

Chewy and juicy all in one bite.

Cut ciabatta or other good bread into cubes. Chop ripe tomatoes, oil-cured black olives, anchovies, garlic, and capers; combine with red wine vinegar, olive oil, and lots of black pepper. Add the bread, tossing to absorb the dressing. Garnish with fresh chopped basil and shaved Parmesan cheese.

16.

Tuna Tabouleh

Serve on romaine leaves with tomato and yogurt.

Soak about one-half cup of fine-grain bulgur in boiling water to cover. Peel, seed, and chop a cucumber and toss with lots and lots of chopped parsley, scallions, and fresh mint. Squeeze the bulgur dry and add to the cucumber mixture, dressing with lemon juice (again: lots), olive oil, salt, and pepper. Use a fork to add a can or two of good-quality tuna; toss to fluff the salad and serve.

17.

Black Bean and Mango Salad

Super-colorful, and great wrapped in a flour tortilla with shredded lettuce.

Rinse and drain a can of black beans (or use a couple cups of homemade beans) and combine with a diced mango, a chopped red bell pepper, two or three chopped scallions, and some minced fresh chile. Drizzle with olive oil, lime juice, salt, and pepper. Toss with fresh chopped mint or cilantro and serve.

18.

Mexican Dry-Corn Salad

Use frozen corn if you're feeling lazy.

Heat olive oil in a large skillet over medium-high heat. Add a small chopped red onion, a couple of cups of corn kernels, and a diced fresh chile; cook and stir until the corn is browned. Mash an avocado with a dollop of sour cream or plain yogurt and a squeeze of fresh lime or lemon juice; add chopped cilantro and sprinkle with salt and pepper. Toss the avocado mixture with the corn and serve in a bowl with some shredded iceberg lettuce, chopped tomato, and tortilla chips.

19.

Squid Salad with Basil Mayo

Try stuffing this in tomatoes.

Heat a grill or broiler. Toss whole, cleaned squid with olive oil and salt and pepper. Grill or broil for about two minutes on each side or until opaque but still tender. Meanwhile, toss together sliced radishes, chopped red bell pepper, thinly sliced red onion, and a squeeze of lemon; set aside. Finely chop one cup of fresh basil and stir in one-half cup of mayonnaise. When the squid is cool, cut into rings and toss with the radish mixture; serve on salad greens with a dollop of the mayonnaise on top.

20.

Summertime Shrimp Salad

Toss shelled shrimp in olive oil, salt, and pepper, and grill or broil until cooked through. Zest and juice a lemon and combine with olive oil, chopped cilantro, salt, and pepper. Add diced red onion, chopped cucumber, and chunks of ripe peaches, plums, or melon. Serve the shrimp on top or chop it up a bit and mix it right in the salad.

21.

Soba Noodles and Cucumber with Dipping Sauce

Perfect hot-weather food; add a bit of freshly grated ginger or wasabi for more spice and top with bits of cooked meat or tofu if you like.

Boil and salt water for pasta; meanwhile, combine a quarter cup of chicken stock or water, three tablespoons of soy sauce, two tablespoons of mirin, and a teaspoon of sugar in a bowl; mix to dissolve the sugar. Cook the noodles for about four minutes, then rinse under cold water. Serve a nest of the noodles along with sliced cucumbers in a bowl (set over ice cubes if you like), with a small bowl of the dipping sauce on the side, garnished with chopped scallions.

22.

Four-Bean Salad

A great picnic salad, because the beans only get better as they marinate in the dressing.

Cut about a cup of green beans into one-inch pieces and blanch in boiling, salted water until crisp-tender; drain and run under cold water to stop the cooking. In a bowl, combine a cup or two each of cooked or canned (drain first) kidney or other red beans, cannellini or other white beans, and chickpeas. Add the green beans, a small, diced red onion, and some chopped parsley or chives. Dress with olive oil, sherry vinegar or some other good strong vinegar, Dijon mustard, salt, and pepper.

23.

Prosciutto, Peach, and Mozzarella Salad

Salty, sweet, creamy, and unbeatable.

For each person, cut a fresh peach into eight wedges. Tear prosciutto and sliced mozzarella into bite-size pieces. Dress mixed greens with olive oil, lemon juice, and salt and pepper. Toss in the peaches, prosciutto, and cheese and serve.

24.

Warm Corn Salad with Ham

Like substantial succotash.

Put a half pound or so of good chopped ham into a hot skillet with a little olive oil and a chopped onion. Brown, stirring once in a while. Add the kernels stripped from four ears of corn, along with a handful of frozen lima or fava beans; sprinkle with salt and pepper. Remove from heat and stir in a splash of wine vinegar and some chopped fresh parsley or sage. Serve with thick tomato slices.

25.

Avocado Crab Salad
with Mixed Herb Salad

An impressive, restaurant-style dish.

Whisk together sherry or rice vinegar, Dijon mustard, olive oil, minced shallot, and some salt and pepper. Halve avocados and remove the pits (leave the skin on); cut a thin piece off the bottom of each half so it sits on a plate. Make a salad of fresh herb leaves and sprigs, using chervil, parsley, tarragon, dill, mint, or basil in any combination. Fill each avocado half with lump crabmeat and put a handful of the herbs and a few thin slices of lemon alongside. Drizzle the dressing over all.

26.

Shrimp and Cherry Tomato Salad

Soy sauce is the secret ingredient here.

Stir-fry peeled chopped shrimp and grated ginger in a little sesame oil. Set aside while you halve a pint or two of cherry tomatoes and toss in a salad bowl with a splash of soy sauce. Add the shrimp mixture and a handful of fresh basil (preferably Thai); let rest for a couple of minutes and then serve, with rice crackers.

27.

Arugula with Balsamic Strawberries and Goat Cheese

A surprisingly wonderful salad.

Hull and slice a pint of strawberries and put them in a large salad bowl. Toss with two tablespoons balsamic vinegar and several grinds of black pepper. Let sit for five minutes. Add a bunch of arugula, some crumbled goat cheese, and a sprinkle of salt; drizzle with olive oil, toss, and serve.

28.

Feta and Watermelon Salad

A terrific combination.

Combine watermelon balls (or cubes) in a bowl with crumbled feta cheese, sliced radishes, chopped fresh chives, and a few drops of olive oil; toss well. Spoon over a crisp wedge of iceberg lettuce, making sure to use all the extra juices left in the bottom of the bowl.

29.

Broiled Eggplant with Miso-Walnut Vinaigrette

Toss with soba noodles or serve on a bed of greens.

Heat the broiler. Halve small eggplants lengthwise (or slice large ones) and rub them all over with vegetable oil and salt. While they're broiling, whisk together some miso, chopped walnuts, soy sauce, and rice vinegar. Cook the eggplant until it's browned and soft, then remove to a platter and pour the dressing over all. Garnish with chopped scallions.

30.

Duck Wraps with Plums

Fresh fruit updates Peking duck.

Buy roast duck and take the meat off the bones. Cut several ripe plums into wedges. Heat vegetable oil in a skillet and add some thinly sliced leeks (the white part only). When soft, add the duck and stir-fry for a minute or two, then add the plums, cooking and stirring until they're just warmed through. Roll in small flour tortillas or lettuce leaves, and serve with hoisin sauce for dipping.

31.

Summer Rolls with Barbecued Pork

An excellent use for any leftover meat or seafood.

Shred the pork and toss with a splash of fish sauce, some chiles, a squeeze of lime, and some chopped mint. Dip a sheet of rice paper into a bowl of hot water for about two seconds. Turn it and dip the piece you were holding in the water; lay on a damp towel. Put a little of the pork mixture at the bottom of the wrapper; roll and fold as you would a burrito. Serve with salted shredded cabbage tossed with sesame oil and rice vinegar.

32.

Sausage and Grape Bruschetta

Red grapes are prettier here.

Squeeze two Italian sausages from their casings and break the meat into a hot skillet with a little olive oil and a chopped red onion. Cook, stirring once in a while, until browned all over. Meanwhile, cut several thick slices of good Italian bread, brush with olive oil, and toast or broil until crisp outside but tender inside. When the sausage is done, stir in about a pound of grapes, mashing a bit to break some of them up. Cook until just warmed through. Top the bread with the sausage mixture and pan juices.

33.

Fish Tacos

Any firm white fish works well here; or try crab or shrimp.

Cook a chopped red onion in olive oil for a minute or two. When it's soft, add a big pinch of ground cumin or coriander and some salt and pepper. Keeping the heat relatively high, add a pound or so of fish fillets and stir to break them into chunks, cooking until they're just opaque. Off heat, squeeze lime juice over the mixture and scrape up any browned bits from the bottom of the pan. Warm corn tortillas and fill with the fish mixture. Top with shredded cabbage, chopped tomato or tomatillos, a splash of hot sauce, and a dollop of sour cream.

34.

Tuna-Anchovy Sandwich

You can use this to stuff celery sticks, too.

Mash olive oil–packed tuna with some anchovy fillets and minced garlic. Squeeze lemon juice over all and fold in some chopped black olives, halved cherry tomatoes, and chopped fresh basil or parsley. Spread on good crusty bread or serve with crisp lettuce cups for wrapping.

35.

Grilled Tomato Sandwich with Blue Cheese Spread

Thinly sliced roast beef will bulk this up considerably.

Mash blue cheese with a little softened cream cheese, chopped chives, and just enough milk to make it spreadable. Smear a thin layer on slices of good bread. Top with ripe tomato, salt, and pepper. Make sandwiches and slip into a buttered hot frying pan. (If you're making more than one sandwich, assemble them on a baking sheet and broil them on both sides.) Press down gently when you flip the sandwich and keep cooking until golden and gooey. Cut on the diagonal and serve with pickles or chow chow.

36.

Shrimp-Tomato-Arugula Wraps

Just what it sounds like.

Mince garlic and cook in vegetable oil till just fragrant, less than a minute. Add peeled shrimp and cook until pink, about three minutes more. Make a dressing of plain yogurt, lemon juice, chopped cilantro, salt, and pepper. Warm large flour tortillas (whole wheat are nice), then spread yogurt mixture on each tortilla and add arugula, sliced seeded tomato, the shrimp, and some lettuce. Roll tightly, cut in halves or quarters, and serve.

37.

Caramelized Caprese Sandwich

Halve good crusty rolls or squares of corn bread or focaccia and toast under the broiler. Slice ripe tomatoes crosswise into thick rounds; spread out on a broiler pan, drizzle with olive oil, sprinkle with salt and pepper, and quickly brown on both sides. Serve open-faced: bread first (olive bread is awesome), then sliced fresh mozzarella and fresh basil leaves, topped with the tomato slices; drizzle with pan juices.

38.

Portobello Burgers
with Tomato Mayonnaise

You can grill or broil the lettuce and tomato too, if you like.

Stem large portobellos; cut a large onion into thick slices. Brush both with oil and sprinkle with salt and pepper, then grill or broil until tender. Meanwhile, puree a large ripe, seeded tomato in a food processor with good-quality mayo, a clove of garlic, and a few fresh herb sprigs if you've got them handy. Halve rolls or buns, spread them with the mayonnaise, and fill with mushroom and onion, adding lettuce and more tomato. Serve.

39.

Grilled Fish Sandwich
with Chile-Lime-Carrot Relish

*Mayo scented with chile and lime is good as a dressing here too;
and use tomatoes if you can't find tomatillos.*

Grate two or three carrots and combine with lime juice, chili powder, minced garlic, salt, and pepper; press down to soften the carrots a bit. Brush any sturdy white fish with olive oil and grill until done, about three minutes per side. Split good-quality rolls; spread carrot relish on the bottom half and add sliced tomatillos, cilantro sprigs, and the fish.

40.

Five-Spice Lobster Sandwich

Or crab, or shrimp, or mixed seafood.

Combine a large pinch of five-spice powder with two tablespoons soy sauce, one tablespoon rice vinegar, and two teaspoons sesame oil. Add two chopped scallions, grated ginger, minced garlic, and minced fresh chile if you like. Mince a red bell pepper and add it to the dressing along with about two cups shredded cooked lobster. Mix well with a fork, taste, and add some salt and pepper. Spread on split baguette or rice cakes.

41.

Blackened Salmon Sandwich

Grind together some cumin seed, fennel seed, dried oregano, dried thyme, paprika, a little bit of cayenne, and salt; rub all over skinned salmon fillets. Heat a heavy skillet until almost smoking, add a film of oil, and cook salmon until well browned, about four minutes; then flip and cook until medium-done. Layer thickly sliced bread or rolls with thin-sliced onion, plain yogurt, arugula leaves, and salmon.

42.

Black Bean Tostada

In Mexico, this is called a clayuda.

Heat precooked or canned black beans, adding ground cumin, chili powder, fresh oregano, and salt. Shred cabbage and chop a few radishes or a chunk of jicama; grate some Mexican melting cheese like queso Oaxaca or cotija, and slice some smoked chorizo or other cooked sausage. Drain the beans and mash roughly. Lightly toast large tortillas under the broiler, then top with the beans, the cheese, and the meat. Return to the broiler to melt the cheese and serve, topped with the vegetables and a dollop of sour cream; put lime wedges on the side.

43.

Taco Slaw

Not your usual restaurant salad.

Load a big bowl up with shredded cabbage. Add precooked or canned drained pinto beans, a handful of corn kernels, lots of chopped tomatoes and red onions, sliced red bell pepper and avocado, bits of chopped smoked chorizo, and crumbled queso fresco. Break up some tortilla chips on top. Put a bunch of fresh cilantro in the blender with lime juice, olive oil, salt, pepper, and as much fresh or dried chile as you can stand. Give the mixture a good whirl, then use it to dress and toss the salad. Serve with crema for last-minute drizzling.

44.

Microwaved Honey Eggplant

Sort of amazing.

Combine a half cup each of chopped parsley and breadcrumbs with three tablespoons olive oil, two tablespoons honey, one minced garlic clove, and a pinch of salt. Cut one large or two medium eggplants crosswise into one-inch slices; then score the top of each slice. Put the slices in a dish and spread the breadcrumb mixture over the tops, pressing it into the slits. Partially cover with wax paper and microwave on high power for about five minutes. Remove the paper and cook another two or three minutes, until very soft. Sprinkle with lemon juice and serve with yogurt on the side.

45.

Balsamic Beef, Radicchio, and Romaine

Serve as a warm salad, or skip the lettuce and toss the beef mixture with pasta.

Shred a medium head of radicchio and a head of romaine lettuce. Brown about a half pound of ground beef in some olive oil with salt and pepper, then add a chopped red onion, a chopped garlic clove, and a chopped fresh red chile (or use a pinch of dried flakes). When the vegetables begin to get soft, add the radicchio, a splash of balsamic vinegar, and a little water. Cook until the radicchio is caramelized and the sauce thickens. Toss in a big bowl with the lettuce, adding more olive oil if needed; pass grated Parmesan at the table if you like.

46.

Swiss Chard with White Beans and Pancetta

Or bacon.

Dice a quarter pound of pancetta and sear in olive oil until golden and getting crisp. Meanwhile, take a large bunch of Swiss chard and chop, keeping stems and leaves separate. Add the stems to the pancetta; when they soften a bit, add the leaves. Stir until wilted, then add a quarter cup of raisins, a quarter cup of pine nuts, and a couple cups of precooked or canned navy beans (rinsed and drained). Warm until heated through and serve with toasted olive bread or toss with pasta.

47·

String Beans with Bacon and Tomatoes

Like stewed vegetables, only fresher.

Chop a fair amount of thick bacon and fry with some sliced onions in a deep skillet until the meat is cooked and the onions are soft. Pour off some of the fat if there's a lot; add string beans and cook and stir until brightly colored and beginning to soften. Stir in chopped ripe tomatoes and cook until just breaking apart. Garnish with chopped parsley and serve over white rice or thick slices of toast.

48.

Zucchini with Tomatoes and Chorizo

Serve on crusty bread or pasta.

Cut zucchini into quarter-inch disks; cook crumbled (Mexican) chorizo in olive oil for about three minutes, or until beginning to brown, then add diced shallot or onion and minced garlic; continue cooking until the shallot is translucent, a couple of minutes more. Add the zucchini and some chopped tomatoes; cover and cook until the zucchini is tender, about five more minutes. Add some lemon zest and juice, season with salt and pepper, and serve.

49·

Shrimp with Toasted Coconut

Great over a bed of jasmine rice.

Toast some shredded unsweetened coconut, shaking the pan to keep it from burning, until just golden; remove and set aside. Add some oil to the pan, along with peeled shrimp and some curry powder, and cook until the shrimp are pink. Add enough coconut milk to make the mixture saucy, along with some soy sauce and the toasted coconut. Serve garnished with fresh cilantro.

50.
Lettuce Wraps

Incredibly easy and impressive.

Toss good-quality shredded cooked chicken, cooked ground meat, or lump crabmeat with minced shallot or red onion, chopped cilantro, sesame oil, minced Thai chile, salt, and pepper. Take the large outer leaves from heads of Bibb or Boston lettuce, put a couple of tablespoons of the filling mixture in the middle of each leaf, then roll up like a burrito to eat.

51.
Grilled Vegetables with Quinoa

Don't hesitate to add leftover shredded chicken, crumbled sausage,
or even some fried tofu.

Heat the grill and cook the quinoa. Thread quartered shallots or red onions on one skewer, and cherry tomatoes and quartered mushrooms on another (they'll cook more quickly than the onions). Brush the vegetables with olive oil and sprinkle with salt and pepper. Grill the vegetables, turning as needed, until browned and done, about six minutes. Remove the vegetables from the skewers and toss them with the quinoa in large bowl; mix gently, season with more olive oil and salt and pepper as needed, garnish with freshly chopped basil, and serve.

52.
Black and Blue Tuna

Combine sushi-grade tuna steaks with a lot of grated ginger, some minced garlic, and a splash each of oil, soy sauce, fish sauce, and lime juice. Marinate about five minutes, then dredge in sesame seeds. For rare, sear each side for about two minutes on a hot grill or in a lightly oiled, well-seasoned pan. Slice and serve over a bed of watercress.

53.

Tuna with Pineapple, Cucumber, and Avocado

Try using toasted nori instead of lavash for the wrap.

Cut sushi-grade tuna into quarter-inch-thick slices; slice avocado and pineapple into pretty much equal-sized pieces. Very thinly slice a cucumber. Mix together minced ginger, lemon juice, soy sauce, and a little fish sauce. Lay cucumber slices on lavash or other wrap-type bread, overlapping them slightly, then top with the tuna, avocado, and pineapple; drizzle with the dressing, throw in a few sprigs of cilantro, and roll up.

54.

Grilled Fish Kebabs

Try any solid, meaty fish here.

Make a paste from a few cloves of garlic; salt; pepper; lemon juice; chopped fresh oregano, marjoram, or parsley; and olive oil. Cut fish into two-inch chunks, rub well with the paste, and thread onto skewers. Grill for about five minutes, turning as needed, until the fish is firm and slightly blackened. Serve with lemon wedges.

55.

Grilled Fish with Peach and Tomato Salad

Again, use whatever fish is fresh and firm.

Brush the fish with olive oil and season with salt and pepper. Slice an equal number of tomatoes and peaches and put them in a serving dish with diced red onion, chopped cilantro, olive oil, lime juice, salt, and pepper. Grill the fish, turning once, until just done, then serve with the salad and a slice of lemon or lime.

56.

Grilled Sardines with Summer Squash

Fresh sardines are fabulous on the grill.

Brush sardines (figure three or four per serving) with olive oil and sprinkle with salt, pepper, and freshly chopped oregano. Slice zucchini and yellow summer squash into half-inch-thick pieces. Brush the squash with olive oil and sprinkle with salt and pepper. Grill the squash until it's softening, about four minutes per side. Grill the sardines a little less, two or three minutes per side. Serve the sardines over a bed of alternating green and yellow squash, with lots of lemon wedges on the side.

57.

Grilled Fish with Spinach and Tomatoes

Use any white-fleshed fish fillets or steaks here.

Brush the fillets with olive oil and season them with salt and pepper; grill until done. Meanwhile, cook a couple of cloves of garlic in olive oil until fragrant, then add spinach and keep cooking until just wilted, just a couple of minutes; sprinkle with salt and pepper. Thinly slice a couple of tomatoes, and layer on plates; drizzle with olive oil. Top with the spinach and fish and serve with lemon.

58.

Scallop and Peach Ceviche

Plums and pineapple are also terrific here.

Dice high-quality scallops and peaches into equal-sized cubes about a quarter- to a half-inch square. Toss them together in a bowl, along with finely diced red onion, finely chopped tarragon, lots of lime juice (the acid in the lime juice will "cook" the scallops in a few minutes), salt, and pepper. Adjust the seasonings and serve.

59·

Grilled Fish
with Raw Pineapple Chutney

Any sturdy, meaty fish will work.

Combine diced pineapple with chopped scallions, chopped cilantro, salt, pepper, lime juice, and a little cayenne. Brush the fish with olive oil and season with salt and pepper and a squeeze of lime juice. Grill the fish until done. Serve topped with a couple of spoonfuls of the chutney.

60.

Braised Fish with Cherry Tomatoes

A lovely summer dinner served with good bread and a crisp salad.

Cut cherry tomatoes into halves. Sprinkle them and some sturdy white fish steaks or fillets with salt, pepper, and fresh or dried oregano. Heat some olive oil and add the fish; cook until it begins to brown, then turn and add a cup of not-too-dry white wine, some minced garlic, and the tomatoes. Bring to a simmer and cook until the fish is done (a thin-bladed knife inserted into its center will meet little resistance). Serve in soup bowls with the broth.

61.

Grilled Watermelon
and Shrimp Skewers

Nice with basmati rice mixed with toasted coconut.

Light a charcoal or gas grill. Alternate chunks of watermelon and large shrimp on skewers; brush with olive oil and sprinkle with curry powder, salt, and pepper. Grill, turning as needed, until the shrimp is opaque. Garnish with chopped scallions and pistachios and serve with lime wedges.

62.

Crab Cake Burger

*Dredging the patties in breadcrumbs instead of mixing them
with the crab makes for a fantastically crisp crust.*

Combine about a pound of crabmeat with a few tablespoons of mayonnaise, a tablespoon of Dijon mustard, a couple of tablespoons of freshly chopped parsley, salt, and pepper; form into patties. Gently coat the patties in fresh breadcrumbs and sear in hot oil. Cook the patties until they're just golden, turning once. Serve on good-quality buns or rolls topped with lettuce and tomato if you like; garnish with slices of lemon.

63.

Shrimp with Cilantro, Garlic, and Lime

Serve alone, over noodles or rice, or even as part of a salad.

In a large bowl, combine a handful or so of chopped cilantro, some minced garlic, the zest and juice of a lime, a tablespoon of fish sauce, salt, and pepper. In vegetable oil, cook a pound of shrimp until pink and no longer translucent, three or four minutes. (Or use squid; cook it for even less time.) Toss the shrimp in the cilantro mixture and serve.

64.

Shrimp, Scallop,
and Cherry Tomato Kebabs

Use chunks of firm fish here too, if you like.

Skewer shrimp, scallops, and cherry tomatoes, alternating fish and tomatoes. Brush with olive oil and sprinkle with salt and pepper. Grill the kebabs until the fish is done and the tomatoes are soft and slightly blackened, turning as needed. Sprinkle with chopped parsley (or a mixture of parsley and minced onion) and serve with lemon.

65.

Bacon-Wrapped Scallops

Modernizing an old fave.

In a pan, cook the bacon until it's pliable and golden, about five minutes; drain on paper towels and set aside. Season the scallops with salt and pepper, wrap each in a half-slice of bacon, and secure with a toothpick; sear the bundles, turning once, until the scallops are opaque and the bacon is nicely browned, about five minutes total. Dress greens lightly with olive oil and fresh lemon juice and serve the scallops on top.

66.

Stir-Fried Corn and Clams

Fun to eat with chopsticks or your hands.

Cut ears of corn crosswise into one-inch slices. Put a film of vegetable oil in the bottom of a large skillet over medium-high heat. Add some ginger and garlic and the corn and cook and stir until coated and beginning to color, just a minute or two. Add scrubbed clams, a splash each of water and white wine or sherry, and a handful of fermented black beans; cover and cook until the clams open. Taste and adjust the seasoning and serve, garnished with chopped scallions or cilantro and lime wedges.

67.

Grilled Lemon-Tarragon Chicken

Tarragon and chicken are a classic and wonderful marriage.

Mix the zest of a lemon with some chopped fresh tarragon (no more than a teaspoon or so; it's strong). Brush thin chicken breasts with olive oil, smear with the zest and tarragon, and season with salt and pepper. Grill the chicken, turning it once, until cooked through. Squeeze more lemon juice over the chicken, then serve, with coarse-grain mustard on the side.

68.

Grilled Chicken Kebabs

*It takes just a couple of minutes more to slice up some eggplant
and zucchini and throw them onto the grill with the kebabs.*

Cut boneless chicken breasts or thighs into chunks. Combine a teaspoon of paprika, a teaspoon of cinnamon, a dash of nutmeg, salt, and pepper together in a small bowl. Toss the chicken with a few tablespoons of olive oil and some fresh lemon juice; sprinkle well with the spice mixture. Thread the chicken onto skewers and grill until done, then serve with lemon wedges.

69.

Grilled Chicken Paillards
with Endive and Radicchio

The grilled lemons make this spectacular.

Pound chicken breasts to quarter-inch thickness, brush them with olive oil, and season with salt and pepper. Cut the endive and radicchio into halves, brush the cut side with olive oil, and season with salt and pepper. Cut three or four lemons in half and brush the cut side with olive oil. On a hot grill, cook the chicken, turning it once, until it's brown and done, about three minutes per side; cook the endive, radicchio, and lemons, cut side down, until browned, about four minutes. Serve the chicken with the vegetables, squeezing the grilled lemon over everything.

70.

Jerk Chicken

Serve with black beans and rice or couscous.

In a food processor, combine a half cup of white vinegar, two tablespoons of rum, one or two habanero chiles, a red onion, one tablespoon of dried thyme, two teaspoons of salt, one teaspoon of cracked black peppercorns, one tablespoon each of allspice, cinnamon, and ginger, and two teaspoons of molasses. Process until smooth. Cover a pound of boneless chicken (thighs or breasts) in this mixture and let sit for about five minutes (or up to an hour). Grill the chicken, turning once, until browned and cooked through.

71.

Chicken with Chinese Long Beans and Lemongrass

If you can't find Chinese long beans, use regular green beans.

Cut Chinese long beans into one-inch pieces; cook in boiling, salted water until crisp-tender, about two minutes. Drain and shock in ice water; set aside. Soften a diced onion in a little oil, along with some minced garlic, for about a minute; remove. Stir-fry a pound of chicken that's been cut into half-inch strips until the chicken turns white and is partially cooked, about three minutes. Add a tablespoon of minced lemongrass (the tender inner part only), a tablespoon of fish sauce, a teaspoon of ground coriander, a cup of chicken stock, and about two tablespoons of oyster sauce; mix well and continue cooking until the chicken is done, about three more minutes. Add the green beans, the onion, and garlic and toss well so that everything is coated in the sauce. Season with salt and lots of pepper and serve.

72.

Spicy Chicken Tacos
with Chipotle Cream

Chipotles are hot, so use them to taste.

Mix a cup of sour cream with diced canned chipotles, along with a little of their sauce (adobo). Combine two tablespoons of brown sugar, a tablespoon each of paprika and chili powder, salt, and pepper in a small bowl. Pound chicken breasts to half-inch thickness, brush them with oil, and coat them with the spice rub. Grill or broil the chicken, turning once, until it's cooked through, about six minutes; meanwhile, dice a tomato, an avocado, and a red onion. Slice the chicken and serve it on warm corn tortillas with the vegetables, and chipotle cream; garnish with cilantro.

73.

Spiced Chicken with Mango Salsa

*I grill this chicken, but you can just as easily cook it quickly
in a pan with a bit of oil or butter.*

Heat a grill or grill pan. In a small bowl, mix one teaspoon each of cinnamon, cumin, and paprika; a pinch of cayenne; salt; and pepper. Rub quarter-inch-thick chicken cutlets with the spice mix. In another bowl, combine a chopped mango, half a diced red onion, a handful of chopped cilantro, the juice of half a lime, a tablespoon of olive oil, salt, and pepper. Grill the chicken, turning once, until well browned and cooked through. Serve the chicken topped with mango salsa and lime wedges.

74.

Pork Paillards with Grilled Pineapple

Pound boneless pork chops or medallions cut from the tenderloin to quarter-inch thickness; slice a pineapple into half-inch rings. Brush both with olive oil and season with salt and pepper. Grill the pineapple until it's well browned on both sides, about four minutes. Grill the pork until it's cooked through, about two minutes on each side. Serve the pork and pineapple with a good steak sauce.

75.

Grilled Pork Skewers with Worcestershire

Mix a quarter cup of Worcestershire sauce with two teaspoons of lime juice. Slice a lime into eight wedges. Cut pork tenderloin into one-inch cubes, brush with the Worcestershire mixture, and sprinkle with salt and pepper. Thread the pork and lime wedges alternately on skewers. Grill the pork, turning as needed to slightly blacken on all sides and brushing repeatedly with the sauce, until cooked through. Serve, squeezing the grilled lime over the pork.

76.

Spicy Grilled Pork with Peach Marmalade

If you like sweet and savory combos, you'll love this.

Combine a quarter cup of peach (or apricot) preserves with some minced garlic, a tablespoon of olive oil, a tablespoon of soy sauce, a half teaspoon of dry mustard, a pinch of cayenne pepper, and salt. Coat thin, boneless pork chops with the marmalade and grill, taking care not to let the marmalade burn. Slice fresh peaches (or apricots) in half, and remove the pits; sprinkle with salt and grill flesh-side down for a couple of minutes until colored and just softening. Serve the pork with the grilled fruit.

77.

Grilled Pork with Basil Peanut Sauce

Use natural peanut butter, please (peanuts and salt, nothing else).

In a blender, combine a few handfuls of fresh basil, a lump of peanut butter (say, a quarter cup), a tablespoon or two of fish sauce, a clove of garlic, a small piece of fresh ginger, a pinch of red chile flakes, and a little water; process until you have a smooth, thick paste, then taste and add more of whatever you like. Rub the paste over a pound of boneless pork chops (about a half-inch thick) and set aside to marinate for a few minutes. Slice a couple of heads of baby bok choy in half; brush them with peanut or sesame oil and sprinkle with salt, pepper, and lime juice. Grill the pork until it's slightly blackened and cooked through; grill the bok choy until it wilts slightly and is tender when pierced with a knife. Serve together.

78.

Grilled Steaks with Rosemary Plums

Don't bother to skewer the fruit if you're feeling lazy;
just lay the rosemary on top as the pieces cook.

Brush rib eye, strip, or sirloin steaks with olive oil and sprinkle with salt and pepper. Cut plums into quarters, remove the pits, and skewer them on rosemary sprigs. Grill everything, turning once, until the steaks are just done—five minutes or so, depending on their thickness—and the plums are soft and slightly blackened. Serve together, with garlic bread.

79.

Korean Barbecued Beef

Traditionally eaten with white rice, wrapped in lettuce leaves.

Slice a flank (or better: skirt) steak into half-inch pieces. Mix together one teaspoon of sesame oil, one tablespoon of brown sugar, three tablespoons of soy sauce, one tablespoon of mirin (or a little honey mixed with water), two minced cloves of garlic, and a pinch of red chile flakes. Brush the meat with the sauce and grill until it begins to crisp, about two minutes per side, basting frequently. Serve the beef sprinkled with toasted sesame seeds and chopped scallions.

80.

Grilled Skirt Steak with Tomatillo Salsa

Use tomatoes, peaches, or pineapple here.

Season a skirt steak with salt and pepper. In a food processor, puree three or four tomatillos, a handful of cilantro, a clove of garlic, a jalapeño or other green chile, a couple of tablespoons of olive oil, some lemon or lime juice, a dash of sugar, salt, and pepper; process until smooth, then taste and adjust the seasonings. Grill the steak to medium-rare, about three minutes on each side. Serve the steak sliced against the grain and drizzled with the salsa.

81.

A Very Good Burger

In a food processor, coarsely grind a pound or so of sirloin or chuck, cut in chunks, with half of a white onion. Season the meat mixture generously with salt and pepper, and form it into patties, handling it as little as possible. Grill the burgers on each side for about three minutes for rare, and a minute more for each further degree of doneness. Serve on buns or rolls with freshly sliced tomatoes, pickles, lettuce, bacon, avocado, or whatever you like.

82.

Hot-and-Sour Beef and Okra Stir-fry

High heat minimizes okra's slime factor.

Trim okra and cut in half lengthwise. Put a film of vegetable oil in the bottom of a large skillet set over high heat. When hot, add the okra, sprinkle with salt and pepper, and cook without stirring until it sputters and browns a bit; stir and let it go a minute or two more. Meanwhile, cut a sirloin or flank steak into strips and chop up some garlic, ginger, onions, and fresh hot chile. Remove the okra from the pan, adding more oil if needed. Stir-fry the beef until almost done; then add the aromatics and chile and sprinkle lightly with sugar. Splash some rice vinegar and soy sauce in the pan to make a little sauce. Add the okra and some cilantro or Thai basil and give a good stir. Serve over rice.

83.

Grilled Lamb Chops with Lemony Yogurt Sauce

This is a lovely sauce whose flavor profile you can readily change by replacing the spices with chopped dill or mint.

Combine a cup of plain yogurt with a few tablespoons of lemon juice, a quarter cup of diced cucumber, and a teaspoon or so of ground cumin and paprika (or pimentón). Season the chops with salt and pepper; grill until medium-rare, about three minutes per side depending on thickness. Serve the lamb with the yogurt sauce.

84.

Grilled Lamb Chops
with Summer Fruit

Grill whatever's in season—nectarines, plums, peaches, and pears are all delicious.

Season lamb chops with salt, pepper, and a sprinkle of cinnamon; cut the fruit into quarters. Cook the lamb chops, turning once, until medium-rare (timing will depend on how thick the chops are). While the lamb is cooking, add the fruit to the grill and cook until it begins to soften and you have nice grill marks. Serve the lamb topped with the grilled fruit.

85.

Shrimp and Pasta with Pesto

You can always use store-bought pesto; but I wouldn't.

Boil salted water for pasta and cook it. Meanwhile, in a food processor, puree a few large handfuls of fresh basil, a large handful of freshly grated Parmesan, and a small one of pine nuts or walnuts; and salt, pepper, and enough olive oil to reach a smooth consistency—you don't want the pesto too thin. In some olive oil cook about a half pound of small whole or large chopped shrimp. Drain the pasta, reserving some of the cooking water, and toss it with the pesto and shrimp, using some of the pasta water to moisten the mixture if needed. Serve warm or cold.

86.

Pasta with Cherry Tomatoes

This is sublime when summer tomatoes are at their peak.

Boil salted water for pasta and cook it; meanwhile, cook a minced clove of garlic in olive oil for a couple of minutes, until fragrant. Add about a pound of whole cherry or grape tomatoes to the pan and cook over low heat. When a few have burst, turn off the heat. Drain the pasta and toss it gently with the tomatoes. Season with salt and lots of freshly ground pepper; serve with freshly chopped basil and/or freshly grated Parmesan.

87.

Pasta Salad with Beans and Herbs

Serve as a room-temperature salad, or warm as a main course.

Cook cut pasta, like ziti, then drain and rinse. Meanwhile, combine a couple of minced shallots; some drained precooked or canned kidney, garbanzo, and black beans; a few tablespoons of olive oil; some minced garlic; a teaspoon of red chile flakes; and lots of freshly chopped parsley, along with (if you have it) a little dill, mint, and basil. (Add some chopped or cherry tomatoes if you like.) Toss the pasta with the bean mixture and season well with salt and pepper.

88.

Pasta with Spicy Squid

Fastest, of course, with pre-cleaned squid.

Boil salted water for pasta and cook it. Meanwhile, slice fresh squid into rings; cook some minced garlic and a diced red chile in olive oil. Add a splash of dry white wine to the pan and bring to a boil. Reduce the heat and add the squid; cook until just done, about two minutes. Toss in the drained pasta, adding extra olive oil if needed, and season well with salt and pepper, and perhaps a little bit of red chile flakes, before serving.

89.

Cellophane Noodles with Shrimp and Papaya

Add some mango or pineapple, or substitute one for the papaya if you like.

Soak the cellophane noodles in boiling water until tender, rinse, and drain. Peel a papaya and dice it into quarter-inch pieces; thinly slice a few scallions; chop a handful of fresh basil; and mince a Thai (or another) chile. Combine in a bowl with a pound of cooked shrimp. Whisk together a few tablespoons of rice wine vinegar, a teaspoon of sugar, and a pinch of salt; then combine with the shrimp mixture and the noodles. Garnish with chopped peanuts and cilantro, mint, or more basil.

90.

Pasta with Spicy Shellfish

This works with peeled shrimp, squid, or crabmeat or shucked clams, oysters, or mussels.

Boil salted water for pasta and cook it; meanwhile, soften a couple of minced garlic cloves and a pinch of red chile flakes in some olive oil; cook until fragrant, about two minutes. Add about a pound of fresh seafood to the garlic and chile flakes, and continue cooking until the fish is cooked (or in the case of crab, warmed through), anywhere from three to five more minutes. Toss the pasta with the seafood, along with a bit of the pasta cooking water if needed. Drizzle with more olive oil if you like; season with salt, pepper, and more red chile flakes if necessary; and garnish with freshly chopped basil or parsley.

91.

Pasta with Puttanesca Cruda

Boil salted water for pasta and cook it; meanwhile, in a large bowl, mix together two large chopped tomatoes, a handful of pitted and chopped olives (any kind, as long as they're good), a couple of tablespoons of drained capers, a handful each of chopped fresh basil and parsley, several chopped anchovy fillets, a little minced garlic, a pinch of red chile flakes, and about a quarter cup of olive oil. Toss the hot pasta and about a quarter cup of the cooking liquid with the tomato mixture, adding more cooking liquid if necessary. Season with salt and pepper, and garnish with more chopped herbs.

92.

Poached Tofu with Broccoli

Bring a large pot of water to a boil and salt it. Lower a brick of firm tofu into the water and cook until it just floats, five to 10 minutes. Meanwhile, whisk together equal parts soy sauce, sake, lemon and orange juices, and water with a little sugar and a few drops of sesame oil; break a head of broccoli into florets. When you remove the tofu, plunge the broccoli into the pot; count to 20 and then drain. Serve thick slices of the tofu with the florets, drizzling the dressing over all. Sprinkle with panko too, if you like.

93.

Blueberry Ricotta Cheesecakes

One of my favorite ways to make the most of fresh blueberries.

In a food processor, finely grind one sleeve of graham crackers. Combine the crackers with about three tablespoons of melted butter and press the mixture into ramekins. Whisk a cup of ricotta cheese with a cup of cream cheese (an eight-ounce package), a couple of tablespoons of honey, the zest and juice of a lemon, and a pinch of salt. Spread the ricotta mixture evenly in the prepared crust, top with lots of fresh blueberries, and serve, or refrigerate for up to a day before serving.

94.

Apricot Cream Upside-Down Pie

Equally good with fresh or dried apricots.

Halve and pit a pound of apricots; put them in a pan with a half cup of brandy and bring to a boil. Continue cooking until the apricots break down, about eight minutes. Whip a cup of cream, along with a tablespoon of brandy, until thick. In a food processor, pulse about eight graham crackers with a good handful of pistachios (pecans are nice here too), leaving the mixture slightly chunky. When the apricots are done, fold them into the whipped cream. Serve a heaping spoonful of the apricot cream in a bowl sprinkled with the graham cracker–nut crunch on top.

95.

Frozen Hot Chocolate

Serve this with biscotti or other not-too-sweet cookies.

Melt six ounces of good dark chocolate with a quarter cup of cream or half-and-half, being careful not to boil. Once the chocolate is melted, taste and add a little sugar if you like. Put it in the blender with three cups of ice and pulse until an even consistency is reached. Serve in small bowls or cups.

96.

Ginger-Lemon "Ice Cream"

Add more candied ginger if you like.

In a food processor, puree two tablespoons of fresh ginger, peeled and roughly chopped, with a half cup of sugar, two cups of cream, and the juice and zest of one lemon. Add ice, pulsing, and pushing down as necessary, until thick and icy; add a couple of tablespoons of chopped candied ginger at the end and process until just combined. Serve immediately, or freeze for up to several days.

97.

Peach Lemon "Cheesecake"

This works just as well with nectarines, raspberries, strawberries, or even mangoes.

Puree two peaches with the juice of one lemon, two tablespoons of sugar, and about six ounces of goat cheese—you want a nice thick mixture, so use more cheese as needed. Spoon the mixture into individual ramekins, smooth the top, and cover with a layer of chopped pistachios. Sprinkle the nuts with powdered sugar and a drizzle of honey.

98.

Fresh Fruit Gratin

Use stone fruits (peaches, nectarines, plums, or apricots) or berries.

Wash, pit, and prepare the fruit as needed; heat the broiler. Combine one cup of sour cream with about two tablespoons of sugar and one teaspoon of vanilla. Put two to three cups of fruit in a baking dish just large enough to hold it, top with the sour cream mixture, and sprinkle with a teaspoon of sugar; broil for about two minutes, or until the cream begins to brown.

99.

Blackberries with Champagne and Tarragon

Oddly appealing.

Finely chop a couple of teaspoons of fresh tarragon. Toss a quart of rinsed blackberries with a few tablespoons of sugar, a cup or so of sparkling wine, and the tarragon. Let the mixture sit for about five minutes, or longer if you have time, and serve in small bowls with your favorite sugar cookie.

100.

Ice Cream Sandwich

Use different flavors of ice cream or sorbet, or vary the jam (or skip it altogether).

Let vanilla ice cream soften for five minutes. Lay cocoa snaps or gingersnaps (or vanilla wafers) out in two rows and spread raspberry jam thinly on each one. Add a scoop of the softened ice cream to half the cookies and top with the remaining cookies to make sandwiches.

101.

Quick Summer Fruit Ice Cream

All you need is a food processor.

Freeze a pound of fresh sliced fruit (trimmed, seeded, or pitted as needed). When hard, put in the machine along with one-half cup crème fraîche (or yogurt or silken tofu for that matter). Add as much or as little sugar as you like and just enough water, a spoonful at a time, to let the processor do its thing. Scrape down the bowl as needed; but don't overprocess, or the ice cream will liquefy. Serve immediately; or if you freeze for later, let it sit out for 10 or 15 minutes to soften a bit.

FALL

Much of summer's bounty remains

through early fall, and as it starts to dwindle, it's
replaced by the late-harvest fruits and vegetables that
will carry through the winter—apples, pears, winter
squash, and a return of many of the cool-weather
vegetables of spring. The combination of grilling and
braising, of summer and winter, makes this a magical
time to cook, and one with more options than any
other.

1.

Spicy Escarole with Croutons and Eggs

You might add a bit of dried oregano, or garlic, or both to the croutons before toasting.

Cut good-quality bread into one-inch cubes; toss the bread with two tablespoons of olive oil, salt, and pepper and toast them until golden, about three or four minutes. Cook a bunch of chopped escarole in two tablespoons of butter for about five minutes, or until wilted. Toss the escarole with the croutons, a pinch or two of red chile flakes, freshly squeezed lemon juice, olive oil, and freshly grated Parmesan cheese. Serve the greens and croutons in bowls with a soft-boiled or poached egg on top, along with more Parmesan.

2.

Mediterranean Poached Eggs

This is fine when the eggs are scrambled, too.

Slice a cup or so of mushrooms and a handful of black olives; chop an onion and two or three plum tomatoes. In a couple of tablespoons of olive oil, cook a smashed clove of garlic and the onion for about two minutes. Add the olives, mushrooms, and tomatoes and let the mixture simmer over medium heat. Poach four eggs and toast thick slices of peasant bread. Add a handful of chopped fresh basil and a couple of tablespoons of capers to the vegetable mixture; season with salt and pepper. Serve the vegetables and eggs on the bread, with lemon wedges on the side.

3.

Egg and Carrot Cake with Soy

Made with common ingredients, but unusual and delicious.

Grate a large carrot while you melt a tablespoon of butter in a skillet over medium heat; add the grated carrot and some minced garlic. Whisk four eggs with a couple of tablespoons of milk in a bowl and add them to the carrots; cook as you would a frittata. When the eggs are almost set, add a few dashes of soy sauce and a sprinkle of scallions and serve. (Good at room temperature, too.)

4.

Huevos Rancheros

*For a less conventional version, replace the tomatoes
in the salsa with peaches or pineapple.*

Chop two large tomatoes, half a red onion, a small chile, and a handful of fresh cilantro; mix together with freshly squeezed lime juice, salt, and pepper. Warm a can of black beans (if you have homemade, all the better). While the beans are warming, make eggs any way you like: fried, poached, or scrambled. Top a warm tortilla with some beans, the eggs, and the salsa; garnish with fresh avocado and more cilantro.

5.

Breakfast Burritos

Basically a tortilla filled with eggs and other stuff.

Heat a can of black, red, or refried beans (or use homemade). Warm large flour tortillas in the oven, in the microwave, or in a dry skillet until just soft. Scramble a couple of eggs and cook them to the desired doneness. Spread some beans down the middle of a tortilla, top with grated cheese, eggs, and then anything else you like: olives, scallions, avocado, tomatoes, cilantro, bacon, sausage, salsa—you get the picture. Fold the short sides of the tortillas in, roll lengthwise, and serve.

6.

Brunch Baked Eggs

Really substantial.

Heat the oven to 400°F. In a pan over medium-high heat, melt a tablespoon or two of butter. Add a bunch of chopped spinach; cover the pan and let the spinach wilt. Add a half cup of cream, a cup of ricotta cheese, a handful of grated provolone, a couple of tablespoons of cognac (optional), salt, pepper, and a sprinkle of nutmeg. Bring this mixture to a simmer, stirring often, for about two more minutes. Divide the spinach mixture among four oven-safe bowls or ramekins (or cook in one big bowl); crack an egg over the top of each. Put the bowls on a cookie sheet and bake them for eight to 10 minutes, or until the whites of the eggs are just set. Serve with toasted bread.

7.

In-Shell Clam Chowder

A rustic spin on the classic.

Heat some olive oil in a pot, and cook a chopped onion for a couple of minutes until soft. Stir in some chopped celery, four cups of fish or clam broth (or water), and a cup each of heavy cream and dry white wine; add a few thyme sprigs, and a pound of potatoes, cut into quarter-inch dice. Bring to a boil, then reduce the heat to medium and cook until the potatoes are tender, about 10 minutes. Add a couple dozen scrubbed clams, season well with salt and pepper, and cover and cook until the clams pop open, just a couple of minutes more. Serve in shallow bowls, garnished with chopped parsley and lemon wedges.

8.

Mushroom and Nori Soup

Light, delicate, flavorful, and unusual.

In a pot over high heat, cook about three cups of mushrooms (any combination works; oyster and shiitake is especially good) in a couple of tablespoons of butter until they begin to release their liquid; add a diced onion, a minced garlic clove, and a chopped celery stalk and cook until the onion is translucent. Add about four cups of vegetable or chicken stock, a quarter cup of soy sauce, the juice of a lemon, a pinch of celery seed, salt, and pepper. Cook until the vegetables are tender. Tear or slice a sheet of nori into strips and put in soup bowls; pour soup over the nori (it will mostly dissolve) and serve.

9.

Lemony Red Lentil Soup with Cilantro

Red lentils cook very quickly, but allow more time if you substitute any other type.

Cook a chopped onion in olive oil in a saucepan until soft; add one cup of red lentils and four cups of chicken broth and bring to a boil; continue simmering until the lentils are soft. Puree a handful of cilantro with a few tablespoons of olive oil and a pinch of salt; set aside. If you like, puree half the lentils until almost smooth; return them to the pan. Add about two tablespoons of lemon juice or more to taste. Stir in the cilantro puree, adjust the seasonings, and serve with crusty bread or a mound of rice in the center.

10.

Egg Drop Soup

Nothing could be easier.

Bring a quart of stock (chicken or vegetable) to a slow bubble; gently pour four beaten eggs into the stock while stirring. Add soy sauce to taste and garnish with some chopped cilantro or scallions; a little sesame oil is nice, too.

11.

Curried Coconut–Butternut Squash Soup

You can buy pre-peeled, precut squash, and just cut it down to quarter-inch pieces.

Cook two cups of chopped squash in a few tablespoons of vegetable oil, along with a diced onion, a teaspoon of cumin, a half teaspoon of cinnamon, and a teaspoon of curry powder (or more to taste). Cook the vegetables and spices until the onion is soft, about three minutes. Add five cups of chicken broth or water and a cup of coconut milk; bring to a boil and cook for about six minutes or until the squash is tender and easily pierced with a knife. Serve the soup topped with fresh cilantro and crusty bread or a scoop of rice.

12.

Tomato Soup with Chickpeas and Greens

Fresh tomatoes and dried chickpeas cooked by you make this even better.

Drain a can of diced tomatoes and a can of chickpeas (if you cooked the chickpeas yourself, use some of their broth in the soup). Cook a diced onion, a diced carrot, and a diced stalk of celery in olive oil until soft. Add one crushed clove of garlic, the tomatoes, the beans, and about four cups of chicken or vegetable broth. Bring to a boil; add a bunch of chopped chard or beet greens (or spinach), reduce to a simmer, and cook for five more minutes. Meanwhile, brush sliced baguette or another good bread with olive oil, and toast. Serve soup with croutons on top.

13.

Broccoli Rabe and Garlic Soup

Some crushed dried chile flakes are nice here.

In a 450°F oven, roast a handful of smashed garlic cloves with a little olive oil for about five minutes. Bring about six cups of stock to a boil; add the garlic, stir in about a half cup of orzo or other small pasta, and a bunch of chopped broccoli rabe; continue cooking until the pasta and rabe are tender. Add lemon juice to taste, along with some salt and pepper. Serve, garnished with freshly grated Parmesan cheese if you like.

14.

Cream of Turnip Soup

This can be rich and creamy, or light and brothy.

Soften half a chopped onion in a couple of tablespoons of butter in a pot over medium heat, along with a smashed clove of garlic, two or three chopped white turnips, and a pinch of salt, for three to five minutes. Add six cups of hot broth, a quarter cup of cream, one bay leaf, and a teaspoon of tarragon, and bring to a boil. Simmer and cook until the turnips are tender, about five minutes. Add a cup of chopped turnip or other greens, stir until they wilt, and serve.

15.

Chile Sweet Potato Soup

Peel about a pound of sweet potatoes and grate or mince them in the food processor. Cook a couple minced cloves of garlic, some diced onion, and a chopped fresh chile in some olive oil until tender; stir in the sweet potatoes and add enough water to cover by about an inch. Bring to a boil, then lower the heat to a vigorous simmer, partially cover, and cook, stirring occasionally, until the sweet potatoes are tender. Stir in some fresh or dried sage and season with salt and pepper. Puree if you like, then add a splash of cream, heat through, and serve with croutons.

16.

Seafood Ramen

Shrimp, calamari, and scallops complement each other beautifully,
but you can use any combination of seafood you like here.

Soak rice noodles in boiling water until tender (two to five minutes, depending on their size), drain, and set aside. Bring four cups of fish, chicken, or other stock and two cups of coconut milk to a boil. Add a pound of seafood to the pot along with a smashed clove of garlic, a handful of chopped scallions, a few dashes of fish sauce, and a thinly sliced hot red pepper. Continue cooking until the fish is done, about three minutes. Divide the noodles among bowls and ladle the soup over the noodles; serve topped with chopped cilantro and a squeeze of lime juice.

17.

Udon Noodle and Miso Soup with Fresh Shiitake Mushrooms

Make this heartier by adding a pound of seafood,
sliced chicken breast or tofu, or thinly sliced beef.

Cook the udon noodles. Bring six cups of vegetable, mushroom, or chicken stock to a boil. Put one-third cup of miso in a bowl and add a ladleful of hot stock to it; whisk until smooth. Add the miso to the stock, along with three cups of sliced shiitake mushroom caps. Cook for about five minutes, then add the drained noodles, garnish with chopped scallions, and serve.

18.

Spinach Salad with Oranges and Goat Cheese

An instant favorite.

Heat the broiler. Finely chop a handful of pecans. Cut a log of goat cheese into half-inch disks; gently pat pecans on all sides of the goat cheese rounds and put them on a greased baking sheet. Broil on both sides until browned and warm, just a couple minutes. Peel two large oranges and separate into sections; thinly slice a small red onion. Whisk together about a quarter cup of olive oil, a few tablespoons of fresh orange juice, a teaspoon or so of mustard, salt, and pepper. In a large bowl, combine a big mound of well-washed spinach, the onion, and the orange slices; toss everything with the dressing and serve topped with a warm disk of pecan-crusted goat cheese.

19.

Endive and Warm Pear Salad with Stilton

Any good blue cheese can take the place of the Stilton here.

Cut three or four pears into eighths; toss them with a couple of tablespoons of olive oil, along with some salt and pepper. Thinly slice a shallot. Cook the pears and shallot in a skillet over medium-high heat until the pears are browning and the shallot slices are wilted; add a tablespoon of maple syrup during the last 30 seconds or so of cooking. Toss the warm pan mixture, and any remaining juices, in a bowl with endive and watercress (or any other greens you like), along with more olive oil and a bit of sherry vinegar. Garnish with crumbled Stilton and serve.

20.

Greek-Style Eggplant Salad

Peeling the eggplant isn't necessary unless the skin is thick and tough.

Heat a broiler or grill (you can use a grill pan, but you'll have to work in batches). Slice an eggplant into quarter-inch rounds; brush with olive oil and sprinkle with salt. Broil or grill until seared on both sides and soft in the center, about five minutes. Thinly slice a small red onion. Put the eggplant, onion slices, crumbled feta cheese, a handful of pitted black olives (oil-cured are good here), and chopped fresh oregano in a bowl. Drizzle with olive oil and season with salt and pepper and serve over greens along with a big squeeze of lemon.

21.

Salad Lyonnaise

A classic.

Bring a pot of water to a gentle boil. Cut bacon or pancetta into small pieces, fry until crisp, and set aside. In a small bowl, combine about a quarter cup of olive oil, a couple of tablespoons of red wine vinegar, a teaspoon of Dijon mustard, salt, and pepper. Crack eggs into the boiling water and poach them for about three minutes, or until set on the outside but still runny on the inside. Remove the eggs with a slotted spoon and drain completely. Toss a few handfuls of frisée or romaine with the bacon and the dressing and serve with a poached egg on top.

22.

Tofu Salad

If you like egg salad, try this.

In a large bowl, whisk together mayonnaise, mustard, soy sauce, and rice wine vinegar with some salt and pepper. Stir in chopped scallions, celery, red bell pepper, and some fresh minced chile if you like. Use your fingers to crumble firm tofu into the bowl and toss with a fork to combine and mash, adding more dressing ingredients if the mixture seems too dry. Serve the salad on a bed of watercress or Bibb lettuce, or rolled up in warmed whole wheat flour tortillas.

23.

Hummus with Pita

There is really no reason to ever buy hummus; homemade is undeniably better, even if you start with canned chickpeas.

Drain a can of chickpeas (or cook some) and reserve the liquid. In a food processor, puree the chickpeas with a few tablespoons of olive oil, a couple of tablespoons of tahini (optional), a large clove of garlic (more or less), a few tablespoons of freshly squeezed lemon juice, and about a teaspoon of cumin, along with salt and pepper. Slowly add chickpea liquid—or water or more oil—until you have a smooth puree; adjust the seasonings. Serve on toasted pita, drizzled with more olive oil and sprinkled with paprika.

24.

Tuna Sandwich with Fennel
and Tarragon

If you don't have tarragon, chop up some of the fennel fronds and toss them in.

Dice a bulb of fennel and a shallot or red onion. In a bowl, mix together about half a cup of plain yogurt, the fennel, the shallot, a drained can of tuna packed in oil, a teaspoon of chopped fresh tarragon, salt, and pepper. Serve in pita pockets, or rolled in large romaine lettuce leaves, with lemon wedges on the side.

25.

White Bean Toasts

Think of this as the Italian version of hummus.

Drain a can of cannellini or other white beans (or cook them yourself), reserving the liquid. In a food processor, puree the beans, some olive oil, a couple of teaspoons of fresh rosemary, fresh lemon juice, salt, and pepper; process until smooth, adding the reserved bean liquid as needed for consistency. Chop a handful of dried tomatoes (they can be dried or reconstituted) into thin strips. Spread the bean mixture on toasted peasant bread, top with a few bits of the tomatoes, and serve.

26.

Kale and Prosciutto Sandwich

*This sandwich gets even better topped with a few slices
of roasted red peppers or softened dried tomatoes.*

Roll four leaves of kale and slice them into half-inch ribbons. Cook in olive oil until wilted and softened; season with fresh lemon juice, salt, and pepper. Toast slices of sourdough or other good-quality bread; spread the toasts with goat cheese and a heaping spoonful of the kale; top with a slice of prosciutto.

27.

Panini with Mushrooms and Fontina

*If you can make grilled cheese, you can make panini; just use another pan
or lid to press on the sandwich while it cooks in a skillet.*

Cook about two cups of sliced mushrooms in butter; season with fresh oregano or thyme, salt, and pepper. When the mushrooms have released their liquid and dried out, divide the vegetable mixture among slices of good-quality whole grain bread with thinly sliced fontina or other semi-hard cheese on top; add another slice of bread on top and brush the outside of both sides with olive oil or softened butter if you like. Cook the sandwich in whatever press you have until the bread is toasted and the cheese is melted, adjusting the heat as needed.

28.

Gruyère Apple Grilled Cheese

Add a couple bacon slices for smokiness (and, of course, meatiness!).

Butter slices of good-quality sourdough bread. Layer Gruyère cheese and thinly sliced tart apples and top with another slice of the buttered bread. Cook the sandwiches in a few tablespoons of melted butter—you can use a press or an ordinary skillet with a bit of weight on top of the sandwich—turning once, until the cheese has melted and the bread is golden brown on both sides, about eight minutes total.

29.

Figs in a Blanket

The name says it all.

Heat the broiler (you can grill these too). In a small pot, bring a cup of red wine, a few tablespoons of honey, a cinnamon stick, and a rosemary sprig to a boil. Wrap half of a fresh fig in half a slice of bacon. Arrange the figs on an oven-safe pan and broil for several minutes per side, until well browned. Serve with the reduced sauce.

30.

Turkey and Pear Wrap
with Curried Aioli

Leftover homemade turkey is ideal, but good-quality deli turkey is fine.

Mix half a cup of mayonnaise (or plain yogurt) with some minced garlic and about a teaspoon of curry powder. Lightly toast flour tortillas in a skillet for about 20 seconds per side. Spread the aioli on the tortillas; evenly layer a lettuce leaf, a thin slice of red onion, thinly sliced pears, and some turkey on top. Roll the tortillas tightly, cut them on the bias, and serve.

31.

Eggplant, Kalamata, Goat Cheese,
and Dried Tomato Sandwich

You can sear the eggplant in olive oil if you like.

Heat the broiler or a grill. Slice an eggplant into one-inch rounds and lightly brush both sides of the rounds with olive oil and sprinkle with salt. Broil or grill for two or three minutes per side, or until golden and softening in the center. In a food processor or blender, puree about a cup of pitted Kalamata olives, some dried tomatoes, and a couple of tablespoons of olive oil to form a paste. Spread goat cheese on ciabatta or other bread; top with a smear of the olive paste and a slice of eggplant.

32.

Seared Cauliflower with Olives and Breadcrumbs

To make this more substantial, start the recipe by frying a sausage or two (or a couple of chunked chicken thighs) in the pan first; break the meat into chunks as it cooks.

Core and roughly chop a head of cauliflower. Heat a film of olive oil in a large skillet over high heat and cook the cauliflower undisturbed, until it browns a little and begins to soften. Add a tablespoon of minced garlic and a handful of pitted olives; cook and stir for a couple of minutes, until the dish comes together and gets fragrant, adding a few more drops of oil to the pan as needed. Add fresh breadcrumbs and keep stirring until they're toasted. Taste and sprinkle with salt if needed, lots of black pepper, and some chopped parsley. Serve hot or at room temperature with lemon wedges.

33.

Broiled Brussels Sprouts with Hazelnuts

For something meatier, fry up a couple of slices of bacon or some diced pancetta and add it along with the hazelnuts.

Heat the broiler. Trim about a pound of Brussels sprouts and pulse in a food processor—or use a knife—to chop them up a bit. Spread out on a rimmed baking sheet, drizzle with two tablespoons olive oil, sprinkle with salt and pepper, and toss. Broil the sprouts for about five minutes, until browning on the edges. Meanwhile, pulse a handful of hazelnuts (or chop them). Shake the pan to flip the sprouts; add the nuts and broil for another three minutes. Sprinkle with freshly squeezed lemon juice and plenty of fresh parsley.

34.

Flatbread Pizza
with Figs, Goat Cheese, and Balsamic

Ripe figs make all the difference here, as does good balsamic vinegar.

Slice a couple of handfuls of figs into quarters. Brush olive oil on lavash or other flatbread and dot generously with goat cheese; spread the figs evenly on top of the cheese. Bake in a 450°F oven until the cheese melts and the figs soften. Drizzle with a tiny bit of balsamic and serve.

35.

Root Vegetable Stir-fry

For a more substantial meal, add strips of cooked chicken when you add the spices.

Use a food processor or box grater to shred a pound or so of one or more root vegetables: waxy potatoes, sweet potatoes, celery root, rutabaga, alone or in combination. Squeeze the shreds dry with your hands. Put a thin layer of vegetable oil in a large skillet over medium-high heat. When it's super hot, add a layer of the vegetables and sprinkle with salt and pepper. Stir-fry without stirring too much so that the shreds brown a bit and clump together. When the vegetables are just tender, season with curry or five-spice powder; stir a couple of times, remove to a serving plate, and repeat in batches with the remaining vegetables. Garnish with chopped cilantro or scallions and serve.

36.

Spiced Vegetables with Raisins

To make this a little more festive, serve on a bed of couscous topped with fresh mint and chopped pistachios.

In a couple tablespoons of olive oil, cook a sliced zucchini; a carrot (chopped into one-inch rounds); a couple garlic cloves, lightly crushed; a teaspoon each of cumin and ginger; half a teaspoon cinnamon; and some salt. Cook for about three minutes. Add a small can of tomato paste and a half cup or so of water, and stir until blended. Add two cups of precooked chickpeas (canned are fine), a handful or two of raisins, the juice of a lemon, and a little more water if necessary; cover and bring to a boil. Reduce to a simmer and cook until the carrot is tender, about five minutes; then adjust the seasoning and serve.

37.

Butter Beans with Prosciutto and Mushrooms

Grate fresh Parmesan over this before serving if you like.

Cut a few slices of prosciutto into pieces about an inch wide, then cook it in a little olive oil until just crisp, about two minutes; remove and set aside. Add a cup or so of sliced mushrooms and drained precooked or canned (or frozen) butter beans to the pan. (There should be some fat left in the pan from the prosciutto; if not, add more olive oil.) Cook until the mushrooms soften a bit, three to five minutes. Add a quarter cup of white wine and continue cooking until the liquid reduces slightly. Sprinkle the vegetables with salt and pepper and serve, topped with the prosciutto.

38.

Stir-fried Mixed Vegetables with Ginger

Replace the broccoli with cauliflower, broccoli rabe, broccolini, or even celery.

Cut broccoli into florets and bok choy into strips. Blanch the broccoli in salted boiling water until crisp-tender; shock in ice water to stop the cooking; drain. Heat two tablespoons of sesame oil in a big skillet; add a tablespoon of freshly grated ginger and some minced garlic and stir; add a few chopped scallions, a diced fresh red chile, a few tablespoons of oyster sauce, a pinch of sugar, and the juice of a lime. Stir to combine well; add the broccoli florets and bok choy strips. Cook until the sauce is reduced slightly and coats the vegetables; add a bit of soy sauce, season with salt and pepper if necessary, and serve over noodles or rice.

39.

Garlicky Rabe with Pancetta and Pine Nuts

Adding more garlic is perfectly acceptable; the same goes for the chile flakes; and of course you can follow these directions for almost any vegetable.

Chop about a quarter pound of pancetta into small pieces and cook in a bit of olive oil until just turning brown, about three minutes. Add some minced garlic and a pinch or two of red chile flakes; continue cooking for another minute or two until the garlic is soft and fragrant. Roughly chop a bunch of rabe and add it to the pancetta: raise the heat a bit and add a splash of water to make some steam. Continue cooking, stirring and adding more water or oil as needed until the rabe is heated and crisp-tender. Adjust the seasonings, toss with toasted pine nuts, and serve.

40.

Fried Endive with Butter and Lemon Sauce

An elegant side dish for almost any fish or meat.

Trim endive heads and halve lengthwise. Cook them in boiling salted water with a squeeze of lemon added for about three minutes. Drain and dip the pieces in milk, then in flour seasoned with salt and pepper. Cook in a few tablespoons of olive oil over medium-high heat for about two minutes per side; set aside. Add a few tablespoons of butter to the pan and continue cooking until it starts to brown, about 30 seconds. Add freshly squeezed lemon juice to taste and chopped parsley; let the sauce continue cooking to thicken a bit. Serve the sauce drizzled over the endive.

41.

Eggplant Stir-fry

Hoisin sauce (think of it as Chinese ketchup) is the main condiment for Peking duck and mu shu pork; it also makes a great dipping sauce for spring rolls.

Dice a medium-size eggplant into one-inch pieces and slice bok choy into strips. Cut firm tofu into one-inch cubes. Cook a teaspoon or so of grated ginger and minced garlic in sesame oil for about two minutes; remove. Add the eggplant and tofu to the pan and continue to cook until both begin to brown (work in batches if the pan is too crowded and add more oil as needed). Add the bok choy and the garlic and ginger, along with a few tablespoons of hoisin sauce and a little water; stir, then cook until the bok choy is wilted. Top with chopped scallions and serve with rice.

42.

Northern Beans with Spanish Chorizo

You can use any cooked sausage you like here, but chorizo is special.

Cut chorizo (Spanish smoked, not Mexican raw) into quarter-inch pieces and sear until slightly browned. Mix together some drained precooked or canned great northern beans or other white beans, a couple of tablespoons of olive oil, and a handful of chopped parsley. Add the chorizo and serve with crusty bread and a mound of arugula.

43.

Crisp Tofu 'n' Bok Choy

They'll take a few minutes longer to cook, but eggplant, broccoli, or green beans can all be substituted for the bok choy, with great results.

Cut firm tofu into thin slices. Shallow-fry the tofu in oil until it browns on both sides. Drain on paper towels; pour off the excess oil (you want about two tablespoons left in the pan). Cook some minced garlic and a teaspoon or so of freshly grated ginger for about a minute before adding a few handfuls of sliced bok choy; continue cooking the bok choy until soft. Add the tofu to the pan to warm and serve over rice or noodles.

44.

Eggplant Rolls

These can be served with tomato sauce, but a drizzle of good balsamic is all they really need.

Heat a grill pan or skillet. Trim a large eggplant and cut into quarter-inch-thick slices *lengthwise*. Brush with olive oil and sprinkle with salt and pepper. Cook with olive oil over medium heat until golden brown and quite tender. Stir together about a cup of ricotta cheese and half a cup grated Parmesan cheese; add a handful of chopped fresh basil and some salt and pepper, and mix well. Spread a few tablespoons of the cheese mixture on each slice of eggplant, roll up, and serve.

45.

Braised Fish with Zucchini

Leave the skin on the fish if at all possible.

Season any sturdy fillets or steaks with salt and pepper. Slice a couple of zucchinis into disks; dice a couple of tomatoes (canned are fine). Heat a few tablespoons of oil in a skillet and cook the fillets, skin side down, until crisp, three minutes or a little longer; remove the fish. Add about a cup of white wine (or, even better, half white wine and half fish stock) to the pan along with the zucchinis and tomatoes and bring to a boil; reduce to a simmer and put the fish back in the pan on top of the vegetables, skin side up. Continue cooking until a thin-bladed knife pierces the fish with little resistance; put the fish in shallow bowls and stir some grated lemon zest and parsley into the sauce. Put the vegetables and broth in the bowls with the fish, drizzle with olive oil and a bit more salt and pepper, and serve.

46.

Walnut-Coated Fish

*Pretty much any nuts—pecans, hazelnuts, peanuts,
and pistachios—can be used to make this type of crust.*

Heat the oven to 400°F. Put about a cup of walnuts in a food processor and pulse a few times until the nuts are just ground, but not too fine. Add a small handful of parsley, a tablespoon or two of chopped thyme (or a teaspoon dried), salt, and a pinch of cayenne; pulse another once or twice to combine. Slice any sturdy fish fillets into large pieces and rub with olive oil, then press the walnut mixture on it to form a crust. Put in an ovenproof dish, drizzle with more olive oil, and cook, turning once, until golden brown and done in the middle, six to 12 minutes depending on their thickness. Serve on a bed of watercress with lemon wedges or vinaigrette.

47.

Baked Fish with Oregano, Lemon, and Olives

Very classic.

Heat the oven to 475°F. Score the skin of some fish fillets (any kind, really). In a mortar and pestle or small food processor, mix together a few cloves of garlic, salt, pepper, and a tablespoon or two of fresh marjoram or oregano; add some olive oil and lemon juice to make a paste. Smear the paste on the fish, covering it well. Bake the fish skin side up for about eight minutes, or until a thin-bladed knife pierces it with little resistance. Chop a handful of good-quality black olives and a little more herb and scatter them over the fish before serving.

48.

Salmon and Sweet Potato with Coconut Curry Sauce

Use a spicy curry powder or a pinch of cayenne if you want more heat.

Heat some vegetable oil and cook a thinly sliced onion and a minced clove of garlic for a couple of minutes until soft; add a tablespoon or so of curry powder and stir until fragrant. Add a can of coconut milk, a couple of diced sweet potatoes, a generous squeeze of lime juice, a few dashes of fish sauce if you like, and some minced fresh ginger; bring to a boil and simmer until the sweet potato is almost tender, about five minutes. Cut a couple of skinless salmon fillets into half-inch cubes and add them to the pan; reduce to a simmer and cook until the fish is just done, about five minutes more. Garnish with fresh chopped cilantro and serve over basmati rice.

49.

Seared Tuna with Capers and Tomatoes

Don't overcook the tuna, or it will become dry.

Sprinkle tuna steaks with salt and pepper, then sear in a very hot skillet or grill pan with a little olive oil, just a minute or so on each side. Add a couple of diced tomatoes (canned are fine), a few tablespoons of freshly squeezed lemon or lime juice, and a tablespoon or two of capers. Cover and reduce the heat to medium for about two minutes; you want to just warm the tomatoes while the tuna cooks a bit more. Serve the tomato-caper sauce spooned over the tuna.

50.

Stir-fried Shrimp with Chestnuts and Napa Cabbage

Frozen chestnuts work nicely in this dish.

Cook a tablespoon each of minced garlic and freshly grated ginger in a couple of tablespoons of hot vegetable oil until they sizzle; add a few handfuls of thinly sliced napa cabbage and cook, stirring, until it just starts to wilt. Add a cup or so of peeled cooked and chopped chestnuts and a handful of shrimp (chopped if they're large). Reduce the heat and continue cooking until the shrimp turn pink, about three minutes. Add two or three tablespoons of water, then soy sauce and sesame oil to taste; top with cilantro and serve.

51.

Pan-Seared Fish
with Spicy Lime Butter

Or try mixing the butter with chopped herbs, capers, anchovies,
or roasted garlic (alone or in combination).

Stir together about a half stick of softened butter, a finely chopped shallot, the zest of a lime and a good squeeze of its juice, a minced red chile, and a pinch or two of salt. Pat any type of fish fillets dry, season them with salt, and cook them quickly in a tablespoon each of olive oil and butter. Turn the fish once and cook until golden and cooked through, about five minutes. Serve the fillets with a generous spoonful of the compound butter on top.

52.

Seared Scallops with Almonds

"Dry" sea scallops are the best.

Sprinkle about a pound of scallops with salt and pepper. Heat a couple of tablespoons of butter until the foam subsides; add the scallops and cook for about two minutes on each side, until nicely browned but still quite rare; remove and set aside. Add a handful of chopped almonds to the same pan and cook, stirring, until the nuts brown. Add a half cup or so of dry white wine and cook over high heat until it's reduced to a syrup; add a bit more cold butter to thicken the sauce. Serve the sauce over the scallops, garnished with chopped parsley.

53.

Mussels in Tomato–White Bean Sauce

A handful of diced Spanish chorizo gives an extra boost if you want one.

Cook a clove or two of minced garlic in a couple of tablespoons of olive oil over low heat for about two minutes, or until fragrant. Add a large chopped tomato (a couple of canned ones are fine), two cups of drained precooked or canned white beans, and two to four pounds of cleaned mussels. Cook, covered, for about five minutes, or until all the mussels open (discard those that don't). Sprinkle the mussels with chopped parsley and serve with lemon wedges and good crusty bread.

54.

Sesame Shrimp Toasts

Better than any version you've had in a restaurant.

Heat the oven to 475°F. Slice a baguette in half lengthwise, put the halves face up on a baking sheet, and set them in the oven while it heats. Put shrimp in a food processor with some butter, scallions, soy sauce, a few drops of sesame oil, and a pinch each of sugar and salt. Pulse until the mixture forms a chunky paste. Smear the shrimp paste all over the bread and sprinkle with sesame seeds. Bake until the shrimp paste is pink and cooked through and the bread is crisp, about 10 minutes. Cool a bit, then cut up and serve with a salad.

55.
Braised Chicken
with Olives and Raisins

Toasted pine nuts make a terrific garnish.

In a food processor, combine about a quarter cup of olive oil, a tablespoon of chopped fresh oregano, a handful of raisins, a handful of pitted green olives, a quarter cup of dry white wine, and a pinch or two of salt; pulse a couple of times—you want large pieces, not a paste. Sear chicken cutlets in a couple of tablespoons of olive oil, about two minutes on each side. Lower the heat, add the olive-raisin sauce, then cover and cook until the chicken is cooked through. Garnish with chopped parsley or toasted pine nuts.

56.
Stir-fried Chicken with Nuts

Cashews are my favorite, but peanuts or walnuts do just as well.

Put vegetable oil in a large skillet over high heat; when it's almost smoking, add about a pound of cut-up boneless chicken and sear without disturbing for about a minute; stir and cook for another minute. When the pieces are well browned, remove from the pan and pour in a little more oil if you need it. Add a sliced red bell pepper, a chopped onion, and some minced ginger or garlic and cook another few minutes, stirring only when necessary, until the vegetables wilt. Return the chicken to the pan, along with about a cup of halved cashews, a couple of tablespoons of water, and a few tablespoons of hoisin sauce. Continue cooking until the sauce bubbles and everything is well coated. Serve, sprinkled with a few chopped cashews or some chopped cilantro, or both.

57.

Lavender-Thyme Braised Chicken

Rosemary is easier to find than lavender and works just as well,
but lavender is a nice change if you can find it.

Season chicken cutlets with salt and pepper, then sear them in a couple of tablespoons of olive oil on both sides until brown, about four minutes total; set aside. Add a tablespoon more of olive oil or butter to the pan, along with some minced garlic, a tablespoon of crushed lavender flowers (or a tablespoon of finely minced fresh rosemary), and a teaspoon of fresh thyme; cook for about a minute. Add a half cup (or more) of Riesling and deglaze the pan. Add the chicken, cover, and continue cooking until it's done, another four minutes or so. Spoon the sauce over the chicken.

58.

Chicken with
Sweet-and-Sour Sherry Sauce

Also great with pork.

Heat the broiler. In a little olive oil, cook about a cup of roughly chopped shiitake or button mushrooms and about a quarter cup of chopped shallots until the mushrooms are browning on the edges. Add a couple of teaspoons each of honey and sherry vinegar and cook for about a minute, stirring to combine. Add about a quarter cup of dry sherry and a half cup of chicken stock and cook five more minutes, continuing to stir. Meanwhile, sprinkle quarter-inch-thick boneless, skinless chicken cutlets with salt and pepper, rub them in olive oil, and broil, turning once, until done, about six minutes. Spoon the sauce over the chicken and serve.

59.

Grilled Chicken with Prosciutto and Figs

One of my favorite flavor combinations.

Heat a grill or grill pan. Pound chicken cutlets to a quarter-inch thickness; season with salt and pepper. Grill the chicken, turning once, for about five minutes or until cooked through. Slice a handful of fresh figs in half and grill them, flesh side down, until soft and warm. Put slices of prosciutto on the chicken cutlets to warm for a few seconds; serve with the grilled figs and a drizzle of good-quality balsamic.

60.

Chicken Curry in a Hurry

Add more curry if you like.

In about a tablespoon of oil, cook a sliced onion, teaspoon of curry powder and some salt and pepper for about three minutes. Season chicken tenders with salt, pepper, and more curry powder. Nestle the chicken between the onions, and cook for about two minutes on each side; remove the chicken and set aside. Add a cup of plain yogurt (or sour cream if you want it a bit richer) to the pan and stir, cooking for another minute or so (do not boil). Return the chicken to the pan and cook for another few minutes, turning once, until everything is cooked and warmed through. Adjust the seasonings and serve over couscous or jasmine rice.

61

Chicken Puttanesca

Cut chicken cutlets into half-inch pieces and toss them with salt and pepper. Chop six or more olive-oil-packed anchovies. Use a bit of the anchovy oil mixed with olive oil to cook the chicken and diced anchovies, cooking until the chicken turns white, about three minutes. Add a tablespoon of minced garlic, a can of crushed tomatoes, a handful of chopped black olives, a few tablespoons of capers, and a pinch of crushed red chile flakes. Cook until the sauce thickens and the chicken is cooked through, just a few minutes. Garnish with chopped parsley and serve.

62.

Sesame-Glazed Grilled Chicken

Serve with wilted bok choy or steamed broccoli.

Heat the grill or grill pan. Pound chicken breasts to a quarter-inch thickness. Mix together minced garlic, soy sauce, hoisin sauce, sesame oil, and cayenne to make a thin paste. Brush on the chicken and grill (or broil) until cooked through, turning once, about five minutes. Lightly toast sesame seeds in a dry pan until just starting to color. Sprinkle the chicken with the sesame seeds and garnish with chopped scallion.

63.

Chicken Teriyaki Skewers

Make this, too, with salmon, tuna, beef, or pork.

Cut a pound of chicken thighs or breasts into chunks; thread them on skewers. Combine four tablespoons of soy sauce, four tablespoons of mirin (or honey thinned with water), two tablespoons of sake, two tablespoons of sugar, and a few gratings of fresh ginger in a bowl. Put the skewers on the grill or under the broiler and baste them with the sauce every couple of minutes; continue cooking (and basting) until the meat is cooked through and a little blackened outside, about eight minutes total.

64.

Braised Pork with Rosemary

These chops won't dry out as long as you don't overcook them.

Rub boneless pork steaks or pork chops with olive oil, a clove or two of minced garlic, a tablespoon of fresh rosemary, and some salt and pepper. Sear in butter or oil until just brown on both sides; remove and deglaze the pan with a cup or so of dry white wine over high heat, being sure to scrape up all the brown bits left from the pork. Return the chops to the pan, along with any juices, reduce the heat, and cover. Continue cooking until the chops are barely pink inside, just a couple of minutes. Remove from the pan, turn up the heat, and reduce the liquid to a syrup; add a tablespoon or two of butter to thicken the sauce and adjust the seasonings. Serve the chops topped with the sauce and garnished with a little more rosemary.

65.

Fennel-Orange Braised Pork

The anise and citrus flavors in this preparation also work well with firm white fish.

Sprinkle boneless half-inch-thick pork chops with salt and pepper. Slice a bulb of fennel and an onion very thinly—a mandoline works well here—and break a peeled orange into segments. In some olive oil, sear the pork chops for about two minutes on each side; set aside. Add the fennel, onion, and orange to the pan and cook for a couple of minutes. Add a half cup of freshly squeezed orange juice and return the pork chops to the pan; cover and continue simmering for another six minutes or so, until the pork is cooked to desired doneness (add a little more juice, or some water or white wine, if necessary). Serve the pork with the sauce, fennel, onion, and orange slices; garnish with minced fennel fronds.

66.

Grilled Pork
with Shredded Brussels Sprouts

*Use a mandoline or slicing blade on a food processor
to make quick work of shredding the sprouts.*

Heat the grill or a grill pan. Rub boneless pork steaks with some minced garlic, salt, and pepper. Very thinly slice about two cups of Brussels sprouts. Heat a few tablespoons of butter, add the shredded sprouts, and cook until just wilted but still crisp-tender, about five minutes. Add a few tablespoons of freshly squeezed lemon juice, a tablespoon of poppy seeds, salt, and pepper. Meanwhile, grill the chops until brown on both sides but still a bit pink in the middle; serve on the sprouts.

67.

Sausage and Cabbage

Savoy or napa cabbage makes this a bit more delicate.

Cut some sausages into chunks and cook them in a large skillet with some olive oil over medium-high heat until crisp and almost done, five to seven minutes. Drain off any excess fat, then add some minced garlic and a small head of sliced cabbage to the pan along with a splash of red wine or water and a sprig of thyme if you have it. Cover and cook for about four minutes. Remove the lid and keep stirring and cooking until the cabbage is tender and the sausages are cooked through. Serve with baked potatoes or thick slices of whole grain toast and lots of mustard.

68.

Sausage with Red Lentils

Red lentils cook very quickly, so you'll want to keep an eye on them.

Slice a couple of sausages and cook them in a bit of olive oil until just beginning to brown; add a chopped onion, a chopped carrot, some minced garlic, and fresh thyme leaves. Cook a cup or so of lentils until done but not falling apart. Whisk together about a quarter cup of olive oil, a couple of tablespoons of red wine vinegar, a bit of Dijon mustard, salt, and pepper. Drain the lentils and add them to the sausage and vegetable mixture; toss with some of the vinaigrette, adding more as needed, and serve.

69.

Pork Tacos with Apple-Fennel Slaw

Pork from the shoulder is best here; and if you can't find fennel, use celery.

Heat a grill or grill pan. In a small bowl, combine a tablespoon each sugar, cumin, chili powder, and paprika, and a bit of salt; rub it into slices of pork. Slice a tart apple and a bulb of fennel (this is a great time to use a mandoline if you have one). Toss the apples and fennel with olive oil and lemon juice. Grill the pork, turning once, until browned and cooked; cut into strips and serve it in warm corn tortillas along with the slaw.

70.

West Indian Pork Kebabs

Fresh fruit salsa is the perfect side here; try chopped citrus, pineapple,
or mango mixed with some red onion, cilantro, chile, salt, and pepper.

Heat the broiler. In a bowl, combine some minced garlic, about a half teaspoon of ground allspice, a pinch of nutmeg, some fresh thyme leaves, a chopped small onion, and the juice of a lime. Toss this mixture with about a pound of pork shoulder cut into one-inch cubes. Thread the pork onto skewers and broil for about six minutes or until cooked through, turning to brown all sides evenly.

71.

Ham Steak with Redeye Gravy

A great way to use the morning's leftover coffee.

Sear a thick ham steak in a hot skillet with a fair amount of butter or olive oil. Remove the ham and use the fat to soften a sliced onion. Add some flour to the pan to coat the onion in a paste, and when the flour begins to turn golden, pour in a cup or so of coffee and stir until it thickens into a sauce. Return the ham to the pan to heat through, then serve the steak with some of the sauce and onion on top.

72.

Grilled Steak with Gorgonzola Sauce

Stilton, Roquefort, Maytag, or any good blue can fill in for Gorgonzola.

Heat the grill or a grill pan. Season a three-quarter-inch-thick steak with salt and pepper. In a small pan, heat a cup of white wine, a couple of handfuls of crumbled Gorgonzola, and a tiny pinch of nutmeg; cook until creamy and slightly reduced. Grill the steak, turning once, to the desired doneness. Serve the steak sliced and drizzled with the Gorgonzola sauce.

73.

Miso Burgers

Really more like mini meat loaves.

Mix about a pound and a half of ground beef (or pork) with a tablespoon of dark miso, a handful of panko, and some chopped scallions. Form several fat burgers and sear them on both sides in a little hot vegetable oil. When browned, add a splash each of sake and soy sauce to the pan, lower the heat, cover, and cook to desired doneness. Serve the burgers and pan sauce over rice or somen, with pickles on the side.

74.

Beef Paillards with Leeks and Capers

Grill the steak quickly and don't let it overcook.

Heat the grill or a grill pan. Cut beef tenderloin into four-ounce pieces and pound them to a quarter-inch thickness; season with salt and pepper. Slice several leeks into coins (be sure to rinse well) and toss with olive oil, lemon juice, and a spoonful of capers; partially cover and cook in the microwave until tender and juicy, just a couple of minutes. Grill the steaks over high heat (in batches if you need to) for a minute or less per side. Serve topped with the leek mixture.

75.

Beef Stir-fry with Ginger Noodles

I like rice vermicelli best here, but any thickness will work;
you'll have to boil them for a few minutes though.

Soak thin rice noodles in boiling water until soft, about 10 minutes; drain. In a tablespoon of sesame oil, cook about a tablespoon of grated ginger and a handful of chopped scallions for a couple of minutes, or until softened. Toss the ginger mixture with the noodles and set aside. In some vegetable oil, stir-fry thinly sliced beef for about two minutes; add a couple of handfuls of bean sprouts and cook for another two minutes. Add a little water and a little soy sauce and continue cooking until the sauce coats the beef and vegetables. Serve the beef and vegetables over the noodles.

76.

Lamb Chops
with Cranberry-Rosemary Reduction

The perfect accompaniment is wild rice,
but you'll need considerably more time if you go that route.

Combine a couple of cups of cranberries, a couple of tablespoons of brown sugar, a cinnamon stick, a sprig of fresh rosemary, and about a half cup of brandy in a saucepan and bring to a boil; continue cooking, stirring occasionally, until the mixture is reduced to syrupy consistency, about 10 minutes. Season lamb chops with salt and pepper; in a skillet with a couple of tablespoons of butter, cook the chops, turning once, for about eight minutes total (you want them well browned but still pink on the inside). Serve the lamb chops drizzled with the cranberry-rosemary sauce.

77.

Grilled Lamb Steak
and White Bean Mash

The bean mash is a perfect bed for the lovely lamb juices.

Heat the grill or broiler; season lamb steaks (from the shoulder preferably, or the leg) with salt and pepper. In a food processor, puree a can of cannellini beans (reserving the liquid) or precooked beans, a large clove of garlic, a tablespoon or two of fresh rosemary, a few tablespoons of olive oil, and freshly squeezed lemon juice to taste. Add a few tablespoons of the reserved bean liquid as needed (half-and-half, cream, stock, oil, or water will all work, too) to get a nice smooth consistency. Season the bean mash with salt and (lots of) pepper and add more lemon juice if needed. Grill or broil the steaks until done (medium or so is best). Slice the steaks and serve alongside the white bean mash.

78.

Braised Lamb Chops with Prunes

Serve with good crusty bread.

Chop a handful of prunes (if they're really tough, soak them in water for a few minutes first). Rub not-too-thin lamb chops with a spice mixture of ground cinnamon, ginger, cloves, salt, and pepper; cook chops in olive oil, turning once, for just a couple of minutes. Add the prunes and a glass of port, red wine, stock, or water; cover and cook until just done. Remove the chops and reduce the liquid to a syrupy consistency. Serve the chops topped with the prunes and liquid.

79.

Moroccan Lamb Chops with Couscous

A lot of chopping, but not much cooking.

Heat the broiler. Season lamb chops with some oregano, cumin, salt, and pepper; put them in one half of a shallow roasting pan. In a bowl, toss together a couple of tablespoons of olive oil, a few smashed cloves of garlic, a couple of handfuls of cherry tomatoes, a small eggplant, cubed, a sliced zucchini, salt, and pepper. When mixed, put the vegetables in the other side of the roasting pan. Broil the lamb and vegetables for about eight minutes; turn the lamb once and toss the vegetables so they brown on all sides. Serve the vegetables on a bed of couscous along with the lamb.

80.

Pasta with Balsamic Onions

This would be a cliché if it weren't so damn good.

Boil salted water for pasta and cook it; meanwhile, in a tablespoon or so of olive oil, sear a couple of sliced onions until nicely browned, stirring almost all the time. Splash some balsamic vinegar over all and sprinkle with salt and lots of black pepper; reduce the heat so the mixture thickens into a sauce. Drain the pasta, reserving some of the cooking water; toss the pasta with the onion sauce, adding some of the reserved cooking water as needed to moisten and serve; Parmesan cheese is optional.

81.

Pasta with Herbed Ricotta and Dried Cherries

For some crunch, garnish with finely chopped hazelnuts.

Boil salted water for pasta and cook it; meanwhile, chop a handful of fresh parsley, some oregano, and a few sage leaves. Mix the herbs with a cup of fresh ricotta and about a half cup of freshly grated Parmesan cheese; season with salt and pepper. In a tablespoon or two of butter over low heat, cook a couple of handfuls of dried cherries and a splash of red wine until the cherries soften a bit, about three minutes. Drain the pasta, reserving some of the cooking water. Add the pasta to the cherry mixture and stir to coat, adding some of the reserved cooking water to make a sauce; taste and season with salt and pepper. Serve the pasta with a dollop of the herbed ricotta on top.

82.

Mushroom Pasta

Some reconstituted porcini added to the fresh mushrooms give this a terrific earthiness.

Boil salted water for pasta and cook it; meanwhile, slice about two cups of fresh mushrooms and cook them in a couple of tablespoons of olive oil with some salt and pepper. When they're dry, add about half a cup of white wine and some minced garlic; cook until the wine reduces and the garlic mellows. Drain the pasta, reserving some of the cooking water. Toss the pasta with the mushrooms along with a handful of freshly chopped parsley; add cooking water if needed to moisten the sauce. Serve with lots of freshly ground pepper and grated Parmesan cheese.

83.

Cheesy Corn Bread Dumplings

Enrich the cooking liquid with leftover chicken, beans, or cut-up vegetables.

Bring a deep skillet of salted water or chicken stock to a boil. Mix together a cup each of flour and cornmeal, with a teaspoon of baking powder and a pinch each of baking soda and salt. Beat an egg with a little buttermilk and a couple of handfuls of grated cheddar. Stir the wet mixture into the dry, adding a little more buttermilk or flour as needed to create a stiff biscuit-like batter. With the help of a rubber spatula, drop large spoonfuls of the mixture into the liquid; bring to a steady simmer; cover and cook until set and a toothpick comes out clean, about 10 minutes. Fish the dumplings out with a slotted spoon and serve, garnished with chopped parsley and some of the stock if you used it.

84.

Penne with Vodka Sauce

A contemporary classic.

Boil salted water for pasta and undercook it slightly; meanwhile, use a big skillet coated with olive oil to cook some minced garlic, a pinch or two of red chile flakes, and a pinch of salt until the garlic is soft and fragrant. Add a can of tomatoes (that you've crushed or chopped a bit) and simmer for about five minutes, then add about a quarter cup each of vodka and cream. Drain the pasta and add it to the pan; toss the pasta well and give it a minute or so to absorb the sauce. Season with salt and pepper and garnish with chopped parsley.

85.

Pasta with Spinach, Currants, and Pine Nuts

Use raisins if you must; and cut pasta (like farfalle or fusilli) really works best here.

Boil salted water for pasta and cook it; meanwhile, toast a couple of handfuls of pine nuts in a dry pan until just fragrant and golden; set aside. In a few tablespoons of olive oil, cook a bunch of chopped spinach until wilted; season with salt and pepper. Add two handfuls of currants and continue to cook until warmed through. Drain the pasta (reserving some of the cooking water) and toss it with some olive oil and the spinach mixture, using enough of the water to moisten everything. Garnish with the toasted pine nuts and serve.

86.

Spicy Pork with Soba Noodles

Soba noodles cook in less than five minutes.

Boil salted water for the noodles and cook them; meanwhile, cut boneless pork into thin strips; toss with salt, pepper, and five-spice powder. In a couple of tablespoons of vegetable oil, stir-fry the pork until it's cooked through, about three minutes. Add a bit more oil and a couple of tablespoons each of soy sauce and rice wine vinegar; cook for 30 seconds more. Drain the noodles and put in a bowl. Top with the pork, a handful of thinly sliced scallions, a handful of chopped cilantro, and a few sliced daikon radishes; season with salt and pepper and serve.

87.

Pasta with Fried Eggs

Add crumbled bacon, some fried pancetta,
or a cup of breadcrumbs toasted in olive oil for a bit of crunch.

Boil salted water for pasta and cook it; meanwhile, fry four eggs in butter, keeping them very runny. Drain the pasta, reserving some of the cooking water, and toss it with a few tablespoons of olive oil or butter, lots of freshly grated Parmesan cheese, salt, pepper, and enough of the reserved water to moisten; top with the fried eggs. Roughly cut the eggs up and toss the pasta again to serve.

88.

Pasta Gratinée

Mac-n-cheese, only more substantial.

Heat the broiler. Bring small cubes of waxy potatoes and a couple of cloves of garlic to a boil in a big pot of salted water; when the water boils, add a pound of cut pasta (like penne or rigatoni). Cook for about four minutes, then add some chopped cabbage. In a couple of minutes more, the pasta should be al dente and the potatoes tender. Drain and drizzle some olive oil over everything, season it with salt and pepper, and toss a couple of times. Transfer the mixture to a shallow ovenproof pan or dish, sprinkle grated Parmesan cheese and breadcrumbs on top, broil until bubbly, and serve with a big salad.

89.

Zucchini and Garlic Fusilli with Pistachios

Equally delicious is a combination of zucchini and yellow summer squash.

Boil salted water for the fusilli and cook it; meanwhile, slice two zucchinis into thin disks. Toast a handful of pistachios in a dry pan until just fragrant and turning golden; set aside. Cook some minced garlic in a couple of tablespoons of olive oil until fragrant, add the zucchini slices and two tablespoons of water, season with salt and pepper, and cook until soft. Drain the pasta, reserving the cooking water. Toss the zucchini and garlic mixture with the pasta, adding more olive oil and water if needed; add the toasted nuts and serve with grated Parmesan cheese and plenty of freshly ground pepper.

90.

Apple Cider and White Wine Slushy

Use any sweet white or sparkling wine you like.

In a blender or food processor, combine a cup of apple cider, a half cup of Riesling, and about a quarter cup of sugar. Add ice and pulse; continue adding ice and processing until the desired thickness is reached (about three cups total). Serve immediately with a sprinkle of nutmeg or a cinnamon stick or an orange slice if you like.

91.

Caramelized Pears with Mascarpone

If you have the time, let the pears cook longer to soften and darken more.

Slice a couple of pears into eight pieces each and toss with a few tablespoons of brown sugar. In a couple of tablespoons of butter, cook the pears, along with a handful of pecans, until they're glossy on all sides, about four minutes. Whip together a half cup of mascarpone, a quarter cup of heavy cream, a tablespoon or two of brandy, and a tablespoon of sugar, until thick. Sprinkle the warm pears and pecans with a bit of allspice and serve them over the cream mixture.

92.

Pumpkin Crème Brûlee

It's not a custard, but it's good and serves a crowd of six to eight.

Turn on the broiler and put the rack about four inches from the heat. With an electric mixer or whisk, beat together a small can of pumpkin, eight ounces mascarpone, and a quarter cup of brown sugar; add a half teaspoon each of ground cinammon and ginger and a pinch each of allspice and salt. Spread evenly into an ovenproof baking dish or ramekins and sprinkle the top with a think layer of brown sugar. Broil for a few minutes, until the sugar melts, forming a crust. Serve immediately.

93.

Dark Chocolate Raspberry Pudding

As decadent as a fast dessert can be.

In a pan, heat two cups of cream with one-quarter cup of chopped dark chocolate. When the chocolate melts, about four minutes, add two tablespoons of cornstarch, two tablespoons of sugar, and pinch of salt. Stir until thickened, about four more minutes. Add a cup or more of fresh raspberries and mix to combine. Fill ramekins or pudding bowls with the chocolate mixture. Serve warm, topped with a few more raspberries and sliced almonds.

94.

Quick Lemon Upside-Down Cheesecake

The same flavors as a creamy cheesecake, but without the structure; serve in bowls.

Combine one cup each of softened cream cheese and ricotta with a teaspoon of vanilla, the zest of a lemon and its juice, and sugar or honey to taste; mix until evenly blended and smooth. Put the cream cheese mixture into a glass pie dish. In a food processor, combine one sleeve of graham crackers and a cup of walnuts; pulse until crushed and somewhat even. Top the cream cheese mixture with the crushed graham crackers and walnuts, chill if you have time, and serve.

95.

Pound Cake with Mascarpone and Marmalade

Also good with strawberry-rhubarb compote.

Spread mascarpone on slices of your favorite bakery pound cake and drizzle with warmed marmalade or honey.

96.

Chocolate Panini

You want excellent bread here, but not sourdough.

Sandwich bits or shavings of bittersweet chocolate between two thick slices of bread (like brioche, country-style French or Italian, or a sturdy whole grain). Butter both sides and grill in a hot skillet, using another pan on top with a couple of cans in it to weigh the sandwich down. When toasted, flip and cook the other side the same way. Meanwhile, thin a little strawberry or apricot jam with brandy, rum, or water. Cut the sandwich in quarters and serve hot, with the jam sauce on the side for dipping.

97.

Dessert French Toast

Called torrijas *in Spain; the technique is slightly different from what you're used to.*

Heat about a half inch of olive oil in a large skillet until hot. Soak thick slices of good bread in a mixture of milk, sugar, and salt; then dip them in beaten eggs, let them drain a bit, and pan-fry until crisp on both sides in the hot oil. (Watch out—they will splatter a bit.) Serve with a sprinkle of cinnamon sugar, or drizzled with honey, syrup, fruit compote, or melted chocolate.

98.

Brown Sugar Apple in the Microwave

Pears work just as well.

Core four apples and stuff the centers with raisins, walnuts, brown sugar, and butter. Set upright in a microwave-safe dish, drizzle some port wine or brandy over each, partially cover and vent, and cook for about five minutes, rotating the apples as necessary and basting with the juices. Serve drizzled with their warm syrup and sprinkled with cinnamon.

99.

Apples à la Mode

Try sprinkling a little cinnamon over the hot apples.

Peel and core four apples and cut them into quarter-inch slices. In a few tablespoons of butter, cook the apples for about four minutes; add about a quarter cup of calvados and sprinkle with brown sugar. When the apples have softened and browned, turn up the heat and reduce the liquid to a syrup. Serve over vanilla ice cream.

100.

Caramel Fondue

Be careful with the sugar—it goes from amber to brown very quickly. And it's hot.

In a pan, heat a cup of sugar with two tablespoons of water; cook until the sugar dissolves, swirling the pan occasionally. When the sugar turns amber, add six tablespoons of butter and carefully whisk until the butter melts. Remove the pan from the heat, add a half cup of cream, and whisk until smooth. Put the sauce in a bowl and serve with slices of apples, pears, or bananas, or with whole dried fruit for dipping.

101.

Sweet Couscous with Dried Fruit

Especially nice made with whole wheat couscous.

Bring three cups of water to a boil. When it does, stir in two cups of couscous, a handful of dried cherries, a pat of butter, and a drizzle of honey. Cover, remove from the heat, and let steep for five minutes or so (a little more for whole wheat couscous). Add some chopped cashews, chocolate chunks, or grated coconut (or all three!); fluff with a fork and serve warm.

Winter

The darkest season is a great one

for cooking. It's true that unless you live in the South or Southwest you're going to have a hard time putting gorgeous fresh vegetables on the table, but it's equally true that the early darkness, combined with the warmth provided by the stove, makes this a time when preparing dinner seems most appealing.

These dishes necessarily rely on traditional long-keeping ingredients like legumes, grains, and eggs, with a higher dose of meat and fish than in other seasons, yet the recipes are, as a group, fresh, light, and contemporary.

1.

Egg in a Hole with 'Shrooms

Heat a couple of tablespoons of butter in a skillet and add a cup of sliced mushrooms along with some salt, pepper, and about a teaspoon of dried oregano. Cook until the mushrooms give up their liquid and begin to brown; remove and set aside. Use a biscuit cutter (or a glass, or the lid of a jar) to make three-inch holes in the center of pieces of thickly sliced white bread. Heat an additional tablespoon or two of butter (more butter is better here), add all of the bread pieces to the pan, and cook for a minute until golden. Flip the bread and crack an egg into the holes of each slice, then cook until the whites are just set. Use a wide spatula to remove the bread from the pan. Season with salt and pepper and serve alongside the mushrooms and the center circles for dipping.

2.

Pancetta and Spinach Frittata

Beat four eggs; add a handful of freshly grated Parmesan, salt, and pepper. Cut about a quarter pound of pancetta into small pieces and fry in a tablespoon of olive oil; add a couple of chopped shallots and continue cooking until the pancetta begins to brown and the shallots have softened. Add a bunch of chopped spinach and cook until wilted and beginning to dry. Pour in the egg mixture and cook slowly until the eggs just set. Run under the broiler to brown for a minute if necessary if the top remains runny; serve hot, warm, or at room temperature.

3.

Japanese Egg Crepes

Serve on rice or in soup.

Put four eggs, a teaspoon sugar, a tablespoon of soy sauce, and a little salt in a bowl; whisk briefly. Pour some peanut or vegetable oil into an eight-inch pan (nonstick or well seasoned) over medium heat. Swirl the oil around when it's hot, and add about an eighth of the egg mixture, swirling again so it covers the pan. Cook till the top is just setting up, then flip and cook for about 15 seconds more. Repeat to make more crepes. Stack the crepes, let cool, cut into strips or roll and slice, and serve at room temperature.

4.

Bacon, Eggs, and Grits

You can also use sausage meat, ham, or Mexican-style chorizo.

Cut a few strips of bacon into one-inch pieces and fry; set aside. Bring four cups of water and a teaspoon of salt to a boil; in a steady stream, add a cup of grits and continue stirring until the mixture begins to thicken, in a few minutes. Remove from the heat, add two beaten eggs (they'll cook in the heat of the grits), about a quarter cup of cream, and a few chopped scallions. Serve the grits topped with the bacon and some chopped parsley.

5.

Eggs 'n' Capers

Cook a small handful of thinly sliced onion in butter for about three minutes. Beat four eggs with some salt and pepper, then pour the eggs over the onion; scatter a couple of tablespoons of drained capers into the pan. Cook the eggs as you would an omelet or scramble until they're no longer runny and just set. Serve on top of toasted bread.

6.

Leek, Sun-Dried Tomato, and Goat Cheese Frittata

Cook the chopped whites of two leeks with a handful of dried tomatoes in two tablespoons of butter, until softened; do not brown. Whisk together four eggs and some salt and pepper and pour over the leeks. Sprinkle with a handful of crumbled goat cheese. Cover the pan and continue cooking until the eggs are set. Remove the pan from the heat and put it under the broiler to brown for a minute before serving.

7.

Peanut Soup

Leftover shredded chicken is terrific here.

In a food processor, combine half an onion, a couple garlic cloves, and a stalk of celery; pulse until a thick paste forms. Cook the paste in butter, stirring, for about three minutes. Add one-half cup of peanut butter (or more), one cup of heavy cream, and about four cups of stock; stir (you might have to whisk) to combine; bring to a gentle boil. Reduce to a simmer; season with salt, pepper, and a little cayenne. Serve, garnished with chopped peanuts and parsley or cilantro.

8.

Cauliflower Soup

You might substitute truffle oil for the olive oil here if you have it.

Cut a cauliflower into small florets, then boil them in salted water until tender, about five minutes. Drain, reserving the cooking water. Put the cauliflower into a blender with a bit of the cooking water and some cream or half-and-half and blend to a smooth puree; add sufficient stock to make six cups. Season with salt and pepper, drizzle with olive oil, and garnish with chopped chives.

9.

Chickpea Soup with Saffron and Almonds

Try adding some diced chorizo with the onions and garlic.

In a couple of tablespoons of olive oil, cook a thinly sliced small onion, some smashed garlic, about a half cup of slivered almonds, salt, pepper, and a pinch of saffron for about five minutes. Add a can of chickpeas (or your own cooked; either with their liquid) and four cups of chicken broth or water; use a potato masher or wooden spoon to break down some of the chickpeas. Cook and stir until warmed through and serve with a sprinkling of chopped parsley if you like.

10.

Mixed Vegetable Soup

Try adding a spoonful of pesto or just really good olive oil right before serving.

Put a film of olive oil in a large skillet over medium-high heat and add some chopped onion, some minced garlic, a few broccoli florets, a chopped carrot, and a chopped celery stalk; cook until everything begins to soften. Add a few tablespoons of tomato paste and cook, stirring almost constantly, for another minute or so. Add a couple of chopped tomatoes (canned are fine; use the liquid, too), about five cups of water or stock, and some freshly chopped oregano and thyme, with some salt and pepper; bring to a boil. Reduce to a simmer and add some fresh or frozen peas and a couple of cups of chopped greens, like chard or kale; continue cooking until the greens wilt. Serve with crusty bread.

11.

Zuppa di Pane (Bread Soup)

I sometimes add an egg or two at the end of cooking, giving them a couple of minutes to cook before adding the croutons.

Heat the oven to 450°F. Cut good-quality bread into large cubes; toss with olive oil, salt, and pepper; and toast on a cookie sheet until golden. Meanwhile, cook some chopped onion in olive oil for about two minutes. Add a can of drained pinto, red, or white beans; six cups of stock; and a sprig of fresh thyme. Continue cooking until warmed through. Add a couple handfuls of chopped spinach and the croutons; stir until the spinach is wilted; season with salt and pepper; and serve, topped with a few more croutons.

12.

White Bean Stew

Pancetta or bacon makes a nice alternative to ham; render the meat in the oil before adding the garlic.

Cook some minced garlic in a little oil over medium heat until fragrant. Add a can of chopped tomatoes with their juice, a cup or two of broth (bean cooking liquid is fine), a couple cups of precooked or canned cannellini or other white beans, a handful of chopped ham, and some salt and pepper; bring to a boil. Cook until hot, then add a couple handfuls of spinach, baby arugula, or other tender greens, and cook, stirring, until the greens wilt. Meanwhile, brush a few slices of baguette or other good bread with olive oil, rub with fresh garlic, and toast until golden. Serve the stew on the bread slices.

13.

Chickpea and Zucchini Tagine

To make a thicker stew that you can serve over couscous, just drain the tomatoes.

Cook chopped onion, a sliced zucchini, some ground cumin, a pinch of saffron, and some salt and pepper in olive oil. When the onion is soft, add a can of drained chickpeas (reserving the liquid), along with a large can of chopped-up tomatoes, with their juice. Bring to a gentle boil, then reduce to a simmer and heat through; serve with a spoonful of plain yogurt and freshly chopped cilantro.

14.

Black Bean Soup

Add any cooked meat as you're heating the soup, to make this heartier.

In a food processor, combine about two cups of precooked or canned black beans with some of their liquid, a teaspoon each of cumin and oregano, and salt and pepper to taste. Puree the beans until smooth, adding a bit of chicken stock (or more liquid) if necessary for a thinner consistency. Heat the mixture, adding a cup of whole beans and enough stock to come to about six cups. Serve garnished with a spoonful of plain yogurt or sour cream and freshly chopped cilantro.

15.

Mixed Bean Soup or Stew

In a couple tablespoons of olive oil, cook a diced onion, carrot, and celery stalk until the vegetables soften, then add about four cups of precooked or canned beans (navy beans, cannellini beans, black beans, pinto beans, black-eyed peas, kidney beans, or chickpeas) with some of their liquid, a couple cups of water or stock, two bay leaves, and a sprig of fresh thyme. Bring to a boil and cook until the flavors blend and the beans are warmed through; add more liquid to achieve the consistency you like. Season with salt and pepper, remove the bay leaves and thyme sprig, and serve.

16.

Lima Bean Stew

Use any tender green you like here; arugula, baby spinach, and dandelion are all perfect.

Cook a package of frozen lima beans in a cup of water with some salt, butter, and minced garlic. When the beans are tender, puree half of them with most of the cooking liquid in a food processor until smooth; add some cream, half-and-half, or chicken broth to thin. Return the pureed bean mixture to the pan with the whole beans and season with salt and pepper. Add a bunch of tender greens and continue cooking until the greens are wilted. Add more liquid if necessary and serve, with a drizzle of good-quality olive oil and crusty bread.

17.

Shrimp Bisque

Shrimp stock is ideal here; make it by simmering shrimp shells in water for 10 minutes or so, then strain.

Bring four cups of shrimp stock to a simmer. Soften a diced onion, a minced clove of garlic, and a bit of fresh thyme leaves in butter until softened. Add about a pound of shrimp and cook for another two minutes, stirring occasionally, until the shrimp begin to turn pink. Stir in a couple of tablespoons of tomato paste, then the stock. Add about a cup of cream, then thin as needed with stock or water; season with salt and pepper, and serve, garnished with chopped parsley.

18.

Quick Cassoulet

This version is far from strictly traditional, but it maintains the spirit of the original and takes less than 20 minutes.

Cook a chopped onion, a couple of diced carrots and celery stalks, and some minced garlic in olive oil for a couple of minutes. Add a sliced smoked sausage and cook for about three minutes more, then add two or three cups of precooked or canned (drained) cannellini or other white beans and a cup or two of chopped-up canned tomatoes, along with a bay leaf, a couple of sprigs of fresh thyme, salt, and pepper. Cover and simmer until everything is warmed through and the vegetables are tender. Toss fresh breadcrumbs with some olive oil, salt, and pepper and toast until golden; serve on top of the cassoulet.

19.

Mixed Bean Chili

You want chili con carne? Just add ground beef to the onion and garlic and cook through before adding the beans.

Cook a chopped onion and some minced garlic in a little olive oil, along with chili powder to taste, a tablespoon or so of cumin, a teaspoon of oregano, salt, and pepper. Add a cup or two each of drained precooked or canned kidney beans, garbanzo beans, and black beans; one or two cups of chopped tomatoes (canned are fine; include their liquid), and some frozen corn kernels if you like. Continue cooking until everything is warmed through; adjust seasonings and serve, topped with grated cheese if you like, and freshly chopped cilantro.

Warm Beet and Goat Cheese Salad

A handful of toasted walnuts makes this even nicer.

Put a few beets in a microwave dish, cover, and cook until just fork-tender (about five minutes). Run under cool water and slip the skins off, then cut into wedges. Mix some crumbled goat cheese with the juice of a lemon, a handful of chopped fresh dill (or a pinch of dried), a couple tablespoons of olive oil, a half cup of plain yogurt, salt, and pepper to taste. Dollop the dressing over the beets and sprinkle with chopped celery (and the celery leaves if you have them), some salt, and lemon zest; serve with toasted pita or good crusty bread.

21.

Seared Scallops with Romaine

Try watercress instead of romaine if you can find it.

Season scallops with salt and pepper, then sear the scallops for a few minutes in butter, turning once, until just browned on both sides. Drizzle a bunch of romaine lettuce with some olive oil, freshly squeezed lemon juice, salt, and pepper. Sprinkle the scallops with a bit more freshly squeezed lemon juice (some zest is nice here too) and some chopped parsley, and serve over the dressed lettuce with the pan juices.

22.

Date, Bacon, and Bean Salad

Arugula or watercress works best here, but endive, escarole, frisée, and so on, are all good.

Cut some bacon into one-inch pieces and fry until browned; drain off most of the fat. Add a can of drained cannellini beans to the bacon along with a handful or more of chopped pitted dates; continue cooking until everything is just warm. Serve over a big bed of bitter greens with good-quality whole grain bread.

23.

Scallop and Citrus Salad

Whisk together about a quarter cup of olive oil, a couple of tablespoons of freshly squeezed orange juice, a dash of balsamic vinegar, salt, and pepper; set aside. Peel a couple of small oranges and separate them into segments. Slice some grape tomatoes in half and dice a small red onion. Toss about a pound of bay scallops with some salt and pepper. Sear the scallops and onion in two tablespoons of butter until no longer translucent and just browning, about three minutes; squeeze orange juice over all. Combine the orange segments and tomatoes with mixed greens and toss with the dressing; serve the scallops and onion with their juices on top of the salad.

24.

Raw Beet Salad

Peel four or five medium beets and a couple of shallots; combine them in a food processor, pulsing until shredded but not pureed. Toss with olive oil, sherry vinegar, Dijon mustard, salt, and pepper. Add minced parsley, chives, tarragon, or dill and serve on top of greens or with toasted pita triangles.

25.

Warm Cabbage Salad with Bacon

You can serve this over greens, like arugula, or not;
I sometimes add a couple handfuls of homemade croutons to this.

Chop a few slices of bacon and cook until brown. Meanwhile, use a food processor to shred a small head of red cabbage and a red onion. Add them to the bacon and cook, stirring occasionally, until the vegetables are wilting. Add a tablespoon of mustard seeds, two tablespoons of sugar, and a quarter cup of red wine vinegar; continue cooking until the cabbage is tender and the liquid has evaporated. Adjust the seasonings and serve.

26.

Avocado, Citrus, and Radicchio Salad

Peel an orange and separate it into segments. Slice an avocado or two; cut a head of radicchio into quarter-inch-thick segments. Arrange the orange, avocado, and radicchio slices on a plate; drizzle with olive oil and any mild vinegar, like rice or Champagne. Season with salt and pepper, garnish with freshly chopped mint, and serve.

27.

White Salad

You can add a handful or two of raisins for a bit of sweetness if you like.

Blanch cauliflower florets in salted, boiling water for about two minutes; drain and shock in ice water to stop the cooking. Chop a small head of napa cabbage and a couple of heads of endive; thinly slice a small white onion. Whisk together about a quarter cup of olive oil, a couple of tablespoons of white wine or sherry vinegar, a teaspoon of coarse mustard, salt, and pepper. Toss the cauliflower, cabbage, endive, and onion with the dressing and serve.

28.

Squid Salad
with Red Peppers and Cilantro

The best store-bought roasted red peppers are piquillos; use them if you can find them.

Slice squid into quarter-inch rings. Whisk together a cup of olive oil, a few tablespoons of lime juice, a minced fresh chile, some minced lemongrass or lime zest, salt, and pepper. Slice roasted red peppers into quarter-inch strips. In a few tablespoons of olive oil, stir-fry the squid until it just turns white, about two minutes; season with salt and pepper. To serve, toss the squid with a couple handfuls of cilantro, the red peppers, and the dressing.

29.

Spinach Salad with Feta and Nutmeg

Try adding a handful of nuts, cherry tomatoes, diced cucumber, olives, raisins, or any chopped dried fruit to this salad.

Put a tablespoon or two of sherry vinegar and a handful of crumbled feta in a bowl. Use a fork to mash up the cheese a bit; add some pepper and a small grinding of nutmeg. Continue stirring while slowly adding about three tablespoons of olive oil. Add about a pound of well-washed and dried spinach to the dressing and toss well; season with salt if needed.

30.

Vietnamese Rice Noodle Salad with Crab

Cleaned crab of all kinds is available all year round; I like vermicelli-size rice noodles here, but any thickness will do if you boil them for a few minutes.

Soak the rice noodles in boiling water until soft, about 10 minutes; drain, rinse, drain, and set aside. Mix two parts rice vinegar with one part fish sauce, a little sugar, and some salt. Toss the noodles with a handful of chopped scallions, a shredded carrot, a handful of chopped cilantro, about a cup of crabmeat, and the dressing. Taste and adjust seasoning, garnish with chopped peanuts and a little more cilantro, and serve.

31.

Pear, Bacon, and Goat Cheese Sandwich

A winning combination.

Fry a few slices of bacon until crisp. Smear slices of good bread with goat cheese and layer with thinly sliced pears and the bacon. Drizzle with a little balsamic vinegar and serve.

32.

Chorizo and Manchego Panini

Sort of like a Cuban sandwich.

Smear slices of good-quality bread with Dijon mustard; top with slices of smoked chorizo, thinly sliced manchego cheese, and thinly sliced dill pickle. Toast the sandwich in a press, in a waffle iron, or in a heavy pan using another pan or lid to weight the sandwich down; serve when the cheese has melted.

33.

White Bean and Salmon Sandwich

Sockeye is the best canned salmon, and it's really quite good.

Combine a drained can of cannellini beans, a drained can of salmon, some minced garlic, some finely chopped fresh rosemary, a tablespoon or two of olive oil, a couple of tablespoons of capers, salt, and pepper. Using a fork to slightly mash the beans, combine well; warm slightly if you like, or don't bother. Serve on toasted bread or on top of torn greens.

34.

Beef Tartar Crostini

Please don't use store-bought ground beef for this.

Pulse about a pound of beef sirloin or tenderloin in food processor. Put in a bowl and toss with an egg, a teaspoon or more of dry mustard, a tablespoon or more of Dijon mustard, a tablespoon or more of Worcestershire, at least a few dashes of Tabasco sauce, a handful of chopped scallions, some capers, a couple of anchovy fillets (optional), a bit of minced garlic, and plenty of salt and pepper; mix until just combined. Serve on thin slices of toasted bread.

35.

Wild Mushroom Crostini

Use any kind of mushrooms you like here; a combination is best.

Slice a pile of mushrooms, and cook them in a few tablespoons of butter with some minced garlic, fresh thyme, salt, and pepper. Continue cooking until the mushrooms release their liquid, then add a splash of dry white wine. Cook a few minutes more or until all the liquid has evaporated and the mushrooms are beginning to brown. Stir in chopped parsley, taste and adjust seasoning, and spoon onto good-quality toasted bread.

36.

Cabbage and Kielbasa (or Salami, or Linguica, or . . .) Sandwich

Sear slices of kielbasa or other garlicky cooked or smoked sausage in a pan. Remove, then cook cabbage slices in the same pan, adding a little oil if necessary (or a splash of beer); season with salt and pepper. Build sandwiches with good-quality sourdough bread, Dijon mustard, and the kielbasa and cabbage.

37.

Meatball Sub

You might add some mozzarella and put the sub in the broiler to melt the cheese just before serving.

In a bowl, combine about a pound of ground beef, an egg, and a handful each of breadcrumbs, Parmesan, and freshly chopped parsley or basil, along with some salt and pepper. Make small meatballs (a melon baller can be helpful). Sear in butter or oil until the meatballs are browned on all sides and cooked through; spread a thin layer of tomato paste on toasted hero rolls and add the meatballs, along with any juices.

38.

Chorizo and Egg Rollup

Some queso fresco or other cheese sprinkled on the egg mixture before rolling is nice.

Squeeze Mexican chorizo from its casing into a hot skillet and toss in some chopped red onion; cook, stirring occasionally, until the meat is done and beginning to crisp. Crack a couple of eggs on top, turn the heat down, and cover; cook for about three minutes, or until the eggs set. Meanwhile, warm large flour tortillas. Carefully scoop the eggs and some of the chorizo onto the tortillas along with a dash or two of Tabasco, salt, and pepper, and a spoonful of salsa if you like; fold in the short ends of the tortilla and roll lengthwise to serve.

39.

Fondue

Use cubes of good-quality bread and lots of freshly cut vegetables for dipping.

Combine about one cup of white wine with a crushed clove of garlic in a pan; bring to a boil and reduce to a simmer. Mix a tablespoon of cornstarch with two teaspoons of water and set aside. Add about two cups each of shredded Gruyère and Emmentaler cheese to the wine mixture, whisking until just melted. Add the cornstarch mixture and cook until creamy (do not boil); add more wine if needed for consistency. Serve, with the bread and vegetables (and if you don't have long forks, skewers!).

40.

Beer Batter Shrimp Po' Boy

As good as it sounds.

Heat oil for frying. In a bowl, mix together one can of beer, one and one-half cups cornmeal and pinches of salt, pepper, and paprika. Dip shrimp into the batter and fry in batches until golden, about three minutes. Serve on split crusty Italian or French loaves with lettuce, tomato, and mayonnaise; lemon juice and hot sauce are also great here.

41.

Prosciutto-Egg Sandwich

Hard-boil eggs; as they're cooking, sear slices of prosciutto in olive oil until crisp, just a couple of minutes. Shell the eggs, slice them, and mix with just enough mayonnaise to moisten, and a sprinkle of salt and pepper. Use the egg mixture to fill hard rolls or toasted brioche; top with the crumbled prosciutto, and finish with a few dashes of good olive (or truffle) oil.

42.

Braised Cabbage
with Spanish Chorizo and Beans

You can use linguica or kielbasa in place of chorizo, and any greens you like.

Slice smoked chorizo into quarter-inch-thick pieces, then cook in olive oil until it begins to crisp. Slice a head of green cabbage into eight wedges and put it on top of the chorizo; add a couple of cups of cooked or drained canned cannellini or other white beans, spreading to surround the cabbage; cover and cook for a few minutes, then flip the cabbage and stir the beans. Continue cooking until everything is warmed through, season with salt and pepper, and serve topped with toasted breadcrumbs or croutons and a drizzle of olive oil.

43.

Tofu with Pineapple and Red Peppers

Use precut pineapple, and this is even faster.

Chop half a pineapple and a large red pepper into half-inch pieces and cook for about three minutes in a bit of oil. Remove. Add more oil if necessary, followed by two cups of cubed firm tofu and a tablespoon each of minced garlic and ginger; cook and stir about three minutes more. Off heat, toss with a splash each of soy sauce and rice vinegar and some chopped scallions. Serve over rice.

44.

Mini Cannelloni

Heat the oven to 400°F. In a bowl, mix together a cup of ricotta cheese, a tablespoon of chopped sage, salt, pepper, and grated Parmesan. Put about a teaspoonful of this mixture in a wonton wrapper, roll into a tube, and put on a baking sheet lined with parchment paper. Brush or spray with olive oil. Bake for about 10 minutes, or until the wontons are crisp. If you don't have tomato sauce to warm up, serve drizzled with balsamic vinegar and sprinkled with lots of black pepper.

45.

Crisp Tofu and Asian Greens
with Peanut Sauce

*Use baby bok choy, Chinese broccoli, or tatsoi here; napa cabbage
is a great alternative too.*

Slice firm tofu into strips or cubes and pat dry; roughly chop a bunch of the greens. Pan-fry the tofu in some vegetable oil until it browns on all sides, about four minutes; remove and pour off all but a little of the oil. Add the greens and a pinch or two of red chile flakes, and continue cooking until the vegetables turn dark green, about three minutes. Mix together a half cup of peanut butter, a couple of tablespoons of soy sauce, and fresh lime juice to taste; add a bit of water if necessary to get a nice consistency. Add the sauce to the pan along with reserved tofu and toss to coat. Garnish with crushed peanuts and serve.

46.

Potato Cumin Curry

For more heat, add a freshly chopped chile along with the onions.

Peel and cut four baking potatoes into half-inch pieces. In oil, cook a thinly sliced onion until just soft, about two minutes; add a couple of tablespoons of curry powder, a tablespoon of cumin, and a pinch of saffron. Add the potatoes and toss to coat with the spices. Then add a can of coconut milk; fill the can with water and add that, too. Bring the mixture to a steady bubble; cover and cook until the potatoes are almost tender, about eight minutes. Add a drained can of chickpeas. Combine well and continue cooking until the potatoes are tender and the beans are warmed through. Serve topped with freshly chopped cilantro.

47.

Lettuce-Wrapped Fish

Any thick white fish fillets will work here.

Blanch large romaine or Bibb lettuce leaves in boiling water—one or two at a time—until tender and flexible, just a few seconds, and drain; then cut out the large central vein if necessary to roll. Put a piece of fish on each leaf and sprinkle with salt and pepper; fold or roll the fish in the leaves so the edges overlap. In a large pan or casserole with a cover, bring one cup of wine to a boil with two tablespoons of butter; reduce to a simmer and add the fish packages. Cover and cook until a knife easily penetrates fish, five to 10 minutes; remove the fish to a warm platter. Over high heat, reduce the liquid; when it thickens a bit, pour it over the fish and serve.

48.

Seared Fish with Cumin and Lemon

Any sturdy fish works here, including salmon, shrimp, scallops, or squid.

Combine about a half cup of flour with a tablespoon of cumin, and some salt and pepper. Lightly dredge the seafood in the cumin-flour mixture; cook the fish in a mixture of butter and oil until golden, turning once, about three minutes on each side. Sprinkle with freshly squeezed lemon juice and parsley, then serve with the pan juices.

49.

Shrimp with Black Bean Sauce

You can find fermented black beans at Asian markets and even most supermarkets.

Soak two or three tablespoons of black beans in about a quarter cup of sherry or white wine (or water in a pinch). Cook minced garlic in vegetable oil, along with a teaspoon of grated ginger and a pinch or two of red chile flakes. When fragrant, add about a pound of small shrimp and fry until just cooked through, about a minute. Add the black beans and their liquid, toss, and remove from the heat. Add a bit of soy sauce and toss again. Serve with jasmine or other rice.

50.

Mussels in White Wine and Garlic

Wild mussels are always more flavorful than farm-raised; wash them well, and discard any with cracked shells or those which don't close when you tap them.

Cook some minced garlic in olive oil for a couple of minutes; add a half cup of white wine and bring to a boil. Add two (or more) pounds of mussels to the pot, cover, and cook for five minutes, or until the mussels open (discard any that don't open). Serve the mussels in bowls with the broth, freshly chopped parsley, and slices of good baguette for soaking.

51.
Broiled Squid

Keep the cooking time very short, and your squid will stay tender.

Heat the broiler. Combine about a half cup of olive oil, a few tablespoons of sherry vinegar or freshly squeezed lemon juice, a tablespoon or so of freshly chopped rosemary, salt, and pepper; add a pound or two of cleaned squid and marinate for about five minutes. Remove the squid from the marinade and broil for about three minutes, shaking the pan once or twice, then serve with bread (toasted bread rubbed with garlic and drizzled with olive oil is quite fine here).

52.
Seafood Couscous

You can use almost any fish or shellfish you like here.

Add a bag of frozen peas, two cups of couscous, and a pinch of saffron to three cups of boiling water; stir, cover, and remove from the heat and let sit for about 10 minutes. Meanwhile, cook a chopped onion, a sliced red pepper, and some minced garlic in some olive oil for about two minutes. Add half a pound each of firm white fish and half a pound of fresh squid rings; stir-fry for about three minutes more. Fluff the couscous with a fork and serve the fish and vegetables over it; garnish with freshly chopped parsley leaves.

53.
Shrimp with Lemongrass

When you're mincing lemongrass, peel off its outer few layers to get to the tender inner core.

Cook a tablespoon of minced lemongrass in some vegetable oil; add minced garlic and a teaspoon or so of lime zest, then a pound or more of shrimp. Stir, then cook until the shrimp are no longer translucent, three to five minutes. Add some fish sauce to taste, then add some black pepper, and serve, sprinkled with cilantro.

54.

Scallop Stew with Couscous

A North African–flavored dish that you can spice up or down depending on your taste.

Cook couscous as in recipe 52, with or without peas and saffron. Soften a diced onion, some minced garlic, a teaspoon of cumin, a pinch of cayenne, half a teaspoon of cinnamon, and salt to taste in a couple of tablespoons of olive oil for about three minutes. Add a large drained can of chopped tomatoes and a handful of golden raisins; bring to a boil and simmer for five minutes. Add about a pound of scallops and continue cooking until they're opaque, three to six minutes depending on their size. Serve the stew over couscous with chopped cilantro on top.

55.

Citrus-Braised Fish Fillets or Steaks

Try orange juice, lime juice, or any other combination of citrus juices here.

Sear sturdy fish fillets or steaks for about two minutes on each side in a little oil, until nicely browned. Add a quarter cup each of grapefruit juice and lemon juice, a tablespoon or two of soy sauce, some minced garlic, and about a teaspoon of freshly grated ginger. Cover and braise for about six minutes, or until the fish is cooked through. Serve over shredded red cabbage and sliced radishes.

56.

Simplest Chicken Kebabs

Lamb, beef, or firm fish all take to this preparation equally well.

Heat the broiler. Cut a pound of boneless, skinless chicken thighs into chunks slightly larger than one inch. Toss the meat with a minced onion, some minced garlic, a few tablespoons of lemon juice, olive oil, salt, pepper, a crumbled bay leaf, and about a teaspoon of oregano (fresh is best, but dried is OK; use less). Thread the chicken pieces on skewers and broil, turning occasionally, until browned and cooked through, about six to eight minutes. Serve with lemon wedges.

57.

Chicken in
Spicy Basil-Coconut Sauce

If you like more heat, don't seed one or both of the chiles.

Season chicken cutlets with half a teaspoon each of ground coriander, ground cinnamon, chili powder, and salt and sear them on both sides in a couple of tablespoons of olive oil. Remove from the pan, add more oil if needed, and cook sliced red onion, three minced cloves of garlic, and two seeded Thai chiles for about four minutes. Return the chicken to the pan along with about a cup of coconut milk, a couple dashes of fish sauce, and a few tablespoons of chopped basil. Cook until the coconut milk begins to bubble; reduce to a steady simmer and continue cooking until the chicken is done. Serve the chicken and sauce over rice with fresh lime wedges, garnished with more basil, or cilantro or mint (or all three).

58.

Chicken Paprikash

This can be served over couscous too, but if you have the time,
bulgur gives this stew a richer earthiness.

In two tablespoons of butter, sear a pound of boneless, skinless chicken pieces, about a minute on each side. Add a thinly sliced large onion, two crushed garlic cloves, a teaspoon of minced ginger (or half a teaspoon of ground ginger), three tablespoons of Hungarian paprika, a bay leaf, and a couple of teaspoons of salt; cook for about three minutes. Add a cup of chicken broth and bring everything to a boil. Reduce the heat and continue cooking until the chicken is just done; stir in half a cup of sour cream and serve over buttered egg noodles.

59.

Chicken Curry with Raisins

I like this topped with a handful or two of chopped peanuts and lots of fresh cilantro.

Cut boneless, skinless chicken breasts into one-inch pieces; sear them in hot vegetable oil until browned all over, just a couple of minutes. Remove from the pan, add more oil if needed, and soften a sliced red onion and a thinly sliced stalk of celery for about two minutes. Return the chicken to the pan along with two tablespoons of curry powder, a good pinch of salt, a cup of raisins, and a quarter cup of apple juice (or water); cover and continue cooking until the chicken is done, about three minutes.

60.

Chicken with Apples and Sage

Peel a couple of tart apples and slice them into pieces. Brown the chicken on both sides in some olive oil, about four minutes total; set aside. Add two tablespoons of butter, the apples, a diced shallot, and a tablespoon of brown sugar to the pan and cook for about three minutes. Add a cup of chicken broth, a tablespoon of cider vinegar, and freshly chopped sage, and stir to deglaze the pan and thicken a bit. Return the chicken to the broth and cook until the chicken is done, the apples are tender, and the sauce is reduced. Serve the chicken and apples with the sauce spooned on top.

61.

Coq au Vin

Classic French flavors.

Pound boneless, skinless chicken breasts (or thighs) to half-inch thickness and season with salt and pepper. Sear on both sides in a bit of butter; set aside. Add two carrots chopped into one-inch pieces and half an onion cut into wedges; cook until the onion begins to soften. Add a cup of red wine, a bay leaf, a teaspoon of fresh tarragon, and a thyme sprig; deglaze the pan, return the chicken to the pan, and cover. Simmer for about six minutes until the meat is cooked through and the vegetables are tender.

62.

Honey-Orange Chicken

Boneless pork chops are also terrific here.

Pound chicken breasts to half-inch thickness and season with salt and pepper. Mix together one-half cup of orange juice, one-half cup of honey, one tablespoon ground cumin, salt, and pepper. Sear the chicken on both sides in two tablespoons of vegetable oil for about four minutes total. Add the orange juice–honey mixture, cover, and allow it to simmer for about six minutes. Serve over mixed greens.

63.

Chicken Livers with Broad Noodles

Fettucine or—even better—pappardelle are what you want here.

Soften a chopped onion and a chopped celery stalk for about two minutes in a little olive oil. Add a half pound of ground meat—pork, beef, lamb, chicken, or turkey, whatever you like—plus four roughly chopped chicken livers and a few sprigs of thyme or sage leaves. Cook until the meat loses its redness, about six minutes. Add a couple of tablespoons of tomato paste along with some water and cook until everything is heated through. Serve over thick noodles sprinkled with freshly grated Parmesan cheese and parsley.

64.

Maple-Ginger Glazed Chicken with Pecans

A side of roasted Brussels sprouts really hits the spot here.

Combine a quarter cup of maple syrup with about a quarter cup of chopped pecans and a teaspoon freshly grated ginger in a bowl; mix to coat the pecans and set aside. Season half-inch-thick chicken cutlets with salt and pepper; sear the cutlets in a couple of tablespoons of butter, until browned, about four minutes total. Add some more butter to the pan and pour the syrup-pecan mixture over the top of the chicken, then cook the chicken for a couple of minutes more on each side, moving the chicken around the pan to coat it evenly. Serve the chicken topped with the warm pecans and the pan juice.

65.

Coconut-Orange Chicken

Nice with mixed greens and fresh orange wedges.

Brush half-inch-thick boneless, skinless chicken breasts with olive oil; season with salt and pepper and dredge lightly in flour. Cook a teaspoon of minced garlic, the minced zest of an orange, and a teaspoon of red chile flakes for about two minutes in olive oil; add the chicken and sear for about two minutes on each side. Add a can of coconut milk, a pinch of saffron, and a bay leaf; stir, cover, and let simmer for about six minutes until the chicken is cooked through. Sprinkle with slivered almonds and cilantro and serve.

66.

Chicken with Bacon, Shallots, and Brandy

Use thick-cut bacon here.

Cut a few slices of bacon into one-inch pieces and fry until crisp; remove with a slotted spoon. Season half-inch-thick chicken cutlets with salt and pepper and sear them in the bacon fat until browned, about two minutes on each side; remove and set aside. Add four sliced shallots and a teaspoon of minced garlic and cook for another two minutes; return the chicken to the pan, add a half cup of brandy, cover, and let simmer for about five minutes, or until the chicken is done and the sauce has thickened somewhat. Serve the chicken topped with the shallots, bacon, and sauce.

67.

Chicken Poached in Port

Pound chicken cutlets to half-inch thickness and season with salt and pepper. Cook a chopped onion in butter with salt and pepper for about two minutes. Add about a cup of port to the pan along with the chicken and a couple of bay leaves; bring it to a boil; reduce to a bubble, cover, and simmer for about four minutes. Spoon the onions and sauce over the chicken and sprinkle with freshly chopped parsley.

68.

Honey Fried Chicken

Freshly made breadcrumbs are best here; panko are also nice.

Combine half a cup of flour, about half a cup of fresh breadcrumbs, a tablespoon paprika, an egg, about half a cup of milk, salt, and pepper; mix until a thick batter forms (add a little more milk if necessary). Pound boneless, skinless chicken breasts to half-inch thickness and dip them in the batter until coated. Shallow- or deep-fry the breasts in oil until golden and cooked through, turning once, about eight minutes total. Warm some honey with some water and a sprig of thyme and drizzle it over the chicken to serve.

69.

Chicken Piccata

Boneless pork chops are also good prepared this way.

Dredge chicken breasts, pounded to half-inch thickness, in flour mixed with salt and pepper. Sear the chicken on both sides in a mixture of oil and butter, about four minutes total. Lay very thinly sliced lemon rounds on top of the chicken, add a cup of white wine, and cover; continue cooking for about five minutes. Remove the chicken from the pan and reduce the wine to a syrupy consistency. Serve the chicken with the lemon slices on top, a spoonful of the sauce, and a sprinkling of capers or chopped olives.

70.

Turkey Cutlets with Walnuts and Sage

*You might puree an apple or two in the food processor with a dash of cinnamon
to serve alongside the turkey.*

In a food processor, combine a handful or so of walnuts with about a half cup of breadcrumbs, a few tablespoons of freshly grated Parmesan cheese, a teaspoon or so of fresh sage, salt, and pepper. Pound turkey cutlets to half-inch thickness; season with salt and pepper; dredge in flour, egg, and the walnut mixture, pressing gently to help the mixture adhere. Heat a few tablespoons of olive oil and fry the cutlets, turning once, until golden and cooked through, about eight minutes.

71.

Sausage and Potatoes

Simply classic.

Heat the broiler. Slice potatoes into half-inch pieces and boil in salted water until soft, just a few minutes. Meanwhile, slice a few Italian sausages—sweet, spicy, or a combination—into two-inch pieces and put them in an oven-safe dish with half of a thinly sliced onion; broil until the sausage is well browned, about eight minutes, turning once. Mix the sausage, onion, and potatoes together in a bowl with a few tablespoons of olive oil and a handful of chopped basil or parsley.

72.

Sweet Sauerkraut with Kielbasa

*A chopped or pureed apple—or good-quality applesauce—can be used instead
of the pear.*

In some butter, sear three-inch pieces of kielbasa, a sliced onion, and a couple of chopped pears (slightly short of ripe is fine); cook for about four minutes. Add a bag or jar of sauerkraut (do not use canned), cover, and heat until warmed through, about six minutes more. Serve with pumpernickel rolls.

73.

Braised Pork Chops
with Celery Root

Use parsnips or carrots if you can't find the celery root.

Cut some celery root into half-inch sticks. Take thin, boneless pork chops and smear them with salt, pepper, and minced garlic. Sear in a mixture of butter and oil, turning once, about two minutes on each side; add the celery root and a splash of dry white wine and cover. Cook for about five minutes; remove the chops to a plate and cook until the celery root is just tender and the remaining liquid is reduced to a syrup. Add a bit of fresh butter and return the chops to the pan, along with any liquid that's accumulated around them. Turn once or twice in the sauce and serve, sprinkled with fresh parsley.

74.

Seared Pork Paillards with Prunes
and Olives

A surprising and good combination.

Pound boneless pork chops to quarter-inch thickness and sprinkle with salt, pepper, and some ground coriander. Sear the chops for about a minute per side in olive oil. Remove from the pan and add about a cup of white wine and a couple of tablespoons of butter; bring to a boil. Reduce to a simmer and add a handful of chopped prunes and a few chopped green olives; cover and cook for a couple of minutes, then add the pork and cook until just done, about three minutes more. Serve the pork drizzled with the sauce and garnished with chopped parsley or chives.

75.

Stuffed Pork Chops
with Broccoli Rabe

A bit of a sprint, but worth the effort.

Remove a couple of sweet Italian sausages from their casings and brown in a bit of olive oil, breaking up the meat with a fork or spoon. Meanwhile, cook a bunch of chopped broccoli rabe in boiling, salted water until crisp-tender, about two minutes; drain. Pound boneless pork chops as thinly as you can; season with salt and pepper. Put a bit of the cooked sausage in the center of each of the chops, roll, and secure with toothpicks. Sear in the same skillet, browning the meat well. Drizzle the broccoli rabe with good-quality olive oil, sprinkle with salt and pepper, and serve with the stuffed pork chops.

76.

Steak au Poivre

The classic (and wonderfully excessive) recipe.

Salt and heavily—really heavily—pepper inch-thick steaks—rib eye, sirloin, or skirt (which will be thinner), and cook them in a grill pan to the desired doneness, turning once. Set the steaks aside. Melt some butter in the same pan with a couple of tablespoons of chopped shallot; cook until the shallot softens, about two minutes. Add a splash of brandy to the shallots, along with any collected juices from the steak, and reduce; lower the heat, add a bit of cream, and cook until it begins to thicken. Serve the cream sauce with the steaks.

77.

Beef Fajita Stir-fry

Some garnishes might include fresh cilantro, sour cream, guacamole, chopped tomato, or black olives.

Fry about a pound of thinly sliced sirloin steak in some olive oil over high heat until seared but still rare. Remove; add more oil if needed; add sliced red bell pepper, chopped onion, and garlic and stir-fry until just soft. Season with dried oregano, chili powder, salt, and pepper, and return the meat to the pan along with a couple handfuls of good tortilla chips and some crumbled queso fresco. Toss until the chips are well coated and serve with salsa drizzled on top.

78.

Scallion-Stuffed Beef Rolls

These are known as negima *in Japan, where they originated.*

Heat the broiler. Cut strips of flank steak into three-by-five-inch pieces about a quarter-inch thick. Brush one side of the beef with a little soy sauce. Cut scallions in half the long way, then into five-inch lengths; put two or three pieces on each piece of beef. Roll the beef lengthwise and secure with a toothpick or two. Broil as quickly as you can until browned, maybe five minutes total, turning halfway through. Serve, garnished with chopped scallions, cilantro, and a drizzle of soy and—if you like—sesame oil.

79.

Seared Calf's Liver with Celery

The nearly universal problem with liver is overcooking;
keep the cooking time short, and it will be delicious.

Heat two tablespoons of butter until the foam subsides; dredge a thick slice of liver in flour, shaking off the excess, and put it in the hot butter, sprinkling with salt and pepper. As soon as the liver browns on one side—two to three minutes—turn it and brown the other side, cooking for another two minutes. The liver should be medium-rare. Remove from the pan and add a couple of sliced celery stalks and the juice of a lemon or two. Stir to cook the celery a bit and make a little pan sauce. Serve over the liver, garnished with parsley or chives.

80.

Apricot-Braised Lamb Chops

Lovely over a bed of arugula or other spicy greens.

In a food processor, make a paste from a handful of dried apricots, some lemon juice, a bit of onion, a teaspoon of ground coriander, and a clove of garlic. Salt and pepper not-too-thin lamb chops and sear them in olive oil for about two minutes on each side until browned; remove and set aside. Add the apricot mixture to the pan along with a splash of white wine and bring to a simmer. Put the chops back in the pan, cover, and braise for about five minutes—they should remain pink inside. Serve, drizzled with the braising liquid.

81.

Red Wine–Braised Lamb Chops

Serve these over a bed of couscous tossed with peas.

Salt and pepper not-too-thin lamb chops and sear them in oil, turning once, until they're brown on both sides; set aside. Add a couple of tablespoons of flour to the pan, stirring constantly, until it's well combined with the drippings. Whisk in a half cup of beef broth or water, a half cup of red wine, some minced garlic, and a teaspoon or two of chopped fresh rosemary; bring to a boil. Return the chops and juices to the pan and cook, turning the lamb over once or twice until it's done.

82.

Indian-Style Lamb Kebabs

This preparation also works well with chicken, beef, and even firm fish.

Heat the broiler. Cut a pound or so of lamb shoulder into one-inch chunks. Toss with a cup of plain yogurt, a chopped small onion, some minced garlic, a teaspoon each of ground cumin, coriander, and paprika, and a pinch of cayenne. Thread the lamb pieces on skewers and broil, turning occasionally, until nicely browned and cooked to desired doneness. Serve with slices of fresh limes and freshly chopped cilantro or mint.

83.

Pasta Jambalaya

You can use any cooked sausage here, but the spiciness of andouille is the most authentic.

Boil salted water for pasta and cook it (use short-cut pasta like orzo, orecchiette, shells, or ditalini). Meanwhile, slice an andouille or another spicy cooked sausage into coins. Heat a fair amount of olive oil and brown the sausage; add a chopped onion, a chopped celery stalk, and a chopped green bell pepper and continue to cook until the vegetables begin to soften. Add some minced garlic, a tablespoon of chopped oregano (or a bit of dried), and enough flour to make a roux (add more oil if the mixture looks too dry). Turn the heat up so the roux browns quickly, but watch it like a hawk. As soon as it darkens and smells toasty add the pasta and enough of the pasta cooking water to keep everything moist. Toss well and garnish with chopped fresh parsley; break with tradition and serve with freshly grated Parmesan cheese if you like.

84.

Banderilla Pasta

This borrows the flavors of the original tapa to make a pasta sauce.

Boil salted water for pasta and cook it, reserving some of the cooking liquid. Meanwhile, chop a few crisp pickled peppers or pepperoncini, a handful of green olives, and a couple of good marinated artichoke hearts (optional). Using a fork, mash up a few anchovies (marinated in olive oil and packed in glass) and add them to the chopped vegetables. Toss the pasta with the vegetables and anchovies, adding a few tablespoons of the reserved liquid as needed to make a sauce; garnish with chopped olives or parsley.

85.

Pasta with Tomato Tapenade

You might crumble some fresh goat cheese over the top of this.

Boil salted water for pasta and cook it. Meanwhile, combine a half pound of pitted black olives in food processor with about a handful of drained capers, four or five anchovies, two cloves of garlic, freshly ground black pepper, and olive oil as needed to make a coarse paste. Put the tapenade in a large skillet over medium heat with several canned tomatoes, breaking them up as you cook, and stir until saucy, only a couple of minutes. Toss the pasta with just enough of the tapenade to gently coat the noodles. Serve with cheese if you like, passing any extra sauce at the table.

86.

Linguine with Butter, Parmesan, and Sage

The antecedent of "Alfredo" sauce, and much lighter (and I think better).

Boil salted water for pasta and cook it, leaving it just short of done and reserving some of the cooking liquid. Meanwhile, melt two tablespoons butter (or more) and add a couple handfuls of fresh sage leaves (about 30 leaves) to the pan; cook until the butter just browns and the leaves have shriveled. Add the pasta to the butter and sage, along with about three-quarters of a cup of the cooking liquid; cook until the pasta is done; it's OK if the mixture remains a little soupy. Stir in a couple of good handfuls of freshly grated Parmesan cheese and mix until it becomes creamy; season with lots of freshly ground black pepper and serve.

87.

Pasta with Chicken, Frisée, and Stilton

Try playing with this combination of greens and cheese; use baby spinach and feta or endive and goat cheese, for example.

Boil salted water for pasta and cook it, reserving some of the cooking liquid. Meanwhile, cut a half pound or more of chicken cutlets into one-inch pieces. Chop an onion and cook it in some olive oil until it begins to soften, then add the chicken; sprinkle with salt and pepper and about a tablespoon of freshly chopped rosemary and cook for about four minutes. Separate a head of frisée. When the chicken is almost cooked through, add the frisée and cook until wilted, just a minute or so. Add the pasta to the chicken mixture, along with a handful of crumbled Stilton or another blue cheese. Add a couple tablespoons of the pasta water if needed to soften the cheese and moisten the sauce. Season with salt and pepper and garnish with toasted walnuts.

88.

Pasta with Walnut Pesto

Incredibly simple and incredibly rich.

Boil salted water for pasta and cook it, reserving some of the cooking liquid. Meanwhile, puree a cup of walnuts, some Parmesan cheese, a small handful of parsley, a few sage leaves, salt, pepper, and olive oil in a food processor; use just enough olive oil to get a nice, almost smooth consistency. Toss the pasta with the walnut sauce, using some of the reserved cooking water as needed to moisten it. Serve, topped with more freshly grated Parmesan cheese and some chopped parsley.

89.

Pasta with Garbanzo Beans, Sausage, and Arugula

One of my favorite "more sauce, less pasta" dishes.

Boil salted water for pasta and cook it, reserving some of the cooking liquid. Meanwhile, remove the casings from a couple of sweet Italian sausages and fry the meat, breaking it up into small pieces, until cooked through. Add a large can of drained, diced tomatoes, a can of drained chickpeas, a tablespoon of crushed fennel seeds, a good pinch of red chile flakes, salt, and pepper. Toss the pasta with a couple handfuls of arugula or another tender green (baby spinach, mizuna, and dandelion are all good) and let it wilt. Add the pasta to the sausage mixture, along with some pasta water if needed to moisten, and serve garnished with chopped parsley.

90.

Pasta with Bacon and Breadcrumbs

This relies on good breadcrumbs, which means homemade or panko.

Boil salted water for pasta and cook it, reserving some of the cooking liquid. Meanwhile, cut bacon into small pieces and fry it in a bit of olive oil until just crisping; remove from the pan and add two or three minced cloves of garlic to the pan; cook over fairly low heat, turning until just fragrant, a couple of minutes. Toss in a cup or so of breadcrumbs and a pinch of red chile flakes; cook, stirring, until the breadcrumbs turn golden (they go fast, so you'll want to watch them). Toss the pasta and the breadcrumb mixture along with the bacon and a little of the reserved liquid. Top with some more olive oil and a bit of chopped parsley or basil.

91.

Linguine with Pea Sauce
and Prosciutto

*Good when you're eager for a taste of spring. I don't bother
to strain the sauce, but you can.*

Boil salted water for pasta and cook it, reserving some of the cooking liquid. Meanwhile, cook a bag of frozen peas and a couple of chopped scallions in just enough salted, boiling water to cover everything; simmer until tender, just a couple of minutes. Puree most of the peas with as much cooking liquid as you need in a food processor or blender. Cut a few slices of prosciutto into matchsticks and cook for about two minutes or until coloring slightly; add the remaining whole peas to the prosciutto. Toss the pasta with the pea puree; mix in the prosciutto and whole peas. Season with lots of freshly ground pepper and salt to taste; serve with freshly grated Parmesan cheese.

92.

Warm Milk Toast

Day-old bread is ideal for this; it won't become soggy.

Warm two tablespoons of butter in a large pot; add a cup of milk, a quarter cup of raw cane sugar, and a quarter cup of raisins. Heat this mixture, stirring until the sugar melts, but don't bring it to a boil. Slice good-quality bread (brioche is nice) into two-inch cubes and put the bread in the pot; add as much bread as needed to soak up the milk without becoming soggy. Transfer everything to a bowl to serve; drizzle with a couple of tablespoons of dark rum or whiskey and sprinkle with cinnamon.

93.

Lemon Mascarpone Mousse

Try substituting orange rind and juice for the lemon and add a touch
of Grand Marnier in place of the cream.

Finely grate the rind of a lemon. Whisk together a cup of mascarpone, the lemon's juice and grated rind, and about a quarter cup of sugar (or more to taste) until smooth. Add a tablespoon or two of heavy cream to moisten if needed. If you have time, chill for a bit before serving in pudding cups; top with a drizzle of honey and serve with ladyfingers.

94.

Candied Citrus Rinds

A combination of different citrus fruit makes for a gorgeous presentation.

Bring a small pot of water to a boil. Slice an orange, a grapefruit, or a lime into quarters and remove the flesh from the peel. (Use it for whatever you like.) Slice each quarter rind into quarter-inch-thick strips; boil for a minute, then remove from the water with a slotted spoon. In a combination of one part sugar to one part water boil the rinds a second time, for about five minutes. Drain, toss with a bit of sugar until lightly coated, and set on a cookie sheet to dry. If you like, melt some dark chocolate and dip the rinds halfway. Serve warm, alongside good butter cookies or shortbread.

95.

Grapefruit 'n' Cream Shake

In spring and summer strawberries and tarragon are also a lovely combination,
though you may have to add a bit of water depending on how juicy your fruit is.

In a blender, combine two cups of grapefruit juice, a half cup of cream, and a couple tablespoons (or more) of sugar. Add a cup of ice and blend until it becomes a slushy consistency. Serve immediately, garnished with a dusting of cayenne if you like.

96.

Whipped Grapefruit Cream
with Chocolate Drizzle

The nuts (use whatever type you like) are optional, but they do add a nice crunch.

Melt four ounces of bittersweet chocolate. Whip two cups of heavy cream along with two tablespoons of fresh grapefruit juice and two tablespoons zest; continue whipping until stiff peaks form. Fold in a handful of chopped pistachios. Spoon the grapefruit cream into serving dishes, drizzle with the warm chocolate, and garnish with a sprig of mint.

97.

Orange Fool

You can let this chill and set, or serve immediately.

Combine one and one-half cups orange juice and two tablespoons orange zest in a medium saucepan; simmer gently over medium-low heat until reduced to half its original volume, about fifteen minutes. Meanwhile, whip one and one-half cups of heavy cream until soft peaks form, then add three tablespoons of powdered sugar and continue beating, forming stiff peaks. Cool the saucepan in an ice bath for a minute or two, then strain the orange reduction into the whipped cream. Add three-quarters cup unsweetened flaked coconut and fold gently to combine everything. Garnish with additional coconut.

98.

Almond Tart

Great for guests, as you can serve it hot or at room temperature.

Heat the broiler. In a medium bowl, mix together four eggs, one-third cup of sugar, one-half cup of ground almonds, three-quarters cup of half-and-half, and a half cup of blanched slivered almonds. Melt two tablespoons of butter and add the almond mixture to the pan; mix to evenly distribute the almonds and cover. Cook until the eggs are set; put the pan uncovered in the broiler for about two minutes or until just golden on top. Sprinkle with powdered sugar and additional almonds to serve.

99.

Aztec Hot Chocolate

Increase or decrease the amount of cayenne as you like.

Whip a half cup of heavy cream with a half teaspoon of cayenne pepper and one teaspoon of vanilla extract until soft peaks form; set aside. In a small pot, warm four cups of whole milk with a half cup of chopped semisweet chocolate, a bit more cayenne, and a half teaspoon of cinnamon. Warm the milk until it just begins to bubble (don't let it boil) and the chocolate is melted. Transfer the chocolate milk to mugs and top with the spicy whipped cream.

100.

Nutella Fondue

For fans of Nutella, this is heaven.

Warm a cup of Nutella with a cup of cream and mix to combine well. Cut your favorite bakery pound cake into cubes and slice a couple of not-too-ripe bananas. Use skewers to dip the pound cake and bananas into the fondue.

101.

Chocolate Chip Pancakes

Topped with rum-infused whipped cream, this breakfast favorite becomes a fabulous dessert.

In a bowl, mix together two cups of flour, two teaspoons baking powder, one-quarter teaspoon salt, one tablespoon sugar, two eggs, one and one-half cups milk, and two tablespoons oil or melted butter; some lumps can remain. Warm a large pan with a tablespoon or two of butter, ladle some batter into the pan, and sprinkle the batter with chocolate chips. When the pancake begins to bubble, flip and cook for another minute more or until golden brown.

Spring

We expect so much of spring,

and though it comes slowly, it brings lettuce and other greens, peas, asparagus, onions, rhubarb, strawberries, broccoli, turnips, beets, and more. After a long winter when almost every vegetable comes from the great Central Valley of California or even farther away, anything local is welcome.

We can do wonderful things with that produce as it becomes available. Everything mentioned above, along with spinach, escarole, endive, citrus, arugula, fennel, and more, makes its way into dishes that draw back the curtain of winter.

1.

Fried Eggs with Lemon and Chervil

Chervil, an herb that tastes like basil, can be hard to find, but tarragon and chives are fine substitutes.

Cook a little minced garlic in butter over medium heat until fragrant, then add a few tablespoons of lemon juice and cook a couple of minutes more. Gently add four eggs to the pan, cover, and cook until just set. Sprinkle with freshly chopped chervil and serve with crusty bread.

2.

Chilaquiles

To avoid frying fresh tortillas, use tortilla chips.

Cut corn tortillas (flour tortillas will do, but they're not as good) into strips. Fry in not too much oil—with a few chopped jalapeños, pickled or not, if you tend in that direction—until crisp, about three minutes, turning; drain on paper towels. Beat a few eggs with a bit of milk or cream and sprinkle with salt and pepper. Heat a tablespoon or so of the frying oil (save or discard the rest) and add the tortilla strips and eggs. Cook, stirring, until the eggs are done, two to four minutes. Garnish with salsa (or stir some salsa in there), chopped avocado, cheese, scallions, sour cream, or whatever else you like.

3.

Mixed Herb Omelet

A combo of thyme, basil, marjoram, and rosemary is also good.

Beat four eggs with two tablespoons of milk. Add a pinch of salt and pepper and a small handful of parsley and mint, along with smaller amounts of tarragon and thyme. Set a medium nonstick pan over medium-low heat and add butter to the pan, followed, a minute or two later, by the egg mixture. Cook, undisturbed, until the eggs are mostly set but still quite runny in the center. Fold the omelet in half, slide it from the pan, and serve topped with more chopped herbs.

4.

Hangtown Fry

Supposedly the breakfast of forty-niners (the gold miners, not the football team).

Cook about one-quarter pound of chopped bacon (slab is best) in a little olive oil over medium heat for a minute or two; add one-half cup mushrooms (shiitakes are good) if you like, and cook until brown, with salt and pepper. Add six or eight shucked oysters, cook for a half minute or so. Stir in four or five beaten eggs, with some parsley. Scramble soft and serve with toast.

5.

Eggs Bhona

Add as much or as little spice as you like to this Bangladeshi take on eggs dish.

Boil eight eggs for about six minutes; meanwhile, cook a chopped onion and a chopped green bell pepper in vegetable oil, just until soft. Add a crushed clove of garlic, one-quarter teaspoon each ground ginger and turmeric, a pinch each of red chile flakes and salt, a bay leaf, and a quarter cup of tomato paste and give a good stir. Then add a cup or so boiling water to make a sauce. Shell the eggs and add to the onion mixture. Cover and cook for five minutes.

6.

Lemongrass-and-Chicken Soup

You can add rice vermicelli or mung bean noodles to this if you like.

Heat chicken stock, about a cup-and-a-half per serving. Trim a stalk of lemongrass per serving; bruise the pieces with the back of a knife. Add the lemongrass and a few slices of ginger to the stock, along with two or three minced hot chiles, or to taste. After a few minutes, remove the lemongrass and ginger and add fish or soy sauce and chopped oyster mushrooms or any other mushrooms and some chunks of cooked chicken (or pork, beef, or cubed tofu). Season with lime juice (lots) and salt, and garnish with cilantro leaves.

7.

Udon Noodles with Green Tea Broth

You can embellish this with bonito flakes,
cucumber or avocado slices, chopped scallions, sesame seeds,
or shredded cooked beef or chicken.

Bring about two quarts of water to a boil in a large pot. Tie three tablespoons of green tea leaves in a piece of cheesecloth or put in a tea ball. Remove the pot from the heat and steep the tea for about five minutes or to desired strength. Discard the tea and return to a boil, adding a pinch of salt. Add eight ounces of udon noodles. Cook, stirring once or twice, until noodles are tender. Taste and add some more salt, pepper, and mirin or sugar if desired.

8.

Miso Soup with Tofu

For more substance, add a few chopped cooked shrimp or some shredded chicken.

Bring four or five cups of water to a boil. Whisk a cup of the water with a quarter cup of miso (more if you like) in a bowl until smooth. Pour the miso mix into the water and add cubed tofu, minced carrots, and minced scallions to serve with soy sauce on the side.

9.

Lime and Chicken Soup

Pretty much a perfect combination of flavors, as long as you're generous with both lime juice and cilantro.

Cut a couple boneless, skinless chicken breasts or thighs into one-half-inch chunks; brown in olive oil; then add a chopped onion, a smashed garlic clove, a pinch of cinnamon, and the zest of a lime; cook a minute or so. Add six cups chicken broth and bring to a boil. Stir in a chopped avocado and the juice from the lime. Serve, sprinkled with lots of cilantro, with tortilla chips on the side.

10.

Spinach and White Bean Soup

Any tender green is fine here; arugula, watercress, or dandelion adds a nice peppery flavor.

Cook half a chopped onion with a smashed clove of garlic in some olive oil for about three minutes. Add precooked or canned white beans (with their liquid) and about five cups of chicken or vegetable broth; bring to a boil. Reduce to a simmer and cook for about five minutes, mashing some of the beans a bit if you like. Add two or three cups of chopped spinach and one-quarter cup chopped parsley. Stir to wilt the greens and serve with a hunk of crusty bread and grated Parmesan.

11.

Asparagus Leek Soup

A nice combination of early spring ingredients.

Slice the white part of a leek and cook it for three to five minutes in a couple of tablespoons of butter or oil along with a smashed clove of garlic, a chopped carrot, and a bunch of chopped fresh asparagus. Add about six cups of chicken or vegetable stock and bring to a boil. Reduce to a simmer and cook until the vegetables are tender, five minutes or so. Puree the ingredients until smooth. You can add a few tablespoons of cream if you want a richer finish.

12.

Soup with Poached Eggs and Greens

It doesn't get much faster or better than this.

Bring six cups of vegetable or chicken stock to a slow bubble. Add two cups of any chopped tender greens (spinach, arugula, and mizuna all work well), then four shelled eggs, along with a couple of smashed cloves of garlic, some freshly grated Parmesan, and red chile flakes to taste. Cook until the whites of the eggs are set but the yolks still soft, about three minutes. Scoop out the garlic cloves if you care, and serve immediately.

13.

Chilled Cucumber and Dill Soup

The fresh dill is what makes this fabulous.

Peel and seed three cucumbers. Chop them up and put in a blender with two cups of buttermilk, a half cup of sour cream, a tablespoon of olive oil, a couple of tablespoons of freshly chopped dill, a pinch of sugar, salt, and a splash of white wine vinegar. Puree and garnish with fresh dill. Serve with crusty bread.

14.

Vietnamese Noodle Soup with Beef

I poach an egg or two in this soup at the end,
but you can also just add a couple of hard-boiled eggs.

Soak rice vermicelli and a handful of snow peas, cut in pieces if you like, in boiling water for about 10 minutes. Drain the noodle–snow pea combination in a colander and rinse with cold water; divide evenly among four bowls. Quickly cook a few slices of fresh ginger and a chopped chile, then add a quart of beef broth along with two cups of water and bring to a simmer. Divide one-half pound of thinly sliced rare roast beef among the four bowls (roast beef from a deli is fine, though leftovers are preferable), along with a few torn basil, cilantro, and mint leaves. Stir a tablespoon or so of Asian fish sauce and fresh lime juice into the simmering broth and ladle into bowls. Serve immediately.

15.

Fast Fish Soup

Not a true bouillabaisse, but a good and very fast knockoff.

In a couple tablespoons of olive oil, soften a chopped onion, a smashed clove of garlic, and half teaspoon paprika for about two minutes. Add four cups of stock (fish, vegetable, or chicken), a can of chopped-up tomatoes with their juice, a pinch of saffron, salt, and pepper; bring to a boil. Reduce to a simmer and cook for five minutes. Add about a pound or a pound-and-a-half of white fish, cut into chunks, to the stock; or a mix of scallops, shrimp, and well-washed clams, with some fish if you like. Simmer until the fish is cooked through, about five minutes more. Serve garnished with chopped parsley and slices of toasted baguette.

16.

Classic Caesar Salad

The quality of your anchovies will make a difference; use those marinated in olive oil and packed in glass.

Rub the inside of a large salad bowl (wooden, preferably) with a clove of garlic. Cook two eggs in gently boiling water for about a minute to a minute and a half (you want them barely coddled). Crack the eggs into the bowl and beat them as you add freshly squeezed lemon juice and a few tablespoons of olive oil. Stir in two or more anchovies (you can chop these first if you like), a dash or two of Worcestershire sauce, salt, and plenty of pepper. Toss with a chopped head of romaine, garnish with lots of freshly grated Parmesan, and serve with Italian bread or croutons.

17.

Salad Niçoise

The classic composed French salad made simple.

Boil and salt a pot of water. Chop a couple of potatoes (peeled or not) into half-inch dice and boil until a knife can be easily inserted, about eight minutes. When the potatoes are nearly done, add a handful of trimmed green beans or haricots verts and cook until crisp-tender, just a minute or two. Drain the vegetables and plunge them into ice water to stop the cooking process. Put a bunch of mixed baby greens in a bowl with the beans, the potatoes, a handful of good-quality black olives, a few chopped anchovies, a diced tomato, and half a sliced red onion. Combine one-quarter cup of olive oil, a few tablespoons of sherry vinegar, a teaspoon or so of Dijon mustard, salt, and pepper and dress the salad. Top the salad with a drained can of tuna packed in olive oil.

18.

Spinach Salad
with Smoked Trout and Apples

You can use either tart or sweet apples; just make sure they're crisp.

Toast a handful or two of sliced almonds in a dry skillet until just fragrant. Core two apples and cut them into thin slices. In a large bowl, whisk together a quarter cup of olive oil, the juice of a lemon, and a tablespoon of Dijon mustard. Add the apples and toss to coat. Break a smoked trout into bite-size pieces and add it to the bowl along with a mound of fresh spinach, the toasted almonds, and a handful of currants or raisins. Season with salt and pepper.

19.

Poached Eggs and Truffled Arugula
Prosciutto Salad

Real truffles are best, of course, but occasionally truffle oil can be nice;
you can also use good-quality extra-virgin olive oil here.

Sear a few slices of prosciutto on high heat to crisp them, about two minutes, then set it aside to drain on a paper towel. Poach four eggs in boiling water for about three minutes. Remove the eggs with a slotted spoon, draining off all the excess water, and set them on a large bed of arugula. Top the eggs with the prosciutto, crumbling it between your fingers. Sprinkle the salad with a few dashes of truffle oil, along with salt and pepper to taste.

20.

Carrot and Couscous Salad

An incredibly easy salad with North African flavors.

Add couscous to a pot of boiling water, turn off the heat, cover, and let sit for 10 minutes. Shred four or five carrots and mix them with the juice of a lemon, a few tablespoons of fresh orange juice, about one-quarter cup of olive oil, a bit of cumin, and salt and pepper. When the couscous is done, drain it if necessary, fluff it gently with a fork, and add it to the carrots along with a handful of raisins. Toss well and serve.

21.

Chive Salad

Add cooked chicken, shrimp, or tofu to make this a meal.

In a large salad bowl, whisk together equal parts soy sauce, water, and rice wine vinegar. Add a few drops of sesame oil and a pinch of sugar. Roughly chop a couple of bunches of chives and add them to the bowl along with some chopped romaine or iceberg lettuce. Toss well and serve.

22.

Asparagus and Sesame Salad

Thinner asparagus works better here; but be careful not to overcook the spears.

Trim a bunch of asparagus, then cut the spears on the bias. Cook them quickly in a bit of vegetable oil for a minute or two, or until they turn bright green (you can also blanch them quickly in boiling water). Toss the cooked spears with a tablespoon or two of sesame oil, a splash of rice vinegar, a drizzle of soy sauce, and a sprinkle of sugar if you like; garnish with toasted sesame seeds and chopped scallions.

23.

Seared Scallops with Escarole, Fennel, and Orange Salad

You can mix this up a bit by using grapefruit, tangerines, blood oranges, or any combination of sweet citrus.

In a large salad bowl, mix together about one-quarter cup olive oil, a few splashes of white wine or sherry vinegar, some salt and pepper, and the zest of an orange. Now peel the orange, getting as much pith off as you can, and divide the fruit into sections. Core and thinly slice a head of fennel and toss this into the bowl with a couple of cups of chopped escarole and the orange sections. Sear eight to 12 scallops in olive oil until nicely browned on both sides, sprinkling them with salt and pepper. Give the salad another good toss and serve the scallops on top.

24.

BLT Salad

The avocado dressing really sets this apart.

Fry a few small cubes of slab bacon for about five minutes or until crisp. Puree an avocado, a handful of basil leaves, a clove of garlic, juice from one—or more—limes, about one-quarter cup of olive oil, salt, and pepper together in a food processor or blender; if you like a thinner dressing, add a few drops of water. Mix a head of Bibb or romaine lettuce with sliced tomatoes and chopped red onions. Add the bacon to the vegetables and dress with the pureed mixture. Serve with warm, crusty bread.

25.

Spicy Pork Salad

For an even spicier version,
add a pinch or two of cayenne or red chile flakes to the rub.

Coat thin, boneless pork chops with a mixture of sugar, cumin, chili powder, and salt and set aside to marinate. Combine a few handfuls of baby spinach leaves with half a thinly sliced red pepper, sections of a navel orange, a sliced avocado, and a small handful of toasted pine nuts. Mix together some olive oil, a good squeeze of fresh lime and orange juices, a teaspoon of Dijon mustard, salt, and pepper to dress the salad. Grill, broil, or pan-cook the pork until it's just done; cut into strips; and serve on top of the vegetables with the dressing drizzled over all.

26.

Lebanese Potato Salad

Frozen favas are a lovely addition to the pot; allow a minute or two more cooking time.

Peel and chop four or five large Yukon Gold potatoes; put them in a pot, cover with salted water, bring to a boil, and cook until tender, adding about a cup of frozen peas during the last couple of minutes of cooking. Drain and run under cold water to stop the cooking. Transfer to a large bowl; dress with olive oil, freshly squeezed lemon juice, minced garlic, chopped parsley and scallions, salt, pepper, and coriander seeds if you like and toss to mix well. Serve warm, cold, or in between.

27.

Greek Stuffed Pita Bread

For a salad skip the pita and toss everything with lots of romaine.

Mix together about a cup of plain yogurt, some chopped fresh mint, lemon juice, salt, and pepper. Slice the pitas in half crosswise to create pockets. Stuff the pockets with chopped tomatoes, feta cheese, cucumbers, oil-cured black olives, and roasted red peppers (the ones from a jar are fine; drain them first). Top with a dollop or two of the yogurt mixture and serve.

28.

Green Papaya Salad, with Shrimp

Green papaya is just unripe papaya, easy enough to find.

Cook a dozen or more medium shrimp in a little vegetable oil. Meanwhile, combine a tablespoon of brown sugar, juice of a lime, a garlic clove, a tablespoon fish or soy sauce, one-half teaspoon chile flakes (more or less), and some peeled ginger in a blender or food processor and puree. Grate (the food processor is good for this) a peeled and seeded green papaya (not one the size of a football) and two carrots. Toss with shrimp, sliced fresh tomatoes, and dressing; season to taste; and top with chopped peanuts.

29.

Tuna and Bean Salad

Tuna packed in olive oil, from Europe, is the key here, as is good olive oil.

Mix a cup or so of precooked or canned cannellini beans (drained) with a can of good tuna, a handful of chopped parsley, salt, pepper, a teeny bit of garlic (optional) or shallot (or red onion, or scallion, or whatever), and, if you have it, a sprig of rosemary. Drizzle with olive oil, toss, adjust seasoning, and serve with good bread or alongside cold cooked asparagus.

30.

Curried Chicken Salad Sandwich

Almost any fairly neutral-flavored cooked chicken is fine here,
or use store-bought rotisserie chicken.

Combine a spoonful or two of plain yogurt and half a fresh chopped mango (it doesn't have to be too ripe) in a large bowl. Add a few squeezes of fresh lime juice and curry powder to taste. Season with salt and pepper. Add shredded chicken, along with fresh chopped scallions and cilantro. Taste and adjust the seasoning; if the mixture is too moist, add more chicken or vegetables; if it's too dry, add more yogurt. Spread the salad on rolls, add arugula or lettuce, and serve.

31.

"Potpie" Chicken Salad Sandwich

Shuck a half cup of fresh peas, or run frozen peas under warm water and drain. Whisk together one-quarter cup chopped parsley, one-quarter cup cream, one-quarter cup mayonnaise, two tablespoons cider vinegar, and some salt and pepper. Chop a stalk of celery, a couple of scallions, and a carrot; add them to the bowl along with two cups chopped cooked chicken and the peas. Stir to combine, moistening with more cream if needed. Serve on bread, rolls, or croissants.

32.

Minted Pea and Prosciutto Sandwich

An unbeatable combination.

Blanch half of a bag of frozen peas in salted, boiling water. Put the peas in a food processor or blender with a couple of tablespoons of olive oil, a handful each of grated Parmesan and chopped mint, salt, and pepper; puree until smooth. Spread the pea mixture onto toasted sourdough bread and layer with slices of prosciutto.

33.

Cheese "Burger"

*I'm not saying you'll never go back to meat, but these are intense. Keep 'em small,
and garnish freely; even traditional burger garnishes are fine.*

Combine two cups grated Parmesan cheese with a handful of chopped parsley and
about a cup good breadcrumbs (all of this can be done together in a food processor).
Add two beaten eggs and gently mold into thin patties. Heat olive oil and cook patties
until brown around the edges, about five minutes. Flip and cook the other side for
another three minutes. Serve with tomato sauce or on a bun with garnishes.

34.

Seared Chicken Arugula Rollups

If you feel inspired, include a slice of prosciutto in each roll.

Flatten some chicken tenders with your hand or the bottom of a pot, brush both
sides with olive oil, and sprinkle with salt and pepper. Crumble some Gorgonzola on
each and top with a couple of arugula leaves. Roll the chicken up tightly lengthwise
and secure with a toothpick. Warm some butter over medium-high heat and sear
rollups until browned on all sides, about six minutes. Serve with toasted baguette
slices rubbed with fresh garlic.

35.

Anchovy Egg Sandwich

Served open-face, this is pretty close to perfect.

Hard-boil four eggs. While they're cooking, smear a slice of rye toast with sour cream
or plain yogurt; top with sliced tomatoes and good-quality anchovies. When the eggs
are done, peel them and slice them onto the sandwich. Drizzle with olive oil and
garnish with fresh dill (a sprinkling of dried dill will work too).

36.

Middle Eastern Pizza

Also known as lahmacun.

Mix together about a half pound of ground lamb, a chopped onion, a chopped tomato (canned is fine), some minced garlic, a couple of tablespoons tomato paste, some chopped fresh mint, salt, and pepper. Spread a thin layer on pocketless pita or lavash bread; bake at 450°F for eight minutes, or until the lamb is fully cooked. Sprinkle with lemon juice and serve.

37.

Italian Tostada

OK, it's not traditional, but it's pretty good, like an extremely thin-crust pizza.

Heat the oven to 400°F. Brush flour tortillas with olive oil and bake until firmed up a bit. Evenly spread thinly sliced mozzarella cheese (preferably fresh), some chopped tomato, and slices of prosciutto on top. Bake again until the cheese melts. Drizzle a bunch of arugula with olive oil and lemon juice. Add the greens to the top of the tostadas and put them back in the oven for about a minute to gently wilt. Serve whole or sliced like a pizza.

38.

Chickpea Burgers

If you like hummus, this is your kind of burger.

Drain a can of chickpeas and put them in a food processor with a chopped shallot or some onion, a bit of oregano, paprika, salt, and an egg. Pulse the mixture until it's slightly grainy but even in consistency. Add enough flour—about a quarter cup—so you can form the mixture into flat burger patties. Sear them in olive oil until golden, about four minutes per side. Serve on good whole grain bread or a bun with tahini (optional), greens, and a squeeze of lemon juice.

39.

Saag Paneer

If you can't find paneer (an Indian cheese), use feta or tofu, which both work wonderfully.

Cut about a cup-and-a-half of paneer, feta, or firm tofu into half-inch cubes and chop a pound of spinach. Cook some minced garlic and ginger in peanut oil or another oil, along with a pinch or two of red chile flakes until soft, about two minutes. Stir in curry powder to taste (at least a tablespoon), along with some salt and pepper; add the spinach and cook until it wilts. Stir in a dusting of flour (use chickpea flour if you have it) and cook until just turning golden. Add a couple of spoonfuls of plain yogurt and a cup of half-and-half or cream; cook gently until the mixture begins to dry out. Add the paneer, feta, or tofu, and continue cooking until warmed through; add more half-and-half or cream if necessary, adjust the seasonings, and serve.

40.

Ketchup-Braised Tofu with Veggies

You can use sugar snap peas or asparagus tips instead of green beans.

Press extra-firm tofu between layers of paper towels for a few minutes, or longer if you have time; cut into one-inch squares. Heat a few tablespoons of vegetable oil in a skillet and sear the tofu until golden and crisp, turning once or twice. Add about one-quarter cup of ketchup, a dash of rice vinegar, a few drops of sesame oil, and enough water to make a little sauce. Stir in a thinly sliced carrot, a couple of handfuls of green beans, and a pinch of red chile flakes. Cover the skillet and reduce the heat; braise for about four minutes or until the vegetables are just tender. At the last minute, toss in a handful of bean sprouts or shredded cabbage, give a good stir, and serve, with soy sauce on the side.

41.

Snap Peas with Walnuts and Roquefort

You can also use slender haricots verts here if you can find them.

Cook about a pound of snap peas in salted, boiling water until crisp-tender, about a minute. Drain and shock in ice water to stop the cooking. Soften a minced shallot in olive oil until it's translucent, for another minute or so. Add a handful of chopped walnuts and cook until fragrant, about another minute. Add the peas, salt, and pepper and warm through. Serve with Roquefort cheese crumbled on top.

42.

Spicy Stir-fried Bean Sprouts

Try starting this dish with ground pork, chicken, minced shrimp or tempeh, or crumbled tofu.

Heat a film of peanut or vegetable oil in a deep skillet and add a mound of bean sprouts with minced fresh ginger and a bit of minced chile if you like; toss to coat with oil. Cook, stirring, for about three minutes, then add a couple of tablespoons of any spice blend (Chinese five-spice, curry powder, etc.) and some salt and pepper. Add a few drops of water if the sprouts begin to stick. Cook another minute. Serve with leaves of romaine or Boston lettuce and make little bundles of the sprouts.

43.

Crisp Fennel Gratin

Heat the broiler and bring a pot of water to a boil. Cut a couple of fennel bulbs into quarter-inch-thick slices and boil for about three minutes or until just tender. Drain and put in a shallow broiler-safe dish; top with a layer of breadcrumbs (homemade are better) and freshly grated Parmesan cheese. Put the dish under the broiler for about three minutes or until the cheese melts and the breadcrumbs are golden. Garnish with some of the chopped fennel fronds if you like.

44.

Broccoli Rabe and Couscous

To add a bit of heft, crumble some cooked Italian sausage (sweet, hot, or a combination) in with the broccoli rabe.

Boil two pots of water. When the first is ready, add the couscous, turn off the heat, cover, and let it sit for 10 minutes. Salt the second pot of water and blanch a bunch of broccoli rabe for about two minutes, until crisp-tender; drain well and chop. When the couscous is done, drain if necessary and fluff it with a fork. Add the rabe along with a few tablespoons of olive oil, some freshly squeezed lemon juice, salt, and pepper. Mix to combine; top with freshly grated Parmesan and serve.

45.

Seared Fish with Lettuce Leaves

Use anything sustainable, good, fresh, and firm.

Warm a couple of tablespoons of sesame oil (or use olive or peanut oil; something with flavor, in any case) in a skillet over medium-high heat. Sprinkle fish chunks with salt and pepper and sear until just done. Wrap at the table in leaves of Boston or other tender lettuce, or grape leaves from a jar, garnished with lemon juice and fresh mint or lime juice and basil, mint, and/or cilantro.

46.

Fish in Spicy Soy Sauce

This easy, useful sauce can work with virtually any fish.

Combine one-quarter cup of soy sauce, one-quarter cup of water, a large pinch of sugar, a couple of chopped scallions, and a diced chile in a deep skillet; bring to a boil. Add the fish and adjust the heat so that the mixture bubbles gently. Cook for about eight minutes, depending on the thickness of the fish, turning it once or twice gently until it's coated with the sauce. Spoon on the sauce, garnish with chopped scallions, and serve.

47.

Fish Braised in Lemon
with Tomatoes and Red Peppers

Try sprinkling a few capers on top of the fish just before serving.

Thinly slice a medium onion and a red pepper, then cook them in olive oil; once they soften, add a handful of cherry tomatoes or grape tomatoes, cut in half. Season any white-fleshed fish with salt and pepper; move the vegetables to the side of the pan and sear the fish for about two minutes. Turn, add freshly squeezed lemon juice, then cover and simmer for another three minutes, or until the fish is cooked through (this may take longer, depending on the thickness of the fish). Adjust the seasonings and serve the fish topped with the vegetables and freshly chopped parsley.

48.

Prosciutto-Wrapped Fish
with Wilted Greens

The prosciutto provides a wonderfully crisp crust to the tender fish,
which can be any white-flesh fish.

Heat the oven to 400°F. Season fish fillets with salt and pepper and wrap them in thin slices of prosciutto (it'll stick to itself, but no problem). In a tablespoon each of butter and olive oil, cook the fish for about two minutes on each side or until the prosciutto begins to color and crisp up; put the fish in the oven and continue cooking until done, another five minutes or so. Cook some minced garlic in olive oil and add a bunch of spinach or other tender greens until just wilted; season with salt and pepper. Serve the fish on top of the greens.

49.

Fish with Edamame Pesto

Blanch a bag's worth of edamame for three to five minutes. Put the beans in a blender with a few tablespoons of olive oil or more, as needed to get a nice puree; a handful of grated Parmesan cheese; and a clove or two of garlic. Blend until smooth and season with salt and pepper. Season any fish fillets or steaks with salt and pepper and cook them in a couple of tablespoons of butter or olive oil for about four minutes on each side or until golden and cooked through. Serve the fish with a spoonful of the pesto and garnished with roughly chopped walnuts.

50.

Seared Fish with Fennel and Orange

More delicate fish are best in this recipe.

Slice a bulb of fennel very thinly (a mandoline works best). Peel two large oranges and segment them. Sprinkle four fish fillets with salt and pepper; dredge in flour, a beaten egg, and then panko. Sear in a mixture of olive oil and butter, turning once until both sides are golden and the fish is cooked through. Mix together a few tablespoons of olive oil, some freshly squeezed lemon juice, salt, and pepper. Drizzle the dressing on the fennel and orange slices and serve alongside the fish.

51.

Cajun-Style Salmon

A flexible rub that will boost the flavor of almost any grilled fish.

Mix together one teaspoon each paprika, coriander, cumin, and dried oregano; one-quarter teaspoon each cayenne and cinnamon; and some salt and pepper. Rub the mixture on salmon fillets and grill or broil on each side for four minutes, or to the desired doneness. Serve the salmon over a bed of mixed greens and garnish with lemon wedges.

52.

Fish with Thai "Pesto"

Use this herb paste on almost any seafood, chicken, or meat; it also works beautifully tossed with noodles.

In a food processor or blender, combine a few good handfuls of Thai basil, some cilantro, a few tablespoons of olive or vegetable oil, a fresh Thai chile, a clove of garlic, and a sprinkle of salt and pepper. Puree until nearly smooth, adding a bit more oil if needed. Season the fish with salt, pepper, and a pinch of cayenne. Heat a couple of tablespoons of butter or oil and cook the fish, turning once, until both sides are golden and the fish is cooked through. Top the fish generously with the pesto and serve.

53.

Crisp Fish with Citrus-Soy Glaze and Wilted Cress

Use any tender green you like here—arugula, mizuna, watercress, and dandelion all add a nice spice.

Stir together two teaspoons sugar, a teaspoon of water, and a couple of tablespoons each of grapefruit juice, lime juice, and soy sauce. Heat a couple of tablespoons of extra-virgin olive oil in a pan and cook any sturdy fish fillets (skin side down, if they have skin) for about two minutes, until crispy. Flip fillets and cook them for another minute; add the citrus-soy mixture and swirl gently until it's reduced to a glaze and the fish is cooked through. In another pan heat a tablespoon or so of olive oil; add a bunch of watercress, sprinkle with salt, and toss until just wilted. Serve the glazed fish over a bed of the wilted cress.

54.

Garlic-Ginger Shrimp

*Fast and fragrant; you can save time by using the tip of a teaspoon
to peel the ginger and a microplane to grate it.*

Cook some grated or minced ginger and garlic in a couple of tablespoons of vegetable oil. Add a pound of shrimp to the pan, along with one-quarter cup of rice or dry white wine; cook until the shrimp turn pink on both sides and are no longer translucent, about three minutes. Add chopped scallions, toss, and serve over noodles.

55.

Mark's Famous Spicy Shrimp

*The best "bring-to-the-grill-party" dish ever,
in my humble opinion; I've been doing it for 25 years.*

Use the side of a knife, a small food processor, or a mortar and pestle to make a paste from a couple of minced garlic cloves, salt, a pinch or two of cayenne, and about a tablespoon each of good paprika or pimentón, olive oil, and lemon juice. Smear the paste all over a pound or so of shrimp. Grill or broil the shrimp for about two minutes on each side and serve with lemon wedges.

56.

Shrimp with Asparagus, Dill, and Spice

Dried dill works just fine here.

Melt a few tablespoons of butter in a skillet; when it's hot, add about a pound of sliced asparagus; stir and cook until crisp-tender, about five minutes, then remove. Add some more butter to the pan and repeat with about a pound of shrimp, cooking until it turns pink, about four minutes. Return the asparagus to the pan and sprinkle with a few drops of Tabasco sauce, Worcestershire sauce, dill, and lemon juice. Serve over a bed of jasmine rice.

57.

Seared Scallops
with White Wine and Chile

A handful of toasted breadcrumbs or slivered blanched almonds makes a nice garnish.

Slice scallops in half along their flat side. Soften some minced garlic and a chopped seeded chile in olive oil for about two minutes and remove. Sear the scallops, turning once. Remove the scallops from the pan and add about a half cup of white wine to the pan along with the garlic and chile mixture, and reduce quickly over high heat. Serve the scallops over pasta, rice, or toasted bread drizzled with the wine reduction (and a bit of good-quality olive oil if needed). Garnish with chopped parsley.

58.

Scallops with Sesame Seeds
and Scallions

Toast sesame seeds in a dry skillet for just a minute or two: they're done when fragrant and golden. Remove. Then heat a couple of tablespoons of olive oil in the skillet and add the scallops, sprinkle with salt and pepper, and cook for two minutes or until lightly browned and opaque inside; set aside. Turn the heat up and add one-half stick of butter and one-half cup of dry white wine; continue stirring, scraping up the brown bits from the bottom of the pan and reducing until the sauce is thickened a bit. Add some chopped scallions and a splash of soy sauce and cook for another 30 seconds. Serve the scallops drizzled with the sauce and garnished with the toasted sesame seeds.

59.

Mussels with Green Curry and Cellophane Noodles

Canned coconut milk is a wonderful thing, and the light versions, which are lower in fat, do just fine here.

Cover the noodles with boiling water and set aside. In a large pot, combine one-quarter cup water, the rind and juice of a lime, a teaspoon or so of sugar, a couple of tablespoons of green curry paste (or to taste), a splash of fish sauce, a can of coconut milk, and two to four pounds of mussels; bring to a boil. Cover and cook for about five minutes or until all the shells are open; discard any that don't open. Stir in a handful of chopped cilantro. Drain the noodles and serve the mussels and sauce on top.

60.

Chicken with Chilaquiles and Green Salsa

Store-bought green salsa is OK, but homemade takes just a couple of minutes.

Puree about a dozen tomatillos (canned are fine) with a large clove of garlic, a handful of fresh cilantro, lime juice, salt, and fresh chile to taste. Stir together a cup of sour cream with just enough milk so it can be poured. Bring a cup or so of the salsa to a boil over medium heat. Add a few handfuls of shredded chicken (leftover or from a store-bought rotisserie chicken), season with salt and pepper, and cook until the chicken is warmed through. Add a few handfuls of tortilla chips and let them soften for about a minute. Serve in bowls garnished with cilantro and more tortilla chips, and drizzled with the sour cream mixture. Pass any leftover salsa around the table.

61.

Chicken Tandoori

Perfect for skewers.

Heat the grill or broiler. In a bowl or dish large enough to hold the chicken, combine a cup of plain yogurt, a teaspoon each minced ginger and garlic, a teaspoon of paprika, a teaspoon cumin, a half teaspoon turmeric, the juice of a lime, and some salt and pepper. Marinate a pound of boneless, skinless chicken in this mixture for about five minutes. Grill or broil the chicken for about three minutes per side or until lightly browned and cooked through. Garnish with fresh cilantro and serve with basmati rice.

62.

Mediterranean Chicken

If you can find preserved lemons, a staple in Moroccan cooking, add some with the parsley.

Pound chicken breasts to one-quarter-inch thickness; sprinkle with salt and pepper and dredge in flour. Heat a few tablespoons of olive oil over medium-high heat and brown the chicken on both sides, about a minute per side, then remove. Stir a small handful of brine-cured green olives into the pan, along with a tablespoon of capers. Add a cup of chicken stock or white wine and bring to a boil; continue cooking over high heat until the liquid is reduced and syrupy, about four minutes. Finish with a couple of tablespoons of butter and chopped parsley and sprinkle with salt and pepper. Return the chicken to the sauce to heat through, then serve sprinkled with more chopped parsley.

63.

Spicy Chicken with Lemongrass and Lime

If you can find galangal (not always easy), it's a fun change from the ginger.

In a food processor, puree half an onion, a clove of garlic, a chunk of peeled ginger, the tender core from a stalk of lemongrass, a pinch of red chile flakes (or more if you like), and a teaspoon each of turmeric, sugar, and ground coriander, until a thick paste forms. Heat a couple of tablespoons of vegetable oil in a skillet; sear pounded chicken cutlets or tenders on both sides until brown. Remove the chicken from the pan and set aside; add the paste to the pan and cook for about two minutes. Return the chicken tenders to the pan and add half a cup of water or chicken stock; cover and simmer about four minutes. Serve the chicken with the sauce.

64.

Panko Chicken with Grapefruit-Honey Sauce

The sweetness of the honey, acidity of the grapefruit, and crunch of the panko really make this special.

Pound chicken breasts to one-quarter-inch thickness; dredge them first in a beaten egg and then in panko breadcrumbs seasoned with salt and pepper. Heat a few tablespoons of olive oil; cook the chicken on both sides until golden and just done, about four minutes total. Wipe the pan clean and soften some minced garlic for a minute in some more oil or butter; add half a cup of grapefruit juice and a tablespoon or so of honey. Season with salt and pepper and reduce until syrupy. Serve the chicken generously drizzled with the sauce and garnished with fresh grapefruit slices.

65.

Pan-Fried Herbed Chicken

Fresh herbs are the key here.

In a food processor, combine a small onion, two cloves of garlic, a tablespoon each of tarragon and sage, the juice of a lemon, a tablespoon of tahini or peanut butter, and a quarter cup of olive oil; puree until smooth. Rub the pureed mixture over boneless, skinless chicken pounded to half-inch thickness; dredge in flour. Fry the chicken in hot olive oil for about four minutes on each side, until well browned and cooked through. Serve over a mixed green salad with fresh lemon wedges on the side.

66.

Chicken with Green Olives

Good-quality European olives (think Greek or Spanish) are what you want here.

Pound chicken breasts to one-quarter-inch thickness. Heat a couple of tablespoons of butter or olive oil in a skillet and sear the chicken on both sides, about a minute per side; remove and set aside. Add to the pan half a diced onion, a teaspoon of minced or grated ginger, some minced garlic, and a half teaspoon each of ground cinnamon, cumin, and paprika. Cook until the onion softens, about three minutes. Add a half cup of chicken stock to the pan and bring to a boil; reduce to a simmer and return the chicken to the pan along with a handful of green olives, pitted and chopped. Continue cooking until the chicken is done, about two more minutes. Serve the chicken topped with the olives and drizzled with the sauce.

67.

Chicken with Almonds and Spinach

*A microwave comes in handy here to steam the spinach
and save dirtying an extra pan.*

Wash and chop a bunch of spinach and steam it; set aside. Pound chicken cutlets to about one-quarter-inch thickness; sprinkle with salt and pepper. Melt a couple of tablespoons of butter over medium-high heat and sear the chicken on each side until golden brown, about a minute per side. Add a couple of large minced cloves of garlic and arrange the steamed spinach and a handful of chopped almonds around the chicken, drizzling with more olive oil if you like; cover and cook for another minute or so until the chicken is done and everything is warmed through.

68.

Lemon Parmesan Chicken

Utterly simple yet sublime.

In a bowl, combine the grated rind from a large lemon, a cup of breadcrumbs (homemade are ideal), about a quarter cup of freshly grated Parmesan cheese, chopped fresh parsley, and some salt and pepper. Pound chicken cutlets to about a quarter-inch thickness; dredge in a beaten egg and the breadcrumb mixture. Cook the crusted cutlets in a couple of tablespoons of butter or olive oil over medium-high heat until golden on both sides and cooked through. Serve with lemon slices.

69.

Chicken Satay with Peanut Sauce

Homemade peanut sauce takes less than five minutes to make.

Pound chicken breasts to half-inch thickness and slice them into four-inch pieces. In a bowl, combine the juice from one lime with a smashed clove of garlic; add the chicken and let it marinate for five minutes. Meanwhile, whisk together a half cup of peanut butter, a couple of tablespoons of freshly squeezed lime juice, a splash of soy sauce, a pinch or two of red chile flakes, a teaspoon of brown sugar, and enough chicken broth or water to make a smooth sauce; adjust the seasoning. Set aside most of the sauce for dipping and smear the rest on the chicken pieces with a little salt and pepper, thread onto skewers, and grill for two minutes on each side or until cooked through. Serve with the reserved peanut sauce and lime wedges.

70.

Chicken with Coconut and Lime

You might thread the chicken onto skewers, then serve the coconut-lime mixture as a dipping sauce.

Heat the broiler. Cut boneless, skinless chicken into four-inch pieces and toss with the juice of a lime. Heat a can of coconut milk along with a pinch of cayenne, the zest of two limes, and the juice of the other lime. Broil the chicken for about six minutes, turning once, until browned and cooked through. Add about a teaspoon of fish sauce to the coconut milk and season with salt and pepper. Serve the sauce over the chicken and top with chopped scallions and sprinkled with freshly chopped cilantro.

71.

Moroccan Spiced Chicken
with Yogurt Sauce

A bed of couscous completes this Moroccan-inspired meal.

Heat the broiler or a grill pan. Rub thin chicken breasts with a mixture of ground cumin, coriander, cayenne, cinnamon, salt, and pepper. Cook the chicken until nicely browned and done, turning once, six to eight minutes total. Mix a cup or so of plain yogurt with a couple of tablespoons of freshly squeezed lemon juice, some chopped fresh mint, and salt to taste. Serve the spice-rubbed chicken with the yogurt sauce and top with more mint and a slice of lemon.

72.

Vietnamese Caramelized
Grilled Pork

This caramel sauce does wonders for shrimp as well; just thread the shrimp on skewers, drizzle with the sauce, and grill.

Pound boneless pork chops to quarter-inch thickness and heat the grill or broiler. In a small, heavy saucepan, combine half a cup of sugar with two tablespoons of water and stir with some grated ginger to make a paste; cook, undisturbed, over medium heat until it turns golden. Add a couple of finely diced shallots, a tablespoon each fresh lime juice and fish sauce, and a pinch of salt (at this point the caramel will harden); continue to cook, stirring constantly, until the caramel dissolves and the shallots are soft, about two minutes. Put the pork on the grill and brush with sauce, turning frequently until the chops are just cooked through.

73.

Beef and Corn Tacos

Unless corn is already in season, this is a good time to go with frozen.

Cook a chopped onion and a diced jalapeño pepper for a couple of minutes, until the onion starts to soften. Add a teaspoon each of chili powder and cumin (or more to taste) and cook for another 30 seconds. Add a pound or so of ground beef to the pan, sprinkle with salt and pepper, and cook through, about four minutes. Meanwhile, chop a tomato and an avocado; grate a cup or so of Jack or cheddar cheese. Add a few handfuls of corn to the meat mixture and continue to cook. Warm corn or flour tortillas and serve by wrapping some of the beef-corn mixture and the other fresh ingredients in each tortilla. Garnish with fresh cilantro and sour cream.

74.

Broiled Steak with Fennel and Shallots

Fennel fronds make a lovely garnish.

Heat the broiler. Trim and slice a fennel bulb into about six wedges (save the fronds for later) and a few shallots into halves or wedges; toss with olive oil, salt, and pepper. Put the vegetables on one side of a broiler-safe pan; sprinkle one or two three-quarter-inch-thick boneless rib eye steaks with salt and pepper and put them on the other side of the pan. Broil for six to eight minutes, turning the steaks and vegetables halfway through cooking. Serve the steaks topped with the vegetables.

75.

Carne Cruda

A rare treat (OK, pun intended).

Cut a pound of filet mignon into quarter-inch cubes and combine in a bowl with a handful each of arugula and parsley, about one-quarter cup of olive oil, and a few tablespoons of freshly squeezed lemon juice. Season with salt and pepper and more lemon juice if needed. Serve with crusty bread.

76.

Steak with Butter and Ginger

Use more ginger here if you like.

Sprinkle one or two three-quarter-inch-thick boneless rib eyes with salt and pepper and sear the steaks in a hot skillet for about two minutes on each side; set aside. Add a couple of tablespoons of butter to the pan to melt; add about a tablespoon of fresh minced or grated ginger, a splash of soy sauce, and a bit of water (to keep the soy from burning); cook for about 30 seconds. Return the steaks to the pan and cook for another few minutes on each side, until done the way you like. Spoon the ginger sauce over the meat, and garnish with fresh cilantro.

77.

Stuffed Burgers

Try this with some sautéed mushrooms on top.

Season a pound or so of ground beef with a good pinch of dill (a handful if it's fresh), salt, and pepper; form the meat into patties (two patties per burger, so make them on the thin side). Put a slice of tomato and some cheese (Gruyère, cheddar, blue, whatever) on one patty and then use a second patty to cover the stuffing—making a sandwich of the patties. Pinch the sides of the burgers together to seal them. Cook the burgers on a hot grill, on a grill pan, or under the broiler, turning them once, until done.

78.

Lamb Kibbe

*Pine nuts and breadcrumbs replace bulgur for a nice twist on this
Middle Eastern–style dish.*

In a food processor, blend a handful of toasted pine nuts, about a cup of breadcrumbs, a half teaspoon of allspice, a teaspoon of cumin, and half a diced onion until everything reaches an even, grainy consistency. Combine this mixture in a bowl with about a pound of ground lamb and a couple of tablespoons of olive oil; form into golf-ball-size balls and flatten a bit into patties. Fry each patty for about three minutes per side, or until crisp and cooked through. Serve with pita bread, shredded lettuce, plain yogurt, and a squeeze of fresh lemon juice.

79.

Lamb "Gyro"

Great using chicken, too.

Cut lamb (preferably shoulder; leg is OK) into two-inch chunks. In a large bowl, combine a teaspoon each dried thyme, and ground cumin and coriander; a tablespoon of minced garlic; and a pinch of red chile flakes. Add the lamb and toss to coat well. Sear the lamb pieces in olive oil until browned on all sides. In a separate pan, cook a sliced onion and a sliced red pepper in olive oil, until just soft. Serve the lamb with the onions and pepper in a pita (or wrapped in fresh lavash bread) with a dash of hot sauce, topped with plain yogurt.

80.

Spring Lamb

Israeli couscous takes longer to cook but makes a nice change if you have the time.

Heat the broiler. Puree together a handful each of fresh mint and basil, a clove of garlic, a teaspoon of cumin, a pinch of cinnamon, and a few tablespoons of olive oil to make a paste. Sprinkle salt and pepper on lamb steaks (from leg or shoulder), pound to half-inch thickness, and coat with the herb paste. Broil the steaks, turning once, until done, about eight minutes. In the meantime, mix a cup of plain yogurt with half a diced red onion and chopped cucumber. Serve the lamb over couscous; top with the yogurt mixture.

81.

Pan-Fried Veal Cutlets

Classic, and perfect served with greens cooked in lots of garlic.

Season veal cutlets with salt and pepper; dredge the cutlets in flour, beaten egg, and breadcrumbs. Heat a few tablespoons of olive oil in a large pan and fry the cutlets over high heat, turning once, until golden and cooked through, about three minutes. Serve with lemon wedges and chopped parsley.

82.

Orzo "Risotto" with Chives

Use this technique for any herb or vegetable.

Heat a mixture of butter and olive oil until foamy; stir in a handful or two of chopped chives and some salt and pepper and cook until the herbs are softened and fragrant. Now stir in a pound of orzo and keep cooking and stirring until it begins to get translucent. Stir in chicken stock (or water), a ladleful at a time, waiting for the pan to get almost dry before adding another. Repeat until the pasta is al dente and most of the liquid is absorbed, about eight minutes. Add butter, grated Parmesan cheese, and enough stock to reach the consistency you like. Serve, passing more cheese at the table.

83.

Pasta with Anchovies and Breadcrumbs

Fresh breadcrumbs (as usual) are superior to store-bought, with more flavor and better texture.

Boil and salt water for pasta, and cook it. Meanwhile, heat a couple of tablespoons of olive oil in a pan and lightly toast a cup or so of breadcrumbs until just golden; set aside. Heat a bit more oil and add a pinch of red chile flakes and a few drained, chopped anchovies (the kind marinated in oil and packed in glass) and cook for a minute or so, smashing up the anchovies with a fork as they cook. Drain the pasta, reserving some of the cooking water. Add the pasta to the anchovy mix and toss, adding pasta water as needed to moisten the mixture into a sauce. Add the toasted breadcrumbs and—optionally—freshly grated Parmesan.

84.

Pasta with Moroccan Tapenade

European tuna, packed in oil, is essential here.

Boil and salt water for pasta, and cook it. Meanwhile, in a food processor, combine a couple of handfuls of pitted green olives, a few tablespoons of capers, a drained can of tuna, a couple of cloves of garlic, a teaspoon cumin, freshly ground black pepper to taste, and olive oil as necessary to get a coarse paste. Put the tapenade in a bowl; drain the pasta, reserving some of the cooking water. Add the pasta to the tapenade, tossing to coat; add pasta water or olive oil as needed to make a sauce.

85.

Pasta Carbonara

Pancetta, guanciale, or bacon will do the trick equally well here.

Boil and salt water for pasta, and cook it. Meanwhile, cut about a quarter pound of pancetta into small pieces and fry in a bit of olive oil until golden. In a bowl large enough to hold the pasta, beat together three eggs, about a half cup of freshly grated Parmesan cheese, and the meat. Drain the pasta, reserving some of the cooking water. Toss the pasta quickly with the egg mixture to combine (the heat from the pasta will cook the eggs); add a few tablespoons of pasta water if needed to moisten. Season with salt and lots of freshly ground black pepper; garnish with chopped parsley and more Parmesan to taste.

86.

Pasta with Lemon Sauce

You might toss in a few shrimp or scallops,
or add a couple handfuls of steamed asparagus tips or peas.

Boil and salt water for pasta, and cook it. Meanwhile, in a large pan, combine a half stick of butter, a half cup of cream, and a quarter cup of freshly squeezed lemon juice. When the butter melts, remove the pan from the heat and set aside. Drain the pasta and add it to the reserved lemon sauce and toss. Add a few teaspoons of grated lemon zest and freshly grated Parmesan. Garnish with chopped parsley or chives and serve.

87.

Arugula and Prosciutto Pasta

Other greens can also be used here as long as they're tender enough
to wilt quickly when mixed with the pasta.

Boil and salt water for pasta, and cook it. Meanwhile, sear a few pieces of prosciutto, chopped, until crisp, about two minutes. In a large bowl, mix together about one-half cup crumbled goat cheese, two cups of chopped arugula, and a few tablespoons of olive oil. Drain the pasta, reserving some of the cooking water. Add the hot pasta to the bowl, wilting the arugula and coating the noodles with the cheese and oil; add pasta water as needed to moisten. Season with salt and pepper and crumble the prosciutto over the top of the pasta to serve.

88.

Rice Noodles with Cilantro Pesto

A little nod to fusion cuisine.

Soak rice vermicelli in boiling water to cover. In a food processor, puree two large handfuls of cilantro, the juice of a lime, a few tablespoons of olive oil, a slice of soft butter, salt, and pepper. Toast a handful of peanuts in a skillet lightly until fragrant and just golden. Drain the noodles and toss with the cilantro pesto; garnish with the toasted nuts.

89.

Shrimp Pad Thai

Use leftover chicken instead of shrimp
if you like: just toss it in with the noodles at the end.

Boil and salt water for pasta and cook a pound of wide rice noodles (they take only a couple of minutes); drain, rinse, and set aside in a bowl of cold water. Dice a couple of green onions and a clove of garlic. In a small bowl, combine a tablespoon of sugar, a few tablespoons of fish sauce, a pinch or two of red chile flakes, and a couple of tablespoons of sesame oil. In a tablespoon or two of vegetable oil, cook a handful of shrimp until just cooked; set aside. Add a bit more oil to the pan and scramble two eggs. Add the shrimp, drained noodles, garlic, onions, a handful of bean sprouts, and the sugar mixture to the pan and cook until warmed through. Sprinkle with chopped peanuts and serve.

90.

Udon Noodles with Seafood and Soy-Lemon Sauce

Udon and soba both work equally well here.

Cook the udon noodles; drain, saving some of the cooking water. Cook about a pound of peeled shrimp or firm white fish in a little sesame oil until just opaque. Stir in about one-quarter cup freshly squeezed lemon juice, a couple of tablespoons of soy sauce, a tablespoon grated ginger, and a minced garlic clove. Add the noodles and enough cooking liquid to make a sauce. Sprinkle the noodles with a pinch of red chile flakes and fresh cilantro.

91.

Cheesy Semolina with Asparagus

Like polenta, only faster.

Bring two cups salted water to a boil with one-half cup milk. Meanwhile, thinly slice a bunch of asparagus spears on the diagonal. When the water boils, whisk in one cup semolina and a pat of butter, cooking and stirring for three minutes; then add the asparagus and some grated Parmesan. Cover and set aside for a few minutes, until the vegetables are crisp-tender. Give a good stir and serve, garnished with more cheese, some chopped mint, and lots of freshly ground black pepper.

92.

Herbed Fresh Cheese Patties

Lovely over a bed of greens.

Dice half an onion and cook it in a tablespoon or so of olive oil until just soft. Using doubled cheesecloth, squeeze all the moisture out of two cups of ricotta or cottage cheese; combine the cheese, the onion, a beaten egg, half a cup of breadcrumbs, and a handful of chopped mixed herbs (chervil, basil, dill, and mint, or any combination you like), salt, and pepper in a bowl. Form the mixture into small patties—about three inches wide—and fry over medium-high heat in the same skillet you used for the onion until brown, turning once and adding more olive oil if needed, about six minutes total.

93.

Deconstructed Raspberry Soufflés

Heat the oven to 400°F. Whip four egg whites and one teaspoon lemon zest until stiff peaks form. Toss two cups of fresh raspberries with two tablespoons brown sugar. Spoon raspberries into individual ramekins, top with a scoop of the whipped egg white, and sprinkle each with a teaspoon of slivered almonds if you like. Bake until tops are just golden, about eight minutes.

94.

Rose Water Whipped Cream
with Honeydew

Just a little rose water works wonders.

Whip a cup of heavy cream with a few drops of rose water and a tablespoon of honey until thick. Cut a honeydew melon in half, scoop out the seeds, and slice into individual servings; serve each slice of melon with a dollop of the flavored whipped cream on top.

95.

Grilled Angel Food Cake
with Fruit Salsa

Obviously, homemade angel food is best, but store-bought can be good enough here.

Mix a cup of pitted halved cherries, a chopped mango, and two chopped peaches in a bowl with a quarter cup of sugar, a half teaspoon of cinnamon, juice from half a lemon, and the zest of the lemon. Smear slices of angel food cake with a little soft butter and grill each slice for about three minutes per side. Serve the fruit salsa over the angel food cake; garnish with chopped mint.

96.

Banana Ginger Granita

This takes only a couple of minutes to make,
but you do have to remember to freeze bananas in advance.

Put two fresh ripe frozen bananas, cut into two-inch pieces, in a food processor. Add two tablespoons of ginger ale or ginger beer and one-quarter cup crushed ice; pulse the mixture until smooth and serve, garnished with a grating of fresh ginger on top.

97.

Macerated Strawberries
with Mascarpone

Any orange-flavored liqueur works here.

In a bowl, mix together a quart of hulled, quartered strawberries, a couple of tablespoons of sugar, one-quarter cup Cointreau, freshly squeezed lemon juice, and lemon zest; let sit for five minutes or so. Serve in small bowls topped with a bit of mascarpone and good biscotti or any other crunchy cookie.

98.

Broiled Bananas

Keep an eye on these as they cook; they can go quickly from golden to overdone.

Heat the broiler and lightly butter a baking dish. Peel four bananas, cut them in half lengthwise, and arrange them on the dish. Dot the bananas with butter and sprinkle with brown sugar; broil about six inches from the flame until lightly browned, about five minutes. Serve hot, sprinkled with lemon or lime juice.

99.

Bittersweet Chocolate Crepes with Smashed Fruit

*Crepes should be set and cooked through, but not crisp;
keep in mind that the first crepe almost never works.*

In a blender, mix together one cup of flour, one-half cup cocoa powder, two eggs, one and one-half cups milk, one teaspoon vanilla extract, two tablespoons sugar, and two tablespoons melted butter; scrape down the sides until the mixture is smooth. Warm a bit of butter in a nonstick pan and ladle a thin coating of batter into the pan; swirl it around so it forms a thin layer on the bottom of the pan. Cook about 15 seconds or until the top looks dry; flip and cook 15 to 30 seconds more; repeat. Top with fresh smashed strawberries, raspberries, blueberries, or bananas.

100.

Chocolate Mousse

For a fruit mousse, substitute four ounces of pureed raspberries for the melted chocolate.

In a pan or in the microwave on low, melt two tablespoons of butter with four ounces of bittersweet or semisweet chocolate; set aside. Beat a cup of heavy cream with two tablespoons of sugar and a half teaspoon of vanilla until soft peaks form. Fold the whipped cream into the chocolate gently and stir until just combined; spoon the mousse into dishes, grate some chocolate on top if you like, and serve.

101.

Chocolate Hot Toddy

Serve with biscotti.

For each serving, melt one or two squares of semisweet chocolate in a cup and a half of milk, being sure not to bring the milk to a boil. Once the chocolate is melted, pour the milk into mugs and add a bit of dark rum or whiskey. Whipped cream is optional.

KITCHEN EXPRESS MENUS

Here are year-round ideas to help you use this book for every type of occasion. Obviously, you won't be able to pull together whole menus in 20 minutes, but you'll be amazed at how fast these meals come to the table, especially since many dishes can be made ahead and quickly reheated or served chilled or at room temperature.

WEEKNIGHT DINNER PARTY			
SUMMER	**FALL**	**WINTER**	**SPRING**
Gazpacho (page 31)	In-Shell Clam Chowder (page 71)	White Salad (page 125)	Snap Peas with Walnuts and Roquefort (page 175)
A Very Good Burger (page 58)		Mini Cannelloni (page 131)	
	Grilled Lamb Steak and White Bean Mash (page 102)	Garlic bread	Cajun-Style Salmon (page 178)
Assorted buns and trimmings bar		Lemon Mascarpone Mousse (page 153)	White rice
Blueberry Ricotta Cheesecakes (page 63)	Broiled Brussels Sprouts with Hazelnuts (page 82)		Green salad
	Dessert French Toast (page 111)		Grilled Angel Food Cake with Fruit Salsa (page 199)

BETTER-THAN-CHINESE-TAKEOUT			
SUMMER	FALL	WINTER	SPRING
Soba Noodles and Cucumber with Dipping Sauce (page 36)	Egg Drop Soup (page 72)	Squid Salad with Red Peppers and Cilantro (page 125)	Chive Salad (page 167)
	Sesame-Glazed Grilled Chicken (page 96)		Garlic-Ginger Shrimp (over Chinese egg noodles or white rice) (page 180)
Black and Blue Tuna (page 47)	Steamed white or brown rice	Crisp Tofu and Asian Greens with Peanut Sauce (page 131)	
Ginger-Lemon "Ice Cream" (page 64)	Apple Cider and White Wine Slushy (page 109)	White rice or rice noodles	Banana Ginger Granita (page 199)
		Grapefruit 'n' Cream Shake (page 153)	

ROMANTIC SUPPER			
SUMMER	FALL	WINTER	SPRING
Arugula with Balsamic Strawberries and Goat Cheese (page 38)	Endive and Warm Pear Salad with Stilton (page 76)	Avocado, Citrus, and Radicchio Salad (page 125)	Asparagus Leek Soup (page 163)
Grilled Lamb Chops with Summer Fruit (page 60)	Lavender-Thyme Braised Chicken (page 94)	Steak au Poivre (page 144)	Seared Scallops with White Wine and Chile (page 181)
		Potato Cumin Curry (page 132)	Crisp Fennel Gratin (page 175)
Frozen Hot Chocolate (page 64)	Pasta with Balsamic Onions (page 104)		
		Nutella Fondue (page 155)	
	Dark Chocolate Raspberry Pudding (page 110)		Bittersweet Chocolate Crepes with Smashed Fruit (page 200)

KIDS' NIGHT			
SUMMER	**FALL**	**WINTER**	**SPRING**
Grilled Chicken Kebabs (page 53)	Stir-Fried Mixed Vegetables with Ginger (page 85)	Meatball Subs (page 128)	Beef and Corn Tacos (page 189)
		Green Salad	
Pasta with Cherry Tomatoes (page 61)	Pasta Gratinée (page 108)	Chocolate Chip Pancakes (page 156)	Lettuce, tomato, guacamole, and all the trimmings
Ice Cream Sandwich (page 66)	Chocolate Panini (page 111)		Broiled Bananas (page 200)

ROOM-TEMPERATURE BUFFET			
SUMMER	**FALL**	**WINTER**	**SPRING**
Feta and Watermelon Salad (page 38)	Greek-Style Eggplant Salad (page 77)	Leek, Sun-Dried Tomato, and Goat Cheese Frittata (page 117)	Carrot and Couscous Salad (page 167)
	White Bean Toasts (page 79)		Lebanese Potato Salad (page 169)
Summertime Shrimp Salad (page 35)			
Pasta Salad with Beans and Herbs (page 61)	Flatbread Pizza with Figs, Goat Cheese, and Balsamic (page 83)	Date, Bacon, and Bean Salad (tossed with greens) (page 123)	Shrimp with Asparagus, Dill, and Spice (page 180)
Balsamic Beef, Radicchio, and Romaine (page 45)	Seared Tuna with Capers and Tomatoes (page 90)	Scallop and Citrus Salad (page 124)	Spicy Pork Salad (page 169)
		Banderilla Pasta (page 148)	
			Deconstructed Raspberry Soufflés (page 198)
Fresh Fruit Gratin (page 65)	Sweet Couscous with Dried Fruit (page 112)	Almond Tart (page 155)	

FINGER-FOOD COCKTAIL PARTY			
SUMMER	FALL	WINTER	SPRING
Deviled Eggs with Crab (page 30)	Figs in a Blanket (page 80)	Eggs 'n' Capers (page 116) served on whole grain toast points	Carne Cruda on toasted baguette (page 190)
	Sesame Shrimp Toasts (page 92)		
Summer Rolls with Barbecued Pork (page 39)			Seared Fish with Lettuce Leaves (page 176)
Sausage and Grape Bruschetta (page 40)			
	Panini with Mushrooms and Fontina (cut into triangles) (page 80)	Shrimp with Black Bean Sauce (to eat with toothpicks) (page 133)	Mark's Famous Spicy Shrimp (served with toothpicks) (page 180)
Duck Wraps with Plums (page 39)	Turkey and Pear Wrap with Curry Aioli (page 81)	Scallion-Stuffed Beef Rolls (page 145)	
			Chicken Satay with Peanut Sauce (page 187)
Shrimp-Tomato-Arugula Wraps (page 41)	West Indian Pork Kebabs (page 99)	Fondue (page 129)	
		Simplest Chicken Kebabs (page 136)	Herbed Fresh Cheese Patties (made bite-size and served with toothpicks) (page 198)

PICNIC OR ROAD TRIP			
SUMMER	FALL	WINTER	SPRING
A thermos of chilled Charred Tomato Bisque (page 33)	Eggplant, Kalamata, Goat Cheese, and Dried Tomato Sandwich (page 81)	A thermos of Mixed Vegetable Soup (page 118)	Minted Pea and Prosciutto Sandwich (page 171)
Tuna Tabouleh (page 34)		White Bean and Salmon Sandwich (page 127)	Kettle-fried potato chips
Pita bread, olives, and feta cheese	Zucchini and Garlic Fusilli with Pistachios (served cold or at room temperature) (page 108)		Macerated Strawberries with Mascarpone (page 199)
		Candied Citrus Rinds (page 153)	
Peach Lemon "Cheesecake" (page 65)			
	Pound Cake with Mascarpone and Marmalade (page 110)		

HOLIDAY BLOWOUT			
SUMMER	FALL	WINTER	SPRING
Melon Soup with Pancetta (page 32)	Gruyère Apple Grilled Cheese (cut into triangles) (page 80)	Wild Mushroom Crostini (page 128)	Tuna and Bean Salad (served with crackers and olives) (page 170)
Avocado Crab Salad with Mixed Herb Salad (page 37)		Shrimp Bisque (page 121)	
	Cream of Turnip Soup (page 74)		Classic Caesar Salad (page 165)
		Pasta with Bacon and Breadcrumbs (page 151)	
Grilled Steaks with Rosemary Plums (page 57)	Seared Scallops with Almonds (page 91)		Spring Lamb (page 192)
Baked potatoes with butter	Fried Endive with Butter and Lemon Sauce (page 86)	Turkey Cutlets with Walnuts and Sage (and pureed apples) (page 142)	Cheesy Semolina with Asparagus (page 197)
			Chocolate Mousse (page 201)
Apricot Cream Upside-Down Pie (page 64)			
	Caramel Fondue (page 112)	Warm Milk Toast (page 152)	

WEEKEND BRUNCH			
SUMMER	FALL	WINTER	SPRING
Mexican Dry-Corn Salad (page 35)	Endive and Warm Pear Salad with Stilton (page 76)	Spinach Salad with Feta and Nutmeg (page 126)	Chilled Cucumber and Dill Soup (page 163)
Migas (page 33)			
Sour cream and assorted salsas	Mediterranean Poached Eggs (page 69)	Bacon, Eggs, and Grits (page 116)	Hangtown Fry (page 160)
			Buttered rye toast
		Biscuits with butter and honey	
Blackberries with Champagne and Tarragon (page 65)	Pumpkin Crème Brûlee (page 109)		Rose Water Whipped Cream with Honeydew (page 198)
		Orange Fool (page 154)	

OVEN TEMPERATURE EQUIVALENCIES

DESCRIPTION	°FAHRENHEIT	°CELSIUS
Cool	200	90
Very slow	250	120
Slow	300–325	150–160
Moderately slow	325–350	160–180
Moderate	350–375	180–190
Moderately hot	375–400	190–200
Hot	400–450	200–230
Very hot	450–500	230–260

ACKNOWLEDGMENTS

Sometime in early summer 2007 I had a conversation with Pete Wells, the *Times*'s Dining editor, which resulted in my writing "101 Summer Express Meals." Neither of us precisely remembers whose idea this was; as is often the case, it was a product of a good discussion, and I certainly won't take full credit for it.

The idea was to produce short, simple, inspiring ideas that would take ten minutes or less to make. Though the ten-minute rule proved difficult to maintain, the story was among the most popular in the paper that year, and remains among the most e-mailed of all time.

I won't take full credit for that, either. For the original article, I asked for ideas from anyone who would give them. This group included Dining colleagues Pat Gurosky, Nick Fox, Trish Hall, Julia Moskin, Pete of course, and Nicki Kalish, who also designed the paper's layout of the original story.

Nor was the idea of building on the concept to make a book mine; credit for that goes to my longtime agent and friend Angela Miller and my editor at Simon & Schuster, Sydny Miner. Others at Simon and Schuster I'd like to thank are David Rosenthal, Michelle Rorke, Alexis Welby and Jessica Abell, Mara Lurie, Michael Accordino, and Linda Dingler.

My colleagues Kerri Conan and Suzanne Lenzer worked hard on *Kitchen Express*, and they both know the depth of my gratitude. Stacey Ornstein helped with original research.

And Kelly Doe not only tweaked the design but lent moral support.

Mark Bittman
New York, Spring 2009

INDEX

INDEX

INDEX

LinkedIn®
Profile
Optimization

by Donna Serdula

for
dummies®
A Wiley Brand

LinkedIn® Profile Optimization For Dummies®

Published by: **John Wiley & Sons, Inc.,** 111 River Street, Hoboken, NJ 07030-5774, www.wiley.com

Copyright © 2017 by John Wiley & Sons, Inc., Hoboken, New Jersey

Published simultaneously in Canada

For general information on our other products and services, please contact our Customer Care Department within the U.S. at 877-762-2974, outside the U.S. at 317-572-3993, or fax 317-572-4002. For technical support, please visit https://hub.wiley.com/community/support/dummies.

Wiley publishes in a variety of print and electronic formats and by print-on-demand. Some material included with standard print versions of this book may not be included in e-books or in print-on-demand. If this book refers to media such as a CD or DVD that is not included in the version you purchased, you may download this material at http://booksupport.wiley.com. For more information about Wiley products, visit www.wiley.com.

Library of Congress Control Number: 2016960164

ISBN 978-1-119-28708-7 (pbk); ISBN 978-1-119-28709-4 (ebk); ISBN 978-1-119-28710-0 (ebk)

Manufactured in the United States of America

10 9 8 7 6 5 4 3 2

Contents at a Glance

Table of Contents

Introduction

P eople are researching you. Perhaps they are headed into a meeting with you, evaluating you for a job opportunity, or looking to purchase a product from you. Perhaps they met you at an event or are simply in the process of doing business with you. Whatever the reason, they want to know more about YOU.

People do business with people and with the dawn of the Internet, it's never been easier to learn more about the people we meet and do business with. All it takes is a couple clicks of the keyboard and you can get a full description of almost anyone or anything.

Not everyone has a personal website or websites devoted to them (well, unless you are a celebrity); however, the LinkedIn profile has become the de facto website for everyday professionals. A simple name search for most people returns their LinkedIn profile on the first page of search results. How does your LinkedIn profile portray you? Your LinkedIn profile is your online reputation, digital introduction, and first impression. The good news is that you have complete control over your profile and can shape how your reader perceives you.

Most people simply copy and paste their resume into their profile because it's easy, but a profile consisting of a copied-and-pasted resume impresses no one. To have a strong and optimized LinkedIn profile, you need to tell your professional story, strategically writing it toward your goals and target audience.

About This Book

This book is a how-to manual that shows you the steps to craft a strategic, compelling, and unique LinkedIn profile. I show you how to take your profile from nothing more than a simple outline to a robust, full-featured profile of you as a professional.

Although you can pick up this book at any point, I highly suggest, at the very least, reading Chapter 1 and Chapter 4. In Chapter 1, I discuss the importance of determining your LinkedIn goal and target audience. If you don't identify your goal, your profile cannot be written strategically and it will not perform adequately.

Likewise, you need to understand your target audience and write to what they need to know about you.

In Chapter 4, I show you how to turn off profile update notifications. You want to ensure that when you start making a lot of changes to your profile, LinkedIn isn't inundating your network with annoying alerts. This is especially important if you are still employed and optimizing your profile for job search.

Regardless of your LinkedIn goal, you will benefit from the information in this book. Although LinkedIn isn't rocket science, it isn't the most intuitive social network either. Plus, writing about yourself is hard! In this book, I break everything down to its core to make it easy for you to use LinkedIn and create an impressive profile that helps you achieve your professional goals.

Foolish Assumptions

Having worked with thousands of professionals, executives, entrepreneurs, and companies from all over the world, I am going to assume that like them you are optimizing your profile for:

>> **Professional branding/reputation management.** You know that people are looking at your profile and you want to showcase yourself in a professional and impressive manner. You recognize that people draw conclusions based upon what they read, and you want to ensure they see you as a thought leader and someone who deserves to be noticed and respected.

>> **Sales and prospecting.** You want to use your LinkedIn profile to help you prospect better and sell more. You know that prospects and clients are looking at your profile, and you want them to see you as a solution provider who can help them achieve their goals. You also know that people may be looking for a service or product that you sell and you want to appear in search results.

>> **Job search.** You are either currently working or displaced, but you are ready to spread your wings and find the next great opportunity that makes you want to get out of bed in the morning and go to work. Recruiters, hiring managers, and human resources professionals are using LinkedIn to find candidates. You want to make sure that your profile stands out in those searches, and that when they click on your profile, what they read is compelling and makes them want to reach out to request your resume. Alternately, you have likely submitted your resume to various job postings and you know that recruiters, hiring managers, and human resources professionals may look at your LinkedIn profile to learn more. You want to make sure your profile is an impressive introduction that compels them to call you for an interview.

How This Book Is Organized

This book is divided into five parts:

Part 1: The Strategy Before the Siege

Most people just jump into writing their LinkedIn profiles, but not you! In this first part, I show you how to immediately stand out by determining your LinkedIn goals, target audience, and keywords.

Part 2: Getting Your LinkedIn Profile Started

In this part I show you how to turn off profile change notifications, choose a professional profile picture, and create a compelling headline. I also show you how to create a personalized link to your profile that makes marketing a cinch.

Part 3: Detailing Your Career Trajectory and Creating the Ultimate First Impression

In Part 3, I walk you through filling out the two LinkedIn profile sections the majority of people find the most challenging: Experience and Summary. You'll learn how to craft impressive experiences that focus on achievements over pure job description. You also learn how to craft a summary that acts as a professional manifesto that engages and impresses your target audience.

Part 4: Rounding Out Your Profile and Adding Finishing Touches

Part 4 is all about the extra flourishes you can add to your profile, such as with sample projects, publications, patents, organizations, and volunteer experiences. I show you how to spice up your profile with a background image and how to add multimedia work samples to take your profile to the next level.

Part 5: The Part of Tens

The Part of Tens is the traditional end of a *For Dummies* book and contains lists of ten items that will help you leverage your profile and LinkedIn even better. This part is packed with links to external websites that provide the tools you can use to create a powerful profile.

Icons Used in This Book

I use a number of icons in this book to draw your attention to pieces of useful information.

This whole book can be considered a series of tips! When I share information that I find especially useful for optimizing your profile, I indicate it with a Tip icon.

This icon is used to flag information that may be useful to remember when you think about and work on your profile.

Whenever something may cause unnecessary work or a headache down the road, I alert you with a Warning icon.

A Technical Stuff icon contains detailed or background information that is not necessary to know to optimize your profile, but is otherwise interesting.

Beyond the Book

In addition to what you're reading now, this book also comes with a free access-anywhere Cheat Sheet that gives you even more pointers on how to optimize your LinkedIn profile. To get this Cheat Sheet, simply go to www.dummies.com and search for "*LinkedIn Profile Optimization For Dummies* Cheat Sheet" in the Search box.

Where to Go from Here

This book was written so that you could open up at any page and immediately get actionable assistance to crank up your profile. I highly suggest beginning with Chapter 1 because it's important to identify your goals and target audience before you begin writing your profile. Also, Chapter 4 shows you how to turn off profile update notifications so you don't annoy your network. After that, check out the Table of Contents to find the profile section areas you want to concentrate on immediately, or simply randomly open the book and see what chance predicts for you.

An optimized LinkedIn profile is more than just your online reputation. A powerfully written LinkedIn profile has the ability to change your life. After optimizing their profiles, I've seen people find amazing jobs and opportunities. They connect with more people and experience the full gamut of what LinkedIn has to offer.

I wish you the very best of luck — now go get optimizing!

1

The Strategy Before the Siege

Understand your LinkedIn goals and target audience to give your profile purpose.

Learn how to use the proper tone in your profile to draw people in, not push them away.

Optimize your LinkedIn search results by discovering your keywords and infusing them throughout your profile.

Learn how to use LinkedIn as a search tool and how to ensure your search result listing catches a reader's eye.

Add skills to showcase your strengths to potential employers or clients.

See why soliciting endorsements and endorsing others boosts your credibility.

Chapter **1**

Determining Your LinkedIn Strategy

When you register for a LinkedIn account, the first thing you encounter is the LinkedIn profile. Most people jump in and immediately fill out the fields of the profile, not giving much thought as to why they are on LinkedIn or who will eventually be reading their profile.

Profiles created without a goal or a target audience in mind lack purpose. These profiles don't catch readers' eyes and compel them to reach out to the person behind the online persona. You see these profiles on LinkedIn every day. Scanning the profile, nothing grabs you or makes you want to learn more about that person.

To experience success on LinkedIn, you must approach your LinkedIn profile strategically. In this chapter, I show you how to determine your LinkedIn strategy by looking at the three most typical goals people are trying to accomplish on LinkedIn. Once you've determined your goal, I show you how to figure out your target audience and discuss the importance of creating a compelling profile tone.

Determining Your LinkedIn Goal

To create a profile that has purpose, you must ask yourself, "What am I trying to accomplish on LinkedIn?" Many people get a LinkedIn account because they want to find a new job. Other people are interested in reputation management and branding. Still other people are on LinkedIn because they are in sales and want to prospect and increase sales through social selling.

To help you determine what you want your profile to accomplish, review the following three most common types of LinkedIn profiles.

Job search

LinkedIn plays a huge role in the job search process. Recruiters, hiring managers, and human resources professionals search LinkedIn looking for potential candidates. They may perform broad-based keyword searches looking for a candidate that matches the skill sets the position requires, or they may already have certain candidates in mind. When they have a person already in mind for a position, a name search is performed on LinkedIn with the goal of learning more about that person than what is stated on his or her resume.

LinkedIn is also a job board. The LinkedIn Jobs section (www.linkedin.com/jobs) is where thousands of jobs from all over the world are posted. These job postings are promoted throughout LinkedIn as well. When you find a job posting that interests you, you can apply for the position by submitting your resume and LinkedIn profile.

TIP

Even if you aren't utilizing LinkedIn's job postings or hoping to collide with a recruiter, potential employers are still looking you up on LinkedIn and reviewing your LinkedIn profile. Think about it: If you are about to hire someone, and available to you is a database in which to look this person up and see a picture of the candidate, a listing of people he or she knows, and recommendations of his or her work ethic, of course you would use it!

Potential employers are looking at your profile. The good news is you have control over how you represent yourself and how they perceive you. A job search profile complements and echoes your resume without being a direct one-to-one copy. The profile is written to the job description of that next position you are targeting and showcases you as the perfect candidate for that role.

To find out more about how to create a powerful job search profile, see Chapter 9.

Reputation management and branding

It's a Google world. At one time, if you needed to find out information, you headed to the library to search the encyclopedias and other reference materials. Now, all you need to do is pull up a web browser and perform an Internet search to get more information than you could ever read or use.

This easy access to information has some side effects. People are doing more research than ever before and they are researching you! Going to the doctor? Most people search the Internet for the doctor's name to see the results that pop up in a search engine. Executives who find their names appearing in press releases or in magazine articles may find that views to their LinkedIn profiles skyrocket by readers wanting to know more about them.

Job candidates' names are entered into search engines all the time by hiring managers looking to discover more than what is provided in the resume. Similarly, hiring managers' names are searched by job candidates wanting to learn more about their potential new employer.

LinkedIn profiles rank high in search results. Not only is it usually the top result when a person searches for your name, but also it's sometimes the only result, as most people don't have a personal website. *You* create your LinkedIn profile. *You* choose what people learn about you. *You* have total control over how people perceive you. A reputation management profile is one that showcases your successes, honors, awards, and accomplishments, and leads people to see you as a credible, impressive professional. See Figure 1-1 for an example.

FIGURE 1-1:
A reputation management and branding profile.

Sales and prospecting

LinkedIn is more than just a job search tool. LinkedIn is a compendium of professional profiles with industry and contact information, which makes it a terrific prospecting tool for sales professionals. However, it's not just for sales people looking for prospects. People use LinkedIn to search for service providers and consultants who can help them.

Most people prefer to do business with someone they know or someone with whom they share a connection. When searching LinkedIn for a service provider, you see how you are connected to that service provider through the degrees of connection. This ability to see shared connections provides a level of trust and comfort.

A sales and prospecting profile shines the spotlight on not just the salesperson, but also on that person's products, services, and company he or she represents. Most important, the sales and prospecting profile focuses on prospective clients and their needs, and solidifies the salesperson as someone clients can feel confident in working with. See Figure 1-2 for an example.

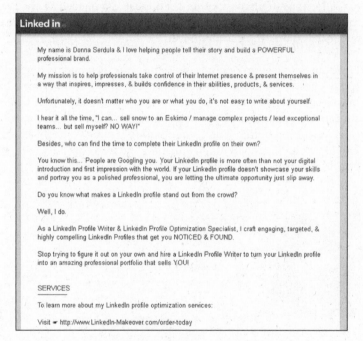

FIGURE 1-2: A sales and prospecting profile.

Figuring Out Your Target Audience

Knowing your goal is only half the battle. Now it's time to figure out your target audience. One of the most common mistakes people make with their LinkedIn profiles is using it to tell the story they want to tell. Instead, you need to use your profile to tell the story your audience *wants to read*. Write for your target audience first.

When you are looking for a job, your target audience is typically recruiters, hiring managers, and human resources professionals. In almost every case, they are armed with a job description. Recruiters want to know that you have the skill sets and experience required to fulfill the job. They also want to know that you are professional, respectful, and capable of doing the job. You want to make it clear in your profile that you are the perfect person for your desired position. After reading your profile, the recruiter should feel confident in your skills and abilities.

When you are on LinkedIn for sales and prospecting, your target audience is your client and prospective client. They are less interested in hearing about your sales expertise and more interested in knowing that you understand their industry and their needs, and can provide solutions to their issues. As you consider your target audience, think in terms of the solutions you offer them and provide them the information they need to feel confident with you as a potential partner.

The sales world has changed in the age of Google and social media. Buyers now educate themselves, researching products and services online. They even research the salesperson, wanting to make sure they are reaching out to someone they can feel comfortable working with. Knowing that you are under a magnifying glass, make sure you provide your target audience with the information they need to feel confident in you and your products or services.

When the goal of your LinkedIn profile is reputation management and branding, your target audience may not be as clear cut as it is with a job search or sale and prospecting. To figure out your audience, you need to determine the type of person you want to cater your profile toward. Is it the executive team and colleagues at your company? Audience members who watched you give a presentation? Readers of articles you wrote? Private equity investors? Once you pinpoint the type of person who you want to target, consider what that person needs to know to take that next step forward.

Do you want your target audience to connect with you on LinkedIn? Perhaps you want them to visit your website and download a whitepaper. You may want your target audience to email you to request your resume. Your target audience could pick up the phone and call you. Figure out what that next step is so you can build it into your profile as a clear call to action.

TIP

Strategically written profiles do not state what you want to say as much as what your target audience needs to know.

Creating a Compelling Tone

LinkedIn is a social network, and writing an impersonal profile filled with business jargon doesn't mesh. Social networks are all about you interacting with your network. And because your network will check out your profile, it's imperative that what they read is from your pen. You don't want to push people away by creating distance between you and your reader.

A powerful LinkedIn profile is written in first person narrative form ("I"). Draw readers in by writing about yourself in the first person. Writing in a conversational, natural tone is a great way to connect with your audience and start forging an easy rapport.

As important as it is to write in first person, you also must be careful not to overuse "I." There is nothing worse than a profile where every sentence starts with I. In my profile, I sometimes use the second person narrative form ("You") because it brings your reader in even closer by speaking directly to them, and it eases the potential overuse of "I."

TIP

The best way to ensure your profile is compellingly written is to read it aloud. Does it sound stilted? Does it sound like it's something you would never say to an acquaintance live in person? If so, the writing is forced and not conversational in tone.

Here is an example of stilted, hard-to-read resume speak:

Creating a clear strategy for leveraging resources to produce the maximum number of insights possible. Integrating contextual analytics to business processes. Centralizing deep analysis expertise for use across the organizational axis but mandating each individual department and line of business takes responsibility for their own reporting needs.

REMEMBER

You want to write your profile as if you are talking directly to your reader. Your words should sound professional yet natural. A profile written in corporate jargon or resume speak is a turn off. Demonstrate your human side and warmth by writing in a natural, conversational tone.

When you see profiles written in the third person, typically the reason is that they simply copied and pasted their biography or resume into the LinkedIn profile. That's a cop-out! Your LinkedIn profile is *not* your resume nor your bio. Your LinkedIn profile is your career future! It's who you are, how you help people, and why you deserve to be noticed. A powerful LinkedIn profile is strategically written for your goals and your target audience. It's not a copy and paste of some other document.

Next up we look at how to get found on LinkedIn.

Chapter **2**

Getting Found on LinkedIn

inkedIn helps people connect with opportunity. Whether it's a new job, a sale, a media interview, a business partnership, or something else entirely, many times the connection starts with a LinkedIn search.

LinkedIn has over 400 million users in over 200 countries. Making sure your profile sticks out and pops up is important. In this chapter I show you how people use LinkedIn as a search engine. I show you the importance of your search result and how to make it attractive and clickable. I also show you how to discover your keywords and how to infuse them into your profile for higher search engine ranking. By the time you finish this chapter, you will have a list of your keywords and the knowledge of how to dominate LinkedIn search results.

Using LinkedIn as a Search Engine

Getting views to your profile doesn't always start through an Internet search. LinkedIn is more than just a professional network and profile listing. LinkedIn is a different type of search engine. Most search engines return websites. Searches conducted via a LinkedIn search return LinkedIn profiles, company pages, job listings, reader-published blog articles, and LinkedIn Groups. LinkedIn search is also used to find potential customers, vendors, service providers, and employees.

Using the search bar

On the top of LinkedIn's website is the search bar. This is where most people enter their search terms. When people search LinkedIn, they search in two different ways: name or keyword. A direct name search is typically performed after a resume has been received or when a person has met you and is looking to connect on LinkedIn. The person doing the search is looking for one, specific person.

Most times, people are searching not for a specific person but for a type of person with distinct skill sets and strengths. In this situation, the person conducting the search enters those skill sets as keywords into the LinkedIn search bar. For example, Figure 2-1 shows the results of a LinkedIn search for the keywords "LinkedIn Profile Writer." The search results display profiles that contain those keywords. Your profile never displays as a search result listing if those keywords do not exist within the profile. Therefore, to get found in searches, your profile must contain the keywords a person is using in the search.

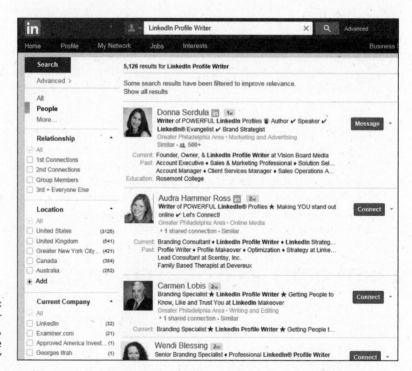

FIGURE 2-1:
Search results for the keywords, "LinkedIn Profile Writer."

Using Advanced People Search

The LinkedIn search bar is not the only search field within LinkedIn. When recruiters search LinkedIn, they often utilize LinkedIn's Advanced People Search. See what the Advanced People Search page looks like in Figure 2-2.

Click the Advanced link to see the
Advanced People Search page

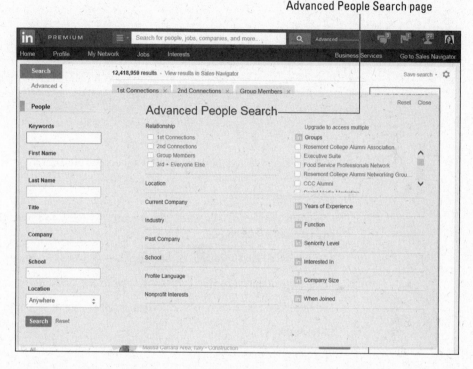

FIGURE 2-2:
Advanced People
Search.

The Advanced People Search page provides additional fields and filters to narrow your search to exactly your target results. You can search by location, current and past company, industry, school, and language. You can also drill in even deeper by searching by First and Last Names or Job Titles. Premium LinkedIn members get access to even more filters such as Years of Experience, Function, Seniority Level, Company Size, and more.

Recruiters typically search by the job titles they are trying to fill. If they are looking for a candidate in a specific area, they will add the Location to make sure they are only finding people within that area.

BOOLEAN SEARCH STRINGS

When super users of LinkedIn, such as recruiters, use Advanced People Search, they often use Boolean search operators and modifiers to limit and widen the scope of their searches so that they can find profiles that more precisely match their target results. The Keywords, First and Last Name, Title, and Company fields support the Boolean search modifiers of quotes and parenthesis, and the Boolean search operators AND, OR, and NOT.

If a recruiter is looking for an account manager, encasing the words "account manager" in quotes ensures he or she finds that exact phrase and not people with simply the words "account" and "manager" in their profiles. To broaden a search so that it includes profiles with one or more specific terms, use the Boolean search operator OR. For example, Sales OR salesperson OR "Account Manager" OR "Business Development."

Follow these steps to use LinkedIn's Advanced People Search:

1. **Go to** LinkedIn.com.

2. **From any LinkedIn page, click "Advanced," which is found to the right of the LinkedIn search bar.**

   The Advanced People Search box opens.

3. **Enter your desired search terms into any of the open fields.**

   Filter the search results by a selected geographic area or industry.

4. **Click Search.**

   The search results page appears.

Ensuring a Compelling and Attractive Search Result

REMEMBER

People use LinkedIn to find other people. They are looking for job candidates, service providers, strategic partnerships, and many other professional relationships. When someone clicks the search button on LinkedIn, he or she is confronted with a list of search results. It's important that your profile turns up in the search results, but it's even more imperative that your search result listing catches the searcher's eye and compels him or her to click your listing to learn more about you.

Your search result listing is comprised of the following:

>> Your profile picture

>> Your name

>> Your headline

>> Your location and industry

>> Your current job title and company

>> Total connections in common

>> A link to similar LinkedIn members' profiles

>> If you are a first-degree connection, a link to the searcher's connection list

TIP

LinkedIn search results show more detail for Premium members. This longer search listing features the last three past professional job titles and companies.

Looking through pages and pages of LinkedIn search results is a daunting task. It's important to make sure your search result listing showcases you in the best light. For example, many recruiters and hiring managers actually skip past profiles that do not have a profile picture. The omission of a profile picture typically means that the LinkedIn user doesn't take the social network seriously, provides little detail to his or her career trajectory, and won't respond when an InMail message is sent. (InMail is a message that you send to a member not directly connected to you. Only Premium members have the ability to send InMail messages.) By including a profile picture, you are proving that you are a serious LinkedIn user and networker. I show you how to upload a profile picture in Chapter 6.

Let's see what your search result listing looks like by performing a name search for you:

1. Type your name into the LinkedIn search bar and click the magnifying glass icon (or press Enter or Return).

While you are typing, LinkedIn may provide you with suggestions from a drop-down list. Do not choose any of these suggestions. Upon pressing Enter or Return, search result listings appear.

2. Find your search result listing.

Your search result listing may be the only result, or if you have a common name, your listing may reside farther down the list of search results.

SHOULD I PAY FOR LinkedIn?

There are two types of accounts on LinkedIn: the free and the paid version. The free account is a good starting point for most users. It allows you to do almost everything the paid version does, only in limited numbers and with limited visibility. For example, a free account can only message people within his or her first-degree network, whereas Premium users have access to InMail and the Open Profile option, which enable them to communicate with people outside their first-degree network.

There are various types of paid accounts ranging from $15.99 per month (Job Seeker; https://premium.linkedin.com/jobsearch) to $899.99 per month (Recruiter Corporate; www.linkedin.com/premium/switcher/recruiter). The higher the price, the more you are able to do with LinkedIn.

Although the free account is a good starting point, if you plan on using LinkedIn for prospecting, recruiting, heavy searching, or to communicate with professionals outside your first-degree network, upgrading is necessary.

Premium account members get a badge on their profiles that identifies them as paid users. This badge is a great way to signal that you are a serious LinkedIn user and someone who is responsive to opportunities.

The Premium plans have many selling points that make the monthly or annual fee reasonable. One of my favorite features of the Premium accounts is the ability to see the full 90-day list of Who's Viewed Your Profile and insights into your audience, such as where they work and their job titles. You also get access to the Open Profile option, which enables you to freely communicate with other Premium members outside your first-degree network.

Depending on the Premium plan you choose, you may get additional search filters, more search result listings, a larger search listing that features more of your profile summary, expanded top profile rankings, job and applicant insights, more saved searches and unlimited profile searches, a larger profile picture (240 x 240 versus 200 x 200), access to the LinkedIn background image gallery, and company page business insights.

My recommendation is to start with the basic, free account. Once you start using LinkedIn more frequently, you will begin to feel restricted by the limits of the free account and upgrading will make sense.

3. **Look at your search result and determine if it showcases you in the best light.**

   Did you upload a professional profile picture? Is your headline engaging? Read through the chapters in Part 2 of this book to learn how to optimize these different areas.

Look at Figure 2-3 to see the difference between an optimized and an unoptimized search result listing and the differences between a free and a paid user listing.

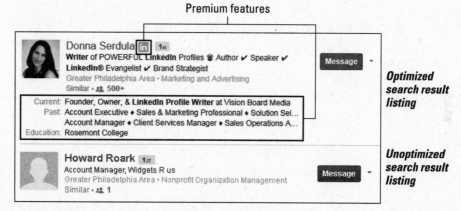

FIGURE 2-3:
An optimized
search result
versus an
unoptimized
result.

Understanding the Importance of Keywords

To appear in search results, you must identify what words people are using to find a person like you. What words would they type into LinkedIn search to find you? These search terms are your keywords.

REMEMBER

Your profile never appears in search results for terms that do not appear in your profile. In order to appear, your profile must contain those keywords people use to search.

How many keywords do you need? I suggest choosing five to ten main keywords to pepper throughout your profile. When you try to rank for too many keywords, you lose keyword density and you end up not ranking for anything.

Keywords don't have to be just one word. A keyword could be a phrase. For example, *profit and loss* may be three words, but it is considered one keyword.

Keywords must be descriptive and exact. *Problem-solver* and *dynamic professional* are not good keywords. These words are too general and can describe anyone from a top executive to an office manager. Good keywords are specific and reflective of key skills, strengths, core competencies, specialties, and abilities that differentiate you.

Here are some questions to help you determine your keywords:

>> In what industries have you worked?

>> What positions have you held?

>> What certifications have you earned?

>> What skill sets were listed on your last job description or resume?

>> What computer applications do you know?

>> What languages do you speak?

>> What services do you provide?

>> What topics are you an expert in?

>> What products do you sell?

>> What additional strengths or skill sets do you have?

Answering these questions provides you with a starting point. Now that you have a few keywords, the next step is to use one of several online keyword tools to find additional, related keywords.

The following is a list of keyword examples to get you thinking. These are real meat-and-potato keywords. Highlight or star the keywords that seem to fit you and your role. Once you have that list, use the keyword tools described in the next section to dive in deeper and find more keywords that fit you.

Accounting	Financial reporting/analysis
Account reconciliation	Financial statements
Auditing	Fixed assets
Budgets/budgeting/budget control	General ledger
Contract management	Internal controls
Corporate governance	Inventory management

Investment finance

Investor relations

Tax accounting

Taxation

Engineering

3D modeling

Assembly design/modification

Conceptualization

Consistency and compatibility

Data collection and analysis

Design methodologies

Efficiency control

Integrated solutions and services

Job costing

Mission-critical programs

Process development

Process improvements

Project management

Prototypes

Resource allocation

Executive

Budgeting

Business plans

Change management

Deal negotiations

International business

IPOs

Joint ventures

Operational streamlining

P&L/Profit and loss

Policy development

Process reengineering

Profit building

Restructuring

Start-up operations

Turnaround strategies

Human Resources

Business reengineering

Compensation management/analysis

Deferred compensation

Dispute arbitration

Employee relations

Job description development

Labor relations

Leadership development

New Hire orientation

Performance management

Recruitment/recruiting

Succession planning

Talent management

US Family and Medical Leave Act

Workforce planning

Information Technology

Data center operations

Database administration

Fault analysis

Information security

Infrastructure development

IT risk management

Multiplatform integration

Network administration

Process reengineering

Quality assurance

Solutions delivery

Systems configuration

Technical documentation

Web-based technology

Yield management

Professor/Teacher

Brain-based learning

Classroom management

Classroom planning

Curriculum design

Curriculum development

Discipline strategies

Educational leadership

Educational technology

In-service training

Interdisciplinary teaching approaches

Lesson planning

Peer mentoring

Process improvement

Teacher-parent relations

Technology integration

Retail

Assortment

Customer service/interpersonal skills

Inventory management

Loss prevention

Marketing strategy

Merchandise planning

Merchandising

Planograms

POS terminals

Sales management

Shrinkage

Store management

Store operations

Team management

Visual merchandising

Sales and Marketing

Account expansion

Account management

Account retention

Channel development

Client relations

Competitive analysis

Contract negotiations

Lead generation

Market analysis

New business development

Post-sale support

Product rollout

Proposal development

Prospecting

Sales forecasting

Supply Chain	**Telecommunications**
Asset management	3G
Cost reduction	Audio visual and peripheral equipment
Demand planning	Broadband
Distribution management	Customer service
Inventory control	Integration
Logistics planning	Internet protocol (IP)
Loss prevention	Network installations
Procurement	Product management
Purchasing	Project management
Quality control/assurance	Telephony
Route management	Value-added service
Shipping/receiving	Voice and data networks
Six Sigma	Voice over IP (VOIP)
Vendor relations	Wireless technology
Warehousing	

Using Online Keyword Tools

Coming up with the right keywords is challenging. The good news is that there are tools designed to assist you in finding the right keywords.

TIP

One of my favorite techniques to determine keywords is the word cloud. A *word cloud* is a way to visualize data. It is an image composed of words used in a particular piece of writing. The size of each word is determined by how many times the word is used or the importance of that word. A word cloud generator is an application that scans through text and provides a graphic output of words. The more often a specific word appears in inputted text, the larger and more colorful the word is shown in the word cloud. (My favorite word cloud generator is found at Wordle.net, which I discuss in the next section.)

To use a word cloud generator, you first need text for it to analyze. Use text from your current job description in digital format or find a similar job description online. If you are looking for your next opportunity, do an Internet search for a job description that fits your dream job. Don't worry whether the position is in your location or already filled. Most job descriptions are the same — right now you are just after the text and not the actual opportunity.

If you are not a job seeker but instead looking to brand yourself more effectively or showcase yourself as an expert thought leader, use the content of your company's website or marketing literature. There are also industry-related articles and whitepapers that you can use. Also check out the LinkedIn profiles of people you admire and copy their LinkedIn profile content into the generator. (But do not copy their content into your own profile!)

There are a number of world cloud generators out there on the Internet. Here are a few examples:

Tagul (`http://tagul.com`)

Tagxedo (`www.tagxedo.com`)

Word It Out (`http://worditout.com`)

Wordel.net (`www.wordle.net`)

Wordsift (`www.wordsift.com`)

Using Wordle.net

Wordle.net is my favorite free word cloud generator. I love it because not only is Wordle.net super easy to use, but also the resulting word clouds are visually beautiful.

Follow these steps to use Wordle.net to generate a word cloud for keyword discovery:

1. **Find and copy the text you want to visualize for keywords by highlighting the text and pressing Ctrl+C (Windows) or Cmd+C (Mac).**

2. **Open your web browser and go to `wordle.net/create`.**

    A large, empty text box appears with the words, "Paste in a bunch of text:". Figure 2-4 shows the text input area of Wordle.net.

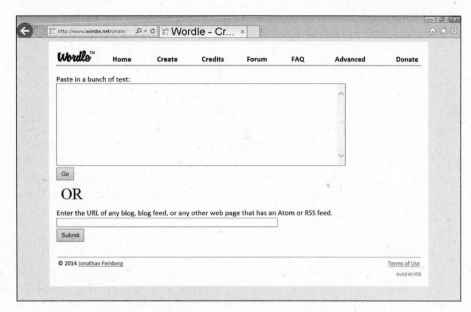

FIGURE 2-4:
Add text to
wordle.net to
create a word
cloud.

3. **Paste the text into the Wordle.net text box.**

   Copy and paste by using the right-click menu or by pressing Ctrl+C/⌘+C to
   copy and Ctrl+V/⌘+V to paste.

The resulting word cloud visually shows you what words hold the most weight.
These words are typically your keywords.

Check out Figure 2–5 to see what a word cloud looks like. I used a job description
text to generate this word cloud. Clearly sales, management, business, and development are important keywords for this position.

FIGURE 2-5:
Here's what a
word cloud
looks like.

Hopefully your word cloud provided you a good strong list of keywords. If not, I
have another keyword tool, and this one is found right in LinkedIn.

Using LinkedIn Topic pages

LinkedIn includes a section on its site devoted entirely to skill development called Topics. LinkedIn collects and analyzes the skills that are listed on the Skills & Endorsements section of members' LinkedIn profile pages. The most popular skills have Topic pages associated with them that present additional information. These Topic pages provide a description of the skill, the top companies where people with this skill work, other skills they share, and where they went to school. Additionally, you can see Lynda.com courses that help you develop the skill, posts members have written that deal with the skill, presentations on SlideShare that relate to the skills, and LinkedIn Groups connected to the skill. And at the very bottom of the Topic page, a list of related skills appears.

TECHNICAL
STUFF

Lynda.com (www.lynda.com) is the leading provider of online video courses specializing in developing business, creative, education, and technical skills. LinkedIn acquired the company in 2015 and has integrated Lynda.com into the LinkedIn site. SlideShare (www.slideshare.net) was also acquired by LinkedIn (in 2012). SlideShare is a presentation slide hosting service where users can upload their presentation slides for others to browse and embed.

The related skills section of the Topic page is a great page to discover additional keywords. By visiting the Business Development Topic page, as shown in Figure 2-6, you'll see that other members with that skill also know: management, new business development, business strategy, strategic planning, and sales. These related skills may also describe your skill sets. If so, add them to your LinkedIn Skills section.

As helpful as the Topic pages are, LinkedIn doesn't provide an easy way to access the Topic page directory. To access the directory, follow these steps:

1. **Go to www.linkedin.com/directory/topics/.**

   The LinkedIn Topic page directory appears.

TIP

   Because LinkedIn doesn't provide an easy way to access such an important page, I recommend creating a browser bookmark.

2. **In the Browse By Name category, click the first letter of the keyword you want to learn more about.**

   A new page displays with a list of keywords starting with that letter.

3. **Click your desired keyword.**

   The Topic page for that keyword appears.

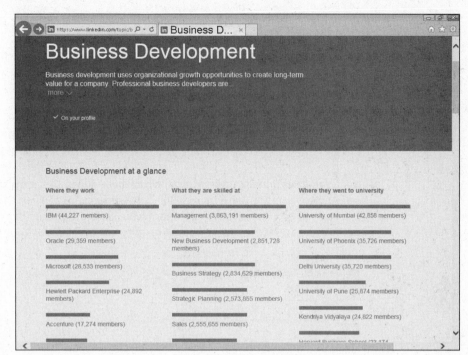

FIGURE 2-6:
Topic pages
provide
additional
information
on skills.

Using Google AdWords Keyword Planner

I have one more site in my arsenal of keyword tools to help you determine your keywords: Google AdWords Keyword Planner. This free online application helps you find keywords by utilizing Google's search history to determine related keywords.

To use Google AdWords Keyword Planner to find keywords, follow these steps:

1. **Go to** `https://adwords.google.com/KeywordPlanner` **and sign into your Google account.**

If you don't have a Google account, create one by selecting "Create an account" in the upper right corner.

2. **Once you are signed in, under the heading, "Find new keywords and get search volume data," expand the section that reads, "Search for new keywords using a phrase, website, or category" by clicking the right arrow.**

The area expands and you see a number of new fields.

3. **In the field marked, Your Product or Service, type the keyword you want to see more related keywords ideas.**

4. **Click the Get Ideas button.**

A graph displaying the average monthly search numbers appears.

5. **Click the Keyword Ideas tab under the graph.**

You see a list of related keywords.

By searching for the keyword, Conflict Resolution, Google AdWords Keyword Planner provides you with *conflict management*, *mediation*, and *dispute resolution*.

Once you determine your keywords, write them down. Don't make the mistake of trying to remember them in your head. It's important to keep these keywords in front of you so you can work them into your LinkedIn profile in an organic, natural manner. In Figure 2-7 is a blank form to use to jot down your keywords.

My LinkedIn Keywords

1. _____
2. _____
3. _____
4. _____
5. _____
6. _____
7. _____
8. _____
9. _____
10. _____

FIGURE 2-7:
Write down your keywords!

Ranking Higher with Profile SEO

SEO stands for *search engine optimization*. It is the process of making certain strategic changes to a profile to boost its search ranking. By putting in a little effort, you can improve your profile's ranking so it appears more often and higher in search. Certain areas within your profile are highly sensitive to the addition of keywords. When you add keywords to these areas, the LinkedIn search algorithm treats these keywords with more weight and your profile ranks higher on the search results page. These highly sensitive SEO fields are:

» Headline

» Summary section

>> Skills & Expertise section

>> Job titles (especially current)

>> Job descriptions

Make sure these five areas are rich in your chosen keywords. Don't just list keywords in the summary and job description fields. Use your keywords intentionally yet naturally in your narrative. Write for your reader first and the search engine second.

The more times a keyword is repeated, the higher you may rank for that keyword in LinkedIn search results. Although repeating keywords is a good thing, it's easy to become obnoxious, so be careful not to overdo it!

Figure 2-8 demonstrates the difference between strategic keyword usage and obnoxious keyword stuffing.

Obnoxious Keyword Repetition	**Unobnoxious Keyword Repetition**
Sales, sales...	As an account manager & sales leader who specializes in the sales & marketing of EMR software, I utilize solution selling and consultative selling in my sales process.

FIGURE 2-8: Don't overstuff your profile with keywords; use them strategically.

WARNING

You can rank higher by repeating your keywords ad nauseam, but when your target reader opens your profile and sees the repetition, they are turned off and exit from your profile and move on to the next search result listing. Keyword abuse doesn't impress anyone. In fact, LinkedIn has been known to delete profiles that are abusive in their keyword stuffing technique. Ultimately, you want to be strategic and smart when peppering your profile with keywords, not obnoxious.

Building Off Profile SEO

In addition to building a powerful profile enriched with keywords, another way to increase your LinkedIn search ranking is to have a large number of connections within your LinkedIn network.

When a person searches LinkedIn, they are not searching the entire LinkedIn database of users. They are only searching their LinkedIn network. Your LinkedIn network extends three degrees. Your first-degree connections are the people who have accepted your LinkedIn connection invitation and ones you have accepted. Second-degree connections are those people who are first-degree connections of your first-degree connections. Third-degree connections are the first-degree connections of your second-degree connections. Additionally, any people who are in a LinkedIn Group that you belong to are also considered part of your LinkedIn network.

Figure 2-9 is a visualization of your LinkedIn network. Your network increases exponentially as you add more first-degree connections.

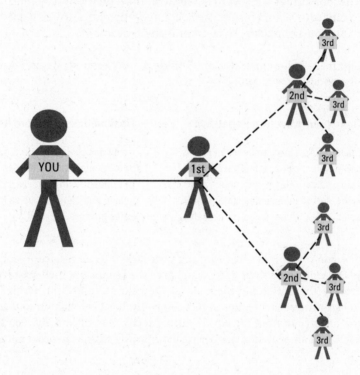

FIGURE 2-9:
There is a clear structure to your LinkedIn network.

When people perform a LinkedIn search, the resulting profiles are from their LinkedIn network. Every now and then you may see a person from outside your LinkedIn network; however, when that happens, you are prevented from seeing that person's full name and that person's profile may not be completely accessible to you.

LinkedIn ranks the profiles of people directly related to you first. This means the more people you are connected to directly, the higher you rank in a LinkedIn search.

LinkedIn cautions that you should only connect with people you know and trust. I agree, but I believe you should remain open to all opportunities. I do not suggest aiming low and wide to connect with everyone and their brothers. However, if a person you do not know sends a connection request, visit his or her profile. Is this person in the same industry? Do you share a similar network of connections or belong to the same LinkedIn Groups? As long as the person doesn't look overly suspicious, it's okay to accept this person into your network. You never know if a connection of theirs may one day be searching for someone like you, and accepting the invitation today means you'll be found tomorrow for a fantastic opportunity.

In the next chapter, let's see how to take your keywords and add them to LinkedIn's Skills & Endorsements section.

Chapter **3**

Understanding Skills and Endorsements

The Skills & Endorsements section is a much maligned area of the LinkedIn profile. Whenever I speak to groups about LinkedIn, there is always someone in the crowd who jumps up and asks, "What is the point of Skills & Endorsements?" The crowd goes wild, and I am left defending this poor section of the profile.

As I show you in this chapter, the bad reputation of the Skills & Endorsements section is not deserved. This section is simply a place to list your skills and strengths and allow your connections to publicly validate them with an endorsement.

In this chapter we look at how to take the keywords you discovered in Chapter 2 and turn them into skills in the Skills & Endorsements section where your connections can endorse them. I show you how easy it is to add and rearrange those skills to expertly showcase your skill sets and strengths. I also show you how to obtain endorsements, how to hide or remove an endorsement you don't necessarily want, and how to endorse others.

Showcasing Your Skills

The skills and strengths you list in the Skills & Endorsements section of your LinkedIn profile are the keywords you discovered in Chapter 2. Think of LinkedIn Skills as your expertise boiled down to just single words. LinkedIn Skills aren't just there to describe you; they are listed for your first-degree connections to validate and endorse. The Skills section is shown in Figure 3-1.

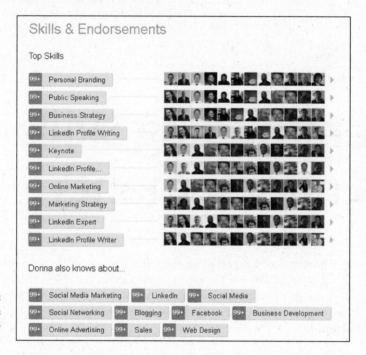

FIGURE 3-1:
The Skills &
Endorsements
section.

The following keywords are examples of excellent skills and strengths in the Skills & Endorsements section:

Change Management

Strategic Planning

Conflict Resolution

Customer Service

Entrepreneur

Employee Relations

Keywords that don't translate so well as skills include:

Problem-solver

Dynamic

Professional

Engaging

Interesting

Friendly

TIP

The excellent keywords are excellent because they are specific and could appear on a job description. Skills should reflect your expertise, competencies, specialties, or abilities that you possess. *Problem-solver*, *dynamic*, *interesting*, and *friendly* aren't great keywords to list. While they are all positive terms, these terms could describe anyone in any industry. The key is to be specific; your listed skills should describe you and your unique abilities and strengths.

Adding skills

To showcase your strengths and get endorsed for your expertise you must add skills to your profile. LinkedIn allows you to add up to 50 skills. If you completed Chapter 2 and have a list of your keywords, get that list out now. If not, no worries!

If you are a job seeker, simply locate a job description of your current position and review it to see the keywords that describe your abilities. For sales professionals using LinkedIn to prospect, visit your company's website. Scan through the pages for words used to describe your service offering or products. Those of you who are interested in reputation management and branding, think in terms of your strengths and expertise.

To add your skills to your LinkedIn profile, follow these steps:

1. **Open your LinkedIn profile.**

   If you already have skills listed on your profile page, go to Step 3. If you don't have any skills listed yet, continue to Step 2.

2. **Click the Skills section that appears toward the top of your profile to add the Skills & Endorsements section.**

   You may need to click View More to find this section. When clicked, the Skills & Endorsements section appears on your profile.

3. **Scroll down to the Skills & Endorsements section.**

4. **Move your cursor over Skills & Endorsements and click the +Add Skill button that appears.**

   An empty Skills & Endorsements screen appears, as shown in Figure 3-2.

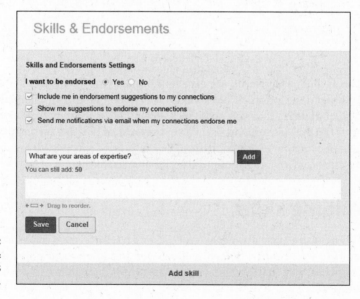

FIGURE 3-2:
An empty Skills & Endorsements section.

5. **Type the name of a skill in the "What are your areas of expertise" text box or choose it from the drop-down list that appears after you type a few letters.**

   If your skill doesn't appear, completely type in the skill name in the field. There is an 80-character limit for each skill.

6. **Click Add.**

   The skill is added to your Skills list.

7. **Click Save.**

TIP

You can add up to 50 skills to your profile. Don't focus on trying to list 50 skills. It's quality versus quantity here. Concentrate on 15 to 20 core skills. When you focus on adding 50 skills, you end up adding some skills of lesser importance. Because LinkedIn allows others to endorse you, you may find some of these lower skills are endorsed and elevated on your profile. If you do get up to 50, that's great, but don't kill yourself trying.

Rearranging skills

Skills are listed in the order in which they are added. Once you start getting endorsements, skills with the most endorsements are listed first. However, you can rearrange the order of endorsed skills by drag and drop. Here's how:

1. **Open your LinkedIn profile.**

2. **Scroll down to Skills & Endorsements.**

3. **Click the pencil (edit) icon next to the skill you wish to move, as shown in Figure 3-3.**

4. **Drag and drop the skills where you want them to appear in the list, as shown in Figure 3-4.**

   When moving skills, make sure you keep your mouse button pressed on the skill you wish to move, drag your mouse to the top or bottom of the list, and then release. Skills without endorsements can't be arranged higher than a skill with endorsement.

5. **When you have finished organizing your skills, click the Save button.**

Click to enter edit mode

FIGURE 3-3:
Click any of the
many pencil icons
to get into
edit mode.

Drag and drop to rearrange skills

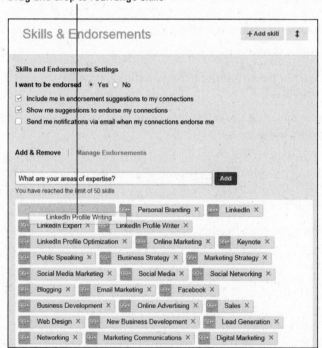

FIGURE 3-4:
Drag and drop
skills to arrange
them in your
desired order.

Obtaining Endorsements

Once you have skills listed on your profile, LinkedIn allows people to endorse you for those skills. By allowing others to endorse you, the Skills & Endorsements section provides credibility and validity that isn't available anywhere else. Sure, you can list your core competencies on your resume, but it's only on your LinkedIn profile where your first-degree connections can endorse you and prove that you really do possess that skill. The more endorsements you have for a skill on your LinkedIn profile, the more credible you appear.

As explained in Chapter 2, LinkedIn search is driven by keywords, and LinkedIn wants its search results to be relevant and valuable to the person searching. By allowing connections to validate skills through endorsements, it allows LinkedIn a way to determine search result listings via a manner that is independent of the owner of the profile. At one time, LinkedIn's search results rankings were based solely on keyword density. As long as you stated your keyword more than anyone else did in their profiles, your profile showed up first. Clearly, this was an easy way to hack and skew the search results in your favor. By providing the ability to endorse others and basing search results on an area that is outside the control of a user, results ranking is harder to hack, thereby creating a better search result.

TIP

There is no maximum limit to endorsements (although you are limited by the number of first-degree connections within your network); however, LinkedIn only shows up to 99. After 99, LinkedIn displays 99+. To display the total number of endorsers of a particular skill, just click the 99+ icon to see the full number and a list of endorsers.

Most people confuse endorsements and recommendations. I like to call endorsements "Recommendations Lite." Endorsements occur with a single click of the mouse. Recommendations on the other hand are a written testimonial from a connection and require much more energy and thought.

TIP

When torn between providing a person with a recommendation or an endorsement, determine how much time you have allotted and what you want to convey. If you only have a few seconds, endorsements work just fine. If you want to say more than just one word and truly convey a message about the person, a recommendation is in order.

Hiding an endorsement

Did someone disreputable endorse you for a skill? Hide that endorsement so it doesn't show on your profile. Here's how:

1. Open your LinkedIn profile.

2. Scroll down to the Skills & Endorsements section.

3. **Hover your mouse pointer over an endorsement you want to hide and click the pencil (edit) icon.**

4. **Click the Manage Endorsements link that appears to the right of Add & Remove.**

5. **Click a skill to show the connections who endorsed you for that skill.**

   In Figure 3-5 you can see all of the connections who endorsed me for *Personal Branding.*

6. **Uncheck the box next to any connections whose endorsements you want to hide.**

7. **Click the Save button.**

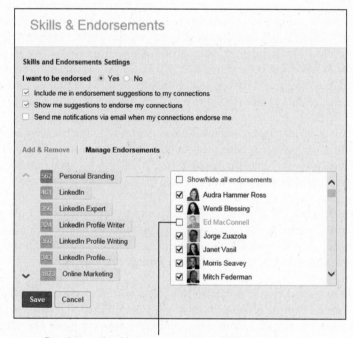

FIGURE 3-5:
Removing an
endorsement is
as easy as
unchecking a box.

Deselect a checkbox to remove an endorsement

Opting out of endorsements

Although I highly recommend embracing endorsements, there are some jobs in which endorsements are frowned upon. Financial advisors, for example, often prefer to opt out of LinkedIn's endorsement feature for compliance and regulation reasons.

If you wish to opt out of receiving endorsements, follow these steps:

1. **Open your LinkedIn profile.**

2. **Scroll down to Skills & Endorsements and click +Add Skill button.**

3. **Under "Skills & Endorsements Settings," click No after "I Want to be Endorsed."**

   After selecting No, LinkedIn indicates that it will show your skills but not your endorsements.

4. **Click the Save button.**

Endorsing a connection

Most people focus on getting endorsements, but it's just as important to give endorsements. Endorsements are a great way to remind connections that you recognize their strengths. By endorsing connections, you are showing acknowledgement and respect for their areas of expertise. Think of endorsements as a "thumbs up" from a business acquaintance. It's an easy way to say, "Hey, I remember you and respect your skill set."

When giving endorsements, read through the person's entire list of skills and endorse those skills that you are able to authentically validate from personal experience with that person.

Here's how to endorse a connection's skills:

1. **Visit the LinkedIn profile of the person you want to endorse.**

2. **Scroll down to the Skills & Endorsement section.**

3. **Hover over the skill you want to endorse and click the plus (+) sign that appears to the right of it.**

   You can endorse numerous skills; just keep clicking the plus (+) signs.

REMEMBER

Endorse your first-degree connections honestly and genuinely. No one wants to be endorsed by someone who is only guessing at their skills. When you make a thoughtful endorsement of a connection you admire, that person is more likely to return the favor in kind.

There may be times you receive endorsements from people within your network that you don't know all that well or at all. This is especially true when you are an open networker and connect with people regardless of whether you know them or not. These first-degree connections that you don't know so well may endorse you because they know of your work and wish to promote positivity in the world. They also may hope that you operate with a quid quo pro mentality and want you to endorse them right back. Do not feel strong-armed! Endorse people because you appreciate their work, not because you feel guilt.

REMEMBER

You are only able to endorse first-degree connections. When you visit a profile of a second-degree, third-degree, or Out of Network profile, you see their skills and endorsements but the plus (+) sign to endorse does not appear.

When viewing your LinkedIn home page newsfeed, every now and then LinkedIn may show you several first-degree connections and provide you the ability to endorse them for skills they have listed on their profiles (see Figure 3-6). This prompt is a great way to keep in touch with connections and show your appreciation for their strengths. By clicking the Show More link, you can cycle through more suggestions.

FIGURE 3-6:
Endorsing others from LinkedIn's newsfeed prompt.

Removing an endorsement

Did you endorse someone only to learn that you would prefer to disassociate from them? Remove your endorsement from their profile by performing a few easy steps:

1. **Visit the LinkedIn profile of the person you endorsed.**

2. **Scroll down to the Skills & Endorsements section.**

3. **Hover your cursor over the plus (+) sign next to the skill you endorsed.**

The words "Remove Endorsement" appear, as shown in Figure 3-7.

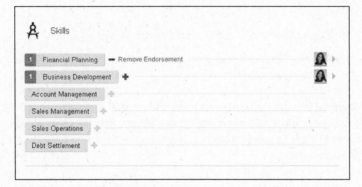

4. **Click Remove Endorsement.**

Don't worry; the recipient is not notified of the removal.

Soliciting endorsements

Are you not receiving endorsements from your connections? Sometimes all it takes is a nudge. Rather than sit and stare at your lonely Skills & Endorsements section, get proactive and send your connections an email. Send a simple LinkedIn message to a few of your close connections and ask them to endorse you. Remember, the squeaky wheel gets the oil!

Following are two sample messages to send to connections with whom you recently finished a project or whom you've recently endorsed. The first is an example of requesting an endorsement after finishing up a project or other work with a client:

> *If you were happy with my work I performed at Widgets, Inc., would you be so kind as to endorse me on LinkedIn?*
>
> *It's just a simple click of a button. The skills and expertise I would like to be endorsed for are Project Management, Leadership Team Building, and SEO.*
>
> *All you need to do is visit my profile and scroll down to the Skills & Endorsements section located under my Summary.*
>
> *Here's the link to my profile:* www.linkedin.com/in/todonna.

The next is an example of requesting an endorsement using the power of quid pro quo:

> *I just endorsed you for Project Management and Leadership Strategy on your LinkedIn profile.*
>
> *If you're comfortable with it, would you do the same for me?*
>
> *There's 50 skills to choose from. All you need to do is visit my profile:* www.linkedin.com/in/todonna.

When your connections do endorse you, make sure you reach out and thank them. Call them on the phone or send them a message via LinkedIn. Use LinkedIn as an excuse to get in touch. This is a great way to continue to network and forge strong relationships.

In the next chapter I show you how to jump in and start building your profile. Don't worry, the very first thing I cover in Chapter 4 is how to turn off profile updates so your entire network isn't alerted to the massive changes about to take place!

2

Getting Your LinkedIn Profile Started

Look at how to optimize the invisible nooks and crannies of your profile, including how to create a customized link to your profile and market your profile for more views.

Learn how to improve your profile's strength, even if you don't have a current position or don't have a school degree.

Set up your digital "calling card" — the upper most section of your profile — and give readers an optimized overview of who you are.

Understand why it is important to include your contact information and how and where to add it to your profile.

See why you need a profile picture and how to present yourself in the best possible light.

Craft a compelling headline to grab your readers' attention and make them want to learn more about you.

Look at how to add flair to your headline, including adding symbols and saturating your headline with keywords.

Chapter **4**

Optimizing the "Behind the Scenes" Sections

Not every part of your LinkedIn profile is there for the whole wide world to see. In this chapter, I take you behind the scenes of your profile to make sure every invisible nook and cranny is optimized for success. You learn how not to bombard your LinkedIn connections with notifications that you updated your profile. You also discover when and how to turn notifications back on and how that helps you rank higher in LinkedIn search.

Managing Profile Changes

When you make changes to your LinkedIn profile, a notification is sent out alerting your network. Activity updates are broadcast to your connections' LinkedIn home page newsfeeds and appear on your profile's Recent Activity page. By seeing your profile updates on their newsfeeds, your connections are reminded of you and they may find themselves compelled to click on your profile to learn more.

LinkedIn updates are broadcast to your connections if you perform the following changes to your profile:

>> Upload or edit your profile picture

>> Add a new link to a website

>> Add a new job position

>> Edit the title of your current position

>> Add additional skills to your profile

LinkedIn also sends notifications if you perform any of the following additional activities:

>> Recommend someone

>> Add a connection

>> Follow a LinkedIn university page

>> Follow a LinkedIn company page

>> Join a LinkedIn Group

>> Post or comment on discussions within a LinkedIn Group

>> Have a current work experience anniversary

>> Upgrade to a premium account (with the exception of Job Seeker)

>> Follow an influencer, channel, or publisher

>> Share content on your newsfeed or as a published post

>> Comment on or like connections' shared content

Turning off update alerts

Regardless of the benefits, there may be times when you don't want people to know you are making changes to your LinkedIn profile. For example, if you are updating your LinkedIn profile in preparation of a new job search, it's best your employer isn't notified of such a change. Or you may be giving your profile page a complete overhaul, and you don't want to bombard your network with information about each and every change. Luckily, LinkedIn provides the ability to turn off the activity updates associated with profile changes and even delete your recent activity notifications.

To turn off LinkedIn update alerts, follow these steps:

1. **Open your LinkedIn profile.**

2. **Locate the Notify Your Network box located in the far right column of your profile page, as shown in Figure 4-1.**

3. **Toggle the Yes/No button so that it reads, "No, do not publish an update to my network about my profile changes."**

   Now, changes that you make to your profile are confidential.

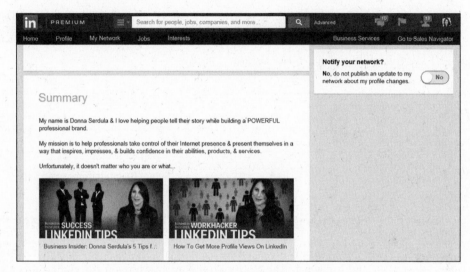

FIGURE 4-1:
Select No to turn
off update alerts.

TIP

Turning off profile updates doesn't turn off your profile visibility. It's the notification of your edits that is turned off; your profile is still on and any changes that you save are visible to visitors of your profile.

Manually removing updates

Did you get excited and start updating your LinkedIn profile without turning off your activity update notifications? Now these changes are on your recent activity screen and quickly hitting your connections' newsfeeds. Don't worry! You can manually remove these updates even after they are broadcast out. Here's how:

1. **Open your LinkedIn profile.**

2. **Move your cursor over the down arrow icon that appears to the right of the View Profile As button.**

3. **Select View Recent Activity.**

   Your recent activity appears.

4. **Hover your mouse pointer over the update you want to delete, and then move your mouse to the upper right corner of the update.**

   A down arrow appears, as shown in Figure 4-2.

5. **Click the down arrow and then select Delete.**

   The selected update is deleted from the Recent Activity log on your profile.

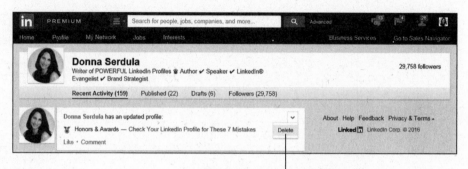

FIGURE 4-2:
Manually remove
an update by
selecting Delete.

Select Delete to remove an update

Knowing when to allow update alerts

Once your profile is optimized and you are ready to unleash it into the world, scroll back down to the Notify Your Network box on the right side of your profile and toggle the button to Yes. Don't worry; all of the updates that you recently made to your profile are not broadcasted out to your connections. Only new changes to your profile since toggling the Notify Your Network box to Yes appear on your connections' LinkedIn home page newsfeeds and your Recent Activity page.

TIP

You may feel the temptation to keep those update notifications set to No all the time, but I highly suggest allowing update alerts. Often when people see you made changes to your profile, they are compelled to visit your profile. Most people want more views to their LinkedIn profile, and this is such an easy way to drive traffic to it. Don't feel shy. Your network wants to stay up to date on your professional career.

Once you are finished updating your profile, toggle the Notify Your Network button to Yes. Go back to your profile and make a single change to trigger an update. My suggestion is to edit the title of your current position. This way you are now alerting your network that a change has occurred, but you are not inundating them with a lot of changes.

CREATING A HIGH-RANKING PROFILE

As I discuss in Chapter 2, LinkedIn is more than a professional social network. It is also a search engine of profiles. As such, it is in LinkedIn's best interest to ensure that the profiles that appear in search results are relevant and pertinent to the person searching. Profiles that are freshly updated are often rewarded with higher placement in search results than a profile that hasn't been touched in years. LinkedIn wants to deliver the right results, and an old, out-of-date profile should never rank high in LinkedIn search.

Get into the habit of updating your profile at least once a month. Not only are you keeping your profile fresh, but also you are ensuring that your profile ranks high for those people looking for someone like you.

Turning On Your Public Profile

Your LinkedIn profile is not just visible within LinkedIn. You can allow the world the ability to see your profile by turning on public version of your profile. Once your public profile is turned on, it is indexed by search engines and returned as a search result for pertinent searches. Anyone can view your public profile regardless of whether they are logged in to LinkedIn or not.

Your profile on LinkedIn is your outpost on LinkedIn. Not everyone is on LinkedIn, and your public profile acts as your outpost on the entire World Wide Web.

If you want your public profile to be found and seen outside of LinkedIn, follow these steps to turn it on:

1. **Open your LinkedIn profile.**

2. **Hover your mouse pointer over the LinkedIn profile URL located under your profile photo and click the gear icon that appears (see Figure 4-3).**

3. **Under the section, "Customize Your Public Profile" located in the right column, select the radio button next to "Make my public profile visible to everyone," as shown in Figure 4-4.**

4. **Click Save.**

   Your LinkedIn profile now appears in search engines and is visible to non-LinkedIn members.

FIGURE 4-3:
Click the gear
icon to customize
your public
profile URL.

Gear icon

FIGURE 4-4:
You can control
how your profile
appears outside
of LinkedIn.

In addition to controlling whether your profile is visible by the public, you determine the profile sections that appear for public consumption. Depending on your privacy needs, you choose what sections appear and which remain hidden.

As shown in Figure 4-4, some sections can be toggled on or off like honors and awards, organizations, interests, and so on. Other sections have enhanced controls.

For example, you can turn off your current experience but leave your past experiences on. You may choose to show your current or past job titles but not the job description details. This works well when you want to show your career trajectory, but not allow the public to see every accomplishment and responsibility.

Although you can toggle sections off, remember, this is only your public profile. Logged-in LinkedIn members see all completed profile sections.

Here's how to preview your public profile and turn sections on and off:

1. **Open your LinkedIn profile.**

2. **Hover your mouse pointer over the LinkedIn profile URL located under your profile photo and click the gear icon that appears.**

3. **In the "Customize Your Public Profile" section, use your mouse to select each checkbox next to the sections you wish to appear in your public profile.**

    Clicking a checked box removes the check and prevents that section from appearing. As you add and remove sections, you can preview what your public profile looks like to the outside world.

4. **Scroll down to see a preview of your profile.**

5. **When you are satisfied with your choices, click Save.**

You may feel compelled to turn off your public profile and prevent people from outside LinkedIn to view it. Your LinkedIn profile is intended to tell your story and control how others see you. I strongly advise you to take a deep breath and leave your public profile on and visible.

It's a different world out there, and people are interested in learning more about you. By providing them with your LinkedIn profile — *your* story told *your* way — you are allowing them to find something out about you on your own terms. By preventing this information, the person looking to learn more about you may decide to dig even deeper and find information about you that you cannot control.

Creating a Personalized URL

There may be times you want to send people directly to your LinkedIn profile. Most people include a link to their profiles in their resume letterhead, email signatures, website bios, or even on business cards. Providing a link to your profile is even more important when you have a common name. Without a link, a person wanting to connect to you on LinkedIn must perform a name search. It's not easy finding the right John Smith or Peter Jones in 10 pages of search results. Alternately, it's hard to find the right Charles or Jennifer. Did they list their name as Chuck, Charlie, Charles, Jenna, Jen, Jenny, or Jennifer?

Whatever you do, don't copy the URL in the address bar of your browser while in edit mode. It looks something like this:

```
https://www.linkedin.com/profile/edit?trk=nav_responsive_sub_nav_edit_profile
```

A person who uses that URL in hopes to find yours will visit their own LinkedIn profile instead. LinkedIn uses dynamic URLs that pull content from their database depending on user input. That dynamic URL works for you now, but it's not static and won't necessarily work in the same way if you copy it and paste it for someone else's use.

Instead, you want to provide a direct link to your public profile with a customized URL. LinkedIn automatically assigns your profile a static web address link. However, this default address is a jumble of letters and numbers that is not easy to remember or market. Luckily, LinkedIn gives you the ability to change this URL to one that is easy to remember and easy to promote, something that looks like this:

```
https://www.linkedin.com/in/firstnamelastname
```

Here's how you create a customized link to your LinkedIn profile:

1. **Open your LinkedIn profile.**

2. **Hover your mouse pointer over the LinkedIn profile URL located under your profile photo and click the gear icon that appears.**

3. **Under the section, "Your public profile URL," which appears in the right column, click the pencil (edit) icon next to your URL, as shown in Figure 4-5.**

4. **Type your new customized URL in the text box that appears (see Figure 4-6).**

   Your custom URL can have 5 to 30 letters or numbers. Spaces, symbols, or special characters are not allowed. The customizable part of the URL is case insensitive. This means DavidJones or davidjones take you to the same profile.

5. **Click Save.**

Pencil icon

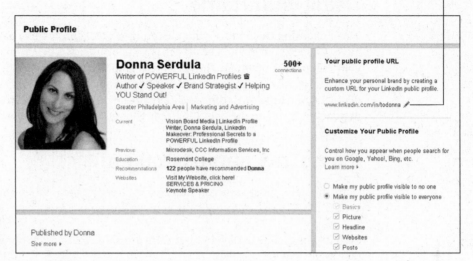

Type the new URL here

TIP

Recruiters often tell me that a personalized URL is a sign that the person has kept up with technology and is a true professional. Recruiters won't pass by a profile because of a non-customized URL, but they may pass silent judgment on that candidate.

Using your name

When choosing the text for your customized URL, don't worry about getting creative. Choose your name because it is *your* profile. Whatever you do, do not use your company's name for the URL. Your public URL is a permanent link to your LinkedIn profile. Companies are not permanent, and although you can change your URL, old links with the old URL may exist for some time. Create a URL that is permanent by using the one thing that is permanent for you: your name.

Oh no, my name is taken*!*

Unfortunately, most common names are already taken. When this happens, you simply must find an alternative way of stating your name.

Pretend your name is David Jones. Here are some ideas of re-phrasing your name that might not yet be taken:

>> First initial and last name: DJones

>> First name, middle initial, and last name: DavidXJones

>> First and middle initial and last name: DXJones

TIP

I highly discourage users from adding numbers to the end of their customized URLs. When I see a number at the end of a URL, I think the person is just one of many. A number gives the feeling of an assembly line of professionals rather than a unique brand. When your name is taken and there is no other way of stating it, utilize a prefix rather than a numerical suffix.

Here are some ideas:

>> ToDavidJones

>> GoDavidJones

>> ImDavidJones

>> theDavidJones

>> SeeDavidJones

>> YourDavidJones

>> VisitDavidJones

Marketing your public profile URL

The beauty of your LinkedIn profile is that when people visit, they can connect with you. By connecting with you, they are subscribing to your activity feed. When you post an activity update or blog, they receive a notification. By driving people to your profile and asking them to connect, you are ensuring a long relationship with them rather than a once-and-done visit.

There are a number of areas you can place your public profile link:

» Brochures

» Business cards

» Email signature

» Facebook profile

» Letterhead

» Resume

» Sales literature

» Tattoo across your forehead (just teasing!)

» Twitter bio

» Website

Improving Your Profile's Strength

LinkedIn cares about your profile. It wants you to take your profile seriously and update it regularly. LinkedIn even provides a rating to your profile to show you how well you are doing. The Profile Strength meter, shown in Figure 4-7, is on the right side of your profile. This meter measures how well you optimized your profile.

There are five levels of profile strength:

» Beginner

» Intermediate

» Advanced

» Expert

» All-Star

The stronger your profile, the more successful your profile. LinkedIn has stated, "Users with complete profiles are 40 times more likely to receive opportunities through LinkedIn." LinkedIn hasn't revealed its search engine algorithms, but knowing how important it is for LinkedIn to provide relevant and complete profiles in search results, it would make sense that stronger profiles are rewarded with high placement on search result listings.

It's worth noting that your profile strength is not broadcast out for everyone to see. Only you, logged in and looking at your profile in edit mode, can see it.

TIP

Your profile strength increases as you add more content to your profile. All-Star is the highest level of strength. In order to achieve a perfect LinkedIn profile that ranks as an All-Star, you must have the following sections completed on your profile:

>> Your industry and location

>> An up-to-date current position (with a description)

>> Two past positions

>> Your education

>> Your skills (minimum of three)

>> A profile picture

>> At least 50 connections

Unfortunately, some of the items that increase your profile strength are outside of your control. If you are a displaced worker looking for your next opportunity, your profile will only rate Expert because you do not have a current experience. Likewise, if you are an entrepreneur who dropped out of college to create a startup, you too are out of luck. Without a college to list on your profile, the highest strength your profile can obtain is Expert.

All-Star is the highest level you can achieve; yet when looking at the graphic LinkedIn uses to illustrate All-Star, the circle isn't complete, leaving a sliver of a gap at the very top. This leads many users to think there is another, higher level. Perhaps LinkedIn is subtly suggesting that one's profile is never truly 100% complete because as a professional, you are always growing and developing skills.

Dealing with a lack of a current position

When you are out of work and looking for a new job, having a strong, complete LinkedIn profile is important. You want your profile to rank high in search results when a recruiter or hiring manager is looking for candidates.

Having a profile that is at Expert level and not an All-Star won't decimate your chances of getting found or finding a new job, but it is certainly annoying. I often hear from job seekers wanting to know what they can do to obtain a 100% complete, All-Star profile.

In this situation, you may decide to add a current position that states you are looking for your next job opportunity. In Figure 4-8, you can see what adding a "seeking new opportunity" experience looks like.

WARNING

Adding a current experience works fabulously; however, I must caution you that adding a current experience also cloaks your unemployed status. I have found that recruiters are divided. Some don't mind seeing a current experience reading "Unemployed." Others find an unemployed current experience devious. Ultimately, there is no right or wrong answer; you must decide what makes the most sense for you.

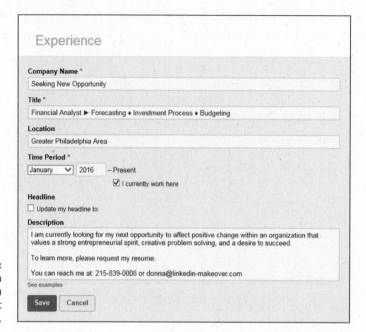

FIGURE 4-8:
Adding an
experience if you
are currently out
of work.

Adding a school without a degree

Whether you opted to not attend college or decided instead to hire someone who did, your profile is also stuck at the Expert strength level. Luckily, there are a few things you can do. My recommendation is to bypass the school list LinkedIn provides and write in your own. If you want to stay on the up and up, enter your high school information. On the other hand, you can get a little cheeky and add a school where you took a class. I have had clients list Sur La Table, Sip and Paint, and The Esteemed School of Hard Knocks. When adding a non-accredited institution of higher learning, leave the degree field empty; it's not a required field.

Expanding your network

The area of the LinkedIn profile that causes the most difficulty in getting to All-Star status is connecting with 50 people. It's important to have a strong network so you can earn an All-Star profile, but a strong network is also the backbone of the site.

REMEMBER

Connections are key to your success on LinkedIn. When you search LinkedIn for people, the results are comprised of people within your LinkedIn network who meet your search criteria. When people search for you or someone like you, you will appear in their search results as long as you reside within their LinkedIn network. The more people you have in your network, the higher you rank in LinkedIn search, and the more often you are found.

LinkedIn uses connections to provide additional insight unlike any other social network. LinkedIn doesn't just show with whom you are directly connected. LinkedIn unveils how you are connected to other people.

Your LinkedIn Network consists of first-, second-, and third-degree connections. These degrees describe how a person is connected to another person. A first-degree connection is someone you have added to your network or someone who has added you to their network. A second-degree connection is a person connected to your first-degree connection but not directly connected to you. If a person is a second-degree connection, that means you have a mutual connection in common. A third-degree connection is someone who is connected to a second-degree connection. If a person is a third-degree connection, they know someone who knows a person you know directly. A person is considered outside of your network if you do not share any connections within three degrees of that person.

To truly leverage LinkedIn and get to All-Star profile strength, you must get your online network to reflect your offline network. Here are some ideas of people you can invite to connect on LinkedIn:

>> Alumni

>> Current colleagues

>> Current employer

>> Family

>> Friends

>> Past colleagues

>> Past employers

LinkedIn provides a tool to make connecting easy. It's called People You May Know. Rather than wracking your brain trying to come up with people to connect, the People You May Know screen provides suggestions based upon commonalities.

LinkedIn shows you the name, current job title, and profile picture of people who you may know. They base these suggestions off of similar profile information such as working at the same company or going to the same school. LinkedIn also looks at the contacts you've imported from your email and mobile address books and offers profiles with the same contact information.

To use People You May Know to help expand your network, follow these steps:

1. **Open your LinkedIn profile.**

2. **From LinkedIn's main navigation bar, hover your mouse pointer over My Network and click People You May Know, as shown in Figure 4-9.**

FIGURE 4-9:
The People You May Know option suggests profile connections.

3. **View the connection suggestions.**

4. **When you see someone you know and would like to add to your network, click the Connect button.**

   Clicking the Connect button immediately sends a default LinkedIn connection request.

You cannot personalize the invitation to connect message from the People You May Know page. If you would like to personalize your invitation to connect message, do the following:

1. **Hover your mouse pointer over the person's name and click.**

   This takes you to that person's LinkedIn profile.

2. **Click the Connect button.**

   You are now at the Invitation screen. If the Connect button doesn't appear in the Summary section, you may have to select the down arrow next to Send InMail and choose Connect from the drop-down list, as shown in Figure 4-10.

FIGURE 4-10:
To send a personal connection invitation, you need to go to that person's profile directly.

3. **Select how you know the person. Your choices are:**
   - Colleague
   - Classmate
   - We've done business together
   - Friend
   - Other
   - I don't know

TIP

Choosing "Other" or "I don't know" prevents you from sending the invitation because LinkedIn only allows you to connect with people you know and trust. If you don't know the person but still wish to connect, you must choose Friend and hope to make it true in the future.

4. **In the Include a Personal Note field, personalize the invitation as you wish (see Figure 4-11).**

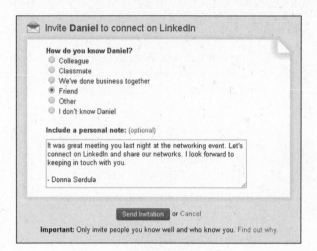

5. **Click the Send Invitation button.**

By expanding your network, you will turn up more often in searches, have more views to your profile, and find more opportunities via LinkedIn. Next, we take a look at setting up your digital calling card.

Chapter **5**

Establishing Your Calling Card

Think of the top part of your LinkedIn profile as your calling card. This upper most section of your profile gives your reader a quick overview of who you are and what you do. This area also provides the information a person needs to reach out to contact you. In a single glance, your reader sees:

» Your profile picture

» Your headline

» Whether you are a premium LinkedIn member

» Your location

» Your industry

» Your current company

» Your previous company

» The last school you attended

» The number of first-degree connections you have

» Your contact information

In this chapter, I show you how to set up this section of your LinkedIn profile in the most optimized manner to ensure the right people are able to find and contact you. Let's start with your name.

Using the Name Field Correctly

What can be easier than adding your name to your LinkedIn profile? Turns out, the name field is an area where people repeatedly make mistakes.

First, when adding your name to your profile, you don't need to use your full, official name. Instead, use your nickname. If your name is Christopher, but everyone knows you as Chris, use Chris on your profile.

Imagine going to a networking event or conference. You meet a man named Ricky. He hands you a business card that states his name is Rick. Later that evening, you log in to LinkedIn to connect with the people you've met, working off the business cards you collected. You type in "Rick" and click through pages of results to no avail. You try Ricky. It, too, yields no results. You try Richard and still nothing. You take a stab in the dark and try Ricardo and bingo!

Don't let this happen to you. Few people are as persistent as our example. Make it easy for people to connect with you by using the name you are known by on your LinkedIn profile.

A good rule of thumb is to make sure your name is consistent across your resume, business cards, website, email signature, and other social media profiles. Make it easy for people to find you by keeping a consistency with your name.

If you have a common name and want to differentiate yourself from others with the same name, adding a middle initial works great. However, don't just add the middle initial to your LinkedIn profile. Make sure you add it everywhere your name is used. It's a Google world out there, and you want to make sure you are easily found.

Editing your name

First things first, check out your LinkedIn profile. How does your name appear? I can't tell you how many times I see profiles that have the first and last name reversed. Once you see how it appears, decide if you want to change it. You may decide to add your maiden name or update your first name to your nickname. Whatever your need, here's how to change your name on LinkedIn:

1. **Open your LinkedIn profile.**

2. **Hover over your name.**

   The edit icon, which looks like a pencil, appears.

3. **Click the pencil (edit) icon.**

   The name field becomes editable, as shown in Figure 5-1.

FIGURE 5-1:
Editing your
name.

4. **Type your first and last names in the open fields.**

   If you have a former name, such as a maiden name, add it to the former name section and then choose who sees it by selecting My Connections, My Network, or Everyone.

   The former name field displays on your LinkedIn profile encased in parenthesis between your first and last name. It does not display on your public profile. This means that if a person performs a search using your former name, your profile will not turn up in the search results; however, if a person searches for you with your former name within LinkedIn, he or she will see your former name on your profile.

5. **Click Save.**

Adding prefixes to your name

Do you have certifications that you want to highlight on your profile? Lots of LinkedIn members like to add "MBA" or "SHRM" as a prefix to their last names. At one time, this was the only way to highlight your credentials on your profile. Now there is a Certifications section of the profile to display this information.

THE DOWN LOW ON LIONs

Some members of LinkedIn subscribe to the *LION connection* philosophy. LION stands for *LinkedIn Open Networker*. Rather than connecting with only the people they know and trust, they connect to anyone and their brother. There aren't any crazy hazing rituals or consideration panels to pass to be considered a LION. All you need to do is follow one rule: Never mark anyone who chooses to connect with you as I Don't Know or SPAM. To show that you are a LION, you simply state it in your profile. Many members add the word "LION" or their email addresses to their name fields. I highly caution against doing this. Not only is it against LinkedIn's user agreement to use the name field for information other than your name, but also doing so potentially makes it harder for people to find you.

I recommend keeping your name field clean. I know you want to shout your MBA from the rooftops, but hold off on putting it in the name field. When people search for you on LinkedIn, they aren't including prefixes. And because LinkedIn is matching the searched name with the name of a member, you want to make it match as best you can.

Keeping your profile confidential

Do you want to maintain your privacy and keep your LinkedIn profile confidential? There is an option that allows you to include only your first name and the first initial of your last name on your LinkedIn profile. Your first-degree connections see your full name, but everyone else sees your first name and last initial.

To access this option, you must first turn off your public profile. Once your public profile is turned off, the option to display your name with only your last initial appears within your Name field.

TIP

If you are on LinkedIn only to connect with a select few individuals and not looking for additional opportunities, displaying just the first initial of your last name may work for you. However, most people use LinkedIn to network and connect with people and to forge business opportunities. Displaying your full name shows you are serious in these goals. Unless you are using LinkedIn under confidential circumstances, my recommendation is to display your full name.

I often hear from people who want to turn their profile off entirely while they work on their profile. Unfortunately, LinkedIn doesn't provide the option to hide your profile. You can turn off your public profile so people outside of LinkedIn can't see your profile. You can hide your last name so people searching for you can't find you. You can turn off your activity feed so people aren't notified that you made changes, prompting them to check out your profile. However, those who are already first-degree connections with you will see your profile if they seek your profile out.

Filling Out Location and Industry

At the top of your profile, right below your headline, LinkedIn displays your location and industry. This information also shows up in search result listings. Location and industry also are used in advanced search. When recruiters search for a candidate, they often filter the search results by location or industry.

If you were sourcing a position located in Texas that doesn't come with a relocation package, why see results with people located in Maine? When searching for a Medical Device Account Manager, a recruiter will narrow the results by industry to ensure they are not looking at Account Managers with backgrounds in Automotive, Telecommunications, or Machinery.

Although these fields would seem easy to fill out, I can't tell you how many times people forget to update their locations when they move or choose the first industry that looks good to them. Medical device sales reps often choose Hospital and Healthcare because it's the first choice they see. Rarely do they scroll down to Medical Devices.

TIP

Because the location and industry fields are front and center and play a big role in search, you want to make sure they are absolutely accurate.

Choosing your location

LinkedIn uses postal codes to determine your location. If you live just outside a major city, LinkedIn provides a couple options. You can choose the actual town and state or the closest major city. When I enter postal code 08075, I can choose Riverside, New Jersey or Greater Philadelphia Area, as shown in Figure 5-2.

Determining which location to choose, think in terms of your market and audience. A small business owner who services clients in a town may prefer to list the town and state. A professional who commutes to the city to work, might prefer to list the greater city location.

FIGURE 5-2:
Choosing your
location.

What do you do if you commute farther than LinkedIn assumes? There are many professionals who take the express train into New York City but live in the northern outskirts of Philadelphia. In this situation, use the zip code where your office is located. Here's how to fill out the location field:

1. **Open your LinkedIn profile.**

2. **Hover your mouse pointer over the location title located directly under your headline and next to your location, as shown in Figure 5-3.**

   The edit icon appears.

FIGURE 5-3:
Getting location
and industry into
edit mode.

3. **Click the edit icon.**

   The industry and location fields become editable.

4. **Enter your postal code, as shown earlier in Figure 5-2.**

5. **Click Save.**

Choosing your industry

The industry section of your LinkedIn profile enables you to choose the industry that most aligns with your career. Remember, this area is used to filter searches, so when you select your industry, think in terms of the person searching for you. What industry would that person choose?

LinkedIn provides a long list of industries from which to choose. To select your industry, follow these steps:

1. **Open your LinkedIn profile.**

2. **Hover your mouse pointer over the industry title located directly under your headline and next to your location and click the pencil (edit) icon.**

    The industry and location fields become editable.

3. **Select your industry from the drop-down list, as shown in Figure 5-4.**

FIGURE 5-4:
Choosing your industry by scrolling through the drop-down list.

4. **Click Save.**

If you are a job seeker looking to make a career transition, you may wonder, "Do I choose my current industry or my desired industry?" When recruiters and other hiring professionals search LinkedIn to find potential candidates, the industry field is one area they often target, as it's a great way to narrow results and drill down to the right people. To get found, choose the industry you are targeting in your job search. This way, you can collide with the right opportunities.

What happens if your work bridges two industries? Sadly, you must make a choice. LinkedIn doesn't allow you to select more than one industry. And no, you can't create a second profile for the other industry. LinkedIn's user agreement forbids more than one profile per user. When you need to choose between two industries, imagine your target audience and what they would choose for you when searching.

Scrolling through the list, don't stop at the very first matching industry you find. Keep scrolling through until you view the entire list. Most professionals find that they fit into multiple industries. Just because you found one industry that matches, that doesn't mean it's the best one. For example, if you are a resume writer, you may notice that there is a Marketing and Advertising industry as well as a Writing and Editing industry. Which one do you choose? You might think, "Well, I help professionals market themselves, so Marketing and Advertising is the best one for me." Instead, think like your target audience. Most regular Joes would categorize a resume writer as a writer and editor, not as a marketer, so Writing and Editing is what you want to use. Don't get too fancy or over-think the industry.

TIP

Still not sure what industry to choose? Visit the profiles of colleagues and competitors to see what they list on their profiles. If you are seeing two different industries listed, go with the one the most successful person has chosen.

Suggesting a missing industry

LinkedIn's industry list is finite, and your industry may not yet be listed. In this situation, LinkedIn welcomes suggestions. To suggest an industry to LinkedIn, follow these steps:

1. **Open your LinkedIn profile.**

2. **Scroll to the bottom of the profile page and click the Send Feedback link (see Figure 5-5).**

   The Send Feedback dialog box appears with two options: Go to Help Center and Send Us Feedback.

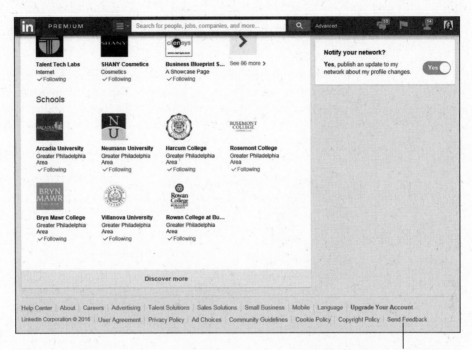

Click to send feedback to LinkedIn

3. **Click the Send Us Feedback button.**

4. **Enter your feedback in the Send Feedback field.**

You may write something like:

Dear LinkedIn,

Please include the missing industry, Super Villainy in the industry list of the LinkedIn profile. Thank you!

—Lex L.

5. **Click Send.**

If you do send LinkedIn a request to add a missing industry, don't expect to get notification that it was added. LinkedIn receives zillions of requests to add industries. After making the request to add an industry, check the industry drop-down list to see if it was added. If after a few weeks it hasn't appeared, LinkedIn may not agree that it makes sense to add it. Go back through the industry drop-down list and see if there is another industry that applies.

Including Your Contact Information

The LinkedIn profile has a dedicated section for your contact information. The Contact Information section is located at the top of the LinkedIn profile on the desktop version and at the very bottom of the mobile version. Clicking the Contact Information box expands the section to reveal the full card of information, as shown in Figure 5-6.

FIGURE 5-6:
The Contact Information section expanded on your desktop.

The area that contains your email address, phone number, instant messaging (IM) address, and mailing address is only visible to your first-degree connections. This means that people who are not directly connected to you cannot see your phone number or email address within the Contact Information section of your profile.

TIP

You can also add your Twitter handle, WeChat address, and three website links. This portion of the Contact Information section is visible to everyone on LinkedIn. The only part of the Contact Information section that shows on your public profile (which is visible to people outside of LinkedIn) are the website links, as shown in Figure 5-7.

Adding your email addresses

It's important to add the email addresses you use on a frequent basis to your LinkedIn account. Whatever you do, don't just add your work email address. Work email addresses are rarely permanent. You can easily get locked out of your LinkedIn account if you forget your password and the only email they have on file for you is the work address that was turned off when human resources handed you a cardboard box.

Alternately, you don't want to just add your personal email address. When people upload their email address books to have LinkedIn autoconnect for them, you want to make sure that whatever email address they have listed for you matches your LinkedIn profile. If you list your personal email address but the person uploading his or her email address book only has your work email, you won't be matched and you will have missed an opportunity to connect. Instead, add all of the email addresses you use frequently, which for most people are their work addresses and personal addresses.

To add your email address, follow these steps:

1. **Open your LinkedIn profile.**

2. **Click Contact Info located in the lower-right corner of your profile calling card.**

   The Contact Information section expands to show the contact information fields.

3. **Hover your mouse pointer over the email field and click the pencil (edit) icon.**

   You are now in edit mode.

4. **Add your email address in the open field.**

5. **Click the Add Email Address button.**

   LinkedIn sends a verification email to the new address.

6. **Open your email client and check for an email from LinkedIn.**

7. **Confirm your email address by clicking the link in the LinkedIn email.**

8. **Go back to LinkedIn and click Done, as shown on Figure 5-8.**

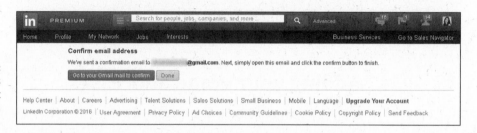

FIGURE 5-8:
LinkedIn's confirmation that a confirmation email was sent.

Within the list of addresses, note that the Send Confirmation link has changed to Make Primary.

9. **Select Make Primary next to the email address at which you want to receive email from LinkedIn.**

   If you have additional email addresses, add them by following Steps 5–7.

10. **Click Close when you have finished adding all of the email addresses you wish to add.**

LinkedIn allows people to upload their email address books to find potential connections. Rather than connecting one by one, uploading your address book is a quick way to connect with many people all at once. However, you need to make sure you add all of your email addresses in your LinkedIn Contact Information section. When a person uploads his or her email address book, the email address he or she has for you might be an old or personal email address. If you don't have that email address associated with your LinkedIn account, LinkedIn will not make the match, and you will lose out on that connection request.

This might seem strange but this is exactly the reason why I also do not recommend removing past work-related email addresses. Sure, that old work email might not work, but that email address may still reside in someone's email address book. Keep it attached to your profile as a secondary email address, not primary. By doing so, people from your past work lives are still able to find you.

REMEMBER

Strong networks = a successful LinkedIn experience. Make it easy for LinkedIn to suggest you as a contact to others by including all your email addresses.

Adding a phone number

LinkedIn provides one field for your phone number. You can designate it as home, work, or mobile. Enter the phone number you want displayed on your profile and accessible to your first-degree connections. To add a phone number to your profile, follow these steps:

1. **Open your LinkedIn profile.**

2. **Click Contact Info.**

   The Contact Information section expands to show the contact information fields.

3. **Hover your mouse pointer over the phone field and click the pencil (edit) icon.**

   You are now in edit mode.

4. **Enter your phone number.**

5. **Select whether the phone number is Home, Work, or Mobile from the drop-down list.**

6. **Click the Save button.**

LinkedIn can be compared to an old fashion Rolodex. People used a Rolodex to store their contacts' contact information. Nowadays, many people hop over to LinkedIn to find contact information. For this reason, it's imperative to include your phone number.

Believe it or not, there are some people who have concerns about adding their phone numbers on their profiles. You might think their concern is rooted in a fear of identity theft, but instead they are more scared of telemarketers!

Yes, by listing your phone number on your profile you may receive a cold call from a salesperson, but you may also receive a call regarding your dream position or an amazing partnership. Are you willing to dismiss potential opportunity because you would prefer to not get bothered by a salesperson?

Success on LinkedIn is getting off LinkedIn. Strong relationships are forged in the real world. Don't be afraid to leave the digital comfort of LinkedIn for a real-world connection. Add your phone number to your profile and make it easy for people to contact you.

TIP

There is another option if you aren't comfortable putting forth your phone number. Consider registering for a Google Voice number and listing that number on your profile instead. Google Voice (www.google.com/voice) is a free service that provides you with a virtual phone number. You may have it forward to your actual phone number or go straight to voicemail. It's an easy way to provide a number while still maintaining your privacy.

Adding your IM address

The next information field is IM, which stands for *instant messaging*. Instant messaging is a way to send and receive short text-based messages instantly either by phone or by using a chat client on your computer. The instant messaging types that LinkedIn accepts are:

>> AIM (AOL)

>> GTalk (Google Talk)

>> ICQ

>> QQ

>> Skype

>> WeChat

>> Windows Live Messenger

>> Yahoo! Messenger

You may choose up to three IM addresses to list. If you have an old AIM username but never use it, don't add it. If you don't IM, leave the field blank.

TIP

Skype is a great IM to add. Not only is it free, but many companies use Skype as an integral part of the hiring process. Skype is used for virtual job interviews. By including a Skype username, you are showing that you are easily available to recruiters and hiring managers and you won't require much help to get up and running. That's definitely a bonus for busy recruiters or human resources professionals. If you don't have a Skype account, don't worry. It's easy to register. Simply visit www.Skype.com and register for a free account.

To add an IM address, follow these steps:

1. **Open your LinkedIn profile.**

2. **Click Contact Info.**

    The Contact Information section expands to show the contact information fields.

3. **Hover your mouse pointer over the IM field and click the pencil (edit) icon.**

    You are now in edit mode where you see empty fields for up to three IM addresses.

4. **In the first IM field, select the IM type from the drop-down list.**

5. **Add your handle or username in the open field.**

   Repeat Steps 4 and 5 to add up to two more IM addresses.

6. **Click the Save button.**

Adding your work address

The Address field in the Contact Information section is for your work or office address. If you work from home, omit the street address and enter just your city, state, and zip. This way people can't get door-to-door directions to your house, but they will know where you are generally located.

If you work from an office complex, but are still hesitant to enter your address on your LinkedIn profile, you may leave the address field empty. However, I've found that the people who hate to add their office address on LinkedIn somehow have no problem tossing their business card into a fish bowl to win a golf club raffle.

To add your work address, follow these steps:

1. **Open your LinkedIn profile.**

2. **Click Contact Info.**

   The Contact Information section expands to show the contact information fields.

3. **Hover your mouse pointer over the address field and click the pencil (edit) icon to enter edit mode.**

4. **Enter your office address information.**

5. **Click the Save button.**

Adding your Twitter account

Not only can you add your Twitter account so people know how to find you on Twitter, you can also enable cross-posting between these two awesome social networks. By linking your Twitter account with your LinkedIn account, you are able to kill two birds with one stone. When you post a LinkedIn status update, you can have that status message go to both LinkedIn and Twitter.

This cross-posting only goes in one direction: from LinkedIn to Twitter. If you want LinkedIn to post your Twitter updates, you need to use a third-party social media aggregator such as Hootsuite (www.hootsuite.com).

To set up this cross-posting ability, you must have a Twitter account already established. If you have more than one Twitter account, you are in luck — LinkedIn allows you to add multiple Twitter accounts.

TIP

If you use Twitter for primarily personal reasons, you should opt not to connect it to your LinkedIn profile. LinkedIn is a professional network. You don't want to lead professional connections to your Twitter account where they can read your tweets about television programs, sports teams, or see pictures of your kitten. On the other hand, if you are tweeting your knowledge, providing advice, directing people to interesting articles, and adding value, absolutely connect your Twitter feed to LinkedIn. Here's how:

1. **Open your LinkedIn profile.**

2. **Click Contact Info to expand the Contact Information section.**

3. **Hover your mouse pointer over the Twitter field and click the pencil (edit) icon to enter edit mode.**

4. **Click Add Your Twitter Account.**

5. **Click the Authorize App button to allow LinkedIn to access the Twitter account you are already currently logged into.**

   Once your Twitter account is successfully linked, you may need to provide your Twitter username and password. You will see it listed in the Contact Information section.

6. **Choose who can see your Twitter account by clicking the drop-down list under your Twitter account name and choosing Everyone or No One, as shown in Figure 5-9.**

   I strongly recommend selecting Everyone unless your Twitter account is used for personal activity. In that situation, choose No One.

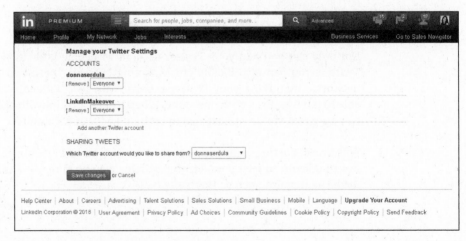

FIGURE 5-9:
Managing your
Twitter settings
within LinkedIn.

7. **If you add more than one Twitter account, select the preferred account LinkedIn uses to share status updates from the drop-down list.**

8. **Click Save Changes.**

Adding WeChat

I had never heard of the WeChat chat client until LinkedIn added it as an option within the Contact Information section. WeChat is popular in China; it's one of the few mobile chat clients the government allows. If you are not familiar with WeChat and don't want or have a WeChat account, feel free to skip this section. If you are already a WeChat user, you can link your WeChat username and QR code to your LinkedIn profile. Here's how:

1. **Open your LinkedIn profile.**

2. **Click Contact Info to expand the Contact Information section.**

3. **Hover your mouse pointer over the WeChat field and click the pencil (edit) icon to enter edit mode.**

4. **Click Add WeChat account with QR code.**

   A QR code displays on your screen.

5. **From the WeChat app on your mobile device, tap Discover and select Scan QR Code.**

6. **Scan the QR code displayed on your LinkedIn profile screen.**

   A confirmation message appears across the top of your Settings page that says you've successfully connected your WeChat with your LinkedIn profile.

7. **Click the edit icon next to WeChat to manage account visibility, and then place a check mark next to Display Your WeChat Account on Your LinkedIn Profile, as shown in Figure 5-10.**

FIGURE 5-10:
Managing
WeChat visibility.

8. **Click Save Changes.**

Adding websites

In addition to all of the other types of contact information, you can also add three website links to your LinkedIn profile. If you have a blog, a company website, an online portfolio, or some other Internet destination, this is the place to add the URL.

When you get into the edit mode of the website area, you see there are two text fields for each website, as shown in Figure 5-11. The first field is a drop-down list for the anchor text, and the other is a text field to enter the website's URL. *Anchor text* refers to the hyperlinked words on a web page. These are the underlined words you click that link you to another website. The drop-down list choices for the anchor text are:

>> Personal Website

>> Company Website

>> Blog

>> RSS Feed

>> Portfolio

>> Other

FIGURE 5-11:
An empty website section.

TIP

You could choose from LinkedIn's drop-down list — it makes sense to choose Personal Website, Company Website, or Blog — but how boring and non-descriptive is that? Instead of accepting the default choices, my recommendation is to ignore all of those choices and instead go with Other. By choosing Other, you are able to enter in more descriptive text to customize your anchor text. Customizing the hypertext helps your reader identify the link easily and makes the link more attractive to click.

Instead of choosing Company, type in the name of the company. For example:

> *Vision Board Media's Website*

Instead of choosing Portfolio, describe exactly what the person will find when clicking the link:

> *Portfolio of Business Headshots*

Instead of choosing Blog, get more descriptive:

> *Supply Chain Mgmt Articles*

Notice how I abbreviated Management? You only have 30 characters available for anchor text so you must be brief.

Check out Figure 5-12 to see how an optimized website section appears in edit mode.

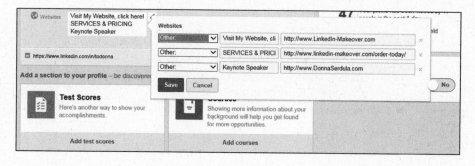

FIGURE 5-12:
This is how an optimized website section appears in edit mode.

To enter up to three website URLs to your LinkedIn profile, follow these steps:

1. **Open your LinkedIn profile.**

2. **Click Contact Info to expand the Contact Information section.**

3. **Hover your mouse pointer over the Websites field and click the pencil (edit) icon to enter edit mode.**

4. **Click the down arrow next to the first drop-down list and choose Other.**

   An additional text box to enter your website title appears.

5. **In the Website Title text field beside the drop-down list, enter the hyperlinked text.**

6. **In the URL text field, enter the URL of the website.**

   Be sure to type the full URL including http://www.

7. **Repeat Steps 4–6 for up to two additional websites and then click Save.**

In the next chapter, get ready to *vogue*! I show you everything you need to know to take a professional profile picture that impresses. Let's go!

IDENTITY THEFT: FEAR IS LEGITIMATE BUT NOT CONCERNING

Identity theft is a legitimate fear. Having your contact information and career trajectory out there for the world to see could invite nefarious behavior from evil people. The thing to remember is that there are over 400 million people on LinkedIn. Identity theft could happen, but with that many people utilizing the service, there are better people than you to target. Plus, you aren't putting your Social Security number out there. (Never put your Social Security number on social media!)

My recommendation is to be smart. Don't list your home address. Instead, simply add your city, state, and zip code. Don't upload your resume to your profile. Instead, let people know they can request it via email or LinkedIn messaging. Don't add your birthdate. Keep the more important information secure, but don't remove the information that prevents opportunity.

» **Choosing and uploading your profile picture**

» **Deciding between a selfie or professional photographer**

» **Presenting yourself in the best professional light**

Chapter 6

Impressing with the Right Profile Picture

Your LinkedIn profile picture is an integral part of your personal branding statement. It's imperative that you get it right, and yet so many people get it wrong. The highest-level executive uploads a snapshot of himself wearing a Hawaiian shirt. A smart entrepreneur uses a photo from her friend's wedding and crops out three-quarters of her date's face. The professional who can manage complex projects chooses a photo of himself holding the family pet.

Your LinkedIn profile picture should showcase you as a professional who commands respect. This chapter walks you through the steps of finding just the right profile picture that presents you in the most professional light and elevates your professional brand. You learn why you need a great photo, how to take your own photo, how to work with a photographer if you get a professional photo taken, and how to upload your photo to LinkedIn.

Why You Need a Profile Picture

Your LinkedIn profile picture can either help or hinder your success on LinkedIn. According to LinkedIn's official blog (https://blog.linkedin.com), profiles with profile pictures get 11 times more views than profiles without a photo. You are also 14 times more likely to be viewed on LinkedIn if you have a profile picture.

The inclusion of a professional profile picture shows the world you are a serious LinkedIn user and networker. It's hard to trust the authenticity of a profile without a photo.

Imagine you are shopping online and the item you want to purchase is for sale, but a photo hasn't been included in the listing. Would you buy it? Not usually! It's hard to trust a sales listing without a photo. The same thing goes for a profile without a profile picture. A professional picture shows your reader that there is a real person behind the profile, and that you are on LinkedIn for business purposes.

REMEMBER

Profile pictures are not just relegated to your profile. When your profile appears in search results, your picture shows up next to your name and subliminally implores your reader to "Read all about me!" Profile pictures also appear along with your LinkedIn Group messages, Network Updates, recommendations, and more.

Because your profile is used in so many places, it really is your digital stand-in. Your profile picture is your visual impression with your network. Although it's important to look good, you don't need to look like a supermodel. Your picture should capture the image of a professional person who looks friendly, clean, and well-adjusted.

Determining If You Need a New Profile Picture

Not sure if you are using the best profile picture? It is difficult to see yourself as others see you. I've created a list of questions to help you determine whether it's time for you to replace your profile picture.

THE DO'S AND DON'TS OF PROFILE PICTURES

Do's

Have a professionally taken photo.

Look straight into the camera.

Use a plain, indistinct background.

Dress professionally.

Zoom in close, frame your face!

Don'ts

Use a picture taken at a wedding.

Wear sunglasses or look away from the camera.

Have a distracting, busy background.

Wear a bathing suit.

Use a full-length shot or have others in the frame with you.

Open your LinkedIn profile and try to look at your profile picture objectively. Answer each question with either Yes or No:

>> Is your profile picture over three years old?

>> Was your profile picture snapped at a family gathering, such as a wedding?

>> Does your profile picture contain another person in addition to yourself?

>> Are there remnants of another person cropped out of your profile picture?

>> Are there animals in your profile picture?

>> Are you wearing a hat or sunglasses in your profile picture?

>> Is your profile picture of a cartoon character, business logo, symbol, or artistic representation?

>> Can you easily discern the background of your profile picture?

>> Are you looking up or down or anywhere other than straight into the camera's lens?

>> Is the quality of the image grainy or dark?

>> Do you look serious (not smiling)?

>> Are you wearing a T-shirt, bathing suit, or jeans in your profile picture?

>> Are your elbows or knees visible in your profile picture?

>> Did you have someone other than a professional photographer take your profile picture?

If you answered "yes" to any of the questions, it's time to get a new profile picture. Even if you answered "no" to all of the questions, there is a good chance you still need a new profile picture. You may be happy with your current picture, but does it truly cast you in the best light? If you aren't sure, keep reading!

TIP

A powerful LinkedIn profile picture is cropped, centered, and recently taken. The image is not too dark, grainy, or taken from afar. Most important, you are the focus of the photograph, and the image spotlights you as a professional!

Using a Photo Already Taken

There are rare occasions when people have a photo already taken that works well as a profile picture. Typically, they have already visited a photographer and had a business headshot taken. Sometimes people have a picture that was snapped at an event or while they were on stage giving a presentation. Perhaps you have a photo from your website's About page that is part of your brand, and you use it across all your social media profiles.

At one time, the rule of thumb was to use the same photo across all of the social media sites — Facebook, Twitter, Instagram, and so on. Now, having that one consistent photo isn't necessary. Each social media site has a different viewpoint and audience. If you use Facebook for family and like to stay more personal, use a personal, informal picture for your profile picture there. It doesn't need to be the same one you use on LinkedIn.

As long as the photo you want to use is professional-looking and casts you in the right light, go ahead and upload it. However, if you are doing this because you are cheap or so busy you don't have time to get a new, better picture taken, stop and keep reading. Your profile picture is an investment in your brand and your future self. Many of my clients fight me over getting a profile picture, but once they have a great one taken, they are amazed at the results and how often they are able to use it even beyond LinkedIn.

Working with a Photographer

A professional photographer has the right equipment and a trained eye and knows how to capture everyone in the best possible light. And the real secret is that most professional photographers are quite affordable! Remember, this is an investment into your future, and it's worth spending money to make yourself look your best.

I know it's hard for busy professionals to find the time to schedule a session with a photographer. As tempting as it might be to ask the photographer to come to your office, resist that urge. Go to the photographer's studio where she has professional lighting and attractive backgrounds.

The right photographer is most likely just down the street from you. All you need to do is an Internet search for photographers in your city or town. Once you have a list of potential photographers, it is important you check out their websites and look at examples of their work. As you peruse their online portfolios, think in terms of the end results. Are you impressed with their work? Do they have good examples of business headshots they've already taken? The photographer may do impressive work with brides and children, but that doesn't mean he can do a professional headshot well.

WARNING

I have a number of clients who chose to go to a department store or a big-box store with a portrait studio for their headshots. In almost every case, the quality of the resulting headshot is embarrassingly bad. The reason for this is that although the photographer at these places is using professional equipment, often the person taking the headshot is not a trained, professional photographer.

Most surprisingly, when all is said and done, these sessions cost about the same as an independent photographer. My recommendation is to use a professional photographer and stay away from the shopping mall.

PROFESSIONAL PHOTOGRAPHER RATES

Photography rates vary by region. A photographer in New York City is going to cost more than a similar photographer in Tupelo, Mississippi. Photography is a creative service, and most photographers set their prices by their reputations. The better the photographer, the higher the cost of his or her session.

Expect to pay somewhere in the ballpark of $100 to $500 a session. You may then have to pay extra for the actual retouched photo or any additional shots. In some instances, expect to pay even more than that. I once spoke to a photographer who charged well over $1,000 for a session. She may have charged a lot, but she guaranteed you would get an amazing portrait that conveys your professional brand and truly impresses.

You may find that you are able to obtain a photographer at a much lower cost. In this situation, do make sure you get examples of his or her work before booking. Remember the adage: You get what you pay for.

Taking Your Own Profile Picture

Professional photographers are really not that expensive. The investment is worth it. Of course, I can say this until I am blue in the face and people still just want to do it themselves. If I haven't yet convinced you to hire a professional photographer to take your headshot, here's how to take a professional-looking profile picture yourself.

My motto when it comes to your profile picture is: Just say no to the selfie. When taking a picture of yourself, it's hard to get enough distance between you and the camera; arms are only so long. When taking selfies, people often look at their images on the camera screen, rather than at the camera lens, thus the resulting image looks slightly off. Plus, it takes a *lot* of pictures to get the right one. If your arm doesn't give up from holding the camera for so long, you might get tired running back and forth from the tripod holding your camera.

The solution is to enlist a friend to take the photo for you. This way you can concentrate on posing and smiling and leave the actual photography to someone else. The less stress you are under, the better you look.

Professional photographers have professional equipment. Sometimes you are lucky to have a digital single-lens reflex (DSLR) camera or know a friend with one. In that situation, consider yourself lucky. When you don't have access to good camera equipment, use what you own. A good point-and-click digital camera or even your smartphone works. When working with amateur equipment, make up for it with good lighting, which I discuss next.

Understanding the importance of light

Good lighting makes all the difference between a great photo and a horrible one. When having your picture taken by a professional, studio lighting can work wonders. When you have a friend taking your photo, and professional lighting isn't available, find an area with lots of natural light. Avoid using the camera's flash or direct sunlight, as both cause harsh shadows.

Good professional photographers make sure to capture a reflection in your eyes from the lights. It's called a "catch light." Without that reflection, eyes look dull (see Figure 6-1). When taking the picture yourself, try to create your own catch light by turning on a nearby lamp. If you don't have a bright enough lamp, add the reflection afterward in a photo editor.

FIGURE 6-1:
A catch light makes the eyes in the left image pop more than those in the right.

Finding the right background

Distracting backgrounds can immediately derail a fantastic picture. When choosing the background, remember that you are the focus of the picture. The background should be as plain and indistinct as possible (see Figure 6-2). When you are taking the picture yourself or with a friend, look for a plain wall to serve as the background. If you are an avid decorator and can't find a wall that isn't full of pictures, consider taking the frames down temporarily. You can always use a photo editor if picture hooks show up in the final image.

When working with a professional photographer in her studio, there should be many different backgrounds available. Avoid backgrounds that are busy or overly colorful. Bamboo trees, laser light shows, and clouds are all backgrounds to pass on. A plain, white background often looks great, but I've also seen black backgrounds look lovely. Use your best judgment when selecting. Take into account the color of your outfit. If you are wearing white, a white background looks odd. Feel free to ask photographers their professional opinions. They do this for a living and are able to guide you.

FIGURE 6-2:
The good, the bad, and the ugly of photography studio backdrops. Less is always more!

Good   Bad   Ugly

Framing the shot

There are many considerations to make when framing your shot. The camera should be around your eye level. You do not want shots taken at too low of an angle or too high of an angle. Too low of an angle makes you appear looming; too high of an angle makes you look diminutive and subservient.

WARNING

Don't zoom in too close just yet. Keep space around your head so you have more cropping options later. The final image on LinkedIn is a perfect square, not a long rectangle. Zooming in too close or shooting with a long rectangle in mind may produce an image that can't be cropped later for LinkedIn's dimensions.

You will not get your ideal photo in one click. It may take hundreds of shots before you get the best picture. Time and time again, my clients come back and tell me that the winning photograph was taken at the very end of the session. It's not a coincidence. Right around the time you start to feel comfortable in front of the camera is when the best picture is snapped. So be patient and stay calm.

As the camera clicks, move around a bit. Keep your shoulders angled, not squared, with the camera. Jutting your jaw out may feel odd but it tightens your jawline and stops that pesky double chin. Vary your expression but always look at the camera. Think in your mind: happy, friendly, confident, calm.

Please smile. The goal is to look professional, not serious. Striving to look serious by not smiling only makes you look angry and unapproachable. When you smile, let your eyes crinkle. A genuine smile engages the entire face. Scared your crow's feet will show? That's what you are aiming for! A smile without eye wrinkles isn't genuine.

Once you have worked your inner supermodel for about 5 to 10 minutes, ask the photographer to review the shots taken thus far. By checking the photos mid-session, you can see if what you are doing is working, and what changes you may want to make.

Finding the right outfit

The outfit you wear in your headshot can make or break your final profile picture. Luckily, a headshot is mainly just your head, so what you wear on the bottom isn't as important as what you wear on the top. Make sure whatever you choose fits well in the shoulders and neck because that is what shows in the photo. When deciding on what to wear, consider an outfit you might wear to a client meeting or a job interview. If you work at an office that does business casual, choose an informal outfit.

When I was starting out in my career, my mother told me, "Don't dress for the job you have, Donna, dress for the job you want!" So although your office environment is a casual one, you still may decide to opt for a more formal business outfit in your profile picture. This is especially true if you have higher aspirations for your career.

My recommendation is to bring two or three different outfits with you to your session. Often what looks nice in person, doesn't translate well to a photograph. By bringing a couple different outfits, you can salvage a studio session gone wrong by the wrong wardrobe choice.

When choosing your outfits, go with soft, neutral colors or stick with gray, navy, or black. If you like bold colors, go for it! Just keep it to one bold color rather than a huge palette of bold colors. Skip the ruffled shirts or crazy prints. Choose ties with either a solid color or simple pattern.

TIP

Here's a tip for men: wear a suit to the photography session. Take the first photos wearing the full suit. After a while, take off the tie, but keep the suit jacket on. Then for the final time remaining, remove your jacket and open the top button of your white shirt. By doing this, you get three different looks with one outfit: formal, semi-dressy, and casual.

People often think they need to remove their eyeglasses when getting their picture taken. I believe your glasses are a part of your brand. People are accustomed to seeing you in your glasses, and you should look familiar in your headshot.

Numerous studies have shown that glasses give the impression of intelligence and professionalism. You might not get a date as Dorothy Parker said, but at least you will get hired.

TIP

However, there can be a problem with glare. When you wear glasses in a studio, many times the glare of the lights reflect on the lenses. If you find this is the case, here is a solution: remove the lenses. Put the lens-free glasses back on your face and smile for the camera.

Choosing and Uploading Your Profile Picture

It's hard to see yourself objectively. When it comes time to choose the right photo for your profile picture, it's often best to ask for help. Friends and family or even colleagues often notice things you miss about yourself, and they can give you insight as to how you appear to others.

Photographers often provide you with a website that hosts all the shots from your session. Share this link with a friend and ask for his or her assistance.

Don't just ask any friend. Make sure you choose a friend who is business-minded and not afraid to speak the truth. There have been a few times where I had to very gently tell a client that the pictures taken were not of the best quality and they needed to be retaken. This is never a comfortable situation, but it's better to hear the truth than to upload a ridiculous-looking profile picture that has people wondering if you are possibly insane or a professional clown.

The final image should not depict a glamorous supermodel, but rather a friendly, happy, approachable, well-adjusted professional. Notice how I did not use descriptors like "serious" or "corporate." When striving for serious or corporate, people end up looking dour and sometimes even downright angry. Opportunities are not given to sourpusses who look sullen and disinterested. The final picture you choose should depict a person who is likeable, happy, and professional.

Cropping to profile picture dimensions

Once you have chosen your final image, it's time to crop it to the perfect dimensions for LinkedIn. When working with a professional photographer, it's a good idea to ask for high-resolution and low-resolution formats. The high-resolution image is for printing. The low-resolution version is for uploading to LinkedIn.

The ideal image size for LinkedIn is 400 x 400 pixels. Photos over 20,000 pixels in either width or height will not upload. The maximum file size is 10MB.

Crop to maximize your face in the frame. Aim for the top of your head down to just above your collarbone, with only a sliver of shoulder showing. By zooming in, you are getting closer to the viewer of your profile. Subliminally you are drawing them closer to you, showing you have nothing to hide.

Another reason to zoom is that the profile picture gets even smaller when viewing on the LinkedIn phone app. By maximizing your face, you are making it easier for people to see and recognize you on the smaller device.

LinkedIn accepts three file formats: JPG, GIF, or PNG. Which one is best? Go with either JPG or PNG. GIF allows for only a limited palette of colors, and you may find your picture looks odd when saved as a GIF.

Resizing and saving a high-res image

Is your final image too big? Whether the image straight out of your camera is too big or the photographer is unable to provide you the image within the proper dimensions, all is not lost. You can always open the file in Microsoft Paint or another image editor and resize the shot yourself.

Follow these steps to resize a high-resolution image in Microsoft Paint:

1. **Open Microsoft Paint.**

2. **Select File ⇨ Open and select the image you wish to resize.**

3. **Click the Resize button that appears in the Toolbar.**

   The Resize and Skew dialog box appears, as shown in Figure 6-3.

4. **Replace the horizontal and vertical dimensions with smaller dimensions closer to 400 x 400.**

   Do not skew the image! You must maintain its dimensions, otherwise the image may elongate or widen.

5. **Click OK to close the Resize and Skew dialog box.**

6. **Select File ⇨ Save As and save the image as a JPG or PNG file.**

FIGURE 6-3:
Resizing profile
picture in
Microsoft Paint.

WARNING

The proverbial "airbrush" is a wonderful thing. If used properly, retouching can make a good photo even better. However, if used improperly, retouching is detrimental. Retouching is best done minimally. Use it to hide dark circles, but don't zap away all of your crow's feet. Use it to hide a zit, but not to reduce the size of your nose. The final image needs to be of you. You don't want to upload an image of a stranger.

Uploading your photo

Now that you have your business headshot ready to go, here's how to upload it to LinkedIn:

1. **Open your LinkedIn profile.**

2. **Hover your mouse pointer over the profile picture area and click Change Photo or Add a Photo if you don't currently have a profile picture uploaded.**

   The Edit Photo dialog box appears.

3. **In the Edit Photo dialog box, click the Change Photo link that appears above the silhouetted picture LinkedIn uses as a space holder or your**

current profile picture. (If you don't currently have a profile picture uploaded, click the Browse button.)

A window opens that enables you to select your photo from your hard drive.

4. **Find your photo and click the Open button.**

A preview of the selected photo appears in the Edit Photo dialog box, as shown in Figure 6-4. Crop your photo by selecting the yellow square on the lower-right corner on top of your picture and resizing the square so that it fits your face, neck, and the top of your shoulders. LinkedIn crops your photo along that yellow dotted line.

5. **When you are happy with your photo, click Save.**

Your picture now appears on your profile page.

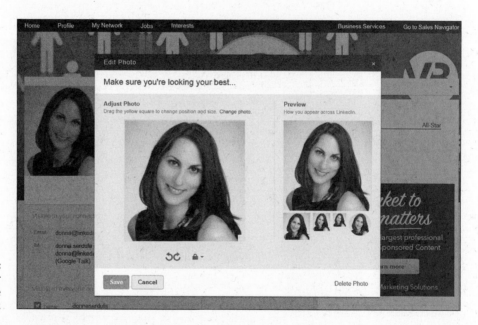

FIGURE 6-4: Uploading your new profile picture.

WARNING

LinkedIn strictly forbids uploading a profile picture that is not a photograph of yourself. The idea behind the profile picture is that it is there to help people recognize you. In Section 8.2 of LinkedIn's User Agreement (www.linkedin.com/legal/user-agreement) it states, "You agree that you will not: Use an image that is not your likeness or a head-shot photo for your profile." Therefore, do not upload photos of company logos, caricatures, cartoon characters, landscapes, animals, illustrations, words, or phrases.

Changing photo visibility settings

Some people are simply uncomfortable having their pictures appear in an online, public forum. When clients of mine objects to uploading their profile pictures, more often than not they are comfortable with their network seeing their pictures but not the whole world. Although I highly recommend making your profile visible to all, LinkedIn allows you some control over who sees your picture. You can't change visibility settings on a person by person basis, but you can choose between your first-degree connections, your LinkedIn network, or everyone. Here's how:

1. **Open your LinkedIn profile.**

2. **Hover your mouse pointer over your profile picture and click Change Photo.**

3. **Click the lock icon that appears below your profile picture, as shown in Figure 6-5.**

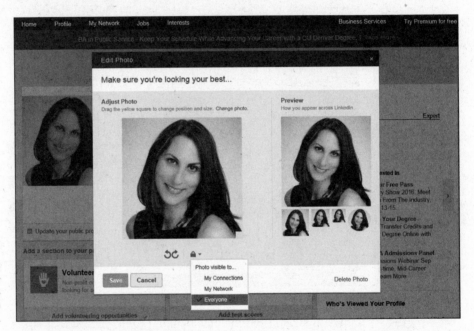

FIGURE 6-5: Changing the visibility options of your LinkedIn profile picture.

4. **Choose between My Connections, My Network, or Everyone.**

My recommendation is to keep it at Everyone, but if you only want people you are directly connected to see your picture, choose My Connections. If you would prefer only people within your LinkedIn network, choose My Network.

Now that you have an impressive profile picture, in the next chapter I show you how to maximize your LinkedIn headline for enhanced search and branding purposes.

Chapter 7

Developing a Compelling Headline

Your LinkedIn headline is extremely important. It is the shortened version of your profile. It shows up right underneath your name on the top of your profile, and it tells who you are in 120 characters or less. It is your readers' first impression of you, and it determines whether they read your profile or click to the next one. This chapter covers how to craft a compelling headline that grabs your readers' attention and makes them want to learn more about you.

Grabbing Your Reader's Attention

The LinkedIn headline is one of the main fields of a LinkedIn search result. It also appears at the very top of a LinkedIn profile. The headline also shows up on invitations to connect, above status updates, on LinkedIn messages, and within Group discussions, Pulse articles, recommendations, Who's Viewed Your Profile stats, and the People You May Know section. Since so many people have the potential to see it, you want to make sure your LinkedIn headline communicates your value and compels people to open your profile to learn more about you.

Your headline sums up your professional identity in just 120 characters (including spaces). You want this phrase to be catchy, bright, and clever. To grab your reader's attention, the headline should alert people to what you are about and how you can help them.

When you first create a profile, LinkedIn automatically populates your headline by using your current job title and company name. Although LinkedIn creates the headline for you, you can override this default, boring headline and add your own.

Take a look at Figure 7-1. See the difference between the default headline LinkedIn added and an optimized one? Which profile would you rather read?

Default and boring

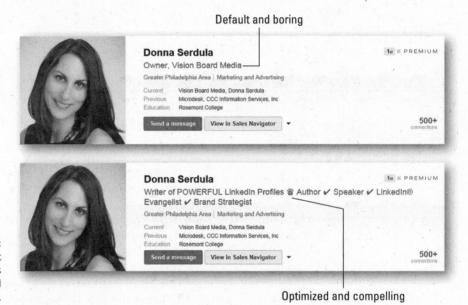

FIGURE 7-1:
The default
headline versus
an optimized
headline.

Optimized and compelling

Ditch LinkedIn's default headline. Your headline should be like a headline in a newspaper — it should compel people to want to read more. Read on to learn how to make your headline a compelling brand statement.

TIP

Adding Flair to Your Headline

A great way to really make sure your headline attracts attention and helps you stand out from the crowd is to use symbols. Take a look at Figure 7-2 for an example of a headline that makes use of symbols. See how boring the first and third headlines are when compared to the second optimized one?

FIGURE 7-2:
FIGURE 7-2:
The middle
profile pops
because of the
symbols in the
headline.

Although there are workarounds, LinkedIn doesn't make it easy to add symbols. In fact, LinkedIn doesn't allow any formatting at all. You can't bold, italicize, or underline text. LinkedIn hasn't ever stated why it doesn't natively allow formatting, but I believe they don't want to become like the old, defunct social network, MySpace.

Back in the early 2000s when MySpace reigned supreme, they allowed not just simple formatting but full on CSS coding to their profiles. Before long, MySpace profiles were twinkling and flashing like the Las Vegas skyline. Most people aren't graphic designers and when given the opportunity to format and prettify, they tend to go overboard. By not providing the ability to format, LinkedIn is keeping their users' tendency to overdo things at a minimum and thus keep their site elegant in its simplicity.

So how do you add symbols to your profile? If you are looking for a magic symbol button, you are out of luck. Instead, the way you add symbols to your LinkedIn profile is through copy and paste.

I discuss adding symbols to your LinkedIn profile in more detail in Chapter 9, when I discuss adding them to your job title, but for now, the easiest way to add symbols to your LinkedIn profile is to visit my LinkedIn profile to find a list of symbols you can use, then copy and paste the ones you like into your headline.

To add symbols to your headline, follow these steps:

1. **Open your web browser and go to** `www.LinkedIn.com/in/todonna`.

2. **Once at my profile, scroll through until you get to the Projects section.**

   I curated a list of different symbols you can use on your LinkedIn profile (see Figure 7-3).

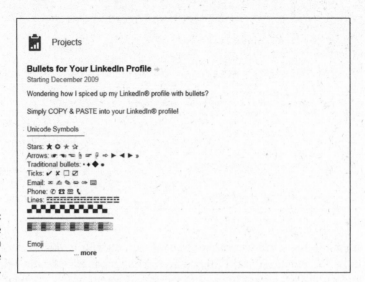

FIGURE 7-3:
Here are the symbols you can copy and paste from my profile.

3. **Highlight a symbol you like and copy it.**

   Copy by using the right-click menu or by pressing Ctrl+C (Windows) or Cmd+C (Mac).

4. **Open your LinkedIn profile and click the edit icon next to your headline at the top of your profile page.**

5. **Paste the symbol into your headline.**

   Paste by using the right-click menu or by pressing Ctrl+V (Windows) or Cmd+V (Mac).

6. **Click the Save button.**

   Your headline now includes the symbols you selected.

Although I have a curated list of professional symbols on my profile, it's by far not a complete list. If you want to see even more symbols, there are a number of sites to check out. Here are just a few:

Copy and Paste Emoji (www.copyandpasteemoji.com)

JRX (http://jrgraphix.net/r/Unicode)

Unicode Character Table (http://unicode-table.com/en)

Wikipedia Symbol Block List (https://en.wikipedia.org/wiki/Unicode_symbols#Symbol_block_list)

WARNING

Choose only one or two types of symbols to use in your LinkedIn headline. The more symbols you use, the cheaper and low level your profile appears. Remember, less is more!

Symbols may appear differently across the different devices and operating systems you use to access your LinkedIn profile. That means what you see isn't necessarily what another person sees when viewing your profile. Smartphones tend to take symbols and convert them to emoji. Emoji are small, colorful icons that are typically used to express ideas and emotions.

If you are viewing your LinkedIn profile on a PC, the symbols in your headline may appear black. Viewing your LinkedIn profile on a smartphone or on a Mac desktop, the symbols in your headline may appear colorful and almost cartoon-like. iPhones and Android phones use different art and so the symbols may look different depending on your smartphone.

TIP

When choosing symbols to populate your LinkedIn profile, the simpler the better. Stars, circles, squares, arrows, and check marks are universal and display with consistency across almost all devices. Using more complex symbols like those of folders, books, phones, paperclips, tools, and other items, you risk the symbol either showing differently on some devices or not at all.

Emoji are standardized, but the differences in display come from the different platforms (smartphone manufacturers, messaging apps, chat clients) designing their own emoji art and interpreting the standard differently.

I remember finding a symbol of a magnifying glass that looked lovely in my headline and on my PC's monitor, but unfortunately it didn't display for everyone. I received numerous emails from people telling me that instead of the symbol, they saw an empty block (see Figure 7-4).

FIGURE 7-4:
What happens when a symbol doesn't display.

As much as I loved using the magnifying glass icon, I had to replace it with a more universal Unicode character that displayed for everyone. When utilizing symbols, the best symbol may not be the right symbol. Choose simple symbols that display for everyone.

Saturating Your Headline with Keywords

As I discuss in Chapter 2, your headline plays a big role in LinkedIn search results. To enhance the likelihood of being found on LinkedIn, your headline should be chock-full of the keywords people are using to find someone like you. I've found that when performing a keyword search on LinkedIn, profiles that contain those keywords in their headlines turn up higher in the search results.

To create a keyword-saturated headline, you must first consider your target audience and why they are looking for someone like you. What are the keywords a person might type into LinkedIn search to find you? These are the words you want to incorporate into your headline. Get out that list of keywords you created back in Chapter 2. If you want to rank high for those words, it is important to work as many of them into your headline as possible.

If you are job seeker, it's important to add your job title to your headline. Your headline is extremely sensitive when it comes to search engine optimization (SEO). Many recruiters and hiring managers, when performing searches for talent, search for job titles. Make sure you include your title so that you increase your chances of being found on LinkedIn.

However, rather than simply stating your current job title, start with an adjective first and then add your title. Here's a bunch of adjectives to get you started:

Accomplished	Expert
Animated	Gifted
Certified	Holistic
Dynamic	Influential
Effective	Innovative
Energetic	Masterful
Engaging	Professional
Exciting	Skilled
Executive	Unabashed
Experienced	

Select one of these adjectives that you feel most accurately describes you in your current role. Then, it's time to add your job title.

Add your job title

Now that you have a good adjective to describe your current role, it's time to add your role/position/business title and follow it with a symbol. It should look like this:

> Accomplished Sales Professional *
>
> Experienced Human Resources Manager *
>
> Creative Marketing Director *

TIP

If you are not a job seeker and don't have a current job title, generalize your position: Healthcare Executive or Client Services Professional. The reason to use your job title is for search and identification. Always think of your target audience and what they need to know about you. Using your exact job title isn't imperative; the right keywords to find you are.

Add your specialty

The next item to add to your headline is another keyword. If you are a sales professional, what do you sell? If you are writing your profile for reputation management, what is your specialty? What are you known for? If you are a job seeker, what is your differentiator? What do you bring to the table that would make a company hire you?

Here are some examples of specialties:

> Accomplished Sales Professional * Office Supplies *
>
> Experienced Human Resources Manager * Organizational Development *
>
> Creative Marketing Director * Product Launches *

If you are struggling to come up with your specialty, think in terms of how people describe you. Do you hear people say things like, "That Tom, he's amazing at customer service!" Most times other people see us clearer than how we see ourselves. If you are struggling, ask other people what they think you do well.

TIP

I have found that most people are blind to their own strengths. Because strengths come rather easily, we expect that everyone else has these strengths — that they aren't unique to us. Talk to other people to get their input. Once you know what they admire about you, stop dismissing your strengths and start developing them into your brand message.

Alternately, when we are good at something, we often describe it in complex terms. When writing your LinkedIn profile, you need to think in terms of the layperson. Talking to others is also a great way to get a simplified view of what you do.

Here are some ideas for specialties:

App Developer	Information Technology
Branding	Internet of Things
Business Development	Marketing
Client Engagement	Product Development
Cloud Computing	Product Marketing
Content Creator	Project Management
Customer Care	Prospecting
Electronic Medical Records (EMR)	Real Estate Development
	SaaS
Financial Forecasting	Scientist
Google Analytics	Social Selling

TIP

Once you have your specialty, add a symbol. You can always use an asterisk (*) or a pipe (|) in the meantime. When your headline is completed, go back and copy and paste real symbols.

Add an extracurricular hobby

Now it's time to take a step on the personal side and add an extracurricular activity. By including a hobby or cause you care about, you turn yourself from a boring corporate creature into a three-dimensional human being. People do business with people, and showing your human side allows people to empathize with you. Here are some examples of headlines that include an extracurricular interest:

Accomplished Sales Professional * Office Supplies * Golfer *

Experienced Human Resources Manager * Organizational Development * Gourmet Foodie *

Creative Marketing Director * Product Launches * Classic Film Buff *

Add a happy ending

The very last piece of a keyword-saturated headline is a happy ending. Conclude your headline on a high note or with a clear call to action. Here are some examples of ending phrases for your headline:

>> Best in Breed

>> Curious? Read On!

>> I Make Things Happen

>> I Move the Needle

>> Learn More, Click Here!

>> Let's Connect

>> Looking to Positively Impact a New Organization

>> Click to Read My Profile!

This is what your keyword-saturated headline looks like:

Accomplished Sales Professional * Office Supplies * Golfer * Let's Connect

Experienced Human Resources Manager * Organizational Development * Gourmet Foodie * Game Changer

Creative Marketing Director * Product Launches * Classic Film Buff * Making Things Happen

REMEMBER

You only have 120 characters for your headline. If you didn't use all 120 characters and have more room, add more keywords! If you don't have enough room, remove the adjective and extracurricular activity.

Creating a Benefit Statement Headline

Instead of infusing your headline with keywords, another way to develop a compelling heading is to create a benefit statement headline. A benefit statement explains to potential readers exactly how you can help them and what they will get from working with you.

When crafting a benefit statement headline, ask yourself, "How do I help individuals or businesses?" "What benefit do others receive from working with me?" Think in terms of the outcome for your audience. If you are selling a service or product, why would a potential client buy from you? What do they get from the service or product?

Benefit statement headlines typically start with an action. Here are some examples:

Accomplishing	Growing
Changing	Helping
Crafting	Maximizing
Creating	Promising
Delivering	Reducing
Developing	Saving
Directing	Teaching
Eliminating	

Once you have the action, what is the core value you provide to your target audience?

A customer service representative might state: "Helping Turn Unhappy Customers into Loyal Clients." A sales person specializing in office supplies might state, "Keeping Offices Running Smoothly with a Complete Catalog of Office Supplies: Whatever You Need, When You Need it!" Individuals using LinkedIn to position themselves as technology thought leaders might use a benefit statement like: "Helping Corporations Embrace Cloud Computing Technologies to Enhance Workplace Productivity and Security."

TIP

When crafting a benefit statement, consider how your target audience reacts to you emotionally. What is it that you do that makes life/work easier and better for your target audience?

Think in terms of your target audience's need for:

Abundance	Peace of mind
Affordability/money savings	Prestige
Being liked	Productivity/time savings
Confidence	Respect
Convenience	Security
Ease of use	

Put these items together and voila! You have a benefit statement headline! To get you started, check out some of these examples of benefit statement headlines:

Insurance Broker & Agent ► Giving You Peace of Mind by Protecting Your Home, Car, and Assets

Financial Advisor ★ Taking Away the Guesswork from Investments ★ Helping You Plan and Achieve Your Future Goals

Real Estate Agent ► Helping Families in New York City Find the Home of their Dreams!

Sales Consultant ► Helping Businesses Develop Strong Sales Forces through Intensive Sales Training Programs

Are you looking for a new job? You can showcase your expertise and value through a benefit statement headline, too. You might be thinking, "But I am a job seeker; I don't help companies or individuals. I just do my job, when I have one." If you truly can't come up with a benefit statement, move back to the keyword-packed headline and go in that direction. However, everyone — no matter what job he or she does, provides value — otherwise, you wouldn't get paid.

TIP

If you don't work directly with clients, consider your colleagues and how you help them. Think also in terms of your department and how it supports the organization and moves the business forward.

Differentiation is also a benefit to employers. Do you provide more than others because of a unique talent, interest, or ability? Your benefit might be that you are bilingual or you are really good with numbers. Perhaps despite being steeped in technology you can effectively interface with sales people and get them to understand complex programs.

Here are some headline examples for jobseekers:

Software Engineer ► Building the Applications that Make Your Business Life Easier

Project Manager with a Passion for Coding and Technical Writing, Looking to Positively Impact a New Organization

IT Specialist Devoted to Creating Stable, Scalable Solutions for Small Businesses

Business Analyst ► Helping Companies Translate Their Business Goals and Ideas to Operational Reality and Positive ROI

Business Advisor ► Helping Manufacturing Facilities Realize Significant Gains through Process Improvement

Interim CEO ► Solving urgent leadership problems. . . when your CEO steps down, I step up!

Adding Your New and Improved Headline to LinkedIn

Now that you have your new and improved headline, it's time to update it on your LinkedIn profile. To add a new headline to your profile, follow these steps:

1. **Open your LinkedIn profile.**

2. **Click the edit icon next to your headline at the very top of your profile.**

3. **Type in your new and improved headline.**

   As you type, if text isn't appearing, you went over the 120-character limit. This means you have too much text and need to cut back.

4. **Click Save when you are finished adding your new headline.**

   Don't forget to add symbols to give your new headline some eye-catching flair!

Your newly updated headline is now acting like a welcoming beacon, directing people to view your profile. In the next chapter, I show you how to make sure that all these new visitors see an optimized experience section that is impressive and interesting.

LINKEDIN HEADLINE GENERATOR

It can be tough coming up with a headline on your own. If you need additional help, I created a free online application that walks you through creating a keyword-saturated headline. In less than 10 clicks of your mouse, you'll have a compelling LinkedIn headline to immediately copy and paste right into your LinkedIn profile. The generator even adds symbols to your headline automatically. Access the app here: www.linkedin-makeover.com/linkedin-headline-generator.

3

Detailing Your Career Trajectory and Creating the Ultimate First Impression

Chapter **8**

Getting Your Experiences Ready

The Experience section on your LinkedIn profile is where you explain your career path and highlight your background, successes, qualifications, and abilities. Most people immediately jump in and start adding experiences without thought to where they've been or where they are going in their career. Before you dive in and start adding your past positions to LinkedIn, it's important to take a step back and look at your complete career trajectory.

Many people, looking to save time, simply copy and paste their resume experiences directly into their LinkedIn profiles. Although copying and pasting from a resume does save time, it is also a huge mistake. The time you save will be made up in lost opportunity.

Not everyone is on LinkedIn for job search. It's important to make sure your Experience section matches your goals as well as your career trajectory. As soon as you paste in your old resume, whatever LinkedIn goal you have suddenly looks like you are desperately looking for a job.

However, when your goal is in fact job search, your LinkedIn profile and resume shouldn't be a one-to-one match. Instead they should work in tandem. The resume and profile should build off of each other.

When a person starts off reading your resume, he or she should want to check out your profile to learn more about you as a person. That profile should provide even more information and compel him or her to reach out directly to you. Conversely, if a person starts off with your profile, he or she should want to request your resume to learn more about your accomplishments and history.

When the resume and profile are a carbon copy of each other, the person reading them may ultimately become disappointed because you haven't shown them anything new or different, and he or she may suspect you have nothing more to provide them. In this chapter, I show you how to determine the career trajectory you want to showcase on LinkedIn. This chapter is all about the important strategic planning you must do before you begin the actual editing of your profile's Experience section.

Referencing Your Resume

As you sit down to work on the Experience section of your LinkedIn profile, it's a good idea to print out your resume. Your resume serves as a reference or outline — a tool to help you flesh out your experiences. If you don't have a resume, don't fret! It's easy to create an outline of your career arc. Simply get out a sheet of paper and create four columns with the following headings: Company Name, Job Title, Start Date, and End Date, as shown in Table 8-1.

TABLE 8-1   **Career Template**

Company Name	Job Title	Start Date	End Date

Then, fill in the chart with your current and past job positions. Start with your most current experience and then move backward in time. If you can't remember a date, don't worry! Skip it and keep moving, recording other positions. Once the list is completed, go back and research the dates and titles you can't remember.

The reason to get out your resume (or create an outline) first, is that it's important to have a master list. With a one-sheet overview of your career arc, you see how your career has unfurled and where it is heading. As you look back on your career, do you have any gaps in which you weren't working? If you were out of work for a year or longer, make sure you provide context around that time off. (See "Dealing with Employment Gaps" later in this chapter for more information on dealing with job gaps.)

Determining Which Experiences to Keep and Which to Merge

Remember, your LinkedIn profile is *not* your resume. Resumes are targeted for specific positions that you apply for. Your LinkedIn profile is your digital introduction, online reputation, and first impression. It should tell your professional story and compel your target audience to take a specific action.

I often see profiles that list a single company multiple times just to show career progression, similar to what is shown in Figure 8-1. Although this is a great way to spotlight promotions, it can look like you jumped around from one company to another, especially if the reader does not notice that all those positions were at the same company.

On the other hand, listing a company multiple times provides you with more opportunity for keyword optimization and potential for higher ranking in search results. The more job titles you have, the more keywords you use, the higher your profile will rise in the search results for those keyword combinations. You have to decide what makes the most sense for you. Do you want to have a high ranking profile? Or do you want to showcase the time you spent with a company?

REMEMBER

How you trace your career trajectory differs depending on your LinkedIn goals. If you are a job seeker, you want to make sure your profile echoes your resume closely in terms of positions and time periods. Recruiters and hiring managers often compare the two, and if they notice a difference, that's a red flag. If you are on LinkedIn for reputation management, highlighting each promotion with a new experience reinforces your successes.

It's less important to dredge up every success when you are on LinkedIn for sales and prospecting or even if you want to be seen as a thought leader. Think in terms of your target audience. What's important to them? Do they need to see every promotion, or is it enough to know you spent time at one company and rose through the ranks?

Once you have an idea of what is most important to your target audience and your goals, go ahead and delete and merge experiences (see Figure 8-2).

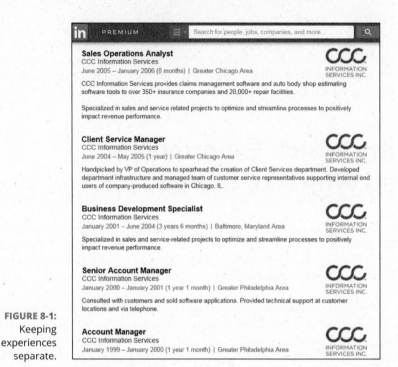

FIGURE 8-1:
Keeping
experiences
separate.

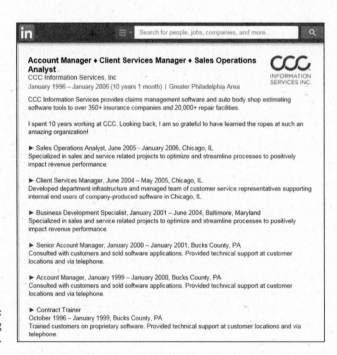

FIGURE 8-2:
Combining
experiences.

Keep your target audience in mind

When you are on LinkedIn for sales or branding reasons (such as reputation management or thought leadership), having a profile that echoes your resume isn't necessary. Certainly you always want to make sure that the information you share on your profile is accurate. But always think in terms of your target audience. As a salesperson looking to prospect and network on LinkedIn, does your target audience of potential clients care that you were promoted three times or made President's Club or that you closed $1.5M in Q1 of 2015, a 25% increase over the previous year? No! They want to know about the services and products you sell and how those services and products help them. In this situation, you don't need to fill your Experience section with a long list of accomplishments and job descriptions. Instead, you want to write for your target audience explaining your role within the organization and how you help your prospects and clients.

On the other hand, if you are a salesperson who is looking to switch companies and you are hoping to intersect with job opportunities, your target audience is now recruiters and human resources professionals. In this situation, you want your profile to align with your resume and show enough information to get your target audience interested in learning more so that they request a full copy of your resume.

Ultimately, when you are on LinkedIn for job search, make sure your resume and LinkedIn profile align and that you include three to five achievements for your more current job experiences. If you are on LinkedIn for executive branding or reputation management, you may not want to concentrate on achievements, but rather showcase your career trajectory and provide a high-level overview of your accomplishments. By providing a high-level overview and not drilling into minutiae, you are differentiating yourself from most other LinkedIn users, especially job seekers. Remember, it's all about what your particular target audience needs to know about you. If you are using LinkedIn for executive branding, your target audience isn't interested in granular, detail-oriented accomplishments as much as your full career trajectory and background. By providing too much information, you may seem like you are in job search mode.

Salespeople should show at least three total positions, but they don't need to go into detail as to their job descriptions or accomplishments unless they also have a desire to attract other job opportunities. Prospects don't want to know that you can sell snow to an Eskimo.

Salespeople looking to use LinkedIn to prospect and sell more effectively can use their current experience descriptions to instead talk about their company and the benefits of their products or services. The job description is also a great area to detail a customer success story.

How far back do I go?

If you have been in business for the last 30 years, it's not necessary to go all the way back to the 1980s. When you started your career, the Internet, technology, and business were different. Also, over 30 years, careers tend to shift and go in different directions. Look at your career path and decide what positions have helped you get to where you are today. Which positions continue you on a forward trajectory into the future? Those early, beginner positions can probably be merged into one position or discarded completely.

It's important to be smart when you identify and document your career journey. Even though you can decide when to start documenting, you always want to be authentic and as transparent as possible.

TIP

At the very least you should have one current position and two past positions. This helps you achieve an All-Star profile ranking, a way LinkedIn rates profiles. I talk more about profile ranking in Chapter 4.

Creating a Work History for Recent Graduates

A complete LinkedIn profile contains one current and two past positions listed in the Experience section. What do you do if you are a recent graduate just starting out in your career or a young professional with limited professional experience?

Don't worry; you can list internships and volunteer positions to flesh out your experience history. You may also consider grouping summer jobs together into one experience. By grouping low-level summer jobs together that are not relevant to your future job search, you are showing that you have employment experience, but you aren't shining a spotlight on jobs that aren't part of your career vision. It's far better to showcase non-paying internships and volunteer experiences over a summer job scooping ice cream. As your career develops, you can delete these positions when you add newer and better positions. Figure 8-3 illustrates an example of how recent graduates might fill out their Experience sections.

TIP

As a young professional currently working, you can break out your current experience to show any promotions you received so that it counts as two experiences rather than just one. By breaking out your experiences, you can achieve All-star profile ranking, which I talk more about in Chapter 11.

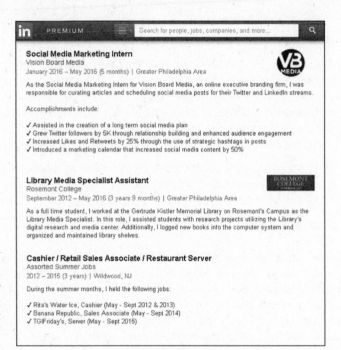

FIGURE 8-3:
An example of how a recent graduate might combine summer positions.

Dealing with Employment Gaps

The dreaded employment gap often keeps people up at night, but I have a fool-proof way to deal with it successfully. Whether you took time off to raise your kids, went back to school, nursed an ailing relative back to health, experienced sickness yourself, or just needed to rest up and enjoyed a radical sabbatical, it's best to explain the employment gap but not dwell on it.

The thing to remember is that employment gaps happen. Hiring managers and human resources professionals know that gaps occur; they just want to understand the reason around it. Mention the gap in the Experience section of your profile and provide context for your reader. It's important to convey that during your downtime, you stayed active in your career and community. List courses you took, books you read, or organizations you participated in. This information can either go in the position listed prior to the gap, or you can create a new position for the gap.

For example, here's how a person with an employment gap caused by a health crisis can explain it on LinkedIn.

Company Name: Health Sabbatical

Title: VP of Marketing

Time Period: January 2009 to June 2009

Description: It was in January of 2009 that I was diagnosed with cancer. The next six months were spent going through treatment and getting myself back to health. During this time, I stayed active in my career by keeping up with industry trends. I read marketing books and attended a number of online webinars. I also mentored a young professional I had hired prior to my diagnosis and am overjoyed that using my advice and support, she received a promotion six months sooner than typical.

Lastly, I took an online course, "Leadership Communication in Organizations," in which I earned a certificate. This four-week course delved into the different communication techniques innovative leadership uses within a corporate setting.

Once my cancer went into remission, I re-entered the workforce in June of 2009.

In this example, the title states *VP of Marketing*. You can't leave a job title blank; this field must be filled in. VP of Marketing is the position she held prior to her sabbatical and most likely is the title she holds upon reentering the workforce. By using her previous title, she reinforces her position and level and increases the chances of ranking highly for that keyword in LinkedIn search. Keywords placed in the job title hold greater strength than in other profile fields.

In the next chapter, I show you the structure of a powerful job experience and walk you through how to optimize your Experience section to really wow your reader and rank higher in LinkedIn search.

Chapter **9**

Creating a Powerful Experience

A powerful experience on your LinkedIn profile is different from a powerful experience on your resume. People are checking you out on LinkedIn to learn more about you. A powerful experience provides just enough information to compel your reader to want to learn more. For that reason, don't simply copy and paste your resume experiences into your LinkedIn profile. Instead, tell a story about your experience. In a conversational voice, explain to your reader your roles and responsibilities. Highlight a few accomplishments. Give readers something different from what they'd find on your resume.

If readers are so moved by what they see on your LinkedIn profile and they request your resume, the worst thing in the world is for your resume to look exactly like what they just saw on LinkedIn. You've left them wanting more only to give them a duplicate of what they already know.

In this chapter I discuss the perfect structure of a job experience description. I show you how to add a new experience to your LinkedIn profile and how to make sure the company logo appears on your profile. You find out how to optimize your job titles to increase your chances of being found. You also find out how to make your accomplishments stand out and wow your reader.

Adding a New Experience

Whether you are starting from scratch or updating your profile with your current position, it's important to know how to add a new experience to your LinkedIn profile. You don't need to worry about adding experiences in chronological order; LinkedIn automatically lists your positions by date, with the most recent on top, receding in time as you scroll down.

Here's how to add a new experience to your profile:

1. **Open your LinkedIn profile.**

   If you already have added an experience to the Experience section, go to Step 3. If you don't have this section on your profile yet, continue to Step 2.

2. **Click the Additional Info section that appears toward the top of your profile to add the Experience section to your profile page.**

   You may need to click View More to find this section.

3. **Scroll to Experiences and click Add Experiences.**

   When clicked, the Experience section appears on your profile within the Additional Information section.

4. **Scroll through your profile until you see the Experience section.**

5. **Click the +Add Position link that appears in the top right corner when you hover your mouse in the Experience section.**

   The Experience section immediately expands to show all of the fields that make up a new experience.

6. **Enter the name of the company where you worked:**

   a. *In the Company Name textbox, begin typing the company name.*

   As you type the name of the company, a drop-down list appears showing all of the companies that have LinkedIn company pages in LinkedIn's vast company page network.

   b. *If the company appears in the drop-down list, select it from the list to link the company to the LinkedIn company page.*

   If several companies have the same name, choose the correct company by confirming the accompanying logo to the left of the name.

   c. *If the company is not listed, select Add as New Company at the bottom of the company drop-down list.*

7. In the Title field, type your job title.

8. In the Location field, type the major city closest to where you worked.

As you type, a drop-down list of locations appears. Choose the location from the list. If the suggested locations are inaccurate, type in the city and state.

9. In the Time Period fields, enter the dates you worked:

a. *Click Choose to choose the month you started followed by a field for the year.*

b. *Enter an end date. If you are currently working at this company, choose Current.*

10. In the Description field, briefly summarize the company where you worked, describe your role and responsibilities, and list a few high-level accomplishments.

11. Click the Save button.

Your new experience is added to your LinkedIn profile's Experience section.

Figure 9-1 illustrates a completed experience.

Click to add another experience

STOPPING LINKEDIN FROM OVERWRITING YOUR HEADLINE

When you add a new current position, LinkedIn updates your LinkedIn headline to match this new job title. As soon as you click the checkbox next to "I Currently Work here," a new option appears directly below. This new option states, "Update my headline to:" and LinkedIn immediately fills in this field with your new job title, as shown in the following figure.

LinkedIn automatically fills this in

Uncheck to leave the current headline unchanged

This might seem like a wonderful idea, but your previous headline will be deleted. If you spent time creating an optimized headline, all that previous work will be lost. In addition, as I describe in Chapter 7, your LinkedIn headline should be different from your current job title. Your job title is just that, a job title. Your LinkedIn headline showcases who you are and it compels people to read the rest of your profile.

I recommend unchecking the "Update my headline to:" box and do not allow LinkedIn to update your headline to your new job title.

Making the start and end dates match your resume

One of the biggest blunders I see on LinkedIn profiles are discrepancies between a person's LinkedIn profile and their resume's start and end dates. If you are searching for a job, it's absolutely imperative that the information on your resume match your LinkedIn profile. Rather than create a one-to-one copy of your resume on your profile, instead, have your profile complement the information on your resume.

TIP

As you add new experiences on your LinkedIn profile, make sure the start and end dates match your resume. When there is a discrepancy between dates, the person reading may wonder if you are simply not a stickler for details or possibly lying. If you can't get the dates right, what else are you fudging?

Using month and year or just year

People often ask if they should use the month and year or just the year for their experiences start and end dates. If you are on LinkedIn with the goal of job search, I highly recommend adding both the month and the year. When a job seeker omits the month, it may send a red flag to recruiters, hiring managers, and human resources professionals. By using just a year, such as 2012, someone might think you started with a month or less left in the year. Most people omit months because they are trying to hide a gap. The best thing to do is own up to a gap and explain it in the job description section of your profile.

When people use LinkedIn for reputation management or to be seen as thought leaders and job search is the furthest thing from their mind, they may omit months if they so choose. When providing a simple trajectory of where and when, it's not important to get caught up in the exact month one's tenure began.

TIP

If you do choose to omit months, omit the months from all experiences. It looks sloppy and inconsistent when some experiences have a month and year and others only have years.

DEALING WITH AGE DISCRIMINATION

Age discrimination is a legitimate fear, and many LinkedIn users figure they can offset age discrimination by cloaking their age by omitting dates on their LinkedIn profile. A profile without dates is a profile that is clearly hiding something. Recruiters see this as unethical. In fact, when a profile is missing information, those who pass by it aren't discriminating against you because of your age, but because you aren't providing accurate information.

Omitting dates is not the right thing to do, but let's say you do it and manage to get asked to interview at a company that doesn't place value on age and experience. Your physical appearance gives away your real age when you show up at the interview. It doesn't matter how well the meeting with the hiring manager goes, you will never get the job. Age discrimination is out there and it's ugly. The good news is, just as there are companies that devalue age, there are plenty of companies who value your wisdom and experience.

Instead of hiding your age and experience, lead with it. Showcase your strengths, your knowledge, your experience, and your true self. You will get discriminated against by some companies and that's okay. Why waste your time on a company that doesn't respect you? The good companies that realize your value and strengths are out there and those are the companies to pursue. They will find your LinkedIn profile and love what they see. Don't hide your age; turn it into a benefit.

Getting the company logo to appear

Scrolling through a LinkedIn profile, it's hard not to notice the company logos sitting to the right of the experiences. These logos add flair and credibility to your profile. Most people assume that the way to get a logo next to their experience is to upload it. Truth is, LinkedIn adds the logo from the company's LinkedIn company page. What this means is if the company hasn't created a LinkedIn company page or didn't upload their logo to their company page, there is no way to add a logo next to your experience. And so if you long ago worked for a now defunct company, there is a very good chance you won't be able to add a logo. If you work for a company that doesn't embrace social media and they don't have a LinkedIn company page, you too are out of luck.

The good news is, it is easy to get a company logo to appear next to your experience as long as the company has a LinkedIn company page created and a logo uploaded. Here's how:

1. **Open your LinkedIn profile.**

2. **Scroll through your profile until you see the experience you want to edit in the Experience section.**

3. **Hover your mouse cursor over the experience you want to edit.**

   The entire experience is highlighted and an edit icon in the shape of a pencil appears to the right of each field within the experience.

4. **Click the highlighted area or the pencil (edit) icon to enter edit mode.**

5. **Directly under Company Name, click the Change Company link.**

   A blank field appears in the Company Name textbox.

6. **Type the name of the company where you worked.**

   A drop-down list appears with companies that match the letters you type.

7. **When you see your company name appear, click the name from the drop-down list to choose it.**

   By selecting the company from the drop-down list, you are allowing LinkedIn to dynamically link your profile to the LinkedIn company page. As long as the company page has a logo uploaded, it shows on your profile next to the experience.

As shown in Figure 9-2, by typing the name of your company into the Company Name field, a drop-down list appears. Selecting the name that LinkedIn provides creates a link that enables the company logo to display on your LinkedIn profile.

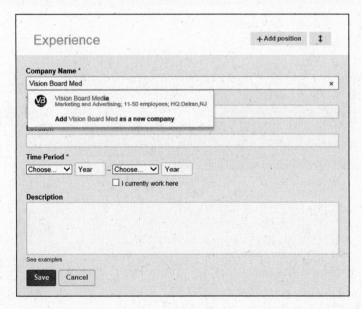

FIGURE 9-2:
Getting a company logo to show on your LinkedIn profile.

Linking to the company page

By linking the company name to the company's LinkedIn company page, you are creating a link from your profile to the company page. When a person clicks the logo or the company name from within your profile, the company's LinkedIn company page opens. When you create this link from your current experience to the company page, LinkedIn recognizes and associates you as a current employee of the company. A section of the company page shows viewers which employees the company is connected to. If you are connected to the viewer of the company page, your profile picture may be displayed.

TIP

The How You're Connected section of the company page is a wonderful way to find inside connections at companies you are interested in. The true power of LinkedIn is that it makes invisible connections visible. Because LinkedIn keeps track of your network and your network's network, you are able to see deeper into relationships and find inside connections that may help you.

When viewing a LinkedIn company page, it's easy to see how you are connected to people within that company (see Figure 9-3). By choosing the Company Name from the drop-down list, LinkedIn is able to link people back to the company page as employees. That's how when viewing a company page, you see who works there and how you are connected to them.

How you are connected to people in the company

FIGURE 9-3: The company page shows how you are connected to a company's employees.

There is a work around when you can't add a company logo. A client of mine worked at MTV China. When we went to add MTV China, only the mother company, Viacom, was available. It was important for my client to showcase his global experience and that meant displaying MTV China's logo. Because the logo wasn't available, only Viacom's, we simply added Viacom to the Company Name field and edited the display name to state MTV China. Then, within the experience we added the MTV logo to the experience. This logo didn't show to the right of the experience but right below the experience's description. It wasn't exactly what he wanted, but it was better than nothing.

Less Is More — Stop Disqualifying Yourself

I often see people filling their LinkedIn profiles to the brim with unending job descriptions and accomplishments. I never advocate an empty profile, but I do believe less is more. When you provide too much information, you may come across as desperate. Contrary to popular opinion, your LinkedIn profile does not qualify you for a position, but it may disqualify you. Saying too much may lower your chances of getting called in for an interview. The goal of your LinkedIn profile is to illicit action from your target audience.

As you write your job descriptions for each experience, write with the goal of getting people interested, whetting their appetite so they want to learn more. Don't give everything away upfront. You want to have enough information left in your back pocket for future conversations.

Summarizing the company with a boilerplate description

You have the company name filled in and the dates added to your experience. It's now time to start writing your company description. Rather than immediately opening with your roles and responsibilities, it's best to start by providing your reader with a quick overview of the company for which you work.

By providing a brief boilerplate description of the company, you are building credibility and providing your reader with important information. Everyone knows Apple, but not everyone knows Applebaum Associates. The best boilerplate language describes the company in the simplest and easiest to understand terms. It should be so clear that a child can understand.

Effective company boilerplate language may contain the following items:

>> Annual revenue

>> Headquarters location

>> Industry

>> Number of employees

>> Number of locations

>> Private company or publicly traded

>> Products and/or services

TIP

Don't wrack your brain trying to come up with this company boilerplate description on your own. Most likely this description exists elsewhere. You just need to find it, copy it, paste it, and then tweak it a little.

Let's find your company's boilerplate description:

1. **In any search engine, type the name of your company into the search field followed by the word *is*.**

   For example, "Applebaum Associates is" or "Vision Board Media, LLC is."

2. **On the results page, you should see a short description of the company:**

   Applebaum Associates is a Philadelphia, PA based accounting company that provides tax preparation services for thousands of small businesses located in the Delaware Valley area. Founded in 2011, Applebaum Associates has three offices and employees over 250 professionals. Applebaum Associates is often cited as a Great Place to Work by Philadelphia Magazine.

   This brief description is nearly perfect and you haven't even opened up the company's website. Sometimes a search engine fails to bring up an adequate description, in which case you have to dig a little further and visit the company website's About page to find a company summary. You can also visit the company's LinkedIn company page to find a brief company description.

3. **Copy and paste the company summary into LinkedIn's company Description field, as shown in Figure 9-4.**

4. **Tweak the company summary so it reads succinctly and incorporates just enough information to give your target audience the information it needs to know.**

It's simple to add a company boilerplate description to the experience's Description field. Just a few sentences provide the context a reader needs to understand more about the company and the work you did there.

By providing a brief company description, your readers now understand the context around where you work and it is easier for them to understand your roles and responsibilities as well as your accomplishments.

So what if you do work for Apple? Should you add a description that states:

> *Apple is a manufacturer of mobile devices and personal computers. With worldwide annual revenue over $233 billion, Apple employs over 80,000 people with offices and store locations all over the world.*

Absolutely not! It's silly to describe Apple. Instead of providing known information, focus in on the unknown by describing the department or division of Apple in which you work. Instead, mention the size of your department, the number of employees, what the division/department specializes in, and how it affects the overall business. Here's an example:

> *The Life Insurance division of Insurance, Inc., employs over 3,500 professionals and is responsible for 25% of the Insurance, Inc.'s total revenues.*

KEEPING WITHIN THE EXPERIENCE CHARACTER LIMITS

LinkedIn gives you 2,000 characters to describe each position in the Experience section. This translates to between 300 to 350 words. Aim for around 200 words per experience. Remember, you are not writing a novel.

It's a balancing act between too much and not enough. Showcase your top-level achievements, but don't go overboard. A person who is interested in learning more can always request your resume.

Describing your roles and responsibilities

Now that you have a boilerplate company description, it's time to dive into your role and responsibilities at your company. It's okay to pull out your resume and take a look at what you have listed, but you don't want to do a direct copy and paste. Instead, speak directly to your reader and describe your role within the company. This is where you provide an overview of the scope of your position. Do not use resume speak or silly corporate jargon. Instead, write in a first person, conversational manner.

Here are some sentence starters:

> In 20XX, I was brought on board to . . .
>
> I was handpicked for this position to . . .
>
> In this role, I . . .
>
> As the XXX, I specialized in . . .
>
> My role within the organization was to . . .
>
> During this time, I . . .
>
> I am most proud to have . . .
>
> My responsibilities included . . .
>
> It was during my tenure at XXX, that I . . .
>
> I was hired to . . .
>
> As the XXX, I was tasked with . . .

By describing your position in just a few sentences, you create context for your reader. Through this description you are painting a picture for your readers and they begin to formulate an idea of who you are and your capabilities.

Crafting an impactful achievement

With your roles and responsibilities described, now it's time to showcase the times you went above and beyond. Achievements describe projects and actions you performed that were exceptional and positively impacted your colleagues, clients, and ultimately, the overall business. This seems so simple, but most people have a hard time telling the difference between an achievement and a responsibility. Responsibilities describe your day-to-day actions. These are those duties that are minimally required of you to keep your job. Achievements describe not just the task but the results of the task.

If you have an up-to-date, professionally written resume, take a look at the achievements that are highlighted. Think in terms of your target audience. Which achievements are the most important to him or her? If you have 15 achievements listed under one position on your resume, you do not want to list all 15 achievements on your LinkedIn profile. First, you don't want to give away the farm to every single viewer of your LinkedIn profile. Second, you want to spotlight only the achievements your target audience finds most interesting and impressive. Aim for three to five achievements per experience. By showcasing only the top achievements, you are whetting your readers' appetites and providing them with a reason to reach out to learn more about you. When you overload your readers with too much information, nothing is left to deliver later.

Once you have chosen your top achievements, you want them to stand out. Because LinkedIn doesn't allow any formatting such as bolding or italicizing text, we need to do something different. Remember those symbols that you used to separate the keywords from your job title in the Title field? Copy one of those symbols again and paste it into your Description field. We are now going to use these symbols to create a bulleted list of accomplishments.

TIP

Make sure you hit the spacebar between the symbol and the first letter of the accomplishment. Also, you want to hit the Enter or Return key on your keyboard twice between accomplishments. This creates an empty line between accomplishments. Whitespace is important and helps make your profile visually attractive and easier to read.

Giving your reader a call to action

Your experience is just about perfect. You have a company boilerplate summary, a description of your roles and responsibilities, and a listing of your greatest accomplishments. What's left? Just one thing: a clear call to action!

Remember how I said we want to whet your readers' appetites and leave them wanting more? We now need to give them a reason to reach out to you:

For a detailed list of accomplishments, please request my resume.

By adding this sentence, you are letting your readers know that you have other accomplishments than just what you listed. You are also letting them know you are open to talking. In fact, if you are interested in job opportunities, you may want to also provide your contact information as well. People outside your first–degree network can view your profile, but if they aren't directly connected to you, they can't see your contact information in the contact information section of your profile nor can they easily message you. By providing your contact information, you are making it easy for that recruiter, hiring manager, or human resources professional to reach out to you.

Editing an Existing Experience

When optimizing your profile, it's not always necessary to add new experiences. Usually you just need to edit older experiences you have previously entered. In this situation, rather than deleting and adding new, you simply want to edit the experience and update it. Perhaps you want to optimize your job title or add an end date or include additional, new accomplishments.

To edit a previously created experience, follow these steps:

1. **Open your LinkedIn profile.**

2. **Scroll through your profile until you see the experience you want to edit in the Experience section.**

3. **Hover your mouse pointer over the experience you want to edit.**

4. **Click the highlighted area or the pencil (edit) icon to enter edit mode.**

    LinkedIn uses inline editing to update information on the profile page. As shown in Figure 9-5, simply hovering your cursor over the experience you want to edit brings you into edit mode. All you need to do is click within the highlighted area to immediately begin making changes.

5. **Make the edits to the experience by clicking your mouse and typing your new content.**

6. **When you are ready to save your work, click the Save button at the bottom of the edited experience to save your work and go back to your profile page.**

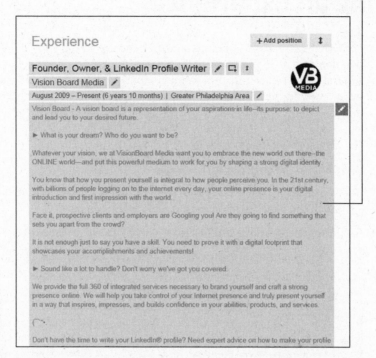

Edit mode

FIGURE 9-5:
Inline editing makes changing your LinkedIn profile a breeze.

Reordering Concurrent Experiences

I often get asked if it's possible to reorder experiences. The short answer is no. LinkedIn sticks with a straight chronological structure with the most current position at top and older positions cascading toward the bottom of the profile.

However, there is one exception to this rule: concurrent, current experiences. If you hold two current experiences at the same time, you can choose the order in which to list them on your profile. Here's how:

1. **Open your LinkedIn profile.**

2. **Scroll through your profile to the Experience section and hover your mouse pointer over the current position you'd like to rearrange.**

3. **Click and hold the Up/Down arrow to the right of your position name and drag it into the desired position.**

   When you reorder experiences, the top-most experience leads in the Current line in the top section of your profile.

Removing an Experience

Sometimes you want to delete an experience. Perhaps a job didn't work out and you don't want to highlight a short stint. Or maybe you added a promotion as a separate experience but now want to consolidate all promotions into one main experience. In these situations, you need to remove the experience. Here's how to do it:

1. **Open your LinkedIn profile.**

2. **Scroll to the Experience section.**

3. **Hover your mouse pointer over the experience you want to delete and click the pencil (edit) icon that appears on the right.**

4. **Click the "Remove this position" link, as shown in Figure 9-6.**

   The link appears to the left of the Cancel button. When you select this link, a dialog box appears asking you if you are sure you want to remove this position.

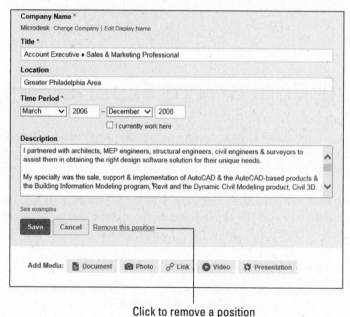

FIGURE 9-6: Removing an experience is easy!

Click to remove a position

5. **To permanently delete the experience, click Yes, Remove.**

    If you change your mind, click Cancel.

Reattaching Recommendations to Different Experiences

Recommendations are an important part of your profile. They create credibility and even respect. LinkedIn users should get at least a few recommendations for each experience they have listed on their LinkedIn profiles.

When it comes to optimizing their profiles and reorganizing and pruning experiences, the loss of an experience stops most people in their tracks. "I can't delete this experience; I have a recommendation attached to it! I don't want to lose those recommendations."

The good news is that recommendations are never lost when the position they are associated with is deleted. They simply become "orphaned" and need to be reattached to a new position.

Here's how to find orphaned recommendations and reattach them to a different experience:

1. **Open your LinkedIn profile.**
2. **Scroll to the Recommendations section.**
3. **Hover your mouse pointer in the Recommendations section and click the Manage button that appears on the right.**

    This takes you to the Manage Recommendations page.

4. **In the Received Recommendations section, find the recommendation you want to reassign, and click Reassign, as shown in Figure 9-7.**
5. **In the resulting window, select the position you want the recommendation attached to from the drop-down list, as shown in Figure 9-8.**
6. **Click Apply.**

    Your orphaned recommendation is now reattached to a new experience.

Click to reassign a recommendation

FIGURE 9-7:
Clicking Reassign
allows you to
reassign an
orphaned
recommendation.

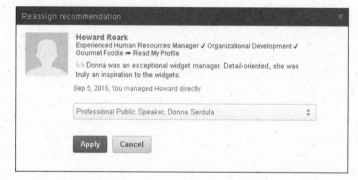

FIGURE 9-8:
Choose the
position to
reassign the
recommendation
from the
drop-down list.

Optimizing Your Job Title with Keywords

The Title field of an experience contains your job title, right? Well, right and wrong. Although most LinkedIn users complete this field with their job titles, they are missing an opportunity to optimize their profile for search and branding purposes.

REMEMBER

The job title is one of those high impact search engine optimization (SEO) fields within LinkedIn. (I discuss SEO in even more detail in Chapter 2.) When a person searches LinkedIn for keywords, LinkedIn returns profiles that match these keywords. When those keywords appear in the job title, that profile turns up higher in search results than a profile that just states that keyword in another less sensitive area of the LinkedIn profile.

In addition, the Title field is at the top of the experience and in a larger font size, so the field pops out at people scrolling through your profile. Truly catch their eye by including more than just your job title.

What do you want to add in addition to your job title? That's easy, keywords!

TIP

A common mistake people make is using abbreviations in their job title. If you are a job seeker, you may choose to play it safe, and so if your title can be abbreviated, enter it both ways. You don't want to list yourself as VP and miss out on appearing in search results because a recruiter searched on Vice President. For example:

VP / Vice President of Marketing

Many companies use different job titles for similar jobs. Some companies prefer using nebulous job titles, while others use job titles that are non-descriptive of the role or responsibilities. Although you never want to lie, it is acceptable to add a more common job title with more description to make it easier for your reader to understand. By using a more common job title, you also improve your chances of getting found by recruiters looking for specific job titles.

I've stated it before and I must state it again: Do not exaggerate or lie when it comes to your job title. Instead aim for more description to assist your reader. For example, look at the differences in these job titles:

BEFORE: *Customer Development Team Member*

AFTER: *Customer Development Team Member ▶ Customer Service Representative ◆ Client Assistance Specialist*

BEFORE: *Lead Generation Specialist*

AFTER: *Lead Generation ▶ Cold Caller ◆ Telemarketer ◆ Business Development ◆ Prospecting*

In the first example, the "Before" title did not adequately describe the job seeker's function. "Customer Development Team Member" might be the official job title, but this is not a common job title used across Corporate America. By adding additional, lateral job titles that are more common, the person is now not only describing exactly his or her role but also making it easier to get found.

In the second example, the job title, "Lead Generation Specialist" is descriptive, but by including a few additional keywords, this person is making sure he or she matches different search terms a recruiter or hiring manager might use instead, such as cold caller, telemarketer, business development, or prospecting.

Job title character limits

There are 100 characters available in the experience Title field. Use as many of these characters as possible. As you type into the Title field within your LinkedIn profile, you will know you hit your character limit because you will suddenly find that no matter what you type, your cursor only blinks and no new characters are added. In this situation you must backspace the word that is incomplete and determine what keywords you want to keep and which you want to remove.

Making your job title pop with symbols

Reading through the job title examples shown throughout this chapter, you may have noticed that they all contained symbols that separate the job title from the keywords and separate keywords from each other. Symbols are a great way to catch the eye and provide flair to your job title.

You can't format your LinkedIn profile. Bold, italic, and underlined text is not allowed. You can't even include a bulleted list. There isn't even a bulleted list option. Even though LinkedIn doesn't provide you with the ability to format text, you can add pizazz by using symbols.

So where do you find these symbols? In addition to the numbers, letters, and punctuation marks that you see on your keyboard, there are additional characters you can use. These extra characters can be added to your profile bypassing your keyboard.

Because directions to get to these symbols vary depending upon your operating system, the easiest way to add symbols to your LinkedIn profile is to visit my LinkedIn profile to find a list of symbols you can use. Here are the steps to do so:

1. **Open your web browser and go to** www.LinkedIn.com/in/todonna.

2. **Once at my profile, scroll through until you get to the Projects section.**

   I curated a list of different symbols you can use on your LinkedIn profile.

3. **When you find a symbol you like, highlight it, copy it, and then paste it into your profile**.

   Copy and paste by using the right-click menu or by pressing Ctrl+C (Windows) or Cmd+C (Mac) to copy and Ctrl+V (Windows) or Cmd+V (Mac) to paste.

In addition to using symbols in your job title and as a bulleted list, you can also use symbols for emphasis. For instance, add symbols around your call to action or use them to break up paragraphs.

Whatever you do, don't go crazy. Using too many symbols makes your profile look silly and juvenile. As they say in the fashion world, less is more. Choose one or two different types of symbols and use them sparingly throughout your profile. Symbols should spotlight your content, not detract from it.

Examples of Great Experiences

It's easy to describe how to do something, but it's not always so easy to actually take the instructions and do it. I'll try to get your creative juices flowing by providing some examples of optimized experiences. As you read each of these examples, take notice of the profile's goals, how each profile is written for the target audience, and how each incorporates keywords.

Salesperson looking for a new opportunity

Company Name: Corporate Leasing, Inc.

Title: Senior Business Development Executive ► Account Management ♦ Social Selling ♦ Prospecting

Dates: November 2007–July 2015 (7 years 9 months) Greater Philadelphia Area

Description: Corporate Leasing is one of the largest equipment finance companies in New Jersey. Providing commercial financing products and services focused on small and mid-size businesses, over 100,000 businesses have used our financing services.

I was initially hired as an Account Executive but in less than 6 months I was promoted to a Senior Business Development Executive. As a Sr. Business Development Executive, my primary job is to identify and close new business opportunities, collaborate with enterprise clients, and support existing clients.

Although I am thoroughly comfortable cold calling, I have found social media to be an amazing channel for prospecting. Utilizing Facebook and LinkedIn, I am able to forge online relationships that yield sales. Social Selling combined with traditional prospecting has allowed me to grow my territory by 200% over a three-year period.

Select major accomplishments include:

► Named Top Regional Performer for the last 2 years.

► My sales pipeline averaged 10MM. The typical deal size was 75K+.

► Closed the largest account in company history totaling over $1.5M over 3-year period

► Consistently attained 100%+ of quota.

If you are interested in learning more about my involvement in these areas, please feel free to connect with me on LinkedIn.

Salesperson looking for more prospects

Company Name: Corporate Leasing, Inc.

Title: Senior Business Development Executive ► Equipment Finance ♦ Commercial Financing ♦ Product Leasing

Dates: November 2007–July 2015 (7 years 9 months) Greater Philadelphia Area

Description: Corporate Leasing provides financing to businesses so they can acquire new equipment and technology while preserving capital. One of the largest leasing companies in New Jersey, Corporate Leasing is committed to helping small business grow.

In 2007, I came on board Corporate Leasing after having spent years focused on sales and marketing for small businesses.

As the Senior Business Development Executive for Corporate Leasing, I am responsible for providing small businesses in New Jersey with financial options that allow them to acquire the equipment and technology they need.

I love keeping in touch with my clients through social media and love providing learning opportunities for them as they grow their businesses.

If you would like to learn more about our company and services, please visit our website at CorporateLeasingInc.com.

Human resources professional using LinkedIn for reputation management

Company Name: Technology Startup, Inc.

Title: Senior Human Resources Manager ► Mergers & Acquisitions ♦ Retention ♦ Employee Relations ♦ Performance Management

Dates: 2015–2016

Description: Technology Startup, Inc., is growing by leaps and bounds. Founded in 2015, Technology Startup, Inc., provides the products and services that shape Startup growth.

In my role as Senior Human Resources Manager, I help support the successful integration of talent from newly acquired companies by focusing on successful onboarding and increasing employee satisfaction. In addition, I recruit top talent and specialize in employee development.

Accomplishments include:

✓ Managed the successful integration of over 100 newly merged employees by creating and delivering workshops and communication tools to educate this new staff of their role in our corporate culture. Attrition from the merger dropped by 75%.

✓ Introduced online tools and social media to the existing traditional tools of employment agencies and job fairs to recruit talent and successfully filled more than 250 positions in a record setting 3-month timeframe.

✓ Created and managed a new employee referral program, which resulted in higher employee referrals and new hires.

For detailed list of accomplishments, please request my resume.

With your Experience section optimized and brimming with impressive results, it's now time to turn to the Summary section of your LinkedIn profile. In the next chapter I show you how to craft a LinkedIn summary that acts as a digital introduction and striking first impression.

Chapter **10**

Writing a Compelling Summary

The Summary section of your LinkedIn profile is where you introduce yourself to your target audience and tell your professional story in a conversational manner. The Summary section is your digital introduction and first impression.

When attempting to write the Summary section, many LinkedIn members are immediately rendered paralyzed. Others find themselves wandering into their kitchen or garage, intent to reorganize. Any task, regardless of how odious, is suddenly more attractive than facing a blank Summary section with the goal of writing about yourself.

In this chapter, I show you how to easily write an impressive, goal-oriented summary that attracts and satisfies your target audience. I discuss why it's important to write your summary in the first person, and I show you how to format your summary so that people find it easy to read and attractive. I also give you the tips you need to conquer the Summary section so that you can get this monumental task off your back.

Editing Your LinkedIn Summary

It's best to draft and edit your summary in a word-processing program rather than directly in the LinkedIn summary text field. My team and I have written thousands of LinkedIn profiles, and more than a few times computers have crashed, Internet connections were lost, LinkedIn went offline, and summaries written in the text field disappear in a blip. It is horrible when it happens, and no amount of cursing or crying brings unsaved work back to life. I know this through direct experience.

The most popular word-processing program in the known universe is Microsoft Word. If you don't have access to Microsoft Word, don't panic. If you are a Mac user, you can use Pages for Mac. Google Docs works great regardless of operating system. Open Office is a free word-processing program that you can download and install. Do try to make sure that whatever program you select, it comes with spelling and grammar check.

After you write your summary in a word processor, copy it and paste it into the Summary section of your profile. Here's how to add your finished summary into your LinkedIn profile:

1. **Open your LinkedIn profile.**

2. **Scroll to the Summary section, hover your mouse pointer over the Summary section text box, and click the pencil (edit) icon.**

   You are now in edit mode, as shown in Figure 10-1.

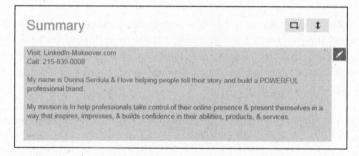

FIGURE 10-1: Editing your summary.

3. **Click your cursor in the text field.**

4. **Open the summary you composed in your word-processing program and copy it to the Clipboard by clicking Ctrl+C (Windows) or Cmd+C (Mac).**

5. **Return to your LinkedIn profile and paste your summary into the Summary text field by clicking Ctrl+V (Windows) or Cmd+V (Mac).**

6. **Click the Save button.**

Now that you know how to add your summary to LinkedIn, let's look at how to draft your best possible summary to catch readers' eyes and compel them to reach out to you.

Writing in First Person

You've probably seen LinkedIn summaries that start like this: "John Gates is a respected executive with an impressive track record of accomplishments . . . ." You know it's his profile. Either he wrote it himself or he copied and pasted it from a bio. Reading it, it feels strange and oddly off-putting. The reason you may react this way is because the profile was written in a third-person narrative voice. In a third-person narration, a narrator tells a story about someone else. Pronouns such as "he," "she," "it," or "they" are used to refer to the characters.

Because the LinkedIn profile clearly belongs to the person writing it, third person is inauthentic and disingenuous. As I mention in Chapter 1, LinkedIn is a social network, and its goal is for members to interact and forge strong relationships with their networks. By writing in third person, you create distance between you and your reader. Instead, be sociable and draw your reader in by writing in the first-person narrative form ("I"). Don't be afraid to use "I." Claim your story and tell it proudly in your voice.

WARNING

With that said, I must warn you, don't start every sentence with "I." It's a balance. Use "I," but don't overdo it. Check out the end of this chapter where I include examples of powerfully written LinkedIn summaries. All the summaries are written in first person, but none abuse "I."

Avoiding Resume Speak

It's hard to write about yourself. That's why so many profiles on LinkedIn are simply copied and pasted from old resumes. The problem then becomes the original resume. Few people actually work with a professional resume writer to create a succinct and clear history of their professional accomplishments. Instead, the majority of resumes use generic, general descriptions that don't spotlight accomplishments or tell an engaging professional history. Here's an example:

> *Results-driven and goal orientated professional commanding over 10 years of progressive leadership success. Top-performing, dynamic manager delivering track record of consistent achievements. Recognized strengths include excellent interpersonal skills, strong client relationship building, and leadership in the effective implementation and use of technology. Exemplary commitment to company and personal success, exhibiting strong leadership, problem-solving, communication, and technical skills.*

Reading that paragraph, do you have an idea what that person does on a day-to-day basis? Do you understand who this person is and what he or she loves to do? Do you have an idea of what industry this person works in, what type of job he or she has, or even what he or she is capable of accomplishing? Do you want to reach out to learn more? No!

That paragraph is a lot of gobbledygook words strung together simply taking up space. To create a powerful, compelling summary, stay away from resume speak. Write instead in a natural, conversational manner.

TIP

Read the paragraph out loud to judge whether it sounds natural or stilted. Ultimately, the goal is for readers to feel that you are speaking to them directly, telling them exactly what they need to know about you.

Even if your resume was professionally written, you still don't want to copy and paste it into the Summary section. Resumes are for job search. If your goal isn't job search, already your profile is portraying you in an inaccurate manner.

If you goal *is* job search, copying and pasting your resume still doesn't work. Let's say a hiring manager discovers your profile on LinkedIn after performing a search for the company's ideal candidate. The hiring manager is impressed and reaches out to you to request your resume. What happens when that resume is a one-to-one copy of your profile? That hiring manager is going to be disappointed.

Here's another scenario. Suppose you submitted your resume for a job listing, and the hiring manager decides to check you out on LinkedIn. Once again, the hiring manager wants to learn more about you, but he is getting the same information he already has in his possession. What a letdown! Here's your chance to make an impression and seal the deal, but instead, by recycling content, an opportunity may be lost.

By creating a unique and high level LinkedIn profile that extends your brand and delivers targeted content, each interaction with your target audience builds interest and confidence and propels the reader through to a successful conclusion.

Revisiting Your LinkedIn Goals and Target Audience

Before you begin writing your summary, it's important to remember why you are on LinkedIn and who is your target audience. As I discuss in Chapter 1, a powerful LinkedIn profile is written toward your goal and target audience. It's not what you want to say, but rather what your target audience needs to know. Your LinkedIn summary should connect to your audience and align with your objectives.

If you haven't already, write down your LinkedIn goal(s) on a piece of paper:

>> I want to find a new job.

>> I want to find new prospects.

>> I want to enhance my reputation.

Next up, who is your target audience? Try to be as explicit as possible. Who are these people, what do they do, what are they looking to achieve, where are they located? For example:

>> Recruiters and hiring managers looking for a data architect with experience in online banking applications located in Fort Worth, Texas.

>> Small business owners in Illinois looking to save money on their credit card processing.

>> Event planning professionals interested in finding oil and gas experts to speak at industry conferences.

Keep this list in front of you as you begin to write your summary. Look at it and write to your goal and write to your target audience. Ask yourself, "What does my target audience need to know about me?" "What do I offer that will get my audience to take notice and feel good about me?" Use that sheet of paper to jot down ideas.

Catching Your Reader's Attention

A strong LinkedIn summary needs to catch a reader's attention immediately. The best way to do this is to introduce yourself and summarize, in a sentence or two, what you do and how it affects your reader. This is known as an *elevator pitch*.

The reason it is called an "elevator pitch" comes from the idea that you are in an elevator with a VIP and you have just the amount of time it takes to ride an elevator a few floors to succinctly and compellingly explain a product, service, person, group/organization/company, or project to gain this person's interest and buy-in.

Let's say you have just met a person and she asks, "What do you do for a living?"

You could answer, "I am a realtor."

Or, you might provide an elevator pitch that would draw the other person in and may even get her interested in you: "As a realtor in the Greater Philadelphia area, I partner with families, helping them get their house ready to attract buyers so that they can sell at the best possible price. I work hard to understand their needs so I can quickly and easily find them their dream home."

REMEMBER

Your reader wants to know who you are and what you do, but more important, what that means to them.

An easy way to get started crafting your elevator pitch is to imagine you are explaining what you do for a living to a small child. Simplify what you do down to the core concepts. Do not use words such as *contextualize*, *organic*, *synergize*, or *paradigm*. And stay away from silly corporate jargon. Instead, concentrate on the results you offer and how what you do helps people and businesses.

Here's an outline to use to create your elevator pitch:

> My name is _____ and I help
>
> individuals/businesses/_____ create/discover/implement
>
> _____ so they can achieve _____.

It may seem odd to state your name, but this introduction does two things. First, it gives your readers a sense that they are really talking to you. They immediately see the profile as coming straight from your pen and not from your boring resume.

Second, by stating your name, you are optimizing the profile for your name in LinkedIn search. Most people share their name with other people. By stating your name in your profile, you are providing more instances of your name than others with the same name. What this means is if a person is searching for your name, there's a greater likelihood your profile will rank higher than others who share your name.

By including an elevator pitch in your LinkedIn summary, your readers will understand who you are and what's in it for them, compelling them to continue reading the rest of your profile.

Creating Your Professional Manifesto

Once you have your introduction and elevator pitch, it's time to tell your professional story. Your reader now has a general idea of who you are and what you do. Next you need to fill in the rest of the pieces. Think of the Summary section as your professional manifesto. Here are some questions to think about to help you create your manifesto:

>> Why do you do what you do?

>> What drew you to your current industry and position?

>> What are you most passionate about accomplishing?

>> What motivates you to succeed?

>> How do you view the future of your industry?

>> What's up ahead and what must a company do to find success?

>> What makes you credible in your industry?

>> What have you accomplished that makes you proud and builds credence to your brand?

>> What is your career philosophy?

>> What quote or concept guides you through your career?

As you brainstorm ideas for your summary, think of author and speaker Simon Sinek's quote:

> People don't buy what you do; they buy why you do it. . . . Very few people or companies can clearly articulate WHY they do WHAT they do. By WHY I mean your purpose, cause or belief — WHY does your company exist? WHY do you get out of bed every morning? And WHY should anyone care?

You could create a summary that simply states what you do and how you do it. The issue with that is it's not compelling or interesting, nor does it portray you as someone who should command respect and notice. By diving deep and truly turning your summary into a professional manifesto, you are shaping your image into one that is high level, interesting, and attractive.

Explain your benefits

Your summary should explain *your* benefits. What strengths do you have? How do they help your reader? What does your reader want to know about you? What are they seeking? The answers to these questions determine what you should write.

Here are some benefit sentence starters:

>> One of my strengths is . . .

>> I gain immense satisfaction from . . .

>> I am equally comfortable setting up a . . . or . . .

>> My mission is to . . .

>> My passion is . . .

If you are looking for a specific job, find a job description for your desired position. Incorporate those skills and qualities the job demands into your summary. You can find job descriptions on the hiring page of a company's website or on a job listing site. By targeting your profile toward that job description, you show that hiring manager or recruiter that you are the perfect person for the job.

WARNING

Whatever you do, you don't want to come across as desperate in your summary. That's a surefire way of scaring off potential employers. How do you change desperation into motivation? Rather than talk about the job you need, tell your reader what you offer in strengths and quantifiable results that intersect with what that job requires. If you cast yourself as the perfect fit, you are ensuring the person sourcing for that job reaches out.

If your goal is sales and prospecting, your target audience is scanning your profile, thinking, "Can this person help me?" Tell your readers how they will benefit from working with you. Include a success story of a past client and what they were able to achieve by working with you. Make your value clear to your reader so that they feel confident in you and the solution you provide.

When your goal is reputation management, you may decide to talk about activities outside of your career's day-to-day functions. You might mention your involvement in your community and your commitment to continuing your education. Your profile is your digital persona. Include the best parts of who you are and showcase them on your profile.

Highlight your top achievements

Although your job experiences contain career successes and achievements, your summary is the place to mention one to three career highlights. A career highlight isn't a simple success, but rather an amazing accomplishment.

By including a few career highlights, you are providing quantifiable evidence of your abilities. You want your reader to come away with a feeling of confidence that you are who you say you are. But whatever you do, don't provide too many career highlights. It's important to leave some successes in your back pocket so there are things to discuss when a person reaches out to you directly. And, it is important not to get too detailed with the highlight — keep the description at a high level.

When you add a career highlight, ask yourself the question, "So what?" It's important the highlight answers that question. It's not enough that you set up a new department. You want to showcase the true impact: You set up a new department with 50 employees that immediately became profitable and brought the company an additional $25M in revenue.

TIP

If you want to really set off your career highlights, preface the highlight with a symbol. (Check out Chapter 7 where I show you how to add symbols to your profile.) A star, arrow, or check mark act as great eye catchers, ensuring your reader pays attention to your accomplishments.

Keep the summary focused on you

I often see LinkedIn profiles that only describe products, services, or a business. It's a good idea to provide additional information for context, but remember, your profile is your own! People are reading it because they want to learn more about *you*. People do business with people. Your summary helps people see you as a real person. If your readers wanted to learn about your company, they would click to the company's LinkedIn company page or website.

For some people, it's scary to open up and talk about themselves. Realize that with your LinkedIn profile, you provide only the information you are comfortable providing. You never have to state anything that makes you uncomfortable. However, it is important to open up somewhat. Decide what you are comfortable sharing. Figure out what you want people to know about you. Once you know how you want to be perceived, create a summary that showcases that persona.

CHARACTER LIMITS

The Summary section can contain up to 2,000 characters. This roughly translates to 350 words. Don't feel that you need to fill your summary with 2,000 characters' worth of content. The most important thing is to tell your story at a high level and leave your reader wanting to learn more. If that's 1,000 characters or 2,000 characters, it's all good.

Create a clear call to action

A successful profile converts. That means the person reading the profile is compelled to do something other than click to another person's profile. If you are a job seeker, this conversion might occur with the reader calling you to request your resume to talk about a potential job opportunity. If you are in sales, the person reading your profile may visit your website to learn more about the products or services you offer. If you are a reputation seeker, the reader could follow you on LinkedIn to read your future long-form blog posts.

To compel your readers to do something after looking at your profile, you must provide them with a clear call to action. If you don't tell your readers what to do, often they just surf away.

What do you want your reader to do?

You have a number of options:

>> Visit my website.

>> Send me an email.

>> Call me.

>> Connect with me on LinkedIn.

>> Follow me on Twitter.

>> Download a whitepaper or marketing literature.

>> Listen to a podcast.

>> Watch a video.

Any information you include in your summary is visible to the world. By providing your email address or phone number, it is available to not just the people in your network, but also to people outside your network and non-LinkedIn users.

Unless you have grave privacy concerns, I suggest including a telephone number or email address. The VIPs of this world are direct people, and when they want to contact you, they want to do it immediately. If they can't find your phone number, they may move on to the next person in their LinkedIn search results. You are on LinkedIn to network and find business opportunities. By trying to avoid the occasional telemarketer, you may also avoid real opportunity.

Once you have your contact method chosen, it's time to conclude your summary. Here's one example:

> *I am currently looking for that next position that allows me to grow revenue, develop strong client relationships, and affect positive change.*
>
> *You can request my resume by contacting me either by phone 215-839-0008 or email donna@gmail.com.*

Or:

> *I am on LinkedIn to forge strong professional relationships. Whether you know me directly or not, please feel free to send me a connection request.*
>
> *Assisting other professionals and acting as a connector is a passion of mine. If I can help you, give me a call or Skype me.*
>
> *Phone: 215-839-0008 / Skype: donna.serdula*

Another way to craft this call to action is by tempting your audience with a carrot. Give your readers a reason to get in touch with you. Will you provide them with a free phone consultation? Do you have experience that you are open to sharing?

Here are some examples:

> *Call me today for a free phone consultation to see if your business can benefit from my services. Let's put the proper solutions into action and together we'll turn your goals into reality.*

Or:

> *I'd love to share with you some of the insights I've gleaned from building and managing datacenters over the last 10 years.*
>
> *Let's talk! My number is: (215) 839-0008*

Perhaps you really don't want your reader to take any action. Some people are on LinkedIn to simply shape how people perceive them, and it's not important for the reader to reach out. In this situation, gently end your summary in a positive way, leaving your reader feeling inspired and impressed.

Here are a few examples:

My success is my clients' success. I gain enormous satisfaction helping my clients optimize their marketing efforts. Building successful campaigns and generating positive word of mouth is what keeps me striving forward in my career.

Or:

The bottom line is I help my clients save money and plan for a secure future.

Or:

My focus moving forward is to continue to improve processes and affect positive change within this amazing organization.

Formatting a Sleek LinkedIn Summary

Formatting? There's no formatting allowed within a LinkedIn profile! That's true, but there are still things you can do to make sure your Summary section is easy to read and attractive to the eye.

For example, space between paragraphs means white space, which makes content look less dense and easier to read. To create an extra line of space between paragraphs in your summary, press the Enter or Return key on your keyboard twice after the end of every paragraph.

You can also use symbols to spice up your text. (I show you how to copy and paste symbols in Chapter 7.) Symbols can be used to create horizontal lines to divide your content. Stars, circles, or check marks can be used as bullets to show off your accomplishments. Check out Figure 10-2 to see how I used symbols to create what appears to be an underline and bullets to draw attention to my call to action.

TIP

A few, well-chosen symbols are a great way to amp up your content, but remember: overdoing symbols can take a great summary and make it look amateurish and tacky.

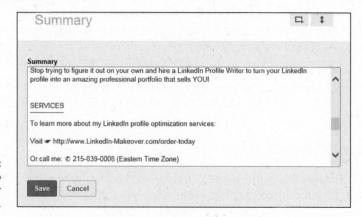

FIGURE 10-2:
Use symbols to
dress up your
profile.

Examples of Compelling and Engaging Summaries

Here are examples of compelling and engaging summaries that you can use to help you create your own.

Product management

My name is Jana Gates and I am a powerhouse in product management. Using my expertise in retail marketing of technology products and my ability to work within the structure of technology companies, I have developed successful programs leading to robust sales of profitable products, and have increased market shares in very competitive markets.

Among other career accomplishments, I am proud to have spearheaded product launches that have paid off for my employers. Being considered a trusted advisor and functional expert in my area of specialization, gives me great satisfaction.

I firmly believe that for today's technology companies to continue to be successful, they must rely on someone like myself who understands the changing dynamics of retail product management, marketing and sales, along with the impact of new technologies.

With the advent of new shopping paradigms such as participatory shopping and new mobile shopping options, it's more important than ever before to drive innovation. My goal is to help shape strategy, achieve higher customer retention and deliver profitability that increases year after year.

As a team leader, I feel it's important to unleash the potential of those working with me and to share my passion for success with them. With our combined energy we can develop better products that respond to and exceed consumer needs.

I am on LinkedIn to meet others who share my commitment to doing great work and to share best practices. Please reach out and let's connect!

Leadership

My name is John Gates and I have never faced a challenge in my work life that I couldn't surmount. I have built a track record over a 10-year career of delivering outstanding results and operational efficiency.

In my current position as VP of Operations for Widgets, Inc., a leading national manufacturer, I've assembled an organization that sets new standards in efficiency and delivers excellent production quality.

I believe that as a leader, the most important success factor is cultivating excellence in people. The employees you hire and train are capable of great things. It's up to the leader to unleash their capabilities in support of the company mission. It's important that they understand business goals and how they can play a part in achieving them.

To that end I work closely with team members and have developed a number of training programs focused on career learning. These programs have received national awards for integrating training execution, results measurement and personal recognition in a way that yields a learning culture. My initiatives were named 2015's Top Training Program by Training Magazine.

My areas of expertise include:

* Employee engagement and culture building

* Operational effectiveness and Six Sigma

* Change management

* Leadership development and organizational growth

I am always looking out for new opportunities that utilize these skills. To explore how my areas of expertise might benefit your organization, please connect with me via LinkedIn.

Retail

My name is Johan Gates and I manage store operations and am a retail leader for Widget Style, a leading U.S. fashion retailer. It is my responsibility to set clear goals and objectives for a team of over 10 associates so that everyone works together to achieve the highest level of customer service.

Every associate at Widget Style is the face of the company to our customers. I pride myself on the training and development opportunities I provide for our team members so that they can fulfill this responsibility. In addition, a key part of my role as retail leader is to inspire the team, maintaining morale and productivity so that they deliver value and service while driving store revenues.

During a career of seven years in retail management, I have developed strengths not only in team building but in leading business operations and building relationships with key influencers. As a result of my solid track record, I've been promoted to positions of increasing responsibility. Today, I am proud to run the flagship store of the company's regional operations.

As a leader of a significant enterprise in our area, fostering community relationships is an important part of my job and I am passionate about supporting the community. In addition, I am on the Board of the Bucks County Orchestra, and have worked with charitable foundations in our area to raise money for worthwhile causes.

I feel that the lessons I have learned in working my way up a retail enterprise can offer valuable insights to others. Please connect with me via LinkedIn and we can share our ideas for creating exceptional customer experiences.

Accounting

My name is Jackie Gates and I am a partner with Thompson, Gates, and Thompson, the leading certified public accounting (CPA) firm in the Dallas, Texas area. We have been in business for 15 years and are the firm of choice for many in our area because of our wealth of experience regarding accounting issues.

As individual and business tax reporting and filing requirements have become increasingly complex, clients know we deliver the highest quality results. They rely on us as strategic partners and reliable advisors. I have been a partner since 2011 and in my tenure have gained expertise in many areas of the tax code, which benefits our clients.

As it relates to the selection of a CPA partner, I would suggest asking the following questions before making a decision:

* How confident are you in managing today's complex tax returns yourself?

* As a business owner, how important is it to you to have confidence in the company managing your firm's tax returns?

* How important is it to you to receive personalized service?

Personalized service is a hallmark of our firm. We assist clients in navigating the complex tax code environment. Long-term clients often express their appreciation for our service. My own priority is to be personally responsible to our clients, understanding their unique situations and making sure each one has the needed services so services are customized to their needs.

To learn more about our services, which include tax preparation, cash flow management, estate planning and preparation of financial statements, among others, please contact me at TGTCPA.com or by phone at 215-839-0008.

Student

My name is Jack Gates. As a recent graduate of Widget University, I am seeking opportunities to apply the wide-ranging skill set I have gained through rigorous academics and multiple internships. My goal is to obtain an entry-level marketing position with a mid-to-large consumer brand company based in New York City.

* Internships Yield Valuable Experiences

While completing my education, I gained real-world experience via multiple internships. These hands-on internships taught me how various departments and functions really work. While successfully carrying out assigned projects in support of company goals I learned accountability. Through internships I expanded my experience, learned new industries and gained invaluable insights from my mentors that I can apply on behalf of a future employer.

* Rigorous Academics Prepare for Meeting Tough Challenges

In the academic world, competition is fierce, and so provides a model for business success. Through university training I have developed critical thinking skills and the ability to prioritize. My degree in Business Administration gave me a strong foundation, and team-based projects taught me that through collaboration, winning outcomes can be achieved for all.

* Contributing in Today's Business World

Self-motivated and self-directed, I am eager to embark on a career where future employers can count on me to deliver my best efforts for the good of their organization.

To discuss how my experiences may be a perfect fit for your company, please connect with me via LinkedIn or contact me directly student@gmail.com.

In the next chapter, I show you how to round out your profile with additional sections like Honors and Awards, Organizations, and more. I'll meet you there!

4

Rounding Out Your Profile and Adding Finishing Touches

Learn how to compile and record all of your professional accomplishments, skill sets, certifications, and abilities to tout on your profile.

See what you need to do to get your profile an All-Star ranking, even if you didn't graduate from college or university.

Look at ways to add multimedia content to turn your profile into a portfolio that showcases your best work and projects.

Understand why it's important to ask for and provide recommendations, and take a look at ways to do so.

Learn how to join LinkedIn Groups, follow the right influencers, and show your allegiance to companies and schools to strengthen your brand vision.

See what finishing touches you should add to your profile, including rearranging sections into a logical order.

Once your profile is complete, learn how to market your profile to get more and more views.

Chapter **11**

There's More to You Than Your Jobs

Most people think of LinkedIn as a place to state the positions they've held throughout their careers. LinkedIn is so much more than just a compendium of where you worked. Your LinkedIn profile is a 360-degree view of you as a professional. Throughout your career you won awards, joined industry organizations, ran projects, received patents, wrote publications, and more.

In this chapter, I show you how to compile and record all these professional accomplishments to create a complete profile of *you*. And it's not just accomplishments; certain professions demand certain skill sets, certifications, and abilities. LinkedIn provides sections for you to record certifications, languages you speak, courses you've taken, and test scores that make you even more marketable. I also show you how to record your education and even show you what to do if you didn't graduate from college or university.

Showcasing Organizations

The Organizations section of your LinkedIn profile is the place to record the real-world associations and clubs to which you belong. Listing professional membership organizations on your profile proves you are an integral force within your community and an involved member within your industry.

I often see LinkedIn members add LinkedIn Groups or their volunteer experience to the Organizations section. This is a mistake. LinkedIn Groups are forums within LinkedIn focused on a specific topic. Within a LinkedIn Group, members post and comment on discussions. It's a great way to come together with like-minded individuals for discussions around shared interests. However, you do not want to list your LinkedIn Groups within the Organizations section, as LinkedIn Groups automatically appear at the bottom of your profile.

The Volunteering Experience section of LinkedIn is where you list those humanitarian organizations to which you donate money or time. Not sure where to add a particular organization? To determine which organization goes into which section, ask yourself the question, "Is this organization's goal philanthropy, and am I donating my time or money?" If so, enter it into the Volunteering Experience section, which I cover later in this chapter in "Adding Volunteer Experiences."

To determine the organizations to list in your profile, answer the following questions:

>> Do you belong to any industry organizations?

>> Do you belong to any user groups?

>> Are you a member of a networking group?

>> Do you pay dues to any association?

>> Are you a part of a local government organization?

>> Do you sit on a board of directors?

Make sure you include organizations that forward you professionally and are interesting to your target audience. It's okay to leave out organizations that are of a personal nature or may alienate your target audience.

TIP

Everyone has causes that move them but you must be smart about what you list on your profile. You may love animals but showing your support of People for the Ethical Treatment of Animals (PETA) may alienate some people. Likewise, listing your National Rifle Association (NRA) membership may upset others. It's certainly fine to stand behind your convictions whatever end of the spectrum they might be on — just realize that not everyone will agree and opportunity might be redacted because of what you list on your profile. You can't please everyone, so be strategic and think through the pros and cons prior to adding organizations to your profile.

To add professional membership organizations to the Organizations section of your LinkedIn profile, follow these steps:

1. **Open your LinkedIn profile.**

2. **If you have the Organizations section already added to your profile, simply scroll to it and click the pencil (edit) icon to enter into edit mode, then go to Step 5.**

3. **If you don't have the Organizations section added to your profile yet, add it by scrolling below the Contact Information section at the top part of your profile.**

    Two sections appear that you can add. If Organizations isn't one of the options listed, click View More (see Figure 11-1) to expand the area to see a full list of sections to add.

4. **In the Organizations section, click Add Organizations.**

    When clicked, the Organizations section appears on your profile.

5. **In the Organization field, type the name of the organization.**

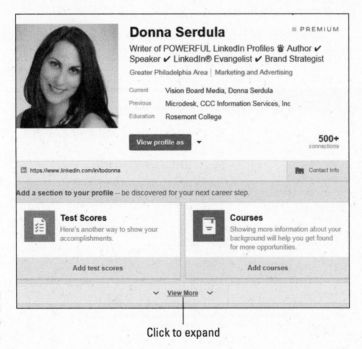

FIGURE 11-1: Add additional sections to your profile.

Click to expand

6. **In the Position(s) Held field, type the position you held.**

If you didn't have an official title, such as President or Treasurer, you can use: Member, Key Contributor, Team Member, Patron, Supporter, Sponsor, Subscriber, Angel, or Backer.

7. **In the Occupation field, select the current or prior experience to connect this organization to a particular role.**

The drop-down list is populated by your current and previous experiences. If you are part of this organization not because of a current or past role, feel free to skip this field.

By linking the organization to a position, the organization shows up in the Organizations section and directly under the position it is paired with.

8. **In the Time Period fields, choose the month and year you started your membership from the drop-down lists.**

LinkedIn defaults to no end date. If this organization is no longer current, enter an end date by deselecting Membership Ongoing.

9. **In the Additional Notes field, enter information about the organization.**

10. **Click the Save button.**

See Figure 11-2 for an example of an organization added to the Organizations section.

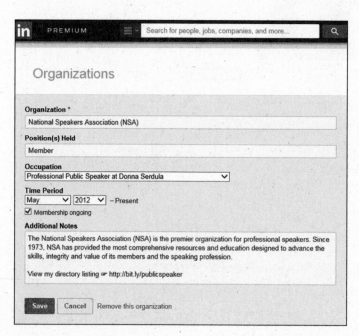

FIGURE 11-2:
Adding an organization membership.

Uncovering Your Honors and Awards

The Honors & Awards section of your LinkedIn profile is the area to enter any honors and awards you earned throughout your career. Working with clients, I find that the Honors & Awards section is one of the hardest areas to fill out. Many people don't keep a list of the honors and awards they have received, and when it finally comes time to list them, they simply can't remember.

Here's something to remember: If you don't record these honors, no one else will. You never know when it might come down to you and another highly lauded individual for a job, promotion, or project. You don't want to miss out simply because they recorded and touted their accomplishments and you didn't.

To determine your honors and awards, think in terms of certificates, plaques, and trophies you received. Open up your closet and check the top shelf — are any of these items collecting dust in a box? Jot down on a piece of paper these awards. Once you have identified any certificates, plaques, or trophies, let's dig deeper. Honors and awards don't have to be tangible items.

Here are some questions to help you remember other types of honors and awards you may have received:

>> Were you ever quoted in a newspaper article?

>> Were you ever profiled in a magazine?

>> Did you ever give a speech or deliver a keynote address?

>> Did you ever sit on a panel or act as a moderator?

>> Were you ever asked to work on a special project?

>> Were you chosen to provide training or mentoring to colleagues?

>> Were you ever appointed to a committee?

Choosing the right honors and awards

Are your brain juices pumping now? Before we start adding all these amazing honors and awards to your profile, we need to take a step back and decide what to add and what not to include.

Look over the list of honors and awards you compiled. Did you list things that occurred over 20 years ago? In the professional world, it's all about what you did lately. With that said, once an Oscar winner, always an Oscar winner. The older awards that are for amazing accomplishments, you may decide to keep. However, if the accomplishments were great at the time but don't point you in the direction of your desired career future or impress your greatness upon your target audience, ditch 'em!

TIP

I can't tell you how many top-level executives have asked me whether to include their Eagle Scout award. Although this award is from childhood, it does showcase perseverance, and I tell them to include it on their profiles. Besides, there are a lot of former Boy Scouts in high places, and the Eagle Scout award impresses them.

Did you earn your black belt in Karate? You might decide to list it under Honors & Awards, especially if it is a recent achievement. However, you could instead add it to your Interests section of your LinkedIn profile, which I cover in Chapter 12. Ultimately it's up to you, but always keep your target audience in mind and consider what they might deem as an impressive professional accomplishment.

Ultimately, it comes down to being smart. If you *only* have awards that are over five years old, include them. As you receive new awards, start deleting the older ones. Also, if you earned President's Club or another top sales award five years in a row, you don't need to list it five times. Condense it into one entry and state it is for multiple years.

REMEMBER

Don't go overboard. It's better to have three to five high-level honors listed instead of 15 to 20 so-so awards.

Creating a strong description

Once you have your final, master list of honors and awards, you now want to do some research to create an optimized description that provides context around the award and showcases your contribution as award worthy.

Start with a boilerplate explanation of the organization that presented the honor or award. Who are they and what do they do? Then describe the honor or award and what you did specifically to get the award. You want to aim for a couple of sentences, not a full-blown novel.

The best way to get this information is to consult the Internet. Run searches on the organization and check its website's About Us page. Then search for the honor or award. Even if it's not the exact award you received, you may find wording that is close to what you need. Rather than plagiarizing, use this content as a springboard and tweak it to make it work for you.

Now that you have descriptions, it's time to enter these honors and awards into your LinkedIn profile. Here's how:

1. **Open your LinkedIn profile.**

2. **If you have the Honors & Awards section already added to your profile, simply scroll to it and click the pencil (edit) icon to enter into edit mode, then go to Step 5.**

3. **If you don't have the Honors & Awards section added to your profile yet, scroll below the Contact Information section at the top part of your profile.**

   Two sections appear that you can add. If Honors & Awards isn't one of the options listed, click the View More link to expand the area and see a full list of sections to add.

4. **In the Honors & Awards section, click Add Honors & Awards.**

   When clicked, the Honors & Awards section appears on your profile.

5. **In the Title field, enter the name of your honor or award.**

6. **In the Occupation field, select the current or prior experience to connect the honor or award to a particular role.**

   The drop-down list is populated by your current and previous experiences. By linking the honor and award to a position, the honor and award shows up in the Honor & Awards section and directly under the position it is paired with.

7. **In the Date field, choose the month and year you received the honor or award from the drop-down lists.**

   If this is an honor and award that spans multiple years, or a date simply doesn't pertain, feel free to leave the date field blank.

8. **In the Description field, enter information about the honor or award.**

   Remember, it's better to add context around your honors and awards, and the easiest way to do that is to search the web for already created content that you can tweak.

9. **Click the Save button.**

    See Figure 11-3 for an example of honors listed in the Honors & Awards section.

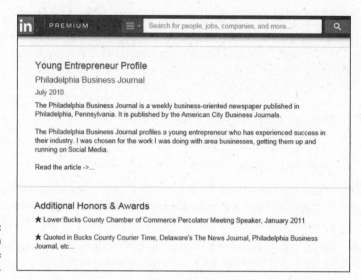

FIGURE 11-3:
Honors listed in the Honors & Awards section.

Keeping your honors and awards updated

TIP

If you take anything away from this chapter, I want it to be this: honors and awards aren't bestowed on just anyone. *Honors and awards are typically given to people who have asked for recognition.*

It's time for you to start strategically identifying honors and awards and doing what it takes to obtain them. Make sure it's known that you are interested and worthy. Keep an eye out for initiatives where you can volunteer to be seen. Honors and awards prove to your audience that you have what it takes to be a success and deserve recognition.

And as you begin to accumulate more honors and awards in your career, revisit this section on your LinkedIn profile. Remove older awards and add new ones. Always include a description. Don't be shy and don't dismiss this section. You are worthy of recognition.

By adding these awards, you aren't bragging; you are merely reporting on what was presented to you. By adding your honors, regardless of how silly they may seem to you, potential employers or customers take notice. No one else will toot your horn, so it's important that you do it!

The Three P's: Projects, Publications, and Patents

There are times when you go above and beyond within your professional life. In these instances, you don't want to group these extraordinary accomplishments with less ordinary accomplishments. Projects, publications, and patents deserve their own spotlighted area on your LinkedIn profile. Keep reading to see what is considered worthy of the spotlight and how to add these "three P's" to your profile.

Adding projects

The Projects section is the perfect place to spotlight your involvement in company-driven initiatives. Long-range, high-yield projects that deserve a bigger spotlight than a simple bullet in your Experience section belong in the Projects section. Choose projects that make you proud and show that you helped move the corporate needle, but most of all, choose projects that will impress your target reader.

TIP

The Projects section is also the perfect section for consultants who have spent time working with different clients. Consultants can't list clients in their Experience section because they didn't work for them directly as an employee. The Projects section is the perfect answer to this conundrum.

This section also allows you to add a URL that links to an external website to add even more context to the project. Another great part of this section is that you can pull in other team members and link them to the project to show the full range of contribution.

To add projects to the Projects section of your LinkedIn profile, follow these steps:

1. **Open your LinkedIn profile.**

2. **If you have the Projects section already added to your profile, simply scroll to it and click the pencil (edit) icon to enter into edit mode, then go to Step 5.**

3. **If you don't have the Projects section added to your profile yet, scroll below the Contact Information section at the top part of your profile.**

   Two sections appear that you can add. If Projects isn't one of the options listed, click the View More link to expand the area and see a full list of sections to add.

4. **In the Project section, click Add Projects.**

   When clicked, the Projects section appears on your profile.

5. **In the Name field, enter the name of the project.**

6. **In the Occupation field, select the current or prior experience to connect the project to a particular role.**

   The drop-down list is populated by your current and previous experiences. By linking the project to a position, the project shows up in the Projects section and directly under the position it is paired with.

7. **In the Date field, choose the month and year you worked on the project from the drop-down lists.**

   If this project spanned a period of time, click Switch to Date Range to add an end date.

8. **In the Project URL field, add the website where more information on this project can be found.**

   If this project doesn't have a web presence, skip this section.

9. **In the Team Member(s) field, place your cursor over +Add Team Member and start typing a name.**

   If the team member is one of your first-degree connections on LinkedIn, his or her name appears in a drop-down list.

10. **Select the team member(s) you wish to add to the project from the drop-down list.**

    You can add team members even if they aren't on LinkedIn, but they will not have profiles dynamically linked within the project.

11. **In the Description field, add context around your project so that your reader has an idea of the extent of your success and why this project was singled out.**

12. **Click the Save button.**

    See Figure 11-4 for an example of adding a project to the Projects section.

TIP

Just as you can add a person to a project you created, others can add you to a project they created. If you aren't happy with your inclusion on a project on someone else's profile, you can't remove it yourself. You must reach out to the person and ask them to remove you from the project.

Adding publications

The Publications section of LinkedIn is the place for writers to add published work. This section is a great place to spotlight your writing ability and showcase your knowledge.

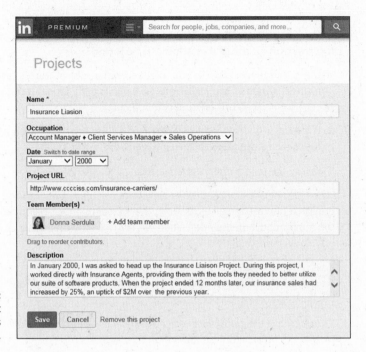

FIGURE 11-4:
Adding a project to the Projects section.

Do not think that this section is only for the books you wrote. If you wrote an article that was published or broadcast in some manner, add it to this section and share it with the readers of your LinkedIn profile. Cite magazine articles, newsletter pieces, guest blog articles, and more. Here's how to add your publication history to your profile:

1. **Open your LinkedIn profile.**

2. **If you have the Publications section already added to your profile, simply scroll to it and click the pencil (edit) icon to enter into edit mode, then go to Step 5.**

3. **If you don't have the Publications section added to your profile yet, scroll below the Contact Information section at the top part of your profile and click the View More link to see a full list of sections to add.**

4. **In the Publications section, click Add Publications.**

   When clicked, the Publications section appears on your profile.

5. **In the Title field, enter the name of the publication.**

6. **In the Publication/Publisher field, enter the name of the publication if it's a magazine or periodical, or the name of the publisher if it is a book.**

7. **In the Publication Date field, choose the month, day, and year the text was published from the drop-down lists.**

8. **In the Publication URL field, add the website address where more information on this publication can be found.**

   If your publication is a book, you might consider adding a link to the book on Amazon. If it is an article you wrote, add a link to the article. If this publication doesn't have a web presence, skip this section.

9. **In the Author(s) field, add the name of a first-degree LinkedIn connection to tie them to the publication, if applicable.**

   If you are the sole author, skip this step.

REMEMBER

   When adding additional authors, they have the opportunity to add the publication to their profiles (or not). The authors' names will not be linked to the publication, and the publication will not show up on the authors' profiles, until they approve.

   Your name is always listed first when you add a publication to your profile. To rearrange the additional author's name, simply click a name and drag it into the desired order within edit mode.

   If you remove the publication after the additional author added it to his or her profile, the publication will remain on that author's profile.

10. **In the Description field, provide some detail around the publication.**

    This is a great place to add a boilerplate description of the books and/or articles you've published, and you can even provide a brief excerpt. LinkedIn allows a maximum length of 2,000 characters, which is approximately 300 words — just enough room to provide context, but not enough room to write a novel.

11. **Click the Save button.**

    See Figure 11-5 for an example of adding a book to the Publications section.

Adding patents

A patent is a professional accomplishment and should be shared on your LinkedIn profile. If you are an inventor with patents to your name, the Patents section is the place to showcase your work.

Here's how to add a patent to the Patents section:

1. **Open your LinkedIn profile.**

2. **If you have the Patents section already added to your profile, simply scroll to it and click the pencil (edit) icon to enter into edit mode, then go to Step 5.**

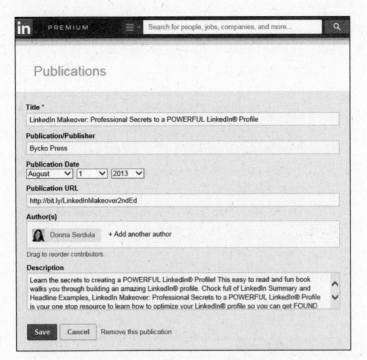

FIGURE 11-5:
Adding a book to the Publications section.

3. **If you don't have the Patents section added to your profile yet, scroll below the Contact Information section at the top part of your profile and click the View More link to see a full list of sections to add.**

4. **In the Patents section, click Add Patents.**

   When clicked, the Patents section appears on your profile.

5. **In the Patent Office field, select the appropriate Patent Office from the drop-down list.**

6. **Under Status, select Patent Issued or Patent Pending.**

7. **Type in the Patent/Application Number.**

8. **In the Patent Title field, enter the name of the patent.**

9. **In the Inventor(s) field, add any additional inventors by placing your cursor over +Add Another Inventor and typing a name.**

   To choose a name from a drop-down list, additional inventors must be first-degree connections on LinkedIn. If they aren't first-degree connections, you can still add their names, but they won't have a profile dynamically linked.

   The additional inventors have the opportunity to add the patent to their profiles (or not). The inventors' names will not be linked to the patent, and the patent will not show up on the inventors' profiles, until they approve.

Your name is always listed first when you add a patent to your profile. To rearrange the additional inventor names simply, click a name and drag it into the desired order within edit mode.

If you remove the patent after additional inventors added it to their profiles, the patent will remain on their profiles.

10. **In the Issue/Filing Date field, choose the month, day, and year from the drop-down lists.**

11. **In the Patent URL field, add the patent's URL where more information on this patent can be found.**

12. **In the Description field, provide some detail around the patent.**

This is a great place to add more description about your patent, and you can even provide a brief sample from the patent itself.

13. **Click the Save button.**

See Figure 11-6 for an example of adding a patent.

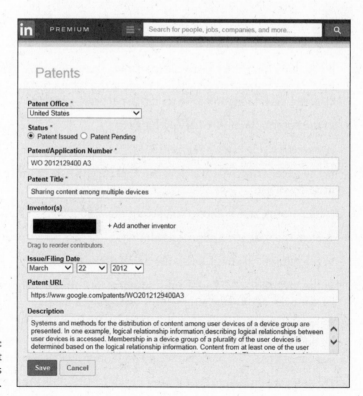

FIGURE 11-6:
Adding a patent to the Patents section.

The Two C's: Certifications and Courses

Certain professions demand certain skill sets and certifications. Increase your marketability by spotlighting your professional development. Add the certifications, licensures, and clearances you've earned and courses you've taken throughout your career to your profile.

WARNING

A common issue I see, however, is that many people enter certifications in the Education section of their profiles. At one time, the LinkedIn profile didn't contain these extra sections, and the only way to record a certification was to add it as part of the Education section. Remember, the Education section is where you enter degrees received. If you received a certificate, enter it in the Certifications section.

Here's how to enter a certification to your profile:

1. **Open your LinkedIn profile.**

2. **If you have the Certifications section already added to your profile, simply scroll to it and click the pencil (edit) icon to enter into edit mode, then go to Step 5.**

3. **If you don't have the Certifications section added to your profile yet, scroll below the Contact Information section at the top part of your profile and click the View More link to see a full list of sections to add.**

4. **In the Certifications section, click Add Certifications.**

   When clicked, the Certifications section appears on your profile.

5. **Type the name of the Certification in the Certification Name field.**

6. **Enter the Certification Authority in the next field.**

   The Certification Authority is the trusted organization or company that issued the certificate. They are the ones guaranteeing your knowledge or ability.

7. **Enter the License Number in the License Number field.**

8. **In the Certification URL field, add the website address where more information on this certification can be found.**

9. **In the Dates field, choose the month and year from the drop-down lists.**

   If the certification has no end date, place a check mark next to This Certificate Does Not Expire.

10. **Click the Save button.**

    See Figure 11-7 for an example of adding a certificate.

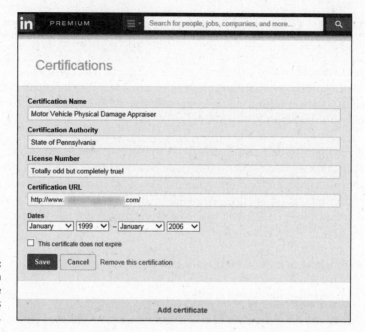

FIGURE 11-7:
Adding a
certificate to the
Certifications
section.

Importing certifications from Lynda.com

LinkedIn acquired Lynda.com (www.lynda.com), the leader in online professional development classes. This acquisition means easy integration of your Lynda.com course completion certificates and your LinkedIn profile. If you're a member of both Lynda.com and LinkedIn, when you complete a course on Lynda.com, you'll receive an email with a link that lets you post your Certificate of Completion to your LinkedIn profile. Click that link and the Certificate of Completion appears in the Certifications section of your LinkedIn profile. Voila!

Adding courses

If you take a one-off course that doesn't deliver a certificate nor is part of a much larger degree program, the Courses section of LinkedIn is for you. In addition, more and more students are joining LinkedIn, realizing the huge opportunities for networking and job search. The Courses section is where you spotlight recent courses that deserve to be highlighted outside of the degree you are working toward.

Here's how to add a course to your LinkedIn profile:

1. **Open your LinkedIn profile.**

2. **If you have the Courses section already added to your profile, simply scroll to it and click the pencil (edit) icon to enter into edit mode, then go to Step 5.**

3. **If you don't have the Courses section added to your profile yet, scroll below the Contact Information section at the top part of your profile and click the View More link to see a full list of sections to add.**

4. **In the Courses section, click Add Courses.**

   When clicked, the Courses section appears on your profile.

5. **In the Course Name field, type the name of the course.**

6. **Enter the course number in the Number field.**

7. **If this course was taken for a position you held, select that position from the drop-down list under the Associated With section.**

   By linking to a past or present work experience, readers can see the courses you took for that position, thus providing even more robustness to your profile and work history.

8. **Click the Save button.**

   See Figure 11-8 for an example of adding a course to the Courses section.

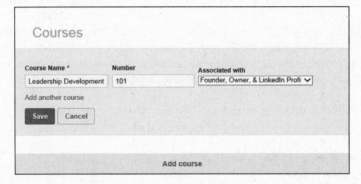

FIGURE 11-8:
Adding a course
to the Courses
section.

Adding the Languages You Speak

Sprechen sie Deutsch? Ja, me neither. But if you do speak other languages, add them to your LinkedIn profile. Simply choose the language(s) from the drop-down list and then indicate your level of proficiency.

Choose from:

>> Elementary proficiency

>> Limited working proficiency

>> Professional working proficiency

>> Full professional proficiency

>> Native or bilingual proficiency

TIP

If you add a foreign language to this section, be sure to also add your native language to the list of languages you speak. You don't want potential alliances to dismiss you because they assume you hired a translator to create your LinkedIn profile and don't speak their language.

Creating a Profile in Another Language

For those global business people who work throughout the world, you can make multiple versions of your profile in different languages. This way, the person viewing your profile sees your profile in the language that matches his or her primary language. If this person is using LinkedIn in a language that doesn't match any of your languages, he or she sees your profile in your primary language.

When you initially created your profile, the language you chose becomes your primary language. Once your primary language is chosen, it can't be changed. However, you can add as many secondary language profiles as you like, provided there are languages available. (Sorry, Klingon is not supported.)

LinkedIn doesn't automatically translate your profile; you are responsible for editing your profile and adding the translated text yourself.

To create a profile in another language, follow these steps:

1. **Open your LinkedIn profile.**

2. **Click the down arrow next to the View Profile As button and select Create Profile in Another Language, as shown in Figure 11-9.**

3. **Choose a language from the drop-down list.**

4. **If your first name and last name are different in the new language, update your name in the First Name and Last Name fields.**

5. **In the Professional Headline field, update your headline in the new language.**

6. **Click the Create Profile button to go to the Edit Profile page of your new language profile.**

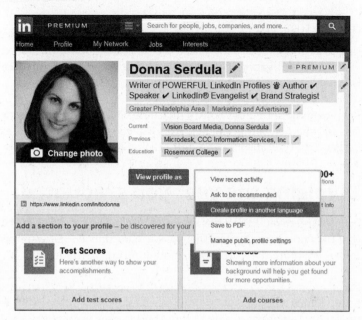

You are now at the new secondary language profile. Your original profile sections have been transferred to the new secondary language profile with the titles, company names, and recommendations intact. When you click into sections, the descriptions remain; you must delete the content and replace it with your translation. Once the original primary language is deleted, LinkedIn provides your primary language text below the fields to aid you in translating.

7. **Refer back to the chapters of this book to optimize your profile in your new language.**

Adding Your Education, or Lack Thereof

Education plays an important role in your LinkedIn profile. Not only is this information placed at the very top of your profile, visible within your search result listing, but also it helps your profile achieve All-Star ranking.

All-Star profiles are profiles that are 100% complete and may perform better in search. When creating an optimized, robust profile, achieving the rank of All-Star is important and a goal to strive for.

Not everyone graduates college, and it's a shame LinkedIn forces you to fill out this section. When I first began working as a LinkedIn profile writer several years ago, I was shocked by the number of executives who didn't have college degrees.

I quickly realized that many movers and shakers of this world aren't content sitting in a college classroom. These "do-ers" have better things to do, such as build businesses and generate revenue. And besides, if they want a college education, they'll hire someone with one.

Keep reading to find out how to make the education section work for you regardless of whether you graduated from college or university, or graduated after a longer than typical spell, or didn't graduate at all.

Divulging the year you graduated

People tend to omit the years they attended college. As I see it, the reason is either that they prefer to disguise their real age, or they do not want people to realize it took them more than the usual amount of time to graduate.

If you are not listing your graduation date because you are trying to hide your age, I say, "Don't worry about it!" Embrace your age. By putting the years you attended university, LinkedIn is able to link you to other people who graduated with you. This means more people to add to your network, which means the potential for more opportunity. And that is a good thing.

WARNING

In addition, a profile that is missing years is a huge red flag to potential employers, recruiters, and human resources professionals. Omitting dates is a sign that something isn't quite right. It's better to be viewed as old than someone who is hiding something.

On the other hand, if you are omitting dates because it took you longer to graduate than the norm, at the very least, enter the year you graduated. This way you are still able to connect with your fellow graduates without divulging the length of time it took you to complete your schooling.

LISTING YOUR HIGH SCHOOL

Every now and then I see clients who come to us with their high school educations listed in their profiles' Education section. Only list your high school experience if:

- You are a recent high school graduate.
- You attended a prestigious high school that provides great networking potential.
- You didn't continue on to college or university.

Listing your high school is not needed if you have a higher-education degree.

Preparing activities and societies

Before we get started adding your Education, let's take a moment to prepare the Activities and Societies and Description sections. It is tempting to leave these fields blank, but profiles that are completely filled out rank better than profiles missing information. This means you should enter *something* in these fields.

In what clubs, activities, fraternities, or sororities did you participate? Determine the activities that portray you as a well-rounded individual and list them. Here are a few examples: Foreign Language Club, Debate Team, Football, Theater, Delta Delta Delta Sorority, Chess Club.

The Description field is where you provide information about your educational background and experience. Did you graduate with honors? Were you the recipient of a scholarship? Take the most interesting notes and add them into your profile. Here are a few examples: Fulbright Scholarship. Graduated cum laude. Study Abroad Program, Junior Year, London, England. Matriculated while working full time. Wrote thesis entitled, *Liberation of Literature during Fin de siècle France.* Minored in English, with a concentration in American Literature.

Don't get too carried away with this section. Just add a couple items and move on.

Adding your education

Whether you graduated from college or not, it's time to add education to your profile. Here's how to do it:

1. **Open your LinkedIn profile.**

2. **Scroll to the Education section of your profile and click the pencil (edit) icon to edit a pre-existing school or select + Add Education to add a new school.**

3. **In the School field, start to type the name of your school.**

   A drop-down list with schools matching the characters you type appears.

4. **Select the school name from the list.**

   By selecting your school from the drop-down list, the school's logo appears alongside your education section, the LinkedIn university page for your school is dynamically linked to your profile, and you are included in the alumni data. LinkedIn also may show you other alumni who graduated with you in the People You May Know page, helping you create an even more robust LinkedIn network.

5. **Under Dates Attended, choose the year you started to attend the school and the year you left the school in the drop-down lists.**

   For the end date, choose the date you graduated or the year you expect to graduate.

EDUCATION FOR THE UNEDUCATED

Houston, we have a problem. In order to obtain an All-Star–ranked, robust profile, one must include education. So what happens if you didn't go to college or earn a degree?

My recommendation is to enter your high school information or whatever was the last bit of education you received. I have clients who enter: The Esteemed School of Hard Knocks. Silly, yes, but if education is what LinkedIn wants, education we will give.

You must put something in the School field. LinkedIn doesn't care if it's the School of Hard Knocks, Cordon Bleu, or Paint and Sip art classes. Add your "school" of choice, leave the degree blank, and move on to the other sections of your profile.

6. **Under Field of Study, start to type your major and choose your major from the drop-down list LinkedIn provides.**

   If your major doesn't match what LinkedIn suggests, add your own major by simply not selecting LinkedIn's suggestions.

7. **In the Grade field, enter your GPA or whether you graduated Cum Laude, Summa Cum Laude, or Magna Cum Laude.**

   If you don't have a respectable GPA or can't remember back that far, don't worry. Leave this field blank. Having written thousands of profiles, I have added information to the Grade field only a few times.

8. **In the Activities and Societies field, enter the clubs and activities you participated in during your time at that school.**

   Refer back to "Preparing activities and societies" earlier in this chapter for more information on how to decide on this information.

9. **In the Description field, enter your educational background and experiences that will impress your reader. (See Figure 11-10.)**

10. **Click Save.**

Reordering education

If you went to multiple schools and want to list them in a specific order, it's easy to reorder them. The first school you list in the Education section is the school that shows at the top of your profile. To change the school at the top of your profile, you need to reorder the schools within the Education section. Here's how to do so:

1. **Hover your mouse pointer over the education entry you'd like to rearrange.**

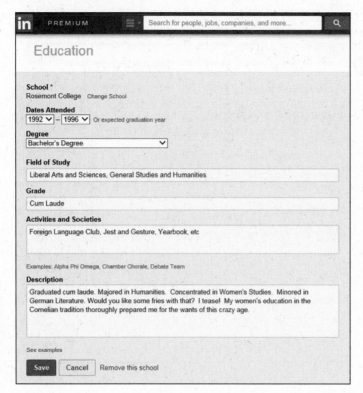

FIGURE 11-10:
Adding
educational
background
and experience
information to
the Education
section.

2. **Click and hold the Up/Down arrow that appears to the right of your school name, as shown in Figure 11-11.**

3. **Drag the school into the desired position.**

REMEMBER

Only one school is listed at the top of your profile.

Adding multimedia

Add documents, photos, links, videos, and presentations to your entries in the Education section. Are you proud of your thesis? Upload it to your profile! Is there a picture you'd like to include? Upload it to your profile!

Follow these steps to add multimedia to your education entries:

1. **Within the Education section of your profile, select the appropriate icon next to Add Media: Document, Photo, Link, Video, Presentation.**

   You can upload documents in the following formats: .pdf, .doc, .docx, .rtf, or odt.

   You can upload photos in the following formats: .png, .gif, .jpg, or .jpeg.

Click and hold to reorder your listed schools

FIGURE 11-11:
Reordering the
schools in your
Education
section.

You can upload presentations in the following formats: .pdf, .ppt, .pps, .pptx, .ppsx, .pot, .potx, or .odp.

2. **Click Upload a File to display the media on your profile or type in a website URL to link to content that exists on another site and then click Continue. (See Figure 11-12.)**

   If you chose to upload a file, select the file from your desktop. A picture of your content displays. LinkedIn automatically populates the Title and Description fields.

3. **If the prepopulated Title and Descriptions fields aren't correct, click and edit them to your liking.**

4. **Click Save.**

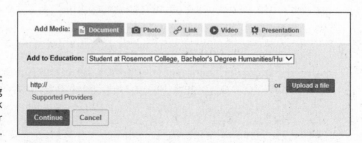

FIGURE 11-12:
Adding
multimedia work
samples to your
education.

Adding Volunteer Experiences

You are more than just a corporate creature. There are causes that you care about and support after work hours. Showing your philanthropic and humanitarian interests proves you are a well-rounded individual, which readers of your profile may find interesting and relatable.

Do you belong to a service organization such as Rotary, Kiwanis, Knights of Columbus, Shriners, or Lions Club?

Do you donate to the Salvation Army, Toys for Tots, Doctors Without Borders, UNICEF, or St Jude Children's Hospital?

Do you take part in the Susan B. Komen Race for a Cure or have donated time to a charitable organization?

The Volunteer section is where you add these items to your LinkedIn profile. Within the Volunteer section of your profile, you can add:

>> Individual volunteer experiences

>> Organizations your support

Individual experiences allow you to showcase the breadth of your work. You can add the name of the organization, your role, the cause it supports, dates of your tenure, and a description. You can also list just the organizations you support, but don't necessarily work one on one with them.

In addition, you can select:

>> Opportunities to donate your time and talent

>> Causes you care about

LinkedIn enables you to select whether you want to donate time or talent to future nonprofit charities. You can also select from a list the causes you hold dear.

Here's how to add a volunteer experience and indicate what volunteer opportunities you are looking for to your profile:

1. **Open your LinkedIn profile.**

2. **If you have the Volunteer section already added to your profile, simply scroll to it and click the pencil (edit) icon to enter into edit mode, then go to Step 5.**

3. **If you don't have the Volunteer section added to your profile yet, scroll below the Contact Information section at the top part of your profile and click the View More link to see a full list of sections to add.**

4. **In the Volunteering Experience section, click Add Volunteer Experience.**

   When clicked, the Volunteer section appears on your profile.

5. **Type the name of the Organization in the Organization field.**

6. **Click Role and add your role or the type of volunteer work you do.**

   This field shows at the top of the individual volunteer experience; it should spotlight either your role or what you are doing specifically. Here are some roles that might work for you: Angel, Backer, Contributor, Supporter, Patron, Donor, Grantor, Giver, Sponsor, Subscriber.

7. **Click the Cause drop-down list and choose the applicable cause from the list.**

   If nothing from the list correctly identifies this volunteer experience, choose the top option that looks like a minus sign to leave this field blank.

8. **In the Date Range fields, choose the month and year from the drop-down lists.**

   LinkedIn defaults to present with no end date. If this Volunteer experience is no longer current, enter an end date by deselecting, I Currently Volunteer Here.

9. **In the Description field, enter information about the volunteer experience.**

   It's better to add context around your experiences and the easiest way to do it is to visit the organization's About Us page on its website.

REMEMBER

10. **Click the Save button.**

11. **Scroll down and hover your mouse pointer over the Opportunities You Are Looking For area and click the pencil (edit) icon to enter into edit mode.**

12. **If you would like to be considered for a nonprofit board or if you would like to offer your skills for free to a nonprofit in need of your specialty, click the boxes to select.**

13. **Click the Save button.**

14. **Scroll down and hover your mouse pointer over the Causes You Care About and click the pencil (edit) icon to enter into edit mode.**

15. **Select the causes you care about by clicking the boxes.**

16. **Under Which Organization(s) Do You Support, enter any additional charitable organizations you would like listed on your profile.**

   The charitable organizations to add are those that you are not actively donating time. Click inside the text field and begin typing. LinkedIn tries to match the organization you are typing with one that already has a page on

LinkedIn. Click the option from the drop-down list or add it free-form if no match is available. To add multiple organizations, press the Tab or Return keys.

17. **Click the Save button.**

    See Figure 11-13 for an example of a completed Volunteer section.

18. **To add additional volunteer experiences, Click Add Volunteer Experience and lather, rinse, repeat.**

Pro bono opportunities

By filling out the Volunteer section, you are able to state whether you are open to joining a nonprofit board or offer your skills pro bono to a nonprofit. This is a great way to get even more involved. When your skills match what a nonprofit is looking for, LinkedIn sends an email to you alerting you of the opportunity.

TIP

Visit the LinkedIn Volunteer Marketplace to find out more about offering your own skills consulting pro bono. Simply visit `Volunteer.LinkedIn.com` to see volunteer opportunities available to LinkedIn members.

Causes you care about

To make it even easier to explain to the world in the simplest language what you truly care about, LinkedIn compiled the top causes in the world and distilled them down to 14 items. For example, within the Volunteer section, you can show the world that you care about Animal Welfare and Economic Empowerment.

Here is the list of causes to choose from:

>> Animal Welfare

>> Arts and Culture

>> Children

>> Civil Rights and Social Action

>> Disaster and Humanitarian Relief

>> Economic Empowerment

>> Education

>> Environment

>> Health

>> Human Rights

>> Politics

>> Poverty Alleviation

>> Science and Technology

>> Social Services

TIP

When working with clients, the biggest mistake I see is choosing all 15 causes. This makes your true interest seem rather dubious. Instead, choose the top three or five causes. If you truly care about all 15 causes equally, think in terms of your target audience and choose the causes closest to their heart.

In the next chapter, I show you how to personalize your profile even more with interests, multimedia work samples, and a background image. I also walk you through how to best leverage recommendations. When you are ready, I'll meet you there!

Chapter **12**

Making Your Profile Personal and Unique

Your LinkedIn profile is more than just text. You can also upload images and multimedia content. In this chapter, I show you how to turn your flat, text-based profile into a graphically attractive profile that is not only eye-catching, but also makes your reader want to learn more about you.

I also show you how to turn your profile from solely professional to one that incorporates your interests and personality so you can create stronger rapport and build an actual relationship with your reader.

Lastly, I take you through the ins and outs of asking for and providing recommendations. I even provide you with my number-one secret to getting tons of glowing recommendations that crank up your credibility and results on LinkedIn.

Leveraging the Additional Information Section

The Additional Information section of your LinkedIn profile is divided into three areas: Interests, Personal Details, and Advice for Contacting. Although LinkedIn is strictly professional, this one section allows for the addition of some personal information. Not only can you add your extracurricular activities, but also you can add your birthday and marital status along with advice for how you would prefer to be contacted by your readers. Filling this section out isn't difficult, but it does present a number of potential issues, and it's important to fill the fields out strategically.

Adding interests

The Interests area of the Additional Information section is where you connect with your reader on a more personal level by adding your hobbies and interests to your LinkedIn profile. I often hear clients say, "But Donna, LinkedIn isn't Facebook; it's professional! I don't want to list my hobbies and interests!"

Remember this: *People do business with people.* That's why when you walk into another person's office for the first time, the very first thing you do is look around. You look for pictures, plaques, trophies, memorabilia, and other objects that give you an idea of his or her personality, likes, and dislikes. As soon as you spy a commonality, you have a conversation starter. For example:

"Oh, I see you swam with dolphins. I love scuba diving. Have you been to Bermuda?"

This is how you forge a connection and build a relationship.

The Interests area allows you to connect with your reader at a deeper, more personal level, and it shows that you have a life outside of work. People love to work with people who are friendly and who lead fun and interesting lives.

The interests you choose should reflect shared characteristics with your target audience. There is no greater way to forge rapport when you have shared interests in common. I am not suggesting that you lie about your interests, but definitely determine what you have in common with your target audience and showcase it in the Interests area.

In addition to shared interests, the interests you choose should reflect how you want to be perceived by your target audience. Prove you are the leader you say you are by choosing interests that reflect the qualities of a leader, like boat captain, Little League coach, or Grand Poohbah of the Loyal Order of Water Buffalo. If you want to appear technically savvy, mention that you enjoy the latest gadgets, building computers, or coding websites for nonprofit organizations.

As you choose your interests, keep your target audience in mind. If your target audience is comprised of animal lovers and members of People for the Ethical Treatment of Animals (PETA), you may want to leave out your love of boar hunting. As much as I am a believer in authenticity and truth, there are times when you must be smart with the information you share. If an interest you list has the potential to spark worry or requires a discussion to explain, it's best to leave it off your profile. You don't want to upset your target audience and risk having them move on to the next profile because of a silly interest.

TIP

When you discuss politics and religion, you risk alienating half of your audience. Even though you may have a strong connection to either, it's sometimes best to leave these interests off your profile entirely.

Here's how to add interests to your LinkedIn profile:

1. **Open your LinkedIn profile.**

   If you have already added information to the Additional Information section, go to Step 3. If you don't have this section on your profile yet, continue to Step 2.

2. **Click the Additional Information section that appears toward the top of your profile to add the Interests section to your profile page.**

   You may need to click View More to find this section.

3. **Scroll to Interests and click Add Interests.**

   When clicked, the Interests section appears on your profile within the Additional Information section.

4. **Scroll to the Additional Information section, hover your mouse pointer over the Interests area, and click the pencil (edit) icon to enter into edit mode.**

5. **Click your mouse inside the text field and start typing your interests.**

TIP

When you enter your interests, separate each term with a comma, as shown in Figure 12-1. LinkedIn automatically links your interests to other profiles that contain those words. By separating your interests with commas, LinkedIn knows what words should be hyperlinked. If you don't include commas, the entire phrase becomes one giant hyperlinked group of words connecting you to no one.

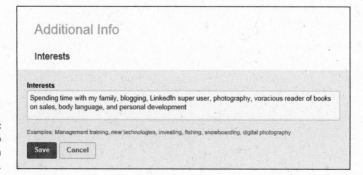

FIGURE 12-1:
Add interests to your LinkedIn profile.

INTEREST IDEAS

Not sure what to list in the Interests section? Here are a bunch of interests categorized by the personality characteristics they convey.

Adventurous

Luger

Rafting

Rock Climbing

Travel

Zip lining

Focused

Blogging

Coin Collector

Electronics

Gadgets

Investments

Model Airplanes

Stamp Collector

Tech Savvy

Web Design

Giver

Fundraising

Helping the Disadvantaged

Humanitarian

Philanthropist

Volunteer work

Healthy

Circuit Training

Hiking

Sailing

Sports

Swimming

Intelligent

Chess

History

Personal Development

Reading Books

Writing

Leader

Community Association Board President

Entrepreneur

Little League Coach

Pilot

Sailboat Captain

Well-Rounded, Cultured

Cooking

Museums

Spending Time with My Kids

Wine Tasting

Now that you have your interests documented in your LinkedIn profile, you can now discover other professionals with similar interests. Here's how:

1. **Open your LinkedIn profile.**

2. **At the top of your profile, click the blue View Profile As button.**

   Your profile now appears as a connection would see it.

3. **Scroll to the Interests area in the Additional Information section and click one of the hyperlinked interests.**

   LinkedIn takes you to a search results page of profiles containing that term.

4. **In the right sidebar, place a check mark next to 1st Connections.**

   LinkedIn filters the list by first-degree connections.

5. **Scroll through the list to see which of your first-degree connections share this interest with you.**

   This is great information. Knowing you have commonality, perhaps you want to ask that client to a round of Frisbee golf?

Providing details that show you are human

The next two fields in the Additional Information section are where you add your birthday and marital status. If you don't already have these fields on your LinkedIn profile, here's how to add them:

1. **Open your LinkedIn profile.**

2. **Click the Additional Info section that appears toward the top of your profile to add the Personal Details section to your profile page.**

   You may need to click View More to find this section.

3. **Scroll to Personal Details and click Add Personal Details, as shown in Figure 12-2.**

   The Personal Details fields appear on your profile within the Additional Info section, as shown in Figure 12-3.

FIGURE 12-2:
Adding Personal
Details to your
profile.

Click to add personal details to your profile

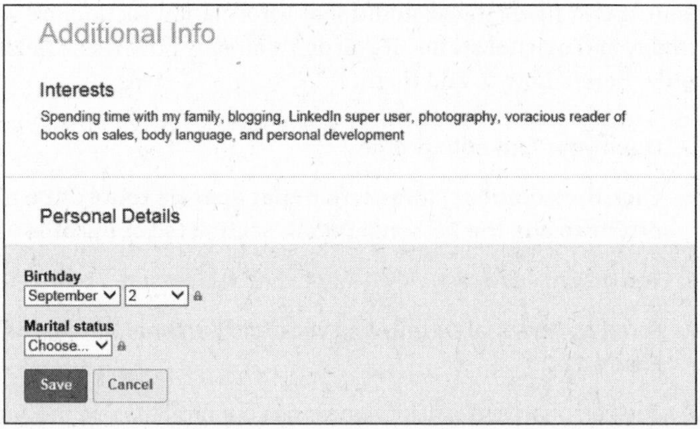

FIGURE 12-3:
The Personal
Details fields.

Your birthday is an event that LinkedIn recognizes and alerts your network so that they can wish you "Happy Birthday!" On my last birthday, my assistant calculated that over 500 birthday greetings arrived in my LinkedIn Messages from my Linke-dIn network.

I highly recommend filling out the Birthday field because it offers the potential for networking and an excuse to get back in touch with people. Plus, LinkedIn doesn't ask for your birth year, so your age isn't front and center, just that you are celebrating a birthday. All you have to do is click the down arrows to select the month and date.

The Marital Status field is an informational field. It isn't searchable within LinkedIn's advanced search. There is potential for it to be used in audience targeting for LinkedIn advertisements; however, currently LinkedIn doesn't offer marital status as criteria for advertisement targeting.

To fill out the Marital Status field, all you do is click the down arrow and choose Married or Single. If your status is something different, select "Choose. . ." to keep the field blank.

The decision to fill out the Marital Status field is one you should approach strategically. When I was single, I left the field blank. My reasoning at that time was that I didn't want to advertise being single. LinkedIn isn't a dating site, and I didn't want people getting the wrong impression. In addition, I felt people might see me as less stable and mature. Now I am married, but I continue to keep my marital status off my profile because I don't want people thinking I am not as committed to my business as I am to my marriage.

Working in a conservative industry where married people are viewed more favorably, it may serve you to add this piece of information to your profile. On the flip side, there are industries where those who are not married are favored, and you may either want to omit your married status or, if you are single, tout that instead.

You have control over who sees the contents of these fields. By clicking the lock icon next to the Birthday and Marital Status fields, you are able to set the visibility to:

>> Only Me (Birthday field only)

>> My Connections

>> My Network

>> Everyone

By selecting Everyone, anyone who views your profile, regardless of whether he or she is connected to you or not, sees the contents of the fields. Selecting My

Connections means that only people who are directly connected to you see the contents of the fields. If you choose My Network, your first-, second-, and third-degree network and members who are in the same LinkedIn Groups as you see this information. Figure 12-4 shows you what this screen looks like.

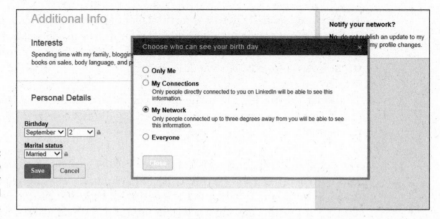

FIGURE 12-4:
Controlling who
sees your
personal
information.

The Additional Information section doesn't appear on your public profile, so people viewing your profile who are not logged in to LinkedIn can't see this information. Think it through and decide if it behooves you to fill these fields in. If you are not comfortable letting people know this information, leave the fields blank.

Offering advice for contacting you

The next area within the Additional Information section is Advice for Contacting. This is a fantastic field that few people ever fill out. This area doesn't show up on your public profile, but it is visible to your LinkedIn network. Just as the name implies, this is where you tell your audience why and how to contact you directly.

REMEMBER

Success on LinkedIn is getting off of LinkedIn. It's in the real world where strong relationships are forged. The Advice for Contacting section helps your reader get off of LinkedIn and start down the path toward real-world communication with you. When you let people know why and how to contact you, you open the door for opportunity.

Rather than leaving it up to your readers, tell them why they should contact you. If you are a job seeker, you can state, "To learn more about my professional history, please request my resume." Or, "If you have a job opportunity to discuss, please contact me directly." If you are on LinkedIn as a salesperson, you might state, "If you are interested in learning more about our services and pricing, contact me today." A thought leader might use, "If you are interested in having me speak at an event, or if you are looking for a snappy quote or interview subject for a news article, please feel free to contact me."

Not everyone prefers the phone. Do you pay more attention to text messages? Do you rarely check voicemail but always check email? Is Skype your communication mode of choice? This is information to share with your readers so they know the most successful way to reach you.

Subtlety doesn't work here. Instead, be direct. For example:

> *The best way to reach me is via Skype. My username is donna.serdula. If email is better for you, my address is donna@linkedin-makeover.com.*

Here's how to edit the Advice for Contacting section:

1. **Open your LinkedIn profile.**

   If you have already added information to the Additional Information section, go to Step 3. If you don't have this section on your profile yet, continue to Step 2.

2. **Click the Additional Information section that appears toward the top of your profile to add the Advice for Contacting section to your profile page.**

   You may need to click View More to find this section.

3. **Scroll to the Advice for Contacting section, hover your mouse pointer below Advice for Contacting, and click the pencil (edit) icon to enter into edit mode.**

4. **Click your mouse inside the text field and start typing your advice to your readers.**

   Figure 12-5 shows you an example of great advice on how to contact me.

5. **Click the Save button.**

The Advice for Contacting section is visible to your full LinkedIn network. This provides the possibility that your phone number or email address might be used for marketing or nefarious purposes. However, there is an even better chance that your contact information will be used to benefit you.

Recruiters, reporters, event planners, hiring managers, angel investors, long-lost colleagues, donors, and others will use it to reach you. If I haven't changed your mind about including your contact information in the Advice for Contacting section, read Chapter 5, where I provide alternative contact information ideas for those troubled by identification theft fears.

Additional Info

Interests

Spending time with my family, blogging, LinkedIn super user, photography, voracious reader of books on sales, body language, and personal development

Personal Details

Birthday   September 2

Advice for Contacting Donna

I welcome all calls and emails. Whether you need someone to help you write your LinkedIn profile, your team's LinkedIn profiles, or something else entirely (resumes, recommendations, blogs, bios, etc) reach me at:

Phone: 215-839-0008
Email: Donna@LinkedIn-Makeover.com

You can find my full contact information here:

★ http://www.LinkedIn-Makeover.com/contact ★

I look forward to hearing from you.

FIGURE 12-5:
Let folks know how best to contact you.

Blocking people from viewing your profile

It's not always identity theft that stops LinkedIn users from wanting to provide their contact information on their profiles. There are times when someone may be dealing with a stalker or an abusive person. In these situations, LinkedIn does allow you to limit a person's access to your profile and LinkedIn activity.

WARNING

You can only block people from your desktop using LinkedIn's website. LinkedIn's mobile application does not yet allow the ability to block people.

Here's how to block a person from seeing your profile on LinkedIn:

1. In the LinkedIn search bar, type the name of the person you want to block and click the search button.

A list of profiles matching the name appear as search results.

2. Open the profile of the person you want to block by clicking the search result.

When you view a person's profile, depending on your settings, that person may be able to see that you viewed his or her profile. Once you block the person, you disappear from his or her Who's Viewed Your Profile section.

3. Hover your mouse pointer over the down arrow next to the button in the top section of the member's profile and select Block or Report from the list, as shown in Figure 12-6.

A Block or Report this person dialog box appears.

4. **Check the box next to Block.**

5. **Click Continue.**

6. **On the next screen, click Agree to confirm your action.**

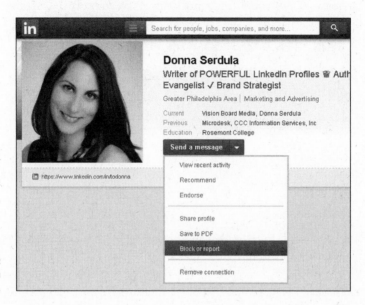

When you block a person from viewing your profile, that person is not alerted and should not know anything is amiss. Only you can unblock a person you blocked. When you block a person, you won't be able to access his or her profile, and that person won't be able to view yours. In addition, you won't be able to see each other's LinkedIn activity or message one another.

If you are connected, that connection goes away along with any endorsements or recommendations that person gave to you or you gave to that person. Any previous views listed under Who's Viewed Your Profile are wiped. Lastly, all suggestions under People You May Know or People Also Viewed stop.

TIP

The block only works when the person is logged into LinkedIn. If he or she logs off LinkedIn and accesses your public profile, that person is still able to see your public information. To keep your profile truly private, you should also hide the public version of your profile that's visible to search engines and people not signed into LinkedIn. Check out Chapter 4 to see how to turn on and turn off your public profile.

Adding Multimedia to Make Your Profile POP!

LinkedIn allows you to add work samples to your profile. Adding multimedia is a great way to further your professional brand on LinkedIn and truly make your profile eye-catching. Types of multimedia samples you can add include:

>> Documents

>> Images

>> Presentations

You can also link to:

>> Images

>> Online videos

>> Rich media (such as foursquare check-ins, polls, Kickstarter campaigns, Tumblr, and so on)

The areas of your profile that allow multimedia work samples are:

>> Education

>> Individual job experiences

>> Summary

Determining what to highlight with multimedia files

Adding multimedia to your profile is a great way to showcase your work and provide your audience with proof of your abilities. Certainly when you are in a creative field, adding work samples is pretty easy. It's your best portfolio pieces that you upload to your Summary and individual Experiences. But what if you aren't in a creative field?

Think in terms of your goals and target audience. If you are on LinkedIn to be seen as a thought leader and expert, upload that podcast interview or link to that video interview on YouTube. Scan that newspaper article in which you were quoted.

Looking to be seen as a leader? Upload a picture of you and your department at a team building event.

Using LinkedIn for prospecting and sales? Upload that presentation slideshow or video demo you created.

On LinkedIn for job search? Showcase your work by uploading a white paper or a dashboard report (minus any confidential or proprietary information) showing your past successes.

Make sure that what you choose makes sense to your reader. It's best to include a title and descriptions for each multimedia file or link you attach to your profile.

Once you decide what to upload, here's how to do it:

1. **Open your profile on LinkedIn.**

2. **Scroll to either your Summary, Experience, or Education section where you want the multimedia work sample to reside.**

3. **Hover your mouse pointer over the section and click the Add Media button that corresponds with the type of media you want to add, as shown in Figure 12-7.**

   If you don't see an Add Media bar, look for an icon in the shape of a little square with a plus sign to the right of the section heading.

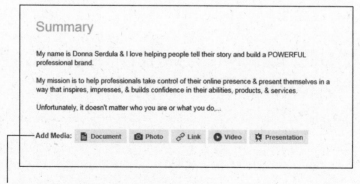

FIGURE 12-7:
Adding
multimedia files.

Select the type of media you want to add

4. **To add a link to external media, paste the URL into the blank URL field and click the Continue button.**

5. **If you would prefer to upload media that resides on your hard drive, click the Upload button.**

An open dialog box appears. Locate the file on your hard drive and click the Open button.

6. **Enter a title and description, as shown in Figure 12-8.**

7. **Click Save.**

FIGURE 12-8:
Adding a description to a work sample media file.

VIDEO RESUMES: WHEN THEY WORK AND WHEN THEY DON'T

Every now and then I see video resumes on LinkedIn profiles. Video resumes are used in addition to the traditional resume and cover letter. Usually one to three minutes in length, a video resume features job candidates talking straight to the camera, introducing themselves, summarizing a success they achieved, and explaining their ideal position.

Many companies tout video resumes as the key to getting that elusive job offer. The problem I have is that few people are comfortable in front of a camera. Just as the possibility is there that a video resume can get you the job, it can also help you lose a job. So often video resumes come across as rather silly, and the person often looks stilted and uncomfortable. If you are exceptionally good-looking and have been trained to work the camera, then by all means, go for it. If you are a regular Joe or Judy, you may decide to steer clear of the whole fiasco. Just because you can, doesn't mean you should.

Resisting the urge to upload your resume

You may run into "experts" who insist you upload a copy of your resume to your LinkedIn profile. I don't agree.

You want your LinkedIn profile to be the hook that gets people to request your resume. That way, you have control and can determine who gets to have access it. Your resume contains your complete career trajectory and you don't want just anyone able to download it.

Recruiters love it when a resume is attached to your profile — this way they can read it without ever contacting you and they can immediately dismiss you without ever talking to you. You want recruiters and hiring managers and human resources people to contact you so that you can show them you are a real person — you can ask questions and make a great impression while engaging in human contact.

TIP

However, if you decide to upload your resume to your LinkedIn profile, consider removing your home address and any confidential information you aren't comfortable sharing with the whole wide world. Your employer may not be too keen on you publicly sharing how you singlehandedly saved them from bankruptcy twice in the past six months.

Although I don't recommend uploading your resume to your profile, you may feel otherwise. If you are clear on the reasons not to and still think it makes sense to do, here's how:

1. **Open your LinkedIn profile.**

2. **Move your mouse pointer over the section to which you want to add your resume and click the Add Media icon in the upper-right corner.**

   I suggest uploading it to your Summary section or to your most current experience.

3. **Select Upload a File.**

   An Open dialog box appears.

4. **Locate and select your resume file from your hard drive and click Open.**

   A picture of your content displays, and sometimes LinkedIn automatically fills in the Title and Description fields with information from the file. Regardless, update the Title and Description fields to something that makes sense for your reader.

5. **Click Save.**

Reinforcing Your Brand with a Background Image

LinkedIn profiles used to be so plain, especially when compared with Twitter and Facebook where you are able to upload large, eye-catching banner images. LinkedIn eventually came around and now allows you to upload a background image to visually spice up your profile.

This background image is only visible to LinkedIn members who view your profile while logged in. The background image doesn't appear on your public profile.

Finding the right image to showcase your brand

When choosing a LinkedIn background image, make sure the image matches your personal/professional brand and conveys your unique message. Choose images that inspire you or reflect what you do.

Here are some ideas:

>> An image of the products you sell or produce

>> A picture of your office building or interior

>> A team photo

>> An illustration or photo that shows an analogy of what you do (lighthouse, magnifying glass, owl, tree, and so on)

>> A picture of you at a podium or presenting in front of an audience

REMEMBER

The image you choose must be professional and it must reflect your personal brand.

LinkedIn's background image is responsive, which means the image can grow and shrink depending on the screen size of the device you are using to view it. Think in terms of the screen size differences between a desktop monitor, a laptop, and a little iPhone. These different devices all have different screen sizes. Utilizing a responsive image means that your profile should look good regardless of what device is used to view it.

Because the background image is responsive, there are areas of the image that you almost always see and other areas where you may only sometimes see. This means you have to be careful with the image you select and the placement of any logos.

Figure 12-9 shows the portion of the background image that is universally visible and the areas that are sometimes visible. To download this image to use as a template, access it here: www.linkedin-makeover.com/tools/background.

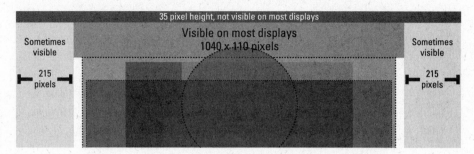

35 pixel height, not visible on most displays

Sometimes visible

Visible on most displays
1040 x 110 pixels

Sometimes visible

215 pixels

215 pixels

FIGURE 12-9:
Background image template.

When choosing your background image, make sure the focal point of the image is not located in an area that is not visible.

Depending on your goals and budget, you may want to reach out to a graphic designer for assistance. www.Fivrr.com and www.99Designs.com are two easy and affordable ways to work with graphic designers. If working with a graphic designer is outside your budget, don't worry! It's easy to create a background graphic yourself using free, online tools, which I discuss in the next section, "Using online graphic tools to create an image."

TIP

Premium LinkedIn members get to choose different background images from a gallery. As wonderful it is to have already created background images, these images are overused and no longer unique. I recommend not using LinkedIn's background images and finding something unique to you and your brand.

Using online graphic tools to create an image

When looking for an image to turn into your LinkedIn background, you must be careful not to steal. Just because you saw an image on Google search or on another person's website doesn't mean it's ripe for the picking. If you found an image you truly love and is perfect for your background image, you can attempt to reach out to the creator of the image and ask permission to use it. Rather than get caught up in finding email addresses and asking permission, it's actually easier to simply visit websites that provide royalty-free stock images.

A few of my favorite sites that specialize in free images are:

- » Barn Images (http://barnimages.com)
- » Raumrot (http://raumrot.com)
- » Pixabay (https://pixabay.com)
- » Unspash (https://unsplash.com)
- » FreeImages (www.freeimages.com)
- » Photocrops (www.photocrops.com)
- » UHD Wallpapers (www.uhdwallpapers.org)

Have you ever heard of the old saying, "you get what you pay for?" With royalty-free stock images, the quality of images isn't always grade A. If you aren't finding any free images you like, you may decide to shop for images instead.

Here are a few sites where you can search and purchase professionally rendered images:

- » GraphicRiver (http://graphicriver.net)
- » iStock (www.istockphoto.com)
- » ShutterStock (www.shutterstock.com)

Are you interested in getting a branded image from your company's website? You can grab images off your company's website fairly easily. Using a print screen tool like Microsoft's Snipping Tool, which is available in the Accessories folder (if you are on a Mac, press Cmd+Shift+4), you can capture images from your website. Depending on how the website is coded, sometimes all you need to do is hover your mouse over the image, right-click your mouse, and choose Save Image As.

REMEMBER

Regardless of how you obtained the image, you must resize it to the requisite dimensions of 1,400 pixels wide by 425 pixels tall. Images sized incorrectly look blurry or pixelated and that comes across as very unprofessional.

My favorite free online tool for resizing images and creating interesting, personalized photo montages is Canva (www.canva.com). Canva is an online graphic design application that offers access to free and paid design tools and templates.

Here's how to use Canva to create an interesting background image for your LinkedIn profile:

1. **Visit Canva.com in your favorite browser.**

   If you have never used Canva before, you need to create an account. It's easy to sign up with your Facebook account.

2. **Click Use Custom Dimension in the top-right corner of the screen.**

   In the Width field enter 1400. In the Height field enter 425.

3. **Click the green Design! Button.**

4. **Click the Uploads tool in the left sidebar.**

5. **Click the green "Upload Your Own Images" button.**

   An Open dialog box appears.

6. **Locate the background image you want to resize, highlight it, and click the Open button.**

   The image uploads to Canva.

7. **Locate the uploaded image and click and drag it to the white canvas on the right side of the screen.**

   The image fills the canvas.

8. **If the image is too small, expand the image by clicking a corner and dragging to resize it, or add another image so that it becomes a montage of images.**

9. **Click the Text tool in the left sidebar to add words to your image.**

   Make sure the text is located in an area that is visible.

10. **Once you are finished designing your image, click the Download button at the top of the screen, and in the drop-down box that appears, click Image:high quality (PNG).**

    A Save As dialog box appears.

11. **Select where on your hard drive you would like to save the image and click Save.**

Adding a background image to your profile

Now that you have a beautiful background image, here's how to add it to your LinkedIn profile:

1. **Open your LinkedIn profile.**

2. **Hover your mouse pointer over the top part of your profile where your background image will go and click the Edit Background button that appears.**

3. **Click the Upload button.**

   An Open dialog box appears.

4. **Locate the background image file from your hard drive and click Open.**

   The image is uploaded and appears in preview mode. Dragging your mouse over the preview image allows you to align it.

5. **Once you are happy with the alignment of your image, click Save.**

   Your background image appears at the top of your profile.

The Importance of Recommendations

Recommendations are testimonials that appear on your profile, showing your reader you are trusted and admired within your network. Recommendations are given by first-degree connections and provide citation to your value and abilities and make your profile more credible.

If you are a job seeker, recommendations from your current or past employer and colleagues sets you apart from other job applicants. When your goal is branding or reputation management, a strong list of recommendations from VIPs and leaders boasting your finer points provides evidence to your reader that you truly are a high performing, impressive professional. If you are promoting your business, products, or services, having recommendations from your current clients touting your strengths impresses your prospects.

You may be thinking, "What's the merit in a LinkedIn recommendation when every recommendation on LinkedIn is glowing?"

The power behind LinkedIn recommendations is it's easy to find out how significant or insignificant the person is who wrote your recommendation by simply clicking on the person's name and visiting his or her LinkedIn profile to learn more. It is not what the recommendation says that's so important, *It's who wrote it*. The short recommendation from someone in a high place is significantly better than the glowing recommendation from a colleague or vendor.

Identifying people to recommend you

The best kind of recommendation comes from employers, VIPs, or customers. These are people with a lot of things on their plates. The fact they took time and wrote you a recommendation speaks volumes and proves that you truly did something important. Recommendations by colleagues and people in lateral or lower positions are useful, but not nearly as powerful. The quid pro quo recommendation, given out of duty, impresses no one. Check out Figure 12-10 to see the types of people you should ask for a recommendation.

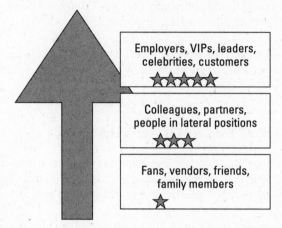

FIGURE 12-10:
Order of
recommenders
by importance.

Here are some questions to help you identify the right people to ask for a recommendation:

>> Who have you helped?

>> Who have you impressed?

>> Who have you inspired?

>> Who have you provided value?

>> Who has recently thanked you?

If you have a large list and don't want to send a recommendation request to each and every one, here's how to narrow the list:

>> Who is on LinkedIn?

>> Who has a large LinkedIn network?

>> Who is active on LinkedIn?

>> Who shares your target audience?

When a person writes a recommendation for you, that recommendation is also listed on that person's profile. By making sure the person has a large network and shares your target audience means more eyes on the recommendation, which might translate to additional opportunity for you.

You can only request recommendations from people who are on LinkedIn and connected to you. However, if you want to add a recommendation from a person who is not on LinkedIn or from someone who has passed on to the great beyond, you can scan the recommendation and add it to the experience as a multimedia file. Directions on adding multimedia files are found in "Adding Multimedia to Make Your Profile POP!" earlier in this chapter.

If you were unable to come up with a list, what are you waiting for? Go out and start impressing people, help others, and start participating in random acts of kindness.

Asking for a recommendation

Now that you have a list of people to ask for a recommendation, don't let shyness get in your way. People love helping other people and you may discover that most people are honored that you asked them to recommend you.

The best and most successful approach when asking for a recommendation is not to simply request a recommendation, but provide the person with a recommendation already written for them.

People often balk when I suggest providing a pre-written recommendation. The truth is, rather than being insulted, more often than not the other person is going to be overjoyed. The vast majority of people out there don't have the time or ability to write you a strong recommendation. Because this person is doing you a favor, it's important to do them a favor by making it as easy for them as possible to help you. And as you struggle to come up with the words for your own recommendation, imagine how difficult it would be for the other person!

The other reason I suggest writing the recommendation yourself is to ensure the recommendation is written with all of the points you want covered. Just because you think your leadership ability and unwavering commitment to customer service is what sets you apart, the person writing your recommendation may instead focus on something else entirely.

In addition, by writing the recommendation yourself, you can infuse the recommendation with keywords that help optimize your profile's searchability. All those keywords can be infused into recommendations to make your profile rank even better. (Refer back to Chapter 2 to find out even more about how to get found on LinkedIn.)

If my arguments to write the recommendation yourself failed to persuade you, at the very least provide the person with some criteria as to what you'd like stated in the recommendation. Consider including language similar to this:

Dear Dave,

I have enjoyed working with you. Would you be open to providing me a recommendation of my work that I can include on my LinkedIn profile?

When you write the recommendation, I would love it if you'd mention my strength in social selling and how I often acted as a trusted advisor to my clients. Perhaps you can even mention how I saved the Wiener deal using my extensive knowledge of widgets and ended up renewing them for an extra two years, which resulted in a $2M uptick in revenue?

Thanks so much! I appreciate it!

—Hal

When requesting a recommendation, it's important that you request the recommendation from within LinkedIn's interface. Whatever you do, don't send the request for a recommendation via an outside email address. Emailing the request makes it difficult for your contact to figure out how to provide the recommendation. By sending the request from LinkedIn's recommendation page, your contacts can easily click the link that LinkedIn provides, making it easy for them to give you a recommendation.

WRITING THE PERFECT RECOMMENDATION

When writing a recommendation for yourself, the best thing to do is list your qualities you want highlighted. If you aren't quite sure what qualities you want highlighted, ask yourself the following questions:

- How does this person know you?

- How long have you known each other?

- How did you work together?

- Detail a singular experience in which you exhibited a high level of leadership as it fits within his or her knowledge of you.

- What one quality of yours proved beneficial to this person? What was the result?

- Did you mentor or work alongside this person? What impact did you have on him or her?

Use the answers to these questions to craft a powerful recommendation.

Here's how to request a recommendation from within LinkedIn:

1. Open your LinkedIn profile.

2. Hover your mouse pointer over the down arrow next to the View Profile As button in the top section of your profile.

3. Select Ask To Be Recommended.

The Recommendations page opens, and the first question you are asked is, "What do you want to be recommended for?"

4. Click the drop-down arrow and select the position the recommendation is for.

The second question you are asked is, "Who do you want to ask?"

5. Enter the name of the person in the empty field.

As you type, LinkedIn suggests contacts with similar names.

6. Select the person from the drop-down list.

TIP

LinkedIn allows you to ask up to three different people per recommendation request. I highly suggest only asking one person per request. It's important to personalize the request, and that is impossible if you are asking numerous people at once.

7. Choose your relationship to the person.

You have numerous options. Read through the list carefully and choose the relationship that most closely echoes yours. Unfortunately, there is no "other" option, so you must determine the best fit. Luckily, the other person has a chance to make changes, so if he or she doesn't feel you used the proper relationship option, he or she can change it for you.

8. Choose the other person's position at the time from the drop-down list.

The drop-down list contains a listing of the person's experiences as listed it on his or her LinkedIn profile.

9. Change the Subject line of the message if you are so inclined.

LinkedIn prepopulates the Subject field with the title, "Can you recommend me?" This is a perfectly acceptable subject for the message, but you may change it if you wish.

Directly below the Subject field is a pre-written recommendation that LinkedIn provides. As I have stated, it is best to add the recommendation for the person or at the very least, guidelines to what you want covered in the recommendation.

Figure 12-11 illustrates an example of the recommendation request form.

10. Click the Send button when you are ready to send your request.

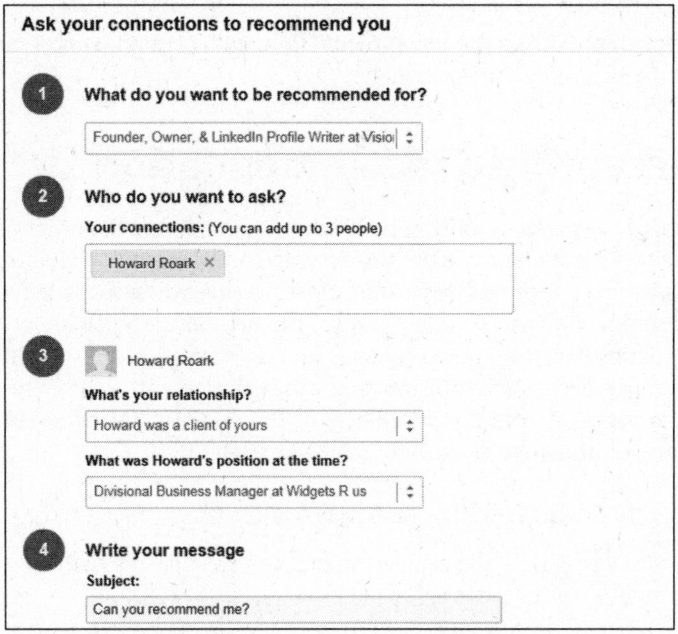

FIGURE 12-11:
LinkedIn's
recommendation
request form.

Your request for a recommendation is sent as a LinkedIn message. Depending on your LinkedIn settings, you may also receive a notification alert via email.

Ditching the default request text

When requesting a recommendation from a connection, LinkedIn provides a pre-written request for you to send. Rather than use LinkedIn's default text, personalize the message instead. Try something like this:

> *Dear Fran,*
>
> *It's been a pleasure working with you and accomplishing so much together. It would be an honor to include a recommendation from you on my LinkedIn profile. I know how busy you are so I took the liberty of writing the recommendation for you. Please feel free to make any edits, and if you would prefer to write your own recommendation, please do so. Thank you in advance and I hope we can do lunch together soon.*
>
> *<insert pre-written recommendation>*
>
> *—Ollie*

Once the recommendation request is sent, rather than wait for the other person to respond, I highly suggest reaching out to the person directly to let them know that you requested a recommendation. Give them a call and walk them through the steps of providing the recommendation. Let them know how appreciative you are of the help they are providing.

Accepting a recommendation

One of the perks of writing the recommendation for the other person is how quick the recommendation is usually accepted and posted. My clients who accepted this advice have reported back that most people, when provided with a pre-written recommendation, post it almost immediately. You'll know when the person responds because LinkedIn sends an email notification. In addition to the email, you also get a LinkedIn message from the person giving the recommendation. This message contains a preview of the recommendation and a link to manage your recommendations. Here's how to accept it:

1. **Go to www.linkedin.com/recs/received.**

   Under Pending Recommendations, you see a picture of the recommender and a preview of the recommendation.

2. **Hover your mouse pointer over the recommendation preview and choose to either Add To Profile or Ask For Changes.**

3. **If you need to request a change, click Ask for Changes.**

   A pop-up message appears.

4. **In the text area, type the reason you are requesting a change.**

   A preview of the recommendation appears below the editable area. To make it as easy for the person as possible, highlight the recommendation and right-click with your mouse to copy it. Paste the recommendation into the editable area and make the change for the person.

5. **Click Send.**

   It may seem insulting and wrong to request a replacement, but it's an important thing to do. You don't want to publish a recommendation filled with typos. That would defeat the purpose of the recommendation.

6. **If the recommendation looks great, click Add to Profile.**

TIP

Sometimes you receive recommendations you do not want on your LinkedIn profile. LinkedIn doesn't easily provide a way to archive or delete recommendations. The best thing to do is to accept the recommendation and then immediately go to the Manage Recommendations area and remove the check mark so that the recommendation does not show up on your profile. If the person recommending you has a poor reputation or the recommendation isn't authentic or genuine, it is best to simply accept it and remove it from view.

Reordering recommendations

Recommendations are listed in the order they were received on your LinkedIn profile. The most current recommendations sit at the top. I've heard from people who stopped accepting recommendations because they want a specific recommendation to remain at the top of their profiles and they don't want another lesser recommendation to take the top spot. You don't have to worry about this because LinkedIn allows you to reorder recommendations. Here's how to do it:

1. **Open your LinkedIn profile.**

2. **Scroll down and hover your mouse pointer over the Recommendations section.**

3. **Click the Manage button that appears.**

    You are now at the manage recommendations page.

    To the right of each recommendation is a small image that looks like two arrows pointing up and down.

4. **Click and hold this icon to drag and drop the recommendation wherever you want it to go within the experience it is located.**

    Unfortunately, you can't move a recommendation to another job utilizing the drag-and-drop method.

Removing recommendations

Careers change, people change, and sometimes, a recommendation you accepted a long time ago may not be a recommendation you want on your profile today. Although it's not possible to delete recommendations, you can prevent them from showing on your profile. Here's how:

1. **Open your LinkedIn profile.**

2. **Scroll down and hover your mouse pointer over the Recommendations section.**

3. **Click the Manage button that appears.**

    You are now at the manage recommendations page.

4. **Remove the check mark that appears to the left of the recommendation you wish to remove, as shown in Figure 12-12.**

Recommendations without check marks do not show on your profile. And don't worry: The other person is not notified that the recommendation was removed.

FIGURE 12-12:
Removing a recommendation from your profile.

Recommending others

Everyone knows it's important to get recommendations, but it's also just as important to give recommendations to other people. Think about it. You want to brand yourself as a leader and executive. Leaders and executives don't just get recommendations, they give them!

Most people only provide recommendations when asked. Instead, give recommendations out of the goodness of your heart. Make it a part of your professional life. Once a month, look back and determine who did good by you. Who inspired and impressed you? Without anyone asking, send a glowing recommendation. You might be surprised by the good things that happen when all that karma comes back to you.

TIP

In addition to good karma, writing recommendations for others is a great way to promote yourself. Within the recommendation, introduce yourself and explain what you do. Not only does this give the recommendation context and credibility, but also it serves to get the word out about you.

Here's an example of a self-promoting recommendation:

> *As a Financial Advisor, I work with many small business owners, helping them reach their financial planning goals. I frequently refer Jill Schwettie to my clients that need a small business advisor. The feedback my clients provide me regarding Jill is always very positive. Jill's marketing advice has been instrumental in helping me expand my business. When you are ready to take your business to the next level, reach out to Jill.*

People who read this recommendation may find themselves not only impressed with the person recommended, but also curious about the person providing the recommendation. Remember, the power of LinkedIn recommendations is the ability to click to learn more about the person providing the recommendation, and when you provide a well-written recommendation, a person may click on your profile to learn more about you, the recommender.

Here's how to give a recommendation:

1. **In the LinkedIn search bar, type the name of the person you want to recommend and click the search button.**

    A list of profiles matching the name appears.

2. **Open the profile of the person you want to recommend by clicking the search result.**

3. **Hover your mouse pointer over the down arrow next to the Send a Message button and select Recommend, as shown in Figure 12-13.**

FIGURE 12-13:
Providing a
recommendation.

The Recommendation Management page opens, as shown in Figure 12-14. The first text area is where you write your recommendation. If the person provided the recommendation for you, this is where you copy it and make any tweaks.

4. **Edit the prepopulated text in the message section of the form if you'd like.**

    This message alerts the person for whom you wrote a recommendation.

5. **In the What's Your Relationship field, choose your relationship to the person.**

    You have numerous options. Read through the list carefully and choose the relationship that most closely echoes yours.

6. **In the What Were Your Positions at the Time field, click the drop-down lists to choose your position and the position of the person you are recommending.**

    The drop-down list contains a listing of the person's experiences as listed on his or her LinkedIn profile.

Give Donna Serdula a recommendation

1 **Write a recommendation**

If needed, you can make changes or delete it even after you send it.

> Ex. Donna is very detail-oriented and produced great results for the company...

Your message to Donna

You can personalize this message if you'd like.

> Hi Donna,
> I wrote this recommendation of your work that you can include on your profile.
> Thanks,
> Howard
> http://www.linkedin.com/recs/received

2 **What's your relationship?**

> Choose...

What were your positions at the time?

You: Choose...

FIGURE 12-14:
Filling out the
recommendation
form.

7. **Click the Send button when you are ready to send your recommendation.**

    LinkedIn displays a banner on top of the page that lets you know the recommendation was sent successfully.

WARNING

Some experts out there may tell you that you can have too many recommendations on your LinkedIn profile. I subscribe to the old adage that you can never be too thin, too rich, or have too many recommendations on your profile. As long as the recommendations are genuine, authentic, come from people within your network, and align you with your career future, you truly can't have too many.

I have over 100 recommendations on my profile. I regularly go through and cull the weaker recommendations. I also make sure that the person who is recommending me is a person who is respectable and professional. Otherwise, I remove the recommendation. The ultimate advice I can give you is to accept and show genuine recommendations from good people and never be afraid to remove a recommendation.

In the next chapter, I show you how to truly trick out your profile by following groups, companies, and influencers. I also show you how to blog directly on your LinkedIn profile. Let's go!

Chapter **13**

Following Groups, Companies, and Influencers

Your LinkedIn activity is reflected on your profile. The LinkedIn Groups you join and the influencers and news topics you follow all show up at the bottom of your LinkedIn profile. Rather than ignore this area, build up your brand and online persona by following the right groups, influencers, news topics, companies, and schools to align with your LinkedIn goals.

In this chapter, you learn the importance of joining LinkedIn Groups (and it's not just for the discussion value) and how to choose the best groups. I also show you how to optimize the Following section by choosing the right influencers, news topics, companies, and schools to complete the construction of your profile to your desired brand vision.

Lastly, I show you how to blog on LinkedIn to further develop your professional presence and showcase yourself as a thought leader. Let's get started!

Understanding the Importance of Groups

The groups you join on LinkedIn are listed toward the bottom of your profile in the Groups section. The group logos appear in a grid pattern, showing your reader your online involvement in your industry and community (see Figure 13-1).

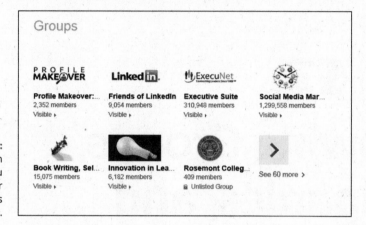

LinkedIn Groups are forums devoted to discussions around a single topic. When reading your LinkedIn newsfeed, you see status updates with discussions, quotes, and links to articles about a myriad of topics. With such a wide range of topics taking place, some people find it overwhelming. On the flip side, when you visit a LinkedIn Group, the discussions are focused on the Group topic, ensuring your interest in the discussions taking place.

When you join the groups that interest you, and you engage successfully, LinkedIn Groups provide you the ability to forge new business relationships with like-minded professionals. Within the group, you can post news, participate in discussions, and network. It is a great way to add value and learn from others.

The only issue when it comes to LinkedIn Groups is your own time limitation. There are a slew of LinkedIn experts and professionals who claim to use LinkedIn Groups to find amazing business opportunity. There is certainly business to be mined, but it takes time and energy that not all of us have in abundance. If you have the time and enjoy interacting in group discussions, do it and reap the rewards. On the other hand, if you are a busy person and do not have the time nor inclination to engage in group discussions, I have another way for you to take advantage of LinkedIn Groups in a passive way that provides real results.

It is not a well-known fact, but LinkedIn Groups expand your LinkedIn network. Your LinkedIn network is comprised of connections within three degrees.

The people you are directly connected to by exchanging and accepting a LinkedIn invite are considered your first-degree connections. The people directly connected to your first-degree connections are considered your second-degree connections. The connections of your second-degree connections are considered your third-degree connections. Your LinkedIn network is also comprised of the members of groups you have joined.

When you perform keyword-based searches on LinkedIn, you are only searching your LinkedIn network. In order to find people and get found, you need to have an extensive network. The fastest and easiest way to expand your network is through joining LinkedIn Groups. People in the same LinkedIn Groups as you are considered part of your LinkedIn network even if they aren't first-, second-, or third-degree connections.

You can join up to 100 LinkedIn Groups. My suggestion is to join 100 groups so you can strengthen and expand your network as wide as possible.

Simply by joining groups, you receive the massive benefit of expanding your LinkedIn network. When you have a strong, large network, you get more views to your profile and collide with more opportunities. You do not have to participate in every single group you join. The only thing you need to ensure is that you join groups that contain your target audience.

Determining the types of groups to join

The LinkedIn Groups you join should contain your target audience — not your competitors. Most people join only groups that reflect their interests and careers. As an example, let's say you are an insurance broker. You may find yourself tempted to join only groups for insurance brokers. When you do that, you are filling your LinkedIn network with your competitors. You don't want to find or be found only by insurance brokers. Instead, think in terms of your target audience. You want to find and be found by prospective customers. Your prospective customers probably belong to LinkedIn Groups for business owners and human resource professionals. Figure out what LinkedIn Groups attract your target audience and join those groups.

Jobseekers should join groups that contain recruiters and human resources professionals. They should research the companies where they want to work and join groups where the employees of their dream companies are members.

Those who are using LinkedIn for executive branding and thought leadership should join groups that contain their target audience. Do you want to be found by reporters and journalists? Join groups for media professionals. Do you want to be asked to speak at conferences? Join groups that cater to conference and event planners. Do you want to be asked for radio interviews? Join groups for radio broadcasters and podcasters.

One of the easiest ways to determine which groups attract your target audience is to visit the profiles of your current customers or target audience members. Scroll to the bottom of their profiles and look at the groups they have listed on the bottom of their LinkedIn profile. After viewing a number of their profiles, you may start to see certain groups repeated across their profiles. Those are the groups you should join.

The other thing to consider when joining LinkedIn Groups is the number of members within the group. Your network grows by the number of people in the group, so choose LinkedIn Groups with the most members. The bigger your network, the more people you find and the more people who find you.

In addition to the groups that fill your network with your target audience, consider joining groups that demonstrate your expertise and industry knowledge. These groups may contain more of your competition than target audience, but that's okay as long as you don't join too many of them.

Another type of groups to join are the groups I like to call "Glory Days." Your university alumni group falls into this category as well as any groups devoted to old companies at which you worked in the past. By joining these groups where old colleagues, schoolmates, and friends are, you are making sure that if you are not directly connected to them yet, they are still in your network. You never know when one of these old relationships may need your new expertise.

Lastly, join a couple groups that are strictly fun. Do you love martial arts? There are a number of great groups devoted to discussions on martial arts. Do you enjoy technology or history or professional development? There are groups related to all of those topics. It's important to have fun on LinkedIn, and it's okay to delve into things you enjoy even if they aren't pertinent to your career. LinkedIn is all about networking, and networking with people who share common interests is a great way to forge real relationships.

Check out Figure 13-2 to see the ideal breakdown of groups you should join on LinkedIn.

If you are so inclined to participate in LinkedIn Groups, choose two or three LinkedIn Groups for your focus. Get into the habit of checking out the group discussions once a week. Participate as you can. Add discussions and comment on already occurring discussions. And guess what? If you simply don't have enough time to keep up with a few groups, don't worry about it. You can still find amazing benefit from LinkedIn Groups without any true participation.

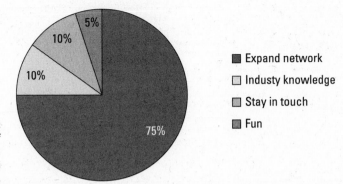

Legend:
- Expand network
- Industy knowledge
- Stay in touch
- Fun

75%
10%
10%
5%

FIGURE 13-2:
A breakdown of the LinkedIn Groups you should join.

TIP

If you love participating in groups, LinkedIn has a LinkedIn Group mobile app. As of 2016, it is available only for the iPhone, but it is slated for release on the Android soon. This mobile app makes it easy to interact with your LinkedIn Groups wherever you are . . . watching TV, in a coffee shop, or trying to look busy during a boring meeting.

Turning off group notifications

Before you start joining groups, especially if you are a currently employed job seeker, it's best to update your notification settings so LinkedIn doesn't notify your network whenever you join a new group. Here's how:

1. **Go to** LinkedIn.com.

2. **Hover your mouse pointer over the thumbnail image of yourself in the upper-right corner of your screen and click Manage next to Privacy & Settings.**

   LinkedIn's settings page opens.

3. **Along the top of the settings page, click Communications.**

4. **Under Groups, click Group notifications.**

   This setting expands to show more information

5. **If "Would you like to publish an update to your network whenever you join a group?" is switched to Yes, click it to select No.**

   By selecting No, when you join a LinkedIn Group your network is not alerted. See Figure 13-3.

Joining recommended groups

There are over two million groups on LinkedIn. Search LinkedIn to find groups that match your target audience and interests or allow LinkedIn to recommend groups to you. LinkedIn looks at commonalities you share with members of different groups such as companies, schools, or industries. Those groups with members that share the most attributes with you are presented as groups you might want to join.

Here's how to discover groups that align with your goals and target audience:

1. **Go to LinkedIn.com.**

2. **Hover your mouse pointer over Interests located in the menu bar at the top of the screen and then click Groups.**

   The My Groups page opens. This is where you see all of the groups you have already joined.

3. **Click Discover on the lower menu bar.**

   The Discover page opens. This is where LinkedIn recommends groups to you.

4. **Scroll through LinkedIn's recommended groups, and if you see a group you would like to join, click the Ask to Join button.**

   Notice the total number of people in the group. The larger the number, the more your network expands when you join. Also, LinkedIn shows you the number of people you know within the group. Are these people your target audience or are they competitors? If they are competitors, you may choose not to join the group. See Figure 13-4.

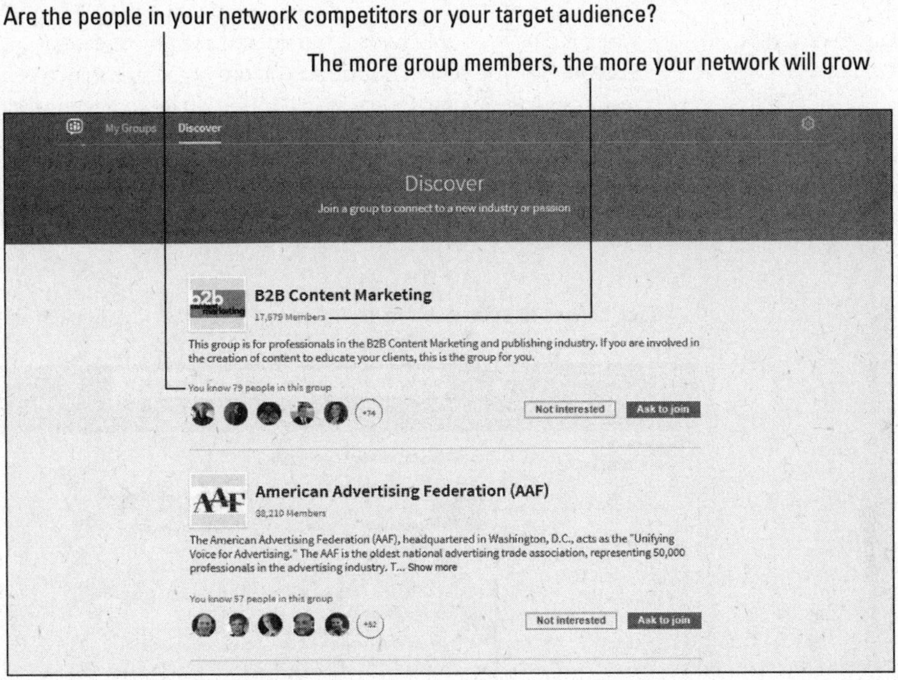

Are the people in your network competitors or your target audience?

The more group members, the more your network will grow

FIGURE 13-4:
LinkedIn
recommends
groups you might
be interested in.

Searching for groups

Rather than just accepting groups that LinkedIn deems worthy of you, search for groups. LinkedIn has two types of groups: standard and unlisted. When searching for groups, you only see standard groups. Unlisted groups are unlisted and do not turn up in Search. The only way to join an unlisted group is to be invited to join.

Here's how to search for groups that match your interests, goals, and target audience:

1. **From any LinkedIn page, click the down arrow to the left of the search bar at the top of the page and select Groups.**

   This filters your search results to only LinkedIn Groups.

2. **Enter a group topic that would attract your target audience in the search bar at the top of the page.**

   Some keyword topic ideas include: Executives, Real Estate, B2B Marketing, CAD, CRM, Sales, Cloud Computing, Supply Chain, Retail, Fashion, Maritime, Military, and so on.

WARNING

When typing in your keywords, do not choose any of the suggested results! Instead, click the search button so you are presented with a page of search results. By clicking on a suggested Group, you are only then visiting that particular Group rather than have numerous options to choose from.

3. **Click the search button.**

Search results display, as shown in Figure 13-5.

Click here to filter search results by type

Click to join a group

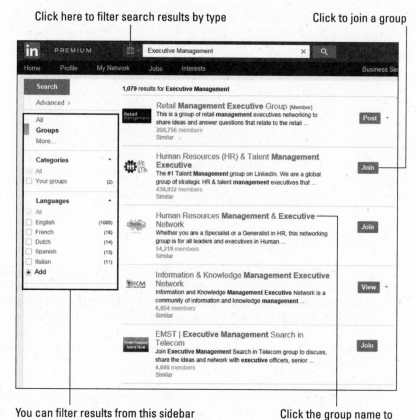

FIGURE 13-5: Going through group search results.

You can filter results from this sidebar

Click the group name to go to the overview page

4. **Scroll through the list.**

The name of the group displays, followed by a brief description. Under the description is the total number of members in the group.

5. **If the group looks interesting, click the Join button to immediately become a member, or if you want more information before joining, click the group name hyperlink to visit the group overview page.**

The group overview page shows you the admins of the group and who within your connections are members. If you wish to join, click the Ask to Join button, otherwise click your browser's back button to go to the previous screen of search results.

Deleting groups

Now that you understand the strategy behind LinkedIn Groups, you may want to delete some groups that aren't providing the value you need. Here's how to delete groups you have already joined:

1. From any LinkedIn page, hover your mouse pointer over Interests located in the top menu bar at the top of the screen and click Groups.

The highlights page displays. This page offers brief summaries of the most popular and trending discussions from all of your groups.

2. Click My Groups on the lower menu bar.

The list of groups that you belong to appears. If you manage any groups, they appear at the top of the list.

3. Scroll through the list until you find the group you want to remove.

4. Click the gear icon that appears to the right of each group listing and select Leave Group, as shown in Figure 13-6.

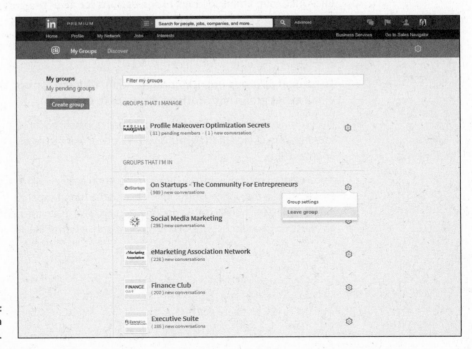

FIGURE 13-6:
Leaving a
LinkedIn Group.

Turning off group communication email

You've joined 100 groups and suddenly you are beginning to see more views to your LinkedIn profile. As wonderful as that is, you are also seeing your email inbox fill up with LinkedIn Group update email. LinkedIn sure does love to fill our inboxes up with notifications, don't they? No worries! It's easy to turn off the LinkedIn Group communication email. Here's how:

1. **Go to** LinkedIn.com.

2. **Hover your mouse pointer over the thumbnail image of yourself in the upper-right corner of your screen and click Manage next to Privacy & Settings.**

   LinkedIn's settings page opens.

3. **Along the top of the settings page, click Communications.**

4. **Under Basics, click Change to the left of Email frequency.**

   The page expands to include different options. This is where you choose what email notifications you want to receive from LinkedIn.

5. **Scroll down to Group updates and click Details.**

   The top five groups you belong to display with the ability to toggle off their email updates.

6. **Click All Group Email Settings to see options for all of the groups you belong to.**

   A page displays with the ability to toggle off communication from all of your groups.

7. **To turn off all group email communication, click the top option, "Receive email about group notifications" from On to Off.**

   If you only want to turn off some group email updates, go through the list toggling from On to Off the groups you no longer want to receive email updates from.

   If you want to receive a weekly digest rather than daily email from some of the groups, toggle the option from Off to On and the menu expands to choose between daily or weekly digest options. You are also given the option to turn off alerts on new discussions and group announcements. See Figure 13-7.

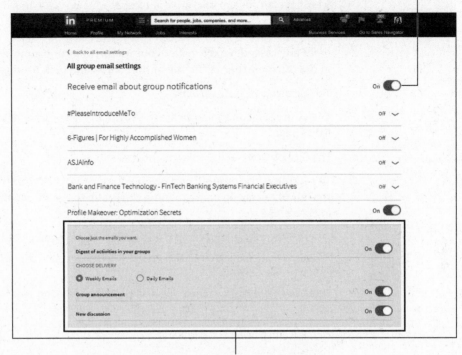

FIGURE 13-7:
Stopping all those
group emails
from deluging
your inbox.

Further limit or expand email updates

Choosing which groups to highlight on your profile

Your profile displays seven group logos on your profile with the option to expand to show the complete list. Although LinkedIn lists the groups on your profile in the order in which you joined them, you can determine the order groups are displayed.

Instead of leaving it to LinkedIn to showcase your group membership, it's important you take control and determine the best groups to populate your profile to impress your target audience. Remember, it's a Google world, and people are looking you up. They want to learn more about you. You control how they perceive you. As a reader scrolls through your profile, you want to make sure that the groups you are associated with build your brand and won't turn anyone off.

In the section, "Determining the types of groups to join," I suggest adding a few groups that showcase your industry knowledge. These groups are great to add to the top of your profile. Always think of your target audience. What group memberships might impress them? Which might make them feel confident in you?

Once you have an idea of the groups to spotlight on your profile, here's how to reorder them:

1. **From any LinkedIn page, hover your mouse pointer over Interests located in the top menu bar at the top of the screen and click Groups.**

The highlights page displays.

2. **Click the gear icon that appears in the upper-right corner of the high-lights page.**

The Groups Order and Display page appears.

3. **To rearrange the order of groups on your profile, click the arrow icon to the left of the group name to jump the group to the #1 position, as shown in Figure 13-8.**

Alternatively, click in the text field and type the order number for the group and press the Return or Enter key on your keyboard to accept the change and see the page update with the new order.

4. **Scroll to the bottom of the page and click the Save Changes button.**

This jumps the group to the first position

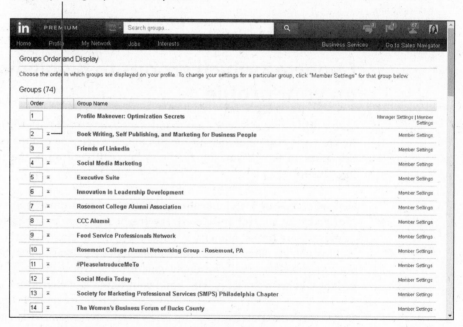

FIGURE 13-8:
Rearranging the
display of groups
on your profile.

Cultivating Your Following Section

When you first log in to LinkedIn, you land on the LinkedIn home page, which is where you post status updates that are potentially seen by your network of connections. It's also where you read your network's status updates. Think of this newsfeed as your own customized newspaper, curated by all of your direct, first-degree LinkedIn connections. You are not limited to just status updates from first-degree connections, however. You can also subscribe to news topics of interest to you, company and school updates, and original content from influencers. To tap into this stream of information, all you have to do is follow companies, news topics, influencers, and schools that interest you.

By following companies, news topics, influencers, and schools, you get their status updates delivered to your LinkedIn home page's newsfeed. You show your interest and allegiance to them on your LinkedIn profile in the Following section, which appears at the very bottom of your profile. Within this section, logos of the companies, news topics, influencers, and news you follow are displayed. To populate this section, you must follow some companies, news topics, influencers, and schools, otherwise the Following section does not appear on your profile, and the opportunity to showcase potential commonality is lost.

You can follow as many as 1,000 companies and an unlimited number of news sources or industries.

Choosing the right companies to follow

Just as individuals have LinkedIn profiles, companies have LinkedIn company pages. A company page is where a company tells its story, mission, and goals on LinkedIn and posts open positions. When employees and past employees list the company in their LinkedIn profiles' experience sections, the logo that is displayed on their profiles comes from this company page. A link is also created from the employees' profiles to the company page.

In addition to providing a digital outpost for the company on LinkedIn, the company page provides the ability to post status updates as the company rather than as an individual. When you visit a company page, you have the ability to follow that page and receive the updates it posts. Some company pages have showcase pages. Most companies post statuses on a large variety of topics, but not all followers want to read such a wide range of topics. Showcase pages are for the different topics a company page might broadcast. Visitors can then subscribe to the showcase page of the topic they are most interested in reading. When you subscribe to a showcase page, that logo is displayed on your profile as a company.

TIP

Follow at least 10 companies and/or showcase pages to demonstrate you are using LinkedIn as a way to get information and updates. These company logos also show your allegiance and interest in the company.

Not sure what companies to follow? No worries; here are some ideas to get you started:

>> Your current company

>> The companies where you worked in the past

>> Your dream company(ies)

>> Companies that are current or prospective customers

>> Companies in the news

>> Companies that are leaders within your industry or customers' industries

>> The companies where your friends and family members work

WARNING

Unlike with groups, you cannot control the order companies are displayed on your profile. If you are not comfortable potentially showcasing a certain company on your profile, don't follow it!

Following companies

It's easy to follow companies on LinkedIn. Here's how:

1. **From any LinkedIn page, click the down arrow to the left of the search bar at the top of the page and select Companies.**

   This filters your search results to only LinkedIn company pages.

2. **Enter the name of a company you would like to follow.**

   As you type, LinkedIn recommends matching company pages.

3. **If the page you are searching for appears, click it to open the company page.**

   If LinkedIn doesn't recommend the correct company page, click the search button to display the search results.

4. **Scroll through the results and click the company page you'd like to follow.**

   The company page opens.

5. **Click the Follow button.**

   The button text changes to Following and the company appears in the Following section on your profile.

Unfollowing companies

If you go overboard and follow more companies than you are able to keep up with, or if you've changed your mind about showing allegiance to a certain company, simply stop following a company and its updates.

To unfollow a company, follow these steps:

1. **From any LinkedIn page, hover your mouse pointer over Interests located in the top menu bar at the top of the screen and click Companies.**

   The Company Recent Updates page displays. This page shows you the most recent updates sent out by companies you follow. This is also where you see the company pages you manage.

2. **Click Following at the top of the page.**

   The list of companies you follow appears. You may need to click the Next button to see more results.

3. **Hover your mouse pointer over the word, "Following," that appears under the logo of the company you no longer want to follow and click.**

   It momentarily changes to Unfollow. Once you click Unfollow, you no longer follow that company and it is removed from your profile's Following section.

Following News

LinkedIn's home page also contains a summary of news items found on LinkedIn Pulse. LinkedIn Pulse is content curated by LinkedIn. These are the top business stories of the day. By following a news source or industry on LinkedIn Pulse, you are customizing the content based upon your preferences.

Here's how to follow different news topics:

1. **Open your LinkedIn profile.**

2. **Scroll down to the Following section and click the Customize News button.**

3. **Scroll down to the list of Channels.**

   Channels are the different news topics you are able to follow to truly customize and personalize the news LinkedIn provides to you via Pulse.

4. **Hover your mouse pointer over a topic that interests you.**

   The plus (+) sign that appears in the upper-right corner of the topic image changes to Follow.

5. **Click Follow.**

   The plus (+) sign becomes a green check mark, showing that you are following this news topic.

Showcasing Influencers on Your Profile

Not only does LinkedIn provide curated content from around the web, you can also tap into original content by big-name thought leaders. These influencers share their knowledge and insights through original articles found exclusively on LinkedIn. When you follow an influencer, you receive their latest articles via your LinkedIn home page's newsfeed. Not only do you get to read their latest missives, but also you get to show your admiration and interest in them on your profile.

When people check out another person's LinkedIn profile, they often scroll to the bottom to check out whether they have any influencers in common. Seeing an admired thought leader on another person's profile shows more than just a common interest; it shows a common philosophy and thought pattern. By following certain influencers, you raise your reputation and viewpoint.

TIP

There is a difference between following and connecting. When you connect, you are sharing your connections with that person and that person is added to your LinkedIn network. As part of your LinkedIn network, when you search LinkedIn, that person potentially shows up in searches as does his or her first- and second-degree network. By following a person, they are not added to your LinkedIn network. You are simply subscribing to their updates and long-form posts. You approve connections; you don't approve followers.

Deciding which influencers to showcase

Unlike with groups, you cannot control the order influencers are displayed on your profile. Just because you adore a certain influencer, consider if that person is a polarizing individual, especially within your industry. Rather than choosing influencers you truly love and want to follow, you may decide to choose influencers who showcase you as you want to be seen.

If you want to be seen as a conservative, traditional leader, you may decide to follow Jack Welch rather than Mark Cuban. Although LinkedIn includes a number of politicians as influencers, you may decide not to follow them and alienate half your audience.

LinkedIn doesn't provide a list of influencers beyond a small list of recommended influencers listed on the Discover page. Rather than have you blindly search for influencers, I've compiled a list of the most popular and prolific (see Table 13-1). See if any strike a chord with you. If they influence you, go ahead and follow them.

TABLE 13-1   ## List of Interesting Influencers

Sallie Krawcheck	CEO and Co-Founder of Ellevest	B2B/Leadership	www.linkedin.com/in/salliekrawcheck
Meg Whitman	CEO of Hewlett-Packard	B2B/Leadership	www.linkedin.com/in/megwhitman
Beth Comstock	Vice Chair at General Electric (GE)	B2B/Leadership	www.linkedin.com/in/elizabethjcomstock
Jonathan Becher	Chief Digital Officer at SAP	B2B/Leadership	www.linkedin.com/in/jbecher
Dr. Marla Gottschalk	Director of Organizational Development, Allied Talent	Human Resources	www.linkedin.com/in/marlagottschalk
Josh Bersin	Principal and Founder, Bersin by Deloitte	Human Resources	www.linkedin.com/in/bersin
Laszlo Bock	SVP, People Operations at Google and author of *Work Rules!*	Human Resources	www.linkedin.com/in/laszlobock
Lou Adler	CEO, Adler Group & author of *The Essential Guide For Hiring and Being Hired*	Job Search	www.linkedin.com/in/louadler
Liz Ryan	Founder & CEO of Human Workplace	Job Search	www.linkedin.com/in/lizryan
J.T. O'Donnell	CEO of CAREEREALISM & CareerHMO	Job Search	www.linkedin.com/in/jtodonnell
Ann Handley	Chief Content Officer of MarketingProfs	Marketing	www.linkedin.com/today/author/6474349
Brian Solis	Principal Analyst, Altimeter Group	Marketing	www.linkedin.com/influencer/2293140
Jonah Berger	Wharton Professor and author of *Contagious* and *Invisible Influence*	Marketing	www.linkedin.com/in/j1berger
Daniel Burrus	Founder and CEO Burrus Research, Inc	Marketing	www.linkedin.com/in/danielburrus

Finding specific influencers

Not all big names are influencers. Check to see if a person you admire is an influencer by following these steps:

1. **From any LinkedIn page, enter the person's name in the search bar at the top of the page.**

   As you type, LinkedIn presents you with name matches.

2. **If the person's name appears, click it to open his or her profile.**

3. **If the person's name doesn't appear, click the search button and review the search results, clicking the person's name to open his or her profile.**

   If the person is an influencer, at the very top of the profile, it says *Influencer*. Although you can connect with influencers, the Follow button is highlighted, as shown in Figure 13-9.

   Just preceding the word, "Influencer," you may see 1st, 2nd, or 3rd, meaning that not only is the person an influencer, but also you are connected to that person and that person is in your LinkedIn network.

4. **Click the Follow button to subscribe to the person's long-form posts and status updates.**

Influencers have an easy-to-see Follow button   The LinkedIn Influencer badge

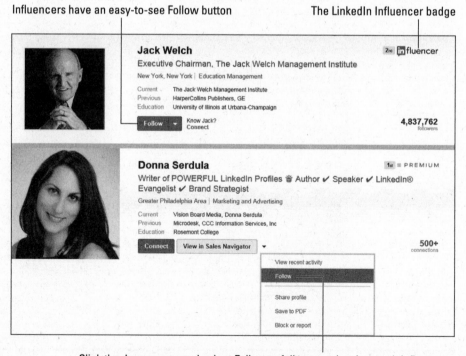

FIGURE 13-9:
Determining if a person is an influencer.

Click the down arrow and select Follow to follow people who aren't influencers

Discovering recommended influencers

LinkedIn provides you with a partial list of recommended influencers. Here's how to access that list and follow those influencers LinkedIn recommends for you:

1. **Open your LinkedIn profile.**

2. **Scroll down to the Following section and click the Customize News button.**

3. **Scroll down to the list of Influencers under Discover More.**

   This is a very small, partial list of some of the top influencers on LinkedIn.

4. **Hover your mouse pointer over an influencer that interests you.**

   The plus sign that appears in the upper-right corner of the influencer's profile picture image changes to Follow.

5. **Click Follow.**

   The plus (+) sign becomes a green check mark, showing that you are following this influencer. See Figure 13-10.

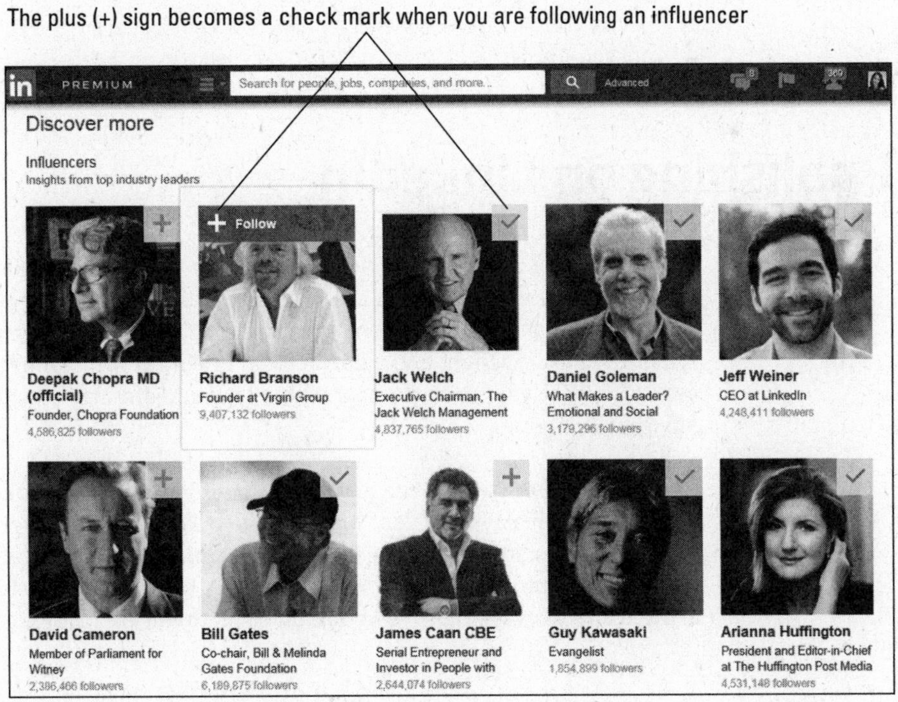

The plus (+) sign becomes a check mark when you are following an influencer

FIGURE 13-10:
Following
Influencers is as
easy as clicking a
plus (+) sign.

Removing influencers

It's a good idea to audit and edit your list of influencers every few months. Not only does LinkedIn add influencers, but also some influencers you follow may lose their luster, and it's best to remove them. Remember, nothing on LinkedIn is written in stone. Not only are you developing as a professional within your career, so are your interests and future vision of yourself. Make sure that you are always keeping your profile updated as to who you are right now in time.

Here's how to remove influencers from your profile:

1. **From any LinkedIn page, enter the person's name in the search bar at the top of the page.**

   As you type, LinkedIn presents you with name matches.

2. **If the person's name appears, click it to open his or her profile.**

3. **If the person's name doesn't appear, click the search button and review the search results, clicking the person's name to open his or her profile.**

4. **Hover your mouse pointer over the Following button, and when it changes to Unfollow, click.**

   Once you click Unfollow, that influencer is removed from the Following section of your profile.

Publishing on LinkedIn

Publishing on LinkedIn isn't relegated to only influencers. LinkedIn's Publishing Platform gives everyone with a LinkedIn profile the ability to publish long-form posts. When you publish a long-form post, the article is listed on your profile under the Posts section, and a notification is sent to your connections and followers. Posts that you write are searchable on LinkedIn and outside of LinkedIn via any search engine.

Check out Figure 13-11 to see how the articles you write on LinkedIn's Publishing Platform are displayed on your profile. If your article gets enough traction through views and likes, it may even be featured on LinkedIn's Pulse. Pulse is a standalone smartphone app, but it's also integrated into LinkedIn's newsfeed. Pulse collects articles and displays them to you in an easy-to-digest content stream.

FIGURE 13-11:
Your three most recent posts are displayed on your profile.

Long-form posts appear here on your profile

The types of information Pulse displays include:

>> Articles from around the web

>> Articles shared by your connections on LinkedIn's newsfeed

>> Popular long-form posts on LinkedIn's Publishing Platform

>> Articles written by LinkedIn influencers

Think of Pulse as a super smart digital newspaper that only displays articles that interest you. How does Pulse know what interests you? You tell it by following news topics, influencers, companies, schools, and people. LinkedIn also utilizes a complex algorithm to determine which articles pertain to your interests.

LinkedIn's goal is to provide tailored and relevant content that interests the reader. When reading articles on Pulse (on your mobile phone app or via LinkedIn's desktop newsfeed) everything you see is customized specifically to you. LinkedIn wants to make sure what you are reading is meaningful to you. If you were to log in as someone else, the information you see would be completely different.

Although all long-form posts can be viewed on Pulse, only popular posts are featured on Pulse and have the ability to truly be seen by thousands of professionals in and out of your LinkedIn network.

Showcasing yourself as a thought leader

At one time, only academics were held to the paradigm of "publish or perish." Now, in the world of rampant social media, professionals who wish to be seen as thought leaders must also publish or perish. By blogging on LinkedIn, you establish yourself as an authority in your specialized field by sharing your expertise, insights, opinions, and professional background. With each share, like, comment, and view, your post is seen, shared, and promoted to your network and beyond.

It's easy to say you are an expert; it's much harder to prove it. Imagine you are on the shortlist for your dream job. The hiring manager visits your profile and the profiles of the other people being considered. Your profile showcases a number of blogs you've written on your specialized field; the other candidates have none. Immediately you have differentiated yourself from the other candidates and have proven your knowledge and authority.

Creating your first blog

The longest journey begins with a single step! Before you create your first long-form post, it's best to consider the topic channels on Pulse. By knowing the different channels people subscribe to, it's easier to choose your topic.

SHARING UPDATES VERSUS WRITING POSTS

Updates are short and quick dispatches that go out to your network via your LinkedIn newsfeed. An update could be a link to an article, webpage, or video; an image or infographic; or an interesting quote, advice, thought, or question you want to share with your connections. Posts on the other hand are longer and more thoughtful, and require more time to create.

Here is a list of the Pulse topic channels:

Leadership & Management	Entertainment
Big Ideas & Innovation	Mobile
Technology	Media
Entrepreneurship	Food & Beverages
Social Media	Apparel & Fashion
Economy	Careers: The Next Level
Professional Women	Automotive
Marketing & Advertising	Oil & Energy
Green Business	Construction
Banking & Finance	Public Relations
Best Advice	Travel & Leisure
Your Career	Management Consulting
Healthcare	Real Estate
Customer Experience	Product Management
What Inspires Me	Logistics & Supply Chain
Big Data	Airlines & Aviation
Software Engineering	Company Culture
Social Impact	Information Technology
Recruiting & Hiring	VC & Private Equity
Law & Government	Pulse
Business Travel	Europe
Careers: Getting Started	Asia Pacific
Productivity	Insurance
India	Operations
Editor's Picks	Pharmaceutical
Retail & E-Commerce	LinkedIn Tips
Accounting	Human Resources
Design	Cloud Computing
Sales Strategies	Public Speaking & Presenting

Writing and Editing	Law Practice
Freelance and Self Employment	Manufacturing
Hospitality	Australia & New Zealand
Business Strategies	Top Videos
United Kingdom	Daily Digest
Global Trade	Millennials
Information Privacy & Security	Africa
Space	The Weekend Essay
US Politics	Middle East
Student Voices	Latin America

You want to choose a topic that resonates with your target audience. Concentrate first and foremost on making the content high quality and meaningful to your audience.

TIP

Articles on LinkedIn shouldn't be overwhelmingly long. Aim for 800 to 2,000 words. If you have a larger vision, break it into a series of articles. Keep yourself focused on your topic and write using a conversational tone. Rather than write for views, write for engagement. A successful post receives feedback in likes, comments, and shares.

Unlike your profile, LinkedIn supports formatting of long-form posts. Make sure your article is thoughtfully formatted. Use headings to outline your overarching points. Add interesting pictures that illustrate your thoughts. Call attention to your important points by using lists and formatting your text in bold and italics.

You can also include links to other websites, and you can embed videos as well as HTML. Here are some items you can embed into your blog post:

>> Charts

>> Images

>> Podcasts

>> Polls

>> Presentations

>> Tweets

>> Videos

By adding multimedia to your article, you are making it visually appealing and providing concrete examples that support your opinion.

TIP

Publishing on LinkedIn isn't a once and done exercise. Publishing is a long-term commitment with no end date. The idea is to commit to a schedule and keep at it. Determine what works for you, and make it a habit whether it's once a week, once a month, or once every three months.

If you are wondering the best days to publish your post to achieve the most views, research points to Thursdays and Sundays. Some of the most successful posts I've written were posted on Fridays and Mondays, so even though research points to Thursday and Sunday, the real differentiator is simply good content.

Now that you have an idea of topic, tone, length, and frequency, follow these steps to create your very first blog post on LinkedIn:

1. Go to LinkedIn.com.

2. **At the top of your home page, click Write an Article (see Figure 13-12).**

A page opens where you write your long-form post, as shown in Figure 13-13. At the top of the page is an area to add a hero image. This image also acts as a thumbnail and proceeds your long-form post on your profile and on status updates and on Pulse, if you are featured.

FIGURE 13-12: Click to start a blog post.

Click to publish a long-form post

3. **Click anywhere within the image area to add an image.**

An Open dialog box appears.

4. **Select your image on your hard drive and click Open.**

The image opens and you can preview how it looks. Hovering your mouse pointer over the image, click at the top to credit the person who made the image.

5. **Click in the area where it says, "Headline," and type in a headline.**

The headline is the title of your article. Make sure it is intriguing and compelling. This field may only contain 150 characters or fewer.

6. **The next area is the body of the post. Click where it says, "Write here. Add images or a video for visual impact."**

This is where you write your article.

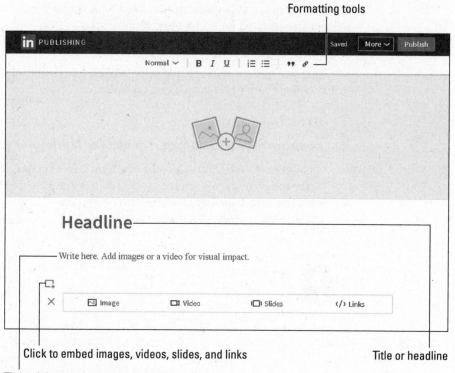

Formatting tools

Headline

Click to embed images, videos, slides, and links

Title or headline

The article goes here

FIGURE 13-13:
Publishing a
long-form post.

7. **Highlight the text you want formatted, and then in the format bar at the top of the screen above the image area, click the Normal drop-down list to expand the text formatting options:**

● **H1:** This is the main heading and produces the largest font size.

● **H2:** This is a subheading and produces the second largest font size.

● **Normal:** This is unformatted body text.

There are other options as well. Click the matching icon to apply the following formatting:

- **B:** This sets the text in bold.
- **I:** This sets the text in italics.
- **U:** This underlines the text. Use this sparingly as most people associate underlined text with hyperlinks.
- **Numbered list:** This creates a numbered list.
- **Bulleted list:** This creates an unnumbered list.
- **Block quote:** This is for a direct quotation. The text is center justified and the font is italics and slightly larger than the normal body text.
- **Link:** This creates a hyperlink to another page on the web.

8. **Once you have finished writing your article, proofread to make sure it's ready to be published.**

9. **Click the Publish button in the upper-right corner of the page to publish your article.**

   A pop up window appears.

10. **In the open text field, provide context around your article so your network knows what it is about, and then click the Publish button.**

    Tell your network what your article is about. Use #tags (hashtags) to help others find it.

TIP

To create a hashtag, all you do is take a word or phrase, remove any spaces, special characters, or punctuation and begin it with a hash mark (#). For example, #LinkedIn #B2B #Leadership #ProfessionalDevelopment.

People search by hashtags to find content that corresponds to subjects they are interested in. By searching for hashtags or just clicking on a hashtag (as long as you are accessing LinkedIn on your mobile device), you are presented with a results page of articles written on that subject utilizing those hashtags.

What happens after you publish?

Take a deep breath, whisper a little prayer to your favorite benevolent god, and hit the Publish button. What happens now? Your post is published to your LinkedIn profile under the Posts section in the top part of your profile. Your profile shows the last three posts you've written. Anyone who views your profile sees your posts.

ADDING AN ENGAGING HERO IMAGE

Sitting atop your long-form post is a hero image that brings visual zest to your article. Make sure you add an image that is interesting and compelling. This image becomes the thumbnail image that follows your article on your profile and throughout the web as it is shared. When chosen well, an image can bring more views than even a great headline.

The dimensions for a long-form post hero image is 744 pixels wide by 400 pixels tall. In Chapter 12 I offer a bunch of ideas for choosing background images. Also check out Flickr's Creative Common images (www.flickr.com/creativecommons) where the images are free to use as long as you attribute the work to the image author.

Now that your post is published, a status update appears on the newsfeed of your followers and connections alerting them of your new post. As newer status updates and long-form posts are published by others, this little update of yours gets pushed down lower and lower on the newsfeed. Depending on the size of your network and how active your connections are on LinkedIn, some people will see it and some will not.

LinkedIn runs your post through a spam and low-quality filter. If your post passes as quality content, LinkedIn begins to individually notify your network. Rather than alert every single connection you have, LinkedIn alerts only the strongest connections that you interact with regularly. This notification appears as a flag on the upper-right corner of the LinkedIn desktop and as an alert on the LinkedIn Pulse smartphone app.

Every day LinkedIn sends out an email entitled, "Pulse's Top Stories." As long as your connections and followers are subscribed to this email, they get a link to your post in their inbox.

And if your article is truly compelling and engaging, you may find that it is chosen for a Pulse channel. When this happens, you'll receive an email alerting you, but most likely you will already know because you'll receive more views, likes, and comments than ever before.

Marketing your blog post

Although LinkedIn does a fair amount of marketing for you by notifying your network of a new blog post, you should also market your post yourself. Use social media as well as email to alert your audience.

Once your article is published, share the link on Facebook, Twitter, and/or Pinterest. Don't just send it out once; send it out a bunch of times on each network. Either schedule a reminder in your calendar to resend the link or use a tool like Hootsuite that allows you to create multiple updates that are scheduled out into the future.

TIP

Don't just post a link — provide some context and include hashtags in the status as well.

Bad:

> *Read my article: www.linkedin.com/today/author/todonna*

Good:

> *Just posted a new article detailing the #Microsoft acquisition of #LinkedIn and what it means to LinkedIn users. Read it here: www.linkedin.com/today/author/todonna*

Email is another great way to get views to your long-form post. If you are a marketer with a double opt-in email list numbering in the thousands, you'll have no difficulty getting word out. But even without a marketing email list you can still send an email out to your friends and colleagues, letting them know you posted an article and providing a link so that they can read it.

When sending email to more than a few people, don't use the To or CC address fields of your email header; instead use BCC. BCC stands for *Blind Carbon Copy*. When you add email addresses to the To or CC fields, everyone can see those email addresses and reply to them. When you use the BCC field, those email addresses aren't visible to others. This is helpful because often people reply not just to you, the person writing the email, but to everyone included as recipients. When this happens, the person replying is unknowingly spamming all of the email recipients. By using BCC, you are stopping people from seeing the other email addresses and mistakenly "replying all."

In the next chapter, it's time for you to review your profile and get ready for the final reveal!

Chapter **14**

The Final Review and Reveal

Your LinkedIn profile is nearly finished! You added a professional headshot and your headline is compelling. The summary is no longer a copy-and-paste of your resume. Instead, it's a digital introduction and an impressive first impression. Your career trajectory is clearly defined in the Experience section of your profile. Your experiences don't dwell on job description, but instead host impactful accomplishments that differentiate you from others in your industry.

You might have thought you were finished, but now it's time to put the final touches on your profile. In this chapter, I show you how to rearrange the different sections of your profile so that the order is clear and aligns your profile with your brand and goals.

I also show you how to market your profile so others see the work you put into it. Lastly, I give you tips and tricks to increase views to your profile so you are more apt to collide with opportunity.

Rearranging Profile Sections

As you build your LinkedIn profile, your summary and experiences are placed at the top, right underneath the section that contains your profile picture and name. After experiences, any new sections are placed in the order in which you added them. This can create a hodgepodge of sections that doesn't make sense to your reader or forward the brand message you are ever so carefully trying to create.

TIP

What most people don't know is that it's easy to rearrange profile sections by simply dragging and dropping them wherever you want the section to appear on your profile.

Follow these steps to rearrange your LinkedIn profile sections:

1. **Open your LinkedIn profile.**

2. **Hover your mouse pointer over the section you'd like to move, then click and hold the Reorder Section icon in the top right (see Figure 14-1).**

3. **Keeping your finger pressed on your mouse button, drag the section to the new location.**

4. **Drop the section into place by releasing your finger.**

   The section is now arranged where you want it within your profile.

Click and drag to rearrange profile sections

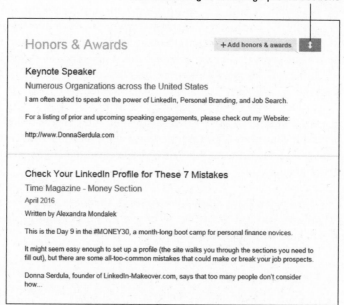

FIGURE 14-1:
Rearranging profile sections is a simple drag and drop.

Think in terms of your goals and target audience. Sections should be moved higher or lower on your profile depending on how pertinent they are to your goals and target audience. Items that are most important to your audience should be at the top, and items that are of lesser importance should be moved to the bottom.

If you aren't sure what sections should rise to the top and which should sink to the bottom, here's my recommended order of profile sections:

1. Summary
2. Experience
3. Projects
4. Patents
5. Publications
6. Honors & Awards
7. Skills & Endorsements
8. Additional Information
9. Organizations
10. Volunteer
11. Certifications
12. Courses
13. Education
14. Test Scores
15. Languages

Keep in mind, when people view your LinkedIn profile, they spend most of their time looking at the top half of your profile. Suppose you are proud of your extensive education and caliber of the schools you attended. Move your education section up higher on your profile. On the other hand, if you didn't receive a college degree and don't want to spotlight your high school diploma, move the education section to the bottom of your profile.

Perhaps you are an author. Move the Publications section below your summary. If you work with nonprofits and want to showcase your volunteer experiences, move up the Volunteering Experience section.

Do keep your summary at the very top of you profile. By straying too far from the default, you may confuse your reader. I remember a time I logged into a client's LinkedIn profile and I couldn't find his Summary section. I clicked back and forth, hit my browser's refresh button, and rebooted my computer, only to find that the Summary section had been dragged to the very bottom of his profile. If you don't see a profile section, it may just be out of order.

Viewing Your Profile as an Outsider

When you log in to LinkedIn and click to view your profile, you are always in edit mode. The profile you see is not what others see when they view your profile. Therefore, to preview your profile, you must decide who you want to view it as. Logged-in LinkedIn users see your profile one way, non-LinkedIn users who are not logged-in to LinkedIn see it a totally different way (if at all).

To view your LinkedIn profile as an outsider, follow these steps:

1. **Open your LinkedIn profile.**

2. **Click the View Profile As button that appears next to your profile picture, as shown in Figure 14-2.**

   You see a preview of your profile as a person logged-in to LinkedIn would see it.

FIGURE 14-2:
The View Profile
As button.

Click to preview your profile

At the top of the page is a bar that reads, "This is what your profile looks like to Connections."

3. **Select Public from the drop-down list, as shown in Figure 14-3.**

    You see a preview of your profile as a person not logged-in to LinkedIn would see it.

Toggle between Public and Connections view

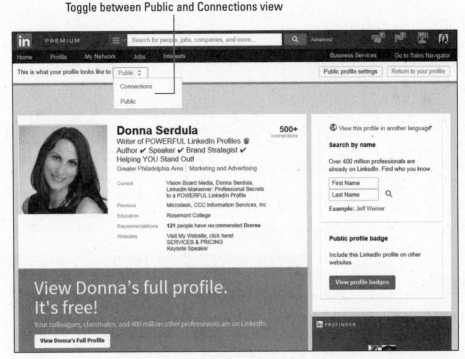

FIGURE 14-3:
Toggling between
Public and
Connections
profile view.

4. **Click the Return to Your Profile button that appears in the top-right corner of your screen to return to edit mode.**

Your LinkedIn Profile Checklist

Now that you can view your profile as your target audience, let's make sure you didn't miss any sections or make any mistakes. Your public profile is your online reputation and digital face to the world. Your profile must be perfect, as this is how people see and judge you. Make sure all the sections are customized completely. As you go through, check off each completed section.

❑ **Profile picture**

   Does your profile picture cast you as a professional? Do you look warm, friendly, and well-adjusted? Is the background neutral and not distracting?

☐ **Name**

Is your name spelled correctly? Is it consistent with your business card, resume, other social media channels, and letterhead?

☐ **Headline**

Is your headline interesting? Does it contain your top keywords? Does it compel a person to open your profile to learn more about you?

☐ **Location and industry**

Is your location correct? Is your industry accurate?

☐ **Customized public profile URL**

Did you customize the link to your public URL? Does the customized URL contain your name?

☐ **Contact information**

Did you include your phone number, email, and IM? Did you add links to your websites and Twitter?

☐ **Summary**

Is your summary engaging and easy to read? Does it introduce you to your reader? Does it provide a clear call to action?

☐ **One current and two past experiences**

Are your experience titles packed with keywords? Do the descriptions contain a boilerplate on the company along with your performance highlights?

☐ **Skills and endorsements**

Did you add your core competencies, strengths, skill sets, and abilities?

☐ **Education**

Did you list at least one education, even if you did not graduate?

☐ **Additional profile sections**

Did you add honors and awards, organizations, volunteer experience and causes, certifications, languages, projects, publications, patents, test scores, and/or courses? Are you showcasing yourself as a well-rounded professional? Did you reorder these sections so the more important ones are listed higher?

☐ **Additional information**

Did you add your interests and advice for contacting you?

☐ **Recommendations**

Do you have glowing recommendations on your profile from people in high places? Have you given recommendations to other professionals?

❑ **Connections**

Do you have at least 50 first-degree connections?

❑ **Groups**

Did you join up to 100 LinkedIn Groups that contain not only your target audience but also large amounts of members?

❑ **Following influencers, news, and companies**

Are you following at least five influencers and companies that interest you? Are you following news items that provide you with information on your industry and interests?

To Pay or Not Pay for LinkedIn

Whenever I speak to groups about the importance of LinkedIn and having a LinkedIn profile, the number one question I get is, "Should I pay for LinkedIn, or is the free version good enough?"

TIP

LinkedIn's free version works well for most people; however, if you plan to use LinkedIn for more than just casual networking, upgrading makes sense.

LinkedIn has restrictions in place on the free account to limit heavy recruiting and prospecting. The commercial use limit is based upon the number of searches you do during a month's time. When you exceed what LinkedIn considers typical usage, you are no longer able to search nor will LinkedIn suggest profiles for you to view until the counter resets the next month.

Unfortunately, LinkedIn hasn't publicly stated the number of searches they consider commercial use versus typical. The number 100 has been bandied around by super users as the maximum search limit for typical use. Here's the thing, if you are a heavy LinkedIn user, you very well may hit the maximum search limit. When this happens, decide if it makes sense to wait for the month to roll over and the search counter resets, or upgrade.

I remember when I hit the commercial use limit — it was only one week into the month. I realized it would be impossible for me to wait three weeks to search again and so that afternoon, I upgraded to Sales Navigator. Ultimately, if you are using LinkedIn to make money, LinkedIn would like you to pay to use its service; it's only fair.

Features of paid accounts

LinkedIn has four types of premium accounts:

>> Job Seeker

>> Business Plus

>> Sales Navigator

>> Recruiter

All four types of premium accounts have features in common. In the following sections I outline the features that exist within all premium accounts.

Open Profile and Open Profile messages

REMEMBER

Free members can view the full names and profiles of anyone in their LinkedIn networks (first-, second-, and third-degree connections). All LinkedIn members can see a user's full profile as long as they searched by that person's first or last name. However, if a person is doing a broad-based keyword search and that person is outside of your network, he or she sees a limited version of your profile.

Premium account holders can turn on Open Profile so that anyone on LinkedIn can see their full profile regardless of how that person searched to find them.

Additionally, anyone with Open Profile turned on can send messages to other members with Open Profile turned on for free, even if they are second- or third-degree connections or outside of your LinkedIn network.

Premium badge

Premium account holders can add a premium badge to their profiles and search result listings so people can see that they are paying members and take LinkedIn and networking seriously. The premium badge appears in the upper-right corner of the person's profile, to the right of his or her name. The badge looks like a yellow square followed by the word: PREMIUM. The premium badge is shown in Figure 14-4.

Premium profile

Free members have a narrower profile picture than premium members. The free member profile picture is sized 200 x 200 pixels, while premium members have a wide screen profile picture sized 240 x 240 pixels. That's 30 percent bigger than a free account's profile picture. Figure 14-4 shows the appearance differences between a premium and a free profile picture.

Free account

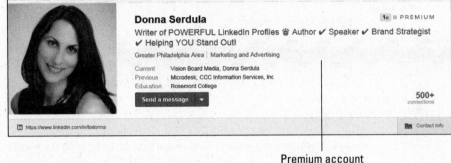

FIGURE 14-4:
Differences
between a
premium profile
picture and free
profile view.

Premium account

When you pay for LinkedIn, you also get access to the Premium Background Image Gallery that provides high-resolution images to use as your background image.

Larger search result listing

Free members have a standard search results listing. Paying members have an enhanced search results listing that shows greater work history detail. Figure 14-5 illustrates the differences between a premium and a standard search listing.

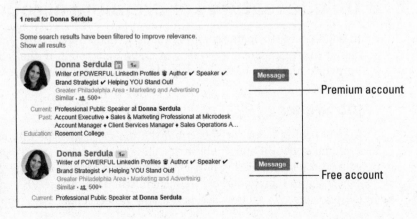

FIGURE 14-5:
Differences
between
premium and
standard search
listings.

Premium account

Free account

Who's viewed your profile

LinkedIn is one of the few social media sites that enables you to see who has viewed your profile. Free members only see the last five profile visitors, whereas premium members get to see everyone who's viewed their profiles within the last 90 days along with additional insights such as the keywords searched that brought them to their profiles and any patterns that may be evident.

If your profile is set to *Anonymous*, you are unable to see who viewed your profile. Basically, LinkedIn goes by the, "If you show me yours, I'll show you mine" rule.

How you rank

Free accounts see the top 10 most viewed connections and the 10 people closest to your ranking. Premium accounts see the full list of top 100 most viewed connections within your network and top 100 "Professionals like you."

InMail

Free members can only communicate directly with first-degree connections. As a paying member, you can use InMail to send a message to LinkedIn users you are not directly connected to. The number of InMails per month differs based on the premium account you have.

Search alerts

Free members have the opportunity to save three searches. Paying members get more saved searches, each plan providing its own number. Great for prospecting, recruiting, or even job search, LinkedIn automatically performs your saved search weekly or monthly and sends you all new search results.

Unique features of premium accounts

In addition to the features all premium accounts offer, LinkedIn provides even more features unique to each type of premium account. In the following sections I provide a rundown of the added features per subscription type.

Job Seeker

A great selling point for subscribing to the Job Seeker premium account is the Featured Applicant and Applicant Insights functionality. As a Featured Applicant, your search results listing puts you at the top of recruiters' applicant lists. Applicant Insights shows you how well you measure up to other current applicants on job postings. You get to see how many other people have applied to the job posting; the other applicants' experience, education levels, and top skills; and how well your profile ranks with other applicants.

Business Plus

The Business Plus premium account provides unlimited profile search so you never hit the commercial use search limit. You also get company page insights that point to the overall health of the organization you are interested in by showing you employee count, employee distribution by function, new hires, notable alumni, and total job openings.

On the advanced search page, Business Plus account owners see additional filters marked with the gold LinkedIn premium badge that are only available to paying members. These filters enable you to further drill down to your perfect target by searching within group members, years of experience, job functions, seniority levels, company size, and more.

Sales Navigator

When you subscribe to the Sales Navigator premium account you get a totally different LinkedIn interface that is focused entirely on sales, lead generation, prospecting, and account management. You can see how this different interface looks in Figure 14-6.

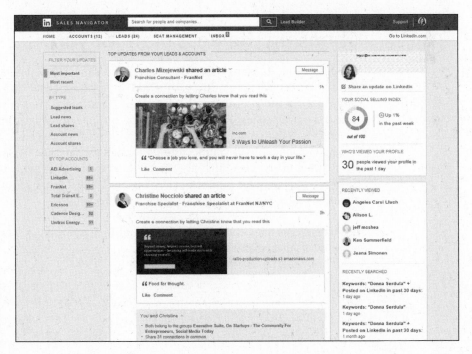

FIGURE 14-6:
Sales Navigator has a different look than LinkedIn.com.

Sales Navigator allows you to save your leads' profiles, which LinkedIn uses to extrapolate and recommend other potential leads for you. You can also build lead lists using premium search filters. Sales Navigator also allows you to drill deep into your target accounts via Account Details Pages that keep you updated on the latest news and information LinkedIn has on those accounts. In addition, Sales Navigator enables you to filter through the noise of your network to see just what's going on with your leads, prospects, and customers via their status updates and news.

This premium account also provides unlimited profile search so you don't hit the commercial use search limit.

Recruiter Lite

LinkedIn has a number of recruiter packages available, but the most popular is Recruiter Lite. Just like Sales Navigator, the Recruiter Lite premium account has a different LinkedIn interface. Recruiter Lite offers unique functionality such as the ability to organize candidates in folders with an area on each profile to take notes and set follow-up reminders.

The Recruiter Lite premium account also allows for unlimited profile searches of your extended network. Recruiter Lite also provides smart search capability that provided additional premium filters and search suggestions to help you find the perfect candidates.

Choosing the best plan for you

By segmenting its plans based upon goal, LinkedIn makes it easy to identify the premium account that works best for you. My recommendation is to use the free version of LinkedIn until you begin to feel constrained. You will know that it's time to upgrade when you start hitting the commercial search limit, or you long to view more than just five of your last profile visitors. Once you realize it's time to pay for LinkedIn, all you need to do is click the upgrade button in the upper-right corner of any LinkedIn page. I often hear from client's who tell me that once they started paying for LinkedIn, they began to take it more seriously. Sometimes you need to get some skin in the game to truly commit.

Ultimately, you may find that it feels good to support a company that lets you network in your pajamas!

Benchmarking Your Profile's Success

You've put a lot of time into improving your profile. Now you want to see if the effort was worthwhile and is bringing enhanced results. The thing is, to determine success, you need to know where you started. Fortunately, LinkedIn provides statistics that show you how well your profile is performing.

You get to see enhanced stats that log the past 90 days of total views. If you are a premium user, you also get to see the individual viewers of your profile over the past 90 days.

TIP

Although LinkedIn tracks your progress for you, the graph only goes back 90 days. Also, the graph does not track the most important information statistic, network total. To truly benchmark your success, you must look past 90 days. For that reason, I suggest going old school — yes, track your progress with a good ol' pen and paper.

Here's how to track your progress with a benchmarking worksheet:

1. **Create a benchmarking worksheet on a blank sheet of paper or download a printable PDF version from my website at** www.LinkedIn-Makeover.com/tools/benchmark_workbook.

    If you are creating your own, divide your paper into a grid that has four columns and several rows.

2. **Label each column with the following:**

    > Date
    >
    > Profile Views
    >
    > Days
    >
    > Network Total

    Your homemade benchmarking worksheet should look similar to the worksheet shown in Figure 14-7.

3. **Hover your mouse cursor over Profile, and in the drop-down list that appears, click Who's Viewed My profile.**

    This page displays your profile stats. The graph shows how many people have viewed your profile in the past 90 days and the actions you did per week (such as added connections, shared updates, commented on updates, liked updates, posted, or commented on group discussions).

4. **Write down the number of people who have viewed your profile and now many actions you took per week into your benchmarking worksheet.**

The number of actions performed

How many people
viewed your profile

Number of
connections

Current date

Date	Profile Views	Actions Taken	Netwotk Total
7/26	23	132	426

FIGURE 14-7: Benchmarking worksheet.

5. **Hover over My Network on LinkedIn's main navigation bar and click Connections.**

   At the top of this page is the total number of first-degree connections.

6. **Write the number of first-degree connections in the Network Total column of your worksheet.**

   The Connections page shows the number of first-degree connections within your LinkedIn network.

7. **Record these stats weekly or with as much regularity as you can into your benchmarking worksheet for the next 180 days.**

The more you use LinkedIn, the better your profile performs. You should see the number of views grow as your network and activity level grow.

Marketing Your Profile

Your profile is a gleaming example of your brand and professionalism. You want your entire network and the whole wide world to look at this amazing profile of you. Now it's time to start marketing it!

I am often reminded of that iconic line from the movie, *Field of Dreams*: "If you build it, they will come!" Unfortunately, that's not always true in the world of social media. Yes, you optimized your profile with keywords so your profile will be easier to find, but there is no promise that people are searching for a person like you every day of the week. To consistently get views to your profile, you need to consistently market your profile.

Alerting your connections of your updated profile

"The squeaky wheel gets the oil." That's an old saying I heard often growing up. This adage holds true in the social media realm as well. If you want people to check out your new and improved profile, you need to speak up and direct them to it. In the following sections I outline how to alert your network and drive traffic to your profile.

Issue a broadcast update

Remember when you toggled off the Notify Your Network button so that LinkedIn would not publish profile change updates to your network? It's time to turn on the notification. Once it's back on, when you make one small change to your profile, LinkedIn notifies people to check out your profile.

Follow these steps to issue a broadcast update:

1. **Open your LinkedIn profile.**

2. **Scroll to the Notify Your Network module that appears on the right side of your profile and click the button to change No to Yes.**

Figure 14-8 shows how the Notify Your Network module changes between on and off mode.

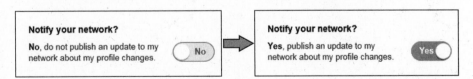

Notify your network?

No, do not publish an update to my network about my profile changes.   No

Notify your network?

Yes, publish an update to my network about my profile changes.   Yes

3. **Scroll to your current position in the Experience section, click in the title field, and make a minor edit to the position title.**

With Notify Your Network turned on, LinkedIn generates an update to your connections stating that you've updated your Experience section.

If you prefer, tweak your profile picture to generate a broadcast update. Simply recropping the image already uploaded generates an update that states you changed your profile picture.

Adding additional skills to your profile also triggers an automatic update to your connections.

By adding a new current job position, an update goes out to your connections announcing the new position and providing a way to "Say Congrats" to you in a LinkedIn message.

Send out a status update

Rather than just letting LinkedIn send out a notification, send out a status update on your own. The real secret in getting people to read and click your update is to send it out multiple times. This ensures that people throughout your network get the chance to see it and act! Here's how to send out a status update. Lather, rinse, and repeat as often as you like!

Follow these steps to send out a status update:

1. **Open your LinkedIn profile.**

2. **Highlight your LinkedIn profile URL that appears at the bottom of your summary and copy it by pressing Ctrl+C (Windows) or Cmd+C (Mac).**

3. **Click Home on LinkedIn's navigation menu to go to the LinkedIn home page.**

4. **At the top of LinkedIn's home page, click the Share an Update button to unveil the text box.**

   Look at Figure 14-9 to see the status update field on your LinkedIn home page.

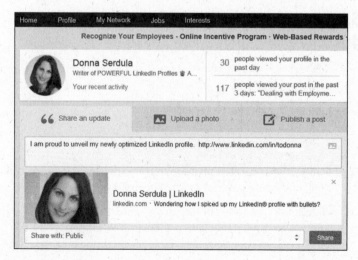

FIGURE 14-9:
Creating a status update.

5. **Type your status update in the Share an Update text field and then paste your LinkedIn profile URL by clicking Ctrl+V (Windows) or Cmd+V (Mac).**

   You may want to use something like this:

   I just updated my LinkedIn profile, check it out: `http://www.LinkedIn.com/in/todonna`

   Or:

   I am proud to unveil my newly optimized LinkedIn profile, view it here: `http://www.LinkedIn.com/in/todonna`

6. **Click the drop-down list underneath the text box to choose your audience: Public, Just Your Connections, or Public + Twitter.**

7. **Click the Share button.**

Message people individually

Are there people within your network that would love to see your updated profile? Why not reach out to them directly? Messaging people individually takes time, but it's a great way to reconnect and get a real response.

Free LinkedIn members can only message people who are direct connections.

Here's how to message people individually on LinkedIn:

1. **Go to** `LinkedIn.com`.

2. **In the search bar at the top of the page, type the name of the first-degree connection you want to message.**

   LinkedIn suggests people.

3. **Click the person's name to open his or her profile.**

4. **Click the Send a Message button at the top of that person's profile.**

   LinkedIn's messaging pane opens, as shown in Figure 14-10. You can add additional recipients by typing their names in the top field.

5. **Type your message in the text field.**

   Some message examples:

   Hey Howard! It's been months since we last chatted, but I wanted to let you know I took your advice and optimized my profile. Check it out when you have a minute.

   Or:

   Hi Deborah! I've always loved your LinkedIn profile. I finally got off my duff and optimized my own. Take a look at it and let me know what you think!

6. **Depending on your messaging settings, you either press Enter/Return on your keyboard, or press the Send button to dispatch your message.**

FIGURE 14-10:
Messaging
connections.

Adding your profile to other social media sites

Most people don't have a personal website, and so LinkedIn becomes their online outpost. If this is true for you, use the other social media websites you frequent as a way to get the word out on your LinkedIn profile.

Instagram, Pinterest, Facebook, Twitter, and other sites all have a website field within the bio section where you can add your LinkedIn profile URL. Check out Figure 14-11 to see how I have my LinkedIn profile URL listed on my Twitter bio.

You can also send out a Facebook status update or tweet the link to your LinkedIn profile so followers on other channels are alerted and can check it out.

FIGURE 14-11:
Add your
LinkedIn profile
URL to other
social media
channels.

MAKING IT EASY FOR PEOPLE TO CONNECT TO YOU

You interact with people every day. Each interaction is a chance to further your brand and direct traffic to your LinkedIn profile. Make sure your LinkedIn profile URL is added to your resume. If you often send out mailed correspondence, place your LinkedIn profile URL on your letterhead.

Do you have a personal website? If so, add a link to your LinkedIn profile. If you have a bio listed on your company's website, check with the webmaster to see if he or she can add a link to your LinkedIn profile.

Emails are such a normal part of business life. It's been stated that the average number of sent and received emails is 121 per day. Make sure that these interactions help further your brand and engage your network by using an email signature. An *email signature* is an automatic line added to the very bottom of the email messages you send that provides your name, contact information, and any other information you wish to include (see the following figure). I highly suggest including your LinkedIn URL at the bottom of your email signature. This way, after reading your emails, people can easily connect with you and stay in touch.

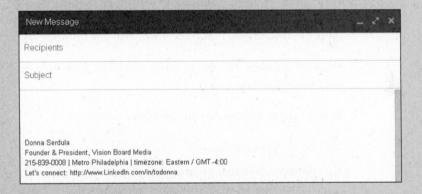

Business cards are another way people trade contact information and stay in touch. If your LinkedIn profile URL isn't on your business card, add it! Some companies simply provide canned cards to employees, and it's not possible to customize the information on the card. If your company won't allow you to add your LinkedIn profile URL to your business card, consider having a thin sticker printed that contains your LinkedIn profile URL and stick it to the bottom or back of your pre-printed business card.

Remember, there is power to your network. You must make a concerted effort to build and nurture your network. By making it easy to connect with you, you are helping to grow your network in a very passive manner.

Getting views to your LinkedIn profile

LinkedIn is one of the few social networking sites where you can remain quite passive and still experience amazing success. Imagine getting on Facebook or Twitter and doing absolutely nothing — nothing would happen. But on LinkedIn, simply by having an optimized profile infused with your keywords, people find you. Your profile's content shapes how people perceive you and compels them to reach out. This is one of the great benefits to LinkedIn, but for some people, it's not enough.

REMEMBER

There are over 400 million users on LinkedIn. It's a veritable ocean of people. In order to drive traffic to your profile, get noticed, and find opportunity, you have to splash around. Your LinkedIn activity is a direct contributor to profile traffic and LinkedIn success. In the following sections I outline a bunch of LinkedIn activities to perform that will increase traffic to your LinkedIn profile page.

View other profiles

LinkedIn is one of the few networks that enables you to see who has checked out your profile. Most people on LinkedIn love looking at the Who's Viewed Your Profile page. Not only do they love looking at who checked out their profile, they also want to learn more about the people with such awesome taste who checked them out! And so, in turn, they click to read their visitor's profile. If you want to drive traffic to your page, view other people's profiles! After you visit a person's profile, more often than not, that person will visit your profile to check you out, too.

However, in order for this to work, you must have your profile set to Visible and not to Anonymous.

Here's how to make sure your profile is visible:

1. **Go to** LinkedIn.com.

2. **Hover your mouse pointer over your profile picture in the upper-right corner of your screen and click Manage next to Privacy & Settings.**

3. **Click Privacy from the top portion of the screen that appears.**

4. **Click Profile viewing options.**

   This is where you choose whether you're visible to other LinkedIn users or viewing in private mode.

5. **Click the top option that shows your name and headline (see Figure 14-12).**

6. **Click the Close link in the upper-right corner of the option to save your setting.**

FIGURE 14-12:
Choose to be
visible on
LinkedIn!

WARNING

By choosing Private mode, not only are you choosing to remain anonymous, but also you are disabling your profile stats so you can't see who has viewed your profile. And when you switch to Private mode, your viewer history is deleted. Premium members can choose Private mode and still see the list of people who viewed their profiles (with the exception of viewers in Private mode). LinkedIn's good when you pay!

It feels weird to let people see that you browsed their profile. Believe me, I know! When I first joined LinkedIn, I kept my profile in Private mode. Eventually, the desire to see who was checking out my profile became so great that I begrudgingly turned my profile from anonymous to full visibility. As I watched my visitor list grow and views to my profile increase, I realized there was nothing to feel weird about. Viewing a profile shows that you are interested in the other person; it doesn't mean you are a stalker. People appreciate that you are doing your due diligence and research to learn more about them. It also provides the person with a link to learn more about you. Try it out after the initial feeling of discomfort passes; you'll be glad you did it.

Post status updates

Keep in touch with your network by posting status updates. As these status updates go out, people will click on your profile to check up and see what you are doing.

Here are some ideas of items to share as a status update:

>> Did you read an interesting article?

>> Did you finish an amazing project?

>> Are you attending a unique event?

>> Did you hear a great piece of advice?

>> Are you reading a life changing book?

These are all things to share on LinkedIn!

One of my favorite tools is the LinkedIn Bookmarklet icon. The Bookmarklet is a little button you drag onto your browser's bookmark tool bar. As you surf the web and find an interesting website or article, simply click the Bookmarklet icon to easily share the information on LinkedIn.

Follow these steps to install LinkedIn's Bookmarklet icon:

1. **Go to www.linkedin.com/bookmarklet.**

2. **Drag the Share on LinkedIn button to your browser's bookmark bar, as shown in Figure 14-13.**

If your browser doesn't have a bookmark bar, go to your browser's settings and turn it on.

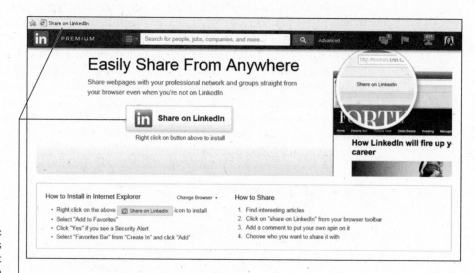

FIGURE 14-13:
Adding LinkedIn's Bookmarklet to your web browser.

Drag the Share on LinkedIn button to the toolbar

3. **While on an interesting website or reading an article that you would like to share on LinkedIn, click the Bookmarklet button on your browser's bookmark bar.**

A LinkedIn window pops up. This window contains the link to the item you want to share along with a brief description and thumbnail image.

Choose to share this as a status update on your LinkedIn newsfeed, post it to specific LinkedIn Groups, or send it via LinkedIn InMail to specific first-degree connections.

4. **To post the link as an update, click to place a check mark next to Share an Update, as shown in Figure 14-14.**

FIGURE 14-14:
Posting an update.

5. **In the text field, type your opinion, input, or reason for sharing.**

Although it's easy not to add your own spin, I highly recommend taking a few moments to share your thoughts.

6. **Click the Share With drop-down menu and select whether you want to share this update with the public or with just your connections.**

If you have a Twitter account connected to your LinkedIn profile, click the Twitter icon to also share this update on your Twitter feed.

7. **Click the Share button.**

In addition to using the Bookmarklet icon to share web pages and online articles as status updates, you can also share as group discussions or direct messages with connections. Placing the check mark by clicking in the Post to Groups box enables you to then choose which group or groups you want to post to. Conversely, click in the Send to Individuals box to send the link via LinkedIn's messaging. It's important when posting to a group or to an individual connection to provide context. If you were posting to a group, you might state, "Do you agree?" "What do you think?" or something that helps the reader respond and create conversation. When sending the link as a message, let the person know why you are sending the link and what result he or she can expect.

Posting status updates is a great way to stay in front of your connections. Make it a part of your professional life. Rather than decide to post an update once a month, once a week, or once a day, resolve to stay connected by sharing the items, events, and happenings that move you. When you read a great article, share it. When you sign up for an event, share it. When you have that Aha! moment, share it. Once you decide that you are on LinkedIn to educate, add value, and inspire people, that's when you start having fun and when opportunities start hurtling toward you.

Blog with the LinkedIn Publishing Platform

Publishing long-form posts gets you in front of large numbers of people quickly as LinkedIn notifies your network of your blog. When you create noteworthy content, it is shared way beyond just your network of connections. As the post catches on, people read it and want to learn more about you, the author. Profile views go up and opportunities appear. Get step-by-step directions on creating a long-from post in Chapter 13 of this book.

Participate in LinkedIn Groups

Believe me, I know it's not easy to find the time to participate in LinkedIn Groups, but when you consider the results of group participation, you may decide it's worth the time investment. Not only do you expand your network by joining groups, but also you meet people, engage in healthy discourse, develop professionally, and drive views to your LinkedIn profile.

By commenting on discussions and creating engaging discussions that compel people to comment, you are showcasing yourself as an interesting individual and expert. I am not suggesting that you market yourself low and wide in a slimy manner. Instead, use the discussions to help and inspire people. When you give your time, advice, and expertise, people take notice of you, which then makes them open your profile to learn more about you.

Recommend people

When you recommend people on LinkedIn, those recommendations display on their profiles as a link back to your profile, right next to your profile picture. The more recommendations you give, the more links you have on LinkedIn pointing back to your profile.

Those profiles attract readers, and many times those readers look at the recommendations received. It's not unusual for people to click the profile link to learn more about the recommender.

Always recommend people out of the goodness of your heart. Recommend people you know and who have impressed you. It's important to use recommendations and endorsements genuinely and authentically.

Endorse people

Endorsements also provide links back to your profile from other profiles. Go out and endorse people for their real skill sets. Not only will they be touched by your generosity, but also your name is now listed next to their Skills & Endorsements section on their profiles. With each link, there's a better than good chance other people will see the endorsement and click to read more about you.

And that concludes this guide for LinkedIn profile optimization. It's been a fun ride, and although it's the end of the guide, you still have the Part of Tens where I give you even more tips and tricks for better leveraging LinkedIn.

5

The Part of Tens

Learn the do's and don'ts to create a professionally impressive profile and create a relatable and likable digital identity.

See what you need to do to take a professional profile picture that portrays you in the best light, including how to photograph your good side, use Photoshop to improve — but not distort — your image, and what you should wear.

Learn the best tips for expanding your network, including improving your contact information, creating an attractive headline, joining groups, and creating great multimedia content.

Discover how you can get the most out of LinkedIn by connecting with as many people as possible.

Get the scoop on some powerful online tools to help you create an impressive profile.

Chapter **15**

Ten Profile Do's and Don'ts

Your LinkedIn profile is your digital identity. Of all the social media profiles out there, LinkedIn's profile is the most in-depth and provides a comprehensive overview of you as a professional person. When people search your name in a search engine, your LinkedIn profile is often returned high in the search results. When it comes to creating a professionally impressive profile that helps you collide with opportunity, here are ten Do's and Don'ts to keep in mind.

Do Use a Professional Profile Picture

The picture on your LinkedIn profile is your public face to your network and the world. It's imperative that it presents you in the absolutely best light. If your budget allows, get a professional photo taken in a photographer's studio. If your budget doesn't allow for it, enlist a friend to take a photo. Make sure you are dressed professionally and the background isn't messy, busy, or distinct. Position yourself near a window to ensure a well-lit image. The camera should be at eye level — not at too high of an angle nor too low of an angle. Look directly into the camera lens and smile. Have the photographer take numerous shots. Usually the winning image is snapped toward the end of the photo session, right when you start to feel comfortable in front of the camera.

Don't Use LinkedIn's Default Headline

LinkedIn automatically populates your headline with your current job title and company name. You couldn't pick a worse headline if you tried! Ditch LinkedIn's default and create a compelling headline — infused with your keywords — that gets your target audience to open your profile and read more.

Do Turn Off Your Update Notifications

Before performing any major updates to your profile, make sure your activity update notifications are turned off. You don't want to inundate your network with change notifications! To turn off update notifications, toggle the Notify Your Network switch that appears on the right sidebar within your LinkedIn profile from On to Off. Once off, you can make changes quietly — LinkedIn will not send updates to your network via email, nor will your changes show up as status updates on your connections' LinkedIn newsfeed.

Do Use Eye-Catching Symbols Sparingly

LinkedIn doesn't allow any formatting within your profile. This means you can't bold or italicize text, create links, or even have a bulleted list. However, you can copy and paste ASCII symbols into your profile to create visual flair. Choose one or two symbols and use them where you want to attract attention to your profile. This might be around your call to action and contact information, or before an accomplishment.

TIP

Less is more when it comes to symbols. Whatever you do, don't go overboard, splashing tons of different symbols throughout your profile. Regardless of how great the content might be, too many symbols may cheapen your profile and may make people not take you seriously.

Do Include Your Contact Information

The Contact Information section of your LinkedIn profile is only visible to your first-degree network of connections. If a second-degree connection, third-degree connection, group connection, someone outside of your network, or someone not on LinkedIn views your profile, they will *not* see your contact information.

TIP

LinkedIn is all about business networking and opportunity development. In order for people to reach out to you, they need to have your contact information. Make sure it's easy for people to reach out by including your contact information not just within the Contact Information section, but throughout your profile.

At the end of your LinkedIn summary, at the end of your current experience, and within the Advice for Contacting section, add your phone number and/or email address. Let people know you are serious by allowing them to contact you off LinkedIn.

Do Add Multimedia Files

Add work examples to your profile to further showcase who you are and what you do. Upload presentations, images, documents, videos, and more to your LinkedIn profile so readers of your profile can get a more robust view of you as a professional. Decide what your target audience would like to see from you and add it. Rich media can be linked to or uploaded to the Summary, Experience, and Education sections.

Don't Stuff Keywords

Strategically placing keywords into your LinkedIn profile is a great way to increase the likelihood of your profile turning up in searches. Although you might be tempted, don't stuff your profile with keywords. Instead, work the keywords into your profile naturally and organically. Profiles that are stuffed with keywords might rank well initially, but they quickly get deleted by LinkedIn. Keyword-stuffed profiles impress no one, and when it's clear you are gaming the system, people click away.

Don't Go Back 30 Years

You don't need to detail your complete work trajectory. Business has changed drastically over the last 30 years. Highlighting your IT accomplishments from 1985 doesn't prepare you for anything today. Your LinkedIn profile should align you with your career future. If you want to showcase your deep history, consolidate all past positions prior to 1985 into one experience. Your history is important, but what really moves mountains is what you did lately.

Do Get Recommendations

Recommendations listed on your LinkedIn profile provide social proof around your accomplishments and background. To get recommendations, you need to ask people to give you recommendations. In fact, if you want to truly make sure that those recommendations are posted to your profile, write the recommendation for the person.

REMEMBER

There is no such thing as too many LinkedIn recommendations; although, you should make sure that the recommendations posted to your profile are current, align with your objectives, and are authentically given.

Do Add Interests

Within the Additional Information section of your profile is where you can list your interests. Don't skip this area of your profile. People do business with people. By adding interests, you show you are human and allow your reader to see what you have in common together. Shared interests allow you to forge a quicker, deeper rapport with your reader.

Yes, LinkedIn is a professional network, but don't skip the Interests section. By providing some insight as to who you are as a person, your business connections may feel a stronger connection to you, which may spur more business and career opportunities.

Chapter **16**

Ten Tips for a Perfect Profile Picture

Say "Cheese!" Your profile picture is your face to the world. Don't settle for an "in the car" selfie. Every reader of your profile inspects your image. Make sure what they see aligns with your brand and portrays you in the best light. Here are ten tips that will help take your so-so profile picture to amazing heights.

Hire a Professional Photographer

So many people tell me that using a professional photographer is outside their budget. I don't buy it! They probably never shopped around. There are zillions of photographers out there offering affordable options.

Do an Internet search for: *Photography [Your Town], [Your State]*

For example, *Photography Delran, NJ*

This produces a listing of all photographers in your local area. Review the list, visit their websites, and check out their portfolios. Call those photographers who feel right to you. Ask for pricing. You'll find that most photographers want your business and will work with you to make your session affordable to you.

In case your Internet search fails you, here are a few online photographer directories to help you search for photographers by location:

>> American Society of Media Photographers (http://findaphotographer.org)

>> Professional Photographers of America (www.ppa.com/findaphotographer)

>> Photographers Index (www.photographersindex.com)

>> Photoshelter (www.photoshelter.com/explore/photographers)

Use Lots of Light

Whether or not you utilize a professional photographer, there should be lots of light where the picture is being taken. Good lighting is what takes a profile picture from mediocre to great. When lighting is adjusted and applied properly, almost everyone looks better.

TIP

Photographs shot in a professional studio often look better than shots taken in a person's office or outside in nature. The reason for this is a professional studio has professional lighting that can be manipulated. When given the option of having your photo taken in a studio or at your home or office, go with the studio. The end result will look much better.

Use a Nondescript Background

The background in your profile picture should be nondescript and plain. You are the focus of the photograph. The background image should never detract from you or provoke questions or judgment in the viewer's mind.

"Is she standing in front of a shed?"

"Gosh that room is messy."

"Is that a bookshelf filled with romance novels?"

"Why is he standing in front of bamboo trees?"

"I think I see the edge of a toilet!"

If you have a friend taking a picture of you, find a bare wall. If working with a professional photographer, find a backdrop that is plain. Pass by the bamboo trees, clouds, and laser-light shows.

Dress to Impress

Choose a professional outfit — clothes that you would wear to a job interview or to a business meeting. Make sure the clothes fit you well in your shoulder and neck area. The image is cropped, so the top area of the outfit matters the most.

I often tell my male clients to wear a suit and to pair it with a tie that complements the color of their eyes. In the beginning of the session, I tell them to have pictures taken with the full suit. After they are sure there is at least one usable image, I tell them to take off their ties and open the top button of their shirts. Then, once another usable image is taken, I have them remove their jackets and take pictures in just the dress shirt. By simply removing the tie and jacket, you are getting three different types of looks: formal, semi-formal, and informal.

When working with my female clients, I tell them to bring a few wardrobe changes to the photography session. Often a dress that looks great in person simply doesn't photograph well. Bringing along two or three different outfits allows them to change clothes and salvage the session if one outfit isn't working out.

TIP

Choosing the right color for your clothing is important. Whatever you do, don't choose a color that is close to the color of your skin. If your clothes too closely match the color of your skin, they can overpower the face and wash you out. Dark colors are usually a safe choice: Dark gray, black, navy blue, green, burgundy, rust, and brown typically work well.

In addition, when choosing your outfit, stay away from bold prints with stripes, plaids, checks, or polka dots. Remember, it's not your clothes but your face that is the focus of the photograph. Choose understated clothes to keep your face the focus of the picture.

Adjust Yourself

Before the photographer starts clicking, look in the mirror. Is your collar straight? Is your necklace clasp behind your neck? Are the backs of your earrings on tight? Is everything smooth and nice?

A client once told me that she was interviewed on television, and unbeknownst to her, her bra strap was clearly visible. As much as she loved the clip, she never used the recording on her website because she was mortified that her bra had a guest-starring role!

And so, in the immortal words of my mother prior to almost every photograph and major event, "Adjust yourself!"

Keep the Camera Close to Eye Level

When working with a photographer, he or she might get on a chair or stoop down a bit to get the right angle. In many situations, this is absolutely fine. However, having worked with thousands of professionals from all over the world, I see too many photos taken at too much of an angle.

The camera should be close to eye level. An image captured at too high of a level makes you look submissive and small. Too low of an angle and you'll look looming and overly dominant. Meet your viewer on equal ground by keeping the level of the image steady.

If the photographer appears to be using too much of an angle, ask to see the pictures on the camera's back screen. If it appears that the angle is too great, tell the photographer that you would like to take a few images with him or her at ground level. Remember, you are the boss.

Say No to the Mug Shot

With the camera close to eye level, position yourself at a slight angle from the camera lens. You don't want your body to be perfectly square with the camera because the resulting images will have the quality of a mug shot, driver's license photo, or passport picture.

The best thing to do is turn your shoulders so that they are at an angle to the camera.

Crinkle, Smile, and Jut

A genuine smile engages the full face and causes the eyes to wrinkle at the edges. To look genuine, give a big smile that crinkles your eyes. Don't worry about crow's feet — it's more important the image looks authentic and real.

As you smile, push your face out, jutting your jaw forward. This might feel weird, but it accentuates your jawline, tightening it and reducing any double chin.

TIP

Two videos by the famous photographer Peter Hurley reveal his secrets and offer advice on how to look more photogenic in portraits. They are found on his website at:

```
https://peterhurley.com/news/2013/who-knew-it-really-all-
about-squinch
```

Use Photoshop Lightly

You've selected your favorite picture and now the photographer will go to work using Photoshop to make you look like an alien. Sadly, most images are over-Photoshopped. The eye crinkles are erased and all lines and definition deleted. You look at the image and it kinda looks like you, but not really.

Instead, use Photoshop to freshen you, smooth hair flyaways, and remove any temporary blemishes. When Photoshop is used too heavily, the resulting image doesn't look authentic or real.

I have asked photographers to remove their Photoshop edits from my images more times than I care to admit. Yes, I have bags under my eyes, but without those bags, I am not me. Accept yourself as you are and don't erase your features — people gravitate to authenticity and the genuine.

Crop Your Image

The headshot is called a headshot for a reason — it should only contain your head. Your profile picture should present your full face and a sliver of your shoulders.

Crop out your ankles, knees, torso, elbows, and chest. The image should span from the top of your head to the bottom of your tie knot or clavicle.

The reason we zoom in is that it brings you closer to your viewer. Plus, that's a nice professional picture you just took — let's show it off!

Chapter **17**

Ten Tips to Expand Your Network

L inkedIn search is a little peculiar. When you search by a person's name in the LinkedIn search bar, it doesn't matter if the person is in your network or not; his or her profile (provided there is one) appears in search results. But as you know, people don't always search by name. When typical users search by keyword, the results that appear are from profiles that are in their LinkedIn networks — not the entire LinkedIn user database.

This means that the profiles that are returned are either first-, second-, or third-degree connections, or members of common LinkedIn Groups. It is true that occasionally you'll see an Out of Network profile appear in your search results, but when that happens, the full name is not provided and the profile isn't completely visible.

You just put a lot of work into optimizing your LinkedIn network. To make sure you get a lot of profile views, you must be able to be found, and to make that happen, you need to make sure you have a strong LinkedIn network.

I am not advocating aiming low and wide, connecting with people for sheer quantity. Instead, I want you to make your online network reflect your offline network. The people you know, the people you knew, and the people you meet every day should be added to your profile.

When you have a strong network, your profile appears in search results more often, and you get more views to your profile. Here's how to get started.

Import Your Address Book

It's hard to connect one by one, remembering the people you met through your life. Rather than rack your brain, LinkedIn allows you to import your online address book. Scanning your email address book shows you who's on LinkedIn already, and LinkedIn allows you to automatically connect with them. I know it seems a little scary to give LinkedIn your email password, but I promise, nothing bad will happen as long as you go slow and read through each screen!

Here are the steps:

1. **On LinkedIn's main toolbar, hover your mouse pointer over My Network and select Add Contacts (some users might see Invite Contacts).**

   The Add Contacts page appears, as shown in Figure 17-1. A list of email providers appears on the right side of the page.

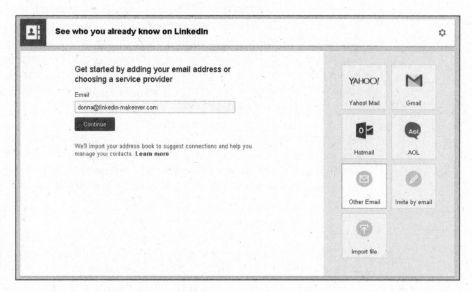

FIGURE 17-1:
This is the page where you add connections via email or csv file.

2. **Click the button for the email providers you use. (If you don't see your provider, choose Other Email.)**

   An authentication window appears.

3. **Enter your email credentials and accept any permission requests.**

LinkedIn scans your email address book looking for profile matches and presents you with a list of people you know who are already on LinkedIn, but not connected to you. (See Figure 17-2.)

FIGURE 17-2:
LinkedIn displays the profile matches based on email addresses in your email address book.

WARNING

LinkedIn automatically selects all contacts. Do not click Add Connections! It's important to first go through this list one by one and select or deselect who you want to invite to connect with you on LinkedIn.

4. **Remove the check marks by clicking in the circle to deselect the individuals you do not want to send a connection request.**

5. **Click the Add Connections button.**

An invitation request is sent, and then LinkedIn displays a list of people from your email address book who are not on LinkedIn that you can invite to join, as shown in Figure 17-3.

6. **Deselect the people on the list you do not want to invite to join LinkedIn and click the Add to Network button, or click Skip to skip this step.**

Invites are sent to those people you selected and you are back at the People You May Know Screen.

TIP

It's absolutely acceptable to skip sending invitations. LinkedIn has over 400 million users. Most times, those people who show up as not on LinkedIn, are on LinkedIn but with a different email address. Rather than bombard people with LinkedIn invitations, skip this step and concentrate on connecting with people who are definitely on LinkedIn already.

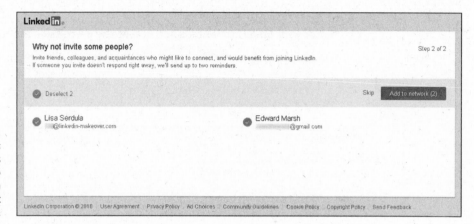

Import a Contact List

To make connecting as easy as possible, LinkedIn lets you upload a .csv, .txt, or .vcf file of email addresses. This is perfect if you have a spreadsheet of email addresses. Simply go to Add Connections under My Network and choose Import file. Select your file and go! If you want explicit directions, simply follow the directions under "Import Your Address Book" starting with Step 4.

Let LinkedIn Help You Connect

Under My Network on LinkedIn's navigation bar is People You May Know. This is a great page that most people overlook.

LinkedIn shows you connection recommendations of people you may possibly know and may like to connect with on LinkedIn. These recommendations are based on similar profile information. You may have gone to school with the person LinkedIn is recommending, or maybe you worked at the same company, or maybe you have similar experiences or work in the same industry.

LinkedIn also extrapolates people you may know from your email and mobile address books. Don't worry: LinkedIn never reads your messages; it just looks for email address matches.

To use People You May Know to make more connections, follow these steps:

1. **Hover your mouse pointer over My Network and click People You May Know.**

2. **Scan through the list of profiles that appear, and click the Connect button when you see a person you want to invite into your first-degree network.**

   By clicking Connect, you are sending a non-personalized invitation. If you want to personalize your invitation, go to step 3.

3. **Click the profile picture of the suggested person.**

   His or her LinkedIn profile opens.

4. **Click the Connect button that appears next to that person's profile picture, as shown in Figure 17-4.**

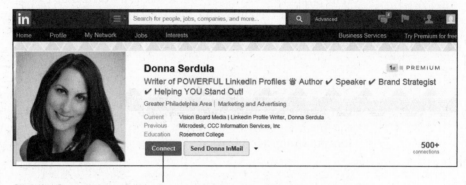

Click the Connect button to invite someone into your first-degree network

FIGURE 17-4: Click Connect to send a personalized connection request.

5. **Choose how you know the person: Colleague, Classmate, We've Done Business Together, Friend, or Other.**

6. **Add a personalized note in the text field.**

7. **Click the Send Invitation button.**

   A personalized invitation is sent.

Join One Hundred Groups

Group members are part of your LinkedIn network. LinkedIn allows you to join up to 100 LinkedIn Groups. If you want to get found and find more people via LinkedIn search, my recommendation is to join the maximum 100 LinkedIn Groups.

REMEMBER

By joining groups, those members are added to your LinkedIn network. This means that when they search for someone like you, the odds of you appearing in their search results are much greater because you are "connected" through the group.

Start a LinkedIn Group

Depending upon your need to grow your network, starting a LinkedIn Group to grow your network might be akin to killing a fly with an anvil. Starting a LinkedIn Group is a huge undertaking, but it can be a worthwhile investment depending on your goals. As the LinkedIn Group administrator, you sit in a unique leadership position, and people within the group get to know you. Who would reject a connection request from the Group administrator?

My only caveat here is there is a lot of work required to create and build a LinkedIn Group. If you are absolutely not interested in creating a group, become very active in an already established group. As you interact with people via group discussions, send them a connection request. It's on a slightly smaller scale than being a LinkedIn Group administrator, but it does allow you to meet people and connect.

Make Connecting a Process

To grow your network, you must make it a systematic process. Don't just focus on connecting with people from your past. Each time you schedule a meeting, make sure the invitees are in your LinkedIn network. Don't just collect business cards at industry events, enter the names into LinkedIn and connect with them. The idea is that you connect with the people you meet along the way.

TIP

Connecting must be part of your professional process, and it's something that you should never stop doing.

Link to Your Profile

Expanding your network is not just about sending connection requests to other people. It's equally important that you make it easy for other people to connect to you. The best way to do that is to provide a link to your LinkedIn profile wherever you are . . . online or off.

Here are a few places you can add a link to your profile:

>> Business card

>> Email signature

>> Letterhead

>> Marketing literature

>> Neck tattoo (just teasing!)

>> Resume

>> Social media networks

>> Website bio

>> Website social media section

Brand Yourself a LION or Just Connect to Them

Surely you've noticed people on LinkedIn with the moniker "LION" next to their names or have it listed in their summaries. No, these people are not actual cat lovers. LION is short for LinkedIn Open Networker. A LION is a person who is willing to connect with anyone on LinkedIn, regardless of whether they know you or trust you.

The one rule LIONs follow is never mark any incoming invitation as SPAM or I Don't Know. When a person marks an invite as SPAM or I Don't Know, that's a black mark against the user. If too many people mark you as SPAM or I Don't Know, LinkedIn restricts your account and you will only be able to add people if you enter in their email addresses.

It's easy to become a LION. All you need to do is add LION or LinkedIn Open Networker to your profile and never choose SPAM or I Don't Know on an incoming invitation to connect.

However, there are pros and cons to becoming a LION. It's something that you need to consider long and hard. If you are only looking to grow a strong network, not a ginormous one, becoming a LION may not be the best option for you.

TIP

Instead of labeling yourself a LION, you can choose to just connect to LIONs. By searching out LIONs and adding them to your network, you are expanding your second-degree network and growing your total LinkedIn network in the process.

Because it's easy to spot a LION, it's easy to find them on LinkedIn. By doing a simple keyword search for "LinkedIn Open Networker," you'll find a slew. Send them a connection request and a short personalized note and they'll be happy to add you to their enormous network.

Join Open Networking Lists and Groups

A number of websites allow you to download a list of LION email addresses. By then uploading that list of email addresses to LinkedIn, you can expand your network very quickly.

Here are two open networking sites:

>> TopLinked (www.toplinked.com)

>> Invites Welcome (www.inviteswelcome.com)

These websites work in a similar manner. It's free to download the list, but it costs money to get your name on the list. The idea is that you want people adding you as a connection rather than having to download the list yourself. By having other people add you, you are able to determine who you want to add, but also, you aren't using up your 5,000 invite limit.

LinkedIn limits the number of invitations you can send out to 5,000. If you hit the 5,000 invitation limit, you can petition LinkedIn's Customer Service for more. If you play nice in LinkedIn's sandbox and have a high rate of invitation acceptance, LinkedIn provides you with an extra 500 invitations. If you don't play nice in LinkedIn's sandbox and have had a high rate of people marking you as Spam or I Don't Know, LinkedIn may refuse your request for more invitations. In that case, to keep growing your network, you have to ask other people to invite you into their network.

If you absolutely must expand your network quickly, only then join an open networking list and pay the money to get your email on the list. By downloading a list of email addresses, you are connecting with pretty much anyone. Paying to get your name on the list affords you a small semblance of control because when people add you, you get to decide of you want them as part of your network.

Whatever you do, don't use your primary email address for the list; instead, use a secondary address. Anyone can download that list, and many people simply use that list for their own spam-y purposes.

Use an App

What makes connecting so gosh darn hard is that it's outside your everyday process. Wouldn't it be great if instead of having to visit LinkedIn.com, you could connect directly with people within your email application? As you receive and read email, you get to see a link to the person's profile and a Connect button? Guess what, there is! It's called Rapportive, a browser extension that works with Gmail.

Rapportive displays profile information on the right side of opened email messages, as shown in Figure 17-5. Not only do you see the sender's headline, location, and current position, but also Rapportive displays links to the sender's LinkedIn profile and Twitter accounts. If you are not currently connected to the sender, Rapportive shows you a Connect button that you can click to send an invitation to connect on LinkedIn.

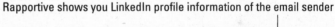

Rapportive shows you LinkedIn profile information of the email sender

FIGURE 17-5: Rapportive makes connecting with people a breeze!

Chapter 18

Ten Tips to Leverage LinkedIn

Your profile is optimized and your network is growing . . . *now what?* Most people optimize their profile and then disappear off LinkedIn. They forget that LinkedIn is more than just a place to house your profile and accomplishments.

LinkedIn is a social network and a business tool. To truly see results and find that elusive opportunity that people claim is "in them thar LinkedIn hills," you must get on LinkedIn and use it.

Here are ten tips to help you leverage LinkedIn like a successful goldminer.

A-B-C . . . Always Be Connecting

In the movie, *Glengarry Glen Ross*, Alec Baldwin's character shouts, "A-B-C . . . always be closing!" I like to think of it a little differently in this brave new social media world. Rather than closing, let's say, "A-B-C . . . always be connecting!"

By connecting with people on LinkedIn, you are able to keep in touch with them. I like to call it *drip-feed marketing*. When connected, that person is subscribed to your LinkedIn activity and updates. Each time you update your profile or send out a status update or get recommended or publish a long-form post, they have the potential to see it and be reminded of you.

There's so much going on in the world today. We are bombarded by messages every second of every day. Just because you met someone doesn't mean she'll remember you when she needs you. But by connecting on LinkedIn, you improve those chances because that person is often reminded of you through notifications, status updates, and search results.

REMEMBER

When you connect with someone on LinkedIn, you aren't just connecting to solely them — you are connecting to his network and his network's network. If either that person or someone within his network searches LinkedIn for someone like you, your profile has a higher likelihood of appearing in the search results because of the network you share.

Connect and Stay in Touch

When starting out on LinkedIn, most people don't put enough focus on connecting and growing a strong network. LinkedIn's People You May Know page is a great way to get connection recommendations.

Here's how to get to LinkedIn's People You May Know page:

1. **Open your LinkedIn profile.**

2. **Hover your mouse pointer over My Network in LinkedIn's main toolbar at the top of the page and click People You May Know.**

   LinkedIn presents you with a page of connection recommendations.

By extrapolating relationships through email matches and shared information on LinkedIn profiles, LinkedIn often provides eerily correct recommendations. Often, the people in the People You May Know page are actually people you had forgotten about, but with LinkedIn's prompting, you can reconnect and reestablish a fruitful relationship.

Another way to reconnect and reestablish professional friendships is through LinkedIn's Connections page. This page shows your list of first-degree connections, but it also shows a list of people with suggested reasons to reconnect.

Here's how to get there:

1. **Open your LinkedIn profile.**

2. **Hover your mouse pointer over My Network in LinkedIn's main toolbar at the top of the page and click Connections.**

    At the top of the page, LinkedIn shows you a grid of people who are celebrating:

    - Birthdays

    - Work anniversaries

    - New positions

    To make it even easier for you, LinkedIn provides a one-click button to wish the person a happy birthday or say congrats.

Now you have no excuses not to stay in touch with people in your network.

Gather Business Intelligence

LinkedIn is a treasure trove of information on people and companies. This is information that you can easily access with just a few simple searches.

TIP

Interviewing at a company and want to learn more about them? Check them out on LinkedIn. Their LinkedIn Company page not only summarizes who they are and what they do, but also you get to see a listing of current employees.

One of the key benefits of LinkedIn is that it turns invisible relationships visible. Looking at the list of employees on a LinkedIn company page, you can see how you are connected to them: first-degree, second-degree, third-degree, or through a group. If you find an employee who's a second-degree connection, visit that person's profile to see the mutual connection you have in common. If it's someone you are on familiar terms, reach out and ask for an introduction. If the employee has provided contact information, use your shared connection's name as an ice breaker.

LinkedIn does not just offer company research. Profiles are brimming with great information, too, even if the person hasn't optimized his or her profile. Back when I was in technology sales, I researched my top 15 prospects on LinkedIn. I checked their LinkedIn Groups and Organizations to see where they belonged online and offline. I then joined those groups and organizations so I could rub elbows with them. Many of those offline organizations afforded me a chance to forge relationships with my prospects that resulted in more clients and sales.

Are you looking to move up within an organization? Look at the profiles of the people in your target positions. What do they have in common? Do they have certain courses, certifications, or degrees to their name that you need? Use their profiles to determine what you need to do professionally to reach their career heights.

Ultimately, do your due diligence. Check out companies and people on LinkedIn so you get a deeper understanding as to who they are and what they do. You'll be surprised at what you find.

Get the News

The newsfeed on LinkedIn's home page is a veritable newspaper, filled with articles and items that have been cultivated and curated by your network. These people with whom you are connected have handpicked the articles, written the posts, and shared news that moves them. This stream of information is brimming with possibilities and opportunities. Scroll through your newsfeed, not just looking at the information being shared, but also at who's sharing it.

TIP

Think of your LinkedIn's home page newsfeed as an online networking party where that tiny little status update is the virtual embodiment of a person standing in the middle of the room, looking for someone to talk to. How do you want to respond to this person? If you simply want to smile and nod, click the Like button. If you want to engage and start a conversation, click the Comment button and type something pithy. If you want to trumpet this person and give her a bigger audience, click the Share button.

Are you ready to do more than just respond to others? Share your own status updates and experience what I like to call *drip-feed marketing*. By sharing links to articles, information on upcoming events, providing advice, quotes, infographics, and more, you provide value to your target audience. Each time you share valuable information, your audience is reminded that you exist. You never know when people might need someone like you. By staying on top on their mind, you are ensuring they reach out to you first!

When you are the one beginning the conversation, people respond to you. Each time a person likes, comments, or shares your update, your potential audience gets bigger and bigger. The more eyes on your update, the more people who may click your profile looking to learn more about you.

Get Social Proof and Credibility

LinkedIn offers something that resumes and recommendation letters can't: social proof. The LinkedIn profile is totally public and visible for all to see. The public nature of the LinkedIn profile acts as an honesty incentive. Who's going to lie when their teammates and colleagues are able to click and see what they are touting?

In addition, recommendations and endorsements add balance to your accomplishments and successes. It's not just you saying you're great; other people can chime in and say it, too. And remember, those people endorsing and recommending you — it's done upfront with their names and faces right next to the endorsement and recommendation. They, too, are incentivized to tell the truth with their public images on the line.

Get Past the Gatekeeper

If you have ever been in sales and had to cold-call potential customers, you know about the Gatekeeper. That's the person hired to keep salespeople and other annoyances away from decision-makers. You call and call but never can get through to the person because the Gatekeeper is keeping you at bay.

Back when I was in sales, I found that LinkedIn offered a great way to get past the Gatekeeper. InMails, OpenLink messages, and group messaging allowed me to directly communicate with the person I couldn't get through to over the phone. LinkedIn allowed me to sidestep the Gatekeeper and get my epistle directly onto the decision-maker's lap.

Even if you aren't in sales, you still will face gatekeepers whose job it is to keep you away from the person you need to reach. LinkedIn is the tool that can get you past that guard. However, it's important to have a compelling message that gets the decision-maker to take notice. Otherwise, even though you got through the door, you still won't make an impact.

Rub Elbows in Groups

LinkedIn Groups are subject-focused forums where like-minded individuals join for discussion and networking purposes. Join groups within your business niche to rub elbows with your target audience. When you join a strong, focused group with serious members, it's a place to learn, develop, inspire, and help others.

If you don't have time to join a group for discussion and interaction, join LinkedIn Groups because they extend your network. By joining a group, those members are added to your network. By having these members in your network, they are able to find you if they are doing a keyword-based search and your search results are enhanced for keyword searches you perform. Joining groups is the easiest way to grow your network and see a real impact in search results.

Find Assistance

When you need a handyman to help fix something in your home, what's the first thing you do? You ask around! You call up the people close to you to see if they know someone. Everybody feels more comfortable working with someone their friends and family have used in the past.

LinkedIn works on this exact same principle!

Are you looking for a marketing consultant to help grow your business? Perhaps you need a financial advisor or an insurance agent? Maybe you need to hire an office manager? Whatever you are looking for, LinkedIn is a searchable database of professionals who are connected to you.

When you use a search engine on the web, the results are all over the board. You'll find websites, blogs, videos, and more. The people you find on a search engine could be located anywhere and without any connection to you.

But search LinkedIn, and the search result listings that are returned are real people within your network. The number after their names tells you how closely connected you are to the people who fit your search criteria. First-degree connections are people directly connected to you. Second-degree connections are people who share with you a mutual connection. Third-degree connections are people who know a mutual connection you share. If the icon next to their name reads *Group*, this person shares a LinkedIn Group in common with you.

Clicking the result gives you a profile that provides everything you need to decide if you want to reach out to learn more.

Showcase Thought Leadership

The problem with blogging is not just coming up with content, it's also finding an audience to read your articles. You can go to Wordpress.com and easily create your own website and start blogging, but it takes time to develop an audience.

The beautiful part of using LinkedIn's Publishing Platform is that when you begin to write long-form posts, you already have a built-in audience — your LinkedIn network! All those people you've connected to over the years are potential readers of your work. Because you have a built-in audience, you can really concentrate on coming up with good topics and content. Your posts are housed on your profile for readers of your profile to see.

Profiles that contain long-form posts showcase thought leadership. Expertise is rare, and by taking the time to create a long-form post, you are differentiating yourself and your profile. Remember:

Blogging = Thought Leadership = Differentiation = Opportunity

Network in Your Pajamas

You always hear about the importance of networking, yet the thought of networking is intimidating. There's this vision of old men in dark suits convening in a club, drinking whiskey and making deals. Do you even want to be a part of that?

Networking is not nearly as complicated or nefarious as it seems. Networking at its most basic level is two things: being friendly and being helpful. That's why so many people fail. They start networking only when they need something. By then, it's often too late. Dig your well before you are thirsty.

Networking used to take place in person or over the phone, one to one. LinkedIn changed the playing field, giving you the ability to network at 3 a.m. in your pajamas.

TIP

Log on to LinkedIn and scroll through your newsfeed. Like, comment, and share your connections' status updates that move you. As you surf the web and find an interesting and pertinent article, send it out as a status update to everyone. Or, select a person from your contacts and message it to him or her specifically with a note, letting this person know you are thinking about him or her.

Join LinkedIn Groups to be part of a larger conversation. Ask for advice. Provide help. Introduce and connect with people with synergy. Share ideas. Add value.

All you need to do is log into LinkedIn. Stop thinking of LinkedIn as a chore or a site that simply houses your profile. LinkedIn is a conduit of information, news, people, branding, and opportunity. LinkedIn is a place to engage and interact. Forge a presence and a reputation on LinkedIn as a giver, and opportunity will begin to flow. Show up and immediately expect quick results, and opportunity will retract.

Chapter **19**
Ten LinkedIn Profile Resources

To achieve a truly optimized LinkedIn profile, it takes more than just sheer writing and typing ability. I've compiled a list of ten resources to help you create the best profile out there. These resources are my secret gems to create an impressive profile. The resources span videos, online tools, and more. The best part? Almost all of them are free.

Get Inspired and Excited

I remember when I watched Simon Sinek's TED talk, "How Great Leaders Inspire Action" the first time. He verbalized something I knew in my heart: *If you want to move someone, don't tell them how, tell them why.* After watching this video, you'll begin to see the bigger picture the LinkedIn Summary section provides, and you will begin to realize your own *why*.

Simon Sinek's TED talk is found here:

    www.ted.com/talks/simon_sinek_how_great_leaders_inspire_action

Carla Harris' presentation, "How to Own Your Power," is one I watch over and over again because it's so inspiring. She provides three pearls of wisdom, and although she's not directly talking about a LinkedIn profile, her pearls absolutely reflect what is possible with your profile. She talks about confidence, risks, and (my favorite) perception.

Carla Harris's "How to Own Your Power" presentation is found here:

https://youtu.be/0rWmtyZXkFg

LinkedIn Headline Generator

I created an online application to help you generate your LinkedIn headline. All you do is check off the descriptive terms that apply to you and . . . bam! A LinkedIn headline is presented to you that you simply copy and paste into your LinkedIn profile.

It doesn't get any easier, folks! My headline generator app is found here:

www.LinkedIn-Makeover.com/LinkedIn-Headline-Generator

Virtual Phone Numbers

Over and over again throughout this book, I told you to add your phone number to your profile. LinkedIn brings opportunity, and often that opportunity is looking to talk to you right this very moment. By not providing your phone number, that hot, heaping spoonful of opportunity will go elsewhere.

However, if you are simply not comfortable providing your home number or mobile number, there are services out there to help.

Google Voice

Google Voice is a free service that provides you with a virtual phone number that you can forward to either voicemail or to your regular phone number. There are many more features as well. Check it out here:

www.google.com/voice

Skype

Most people think of Skype as a way to place video calls to friends and family, but Skype is much more than that. Through Skype, you can purchase your very own phone number. When a person dials that number, it can ring your computer or your mobile phone if you have the Skype app installed. Just like Google Voice, Skype provides even more features, too. Check it out here:

www.skype.com

Say No to AOL and Hotmail Addresses

Believe it or not, your email address says a lot about you. AOL and Hotmail email addresses portray you as an outmoded, tech dinosaur. Is it a fair assumption? Of course not, but there are zillions of articles out there with studies to prove that your email address is a status symbol. Sadly, AOL and Hotmail are equivalent to driving an old-fashioned Buick.

Your own domain

Want to drive a Rolls Royce? Get an email address with your own domain. There's plenty of ways to do it, but the easiest is through Google Apps:

https://domains.google.com

Acceptable free domains

Not a Rolls Royce type? That's okay; you can drive a Lexus with either a Gmail.com or iCloud.com email address:

Gmail (https://mail.google.com)

iCloud (www.icloud.com)

TIP

It's hard to change your email address, and it's something that you can't take lightly. Strategically decide if it makes sense to keep your old addresses, or if it's time to move on. It's a shame to cling to an old email address out of laziness when it's hurting you on the job front.

Symbol Variations

When you paste symbols into your profile, their look changes depending on the device used to view them. What might look like a black check mark to you might look like a bright red check to a person viewing it on a MacBook Pro or an Android smartphone. The reason for this is that some devices display the symbols in black and white Unicode, while others replace them with their emoji equivalent. Every device vendor uses its own emoji art, so what looks one way on Mac looks differently on a PC or Android smartphone.

Check out my website to see the different variations of the most popular business symbols:

`www.LinkedIn-Makeover.com/tools/symbols`

Stop the Typos

Most word processors have a spelling and grammar checker built in, but if you are typing directly into LinkedIn's text fields, only the Chrome browser provides spellcheck through an extension. Grammarly (`https://app.grammarly.com`) is a Chrome extension that enables grammar check within your browser. When Grammarly is running, it catches any grammatical mistakes you type and helps make you look even more professional!

SlideShare

SlideShare is a slide hosting service owned by LinkedIn that allows users to upload slide presentations to share their knowledge. People often ask me for ideas of items to add to their LinkedIn profiles. Most people don't have videos or podcasts to upload, and they are left scratching their head, wondering what to add. I have one word for you: presentations.

Practically every professional has access to PowerPoint or Keynote. Go ahead, get in there and create a presentation! You can paste in report metrics or offer insights into a project you completed. Create a presentation that showcases who you are and what you do. The world is your oyster; get creative and let yourself shine!

Once it's created, share it on SlideShare and link it to your LinkedIn profile. Voila! Instant multimedia content. You can find SlideShare here:

    www.slideshare.net

TIP

You can also access SlideShare from LinkedIn's main navigation bar under Interests.

Photographer Directories

Your profile picture is so important. Working with a professional photographer ensures that this important photograph looks great. Here are a few online photographer directories to help you search for photographers by location:

American Society of Media Photographers (http://findaphotographer.org)

Professional Photographers of America (www.ppa.com/findaphotographer)

Photographers Index (www.photographersindex.com)

Photoshelter (www.photoshelter.com/explore/photographers)

Background Image Libraries

The LinkedIn background image is a great way to brand your profile and really stand out. The issue is finding the right background image. Yes, you can search around and steal an image off the web, but that brings bad mojo. Instead, peruse these online libraries of free images:

Barn Images (http://barnimages.com)

Raumrot (http://raumrot.com)

Pixabay (https://pixabay.com)

Unspash (https://unsplash.com)

FreeImages (www.freeimages.com)

Photocrops (www.photocrops.com)

UHD Wallpapers (www.uhdwallpapers.org)

Here are some libraries where you can purchase images:

GraphicRiver (http://graphicriver.net)

iStock (www.istockphoto.com)

ShutterStock (www.shutterstock.com)

Online Image Apps

Once you have a great background image, you might want to customize it with text. My favorite online image editor is Canva. Canva makes it so easy to create picture montages and place text over images.

Canva isn't the only company out there providing this type of service. PicMonkey and Adobe Spark also offer similar services. You can find them here:

Adobe Spark (https://spark.adobe.com)

Canva (www.canva.com)

PicMonkey (www.picmonkey.com)

Try each service out to see which one is your favorite.

Index

identity theft, 86

IM addresses, adding to Contact Information section, 80–81

Industry section, 71–75, 258

influencers
about, 238
in checklist, 259
choosing which to highlight, 238–239
finding, 240, 241
removing, 242

InMail, 262, 269–270, 305

Interests section
adding to Additional Information section, 194–197
tips for, 284

internships, 120

Invites Welcome (website), 298

iStock (website), 210, 314

J

job search process, using LinkedIn for, 10

Job Seeker account, 20, 260, 262–263

job titles
adding to headlines, 107
optimizing with keywords, 140–143

JRX (website), 104

K

keywords
for headlines, 106–109
importance of, 21–25
online tools for, 25–30
optimizing job titles with, 140–143
for Skills and Endorsements section, 36–37
stuffing, 283

Krawchek, Sallie (CEO), 239

L

languages, 181–183, 258

letterhead, LinkedIn URL on, 271

lighting, for profile pictures, 93, 286

LinkedIn. *See also specific topics*
cost of, 20, 259–264
popularity of, 15
tips for leveraging, 301–307
using as a search engine, 15–18

LinkedIn blog (website), 88

LinkedIn Groups
about, 166, 223
in checklist, 259
deleting, 231
highlighting on profile, 233–234
importance of, 224–234
joining, 228–229, 276, 295–296
participating in, 276
searching for, 229–231
starting, 296
turning off group communication emails, 232–233
turning off group notifications, 227–228
types of, 225–227
using, 305–306

LinkedIn Jobs section (website), 10

LinkedIn Network, 63, 224–225

LinkedIn Open Networker (LION), 70, 297–298

LinkedIn Pulse, 237–238, 242–244

LinkedIn User Agreement (website), 99

LinkedIn Volunteer Marketplace (website), 191

linking, to your profile, 296–297

LION (LinkedIn Open Networker), 70, 297–298

Location section (profile), 71–75, 258

lock icon, 199

Lynda, 28, 180

M

Manage Recommendations section, 218

Marital Status field, 197–200

marketing
adding profile to other social media sites, 270
alerting connections of updated profile, 267–270
blog posts, 250–251
drip-feed, 302, 304
getting views to your profile, 272–277

U

UHD Wallpapers (website), 210, 313
Unicode Character Table (website), 104
Unspash (website), 210, 313
updates
  alerts for, 50–52, 282
  to Honors & Awards section, 172
  manually removing from profile, 51–52
  sharing, 244
uploading profile pictures, 98–99
URL, personalized, 55–59
User Agreement (website), 99

V

video resumes, 206
views, of profile, 202–203, 272–277
virtual phone numbers, 310–311
visibility settings
  for Personal Details field, 199–200
  for profile pictures, 100
  for profiles, 272–273
Volunteering Experience section (profile), 166, 189–192, 258

W

Warning icon, 4
websites, 84–86. *See also specific websites*
WeChat, adding to Contact Information section, 83
Whitman, Meg (CEO), 239
Wikipedia Symbol Block List (website), 104
Word (Microsoft), 148
word cloud generator, 25–26
Word It Out (website), 26
Wordle.net (website), 26–28
Wordsift (website), 26
work address, adding to Contact Information section, 81
work history, 120–121, 283

Y

year
  of graduation, 184
  using in Experience section, 127

About the Author

Donna Serdula pioneered the concept of LinkedIn profile optimization, realizing early on that the LinkedIn profile was so much more than just an online resume. The LinkedIn profile is an amazing opportunity for branding.

Donna spent the first 10 years of her career in sales, marketing, and training. She joined LinkedIn's social network in 2005 where she promptly copied and pasted her resume and wondered what all the fuss was about. A job change in 2006 led her back to LinkedIn as she looked for tools to help her build a sales territory. It was during this time she had her LinkedIn epiphany and forged her LinkedIn profile methodology.

In 2009, she walked away from her successful sales career and founded Vision Board Media and LinkedIn-Makeover.com. Her mission: Help people realize their Internet identity and shape one that makes an impact and leads to opportunity.

From that day on, Donna Serdula became the chief influencer, advocating and evangelizing the importance of taking control of your Internet identity. By presenting yourself in a way that inspires and builds confidence in your abilities, products, and services, you are shaping your future.

Donna is an in-demand speaker throughout the United States, speaking on the topics of LinkedIn, professional branding, online reputation, and job search. Prior to *LinkedIn Profile Optimization For Dummies*, Donna wrote *LinkedIn Makeover: Professional Secrets to a POWERFUL LinkedIn Profile*. Donna has been featured on Business Insider, NBC, and SiriusXM Radio's The Focus Group, and in *Time* magazine's Money Section, the *Wall Street Journal*'s Market Watch, the *Los Angeles Times*, and many other news outlets.

Visit Donna's website www.LinkedIn-Makeover.com for more LinkedIn resources or her website devoted to her public speaking, www.DonnaSerdula.com. You can contact Donna directly at Donna@LinkedIn-Makeover.com.

Dedication

To my sons, Jimmy and Jed — my favorite first degree connections.

Author's Acknowledgments

Thank you to Amy Fandrei and Katharine Dvorak from Wiley for making this book possible. I must also thank Ed Marsh, Lisa Serdula, and Rosalie Serdula (my husband, sister, and mother) for supporting me through this endeavor. A very special thank you to Dionne Carrick who kept Vision Board Media running smoothly while I concentrated on writing this book. Thank you to Cathy Branciaroli and Mary Profy for their special assistance. A huge shout out to all my Branding Specialists, past, present, and future (Audra, Ray, Wendi, Heather, Carmen, Rich, Richard, Judi, Roy, Ellie, Sylvia, Jan, Gwen, Laurel, Ashley, and Jessica) for their dedication to online branding and to all our clients who have entrusted their online reputation and professional story to us.

Publisher's Acknowledgments

Acquisitions Editor: Amy Fandrei

Project Editor: Katharine Dvorak

Technical Editor: Michelle Krasniak

Sr. Editorial Assistant: Serena Novosel

Production Editor: Tamilmani Varadharaj

Cover Image: Billion Photos/Shutterstock